Of Errors and Truth

Or Man Restored to the Universal Principle of Knowledge

A work in which, by pointing out to the Observers the uncertainty of their investigations and their continual misunderstandings, they are shown the path which they should have followed to acquire physical evidence about the origin of Good and Evil; about Man; about material Nature, immaterial Nature and sacred Nature; about the basis of political governments; about the authority of sovereigns; about Civil and Criminal Justice; about the Sciences, Languages and the Arts.

Louis-Claude De Saint-Martin

An English Language Translation from the Original French of the 1775 'Edimbourg' First Edition of *Des erreurs et de la vérité*

Part 1 and Part 2 Combined into a Single Volume

Translated by
Piers A. Vaughan

June 2017

This book is dedicated with great love and gratitude to Sâr Fidentia, Sâr Velle Est Posse, Sâr Semper Paratus Semper Fidelis, Sâr Roca & Sâr Resurrectus

© Piers A. Vaughan 2017

All rights reserved. No part of this publication may be reproduced, distributed, or transmitted in any form or by any means, including photocopying, recording, or other electronic or mechanical methods, without the prior written permission of the publisher, except in the case of brief quotations embodied in critical reviews and certain other noncommercial uses permitted by copyright law. For permission requests, write to the publisher at the address below.

ISBN 978-0-9815421-2-6

Rose Circle Publications
P.O. Box 854
Bayonne, NJ 07002, U.S.A.
www.rosecirclebooks.com

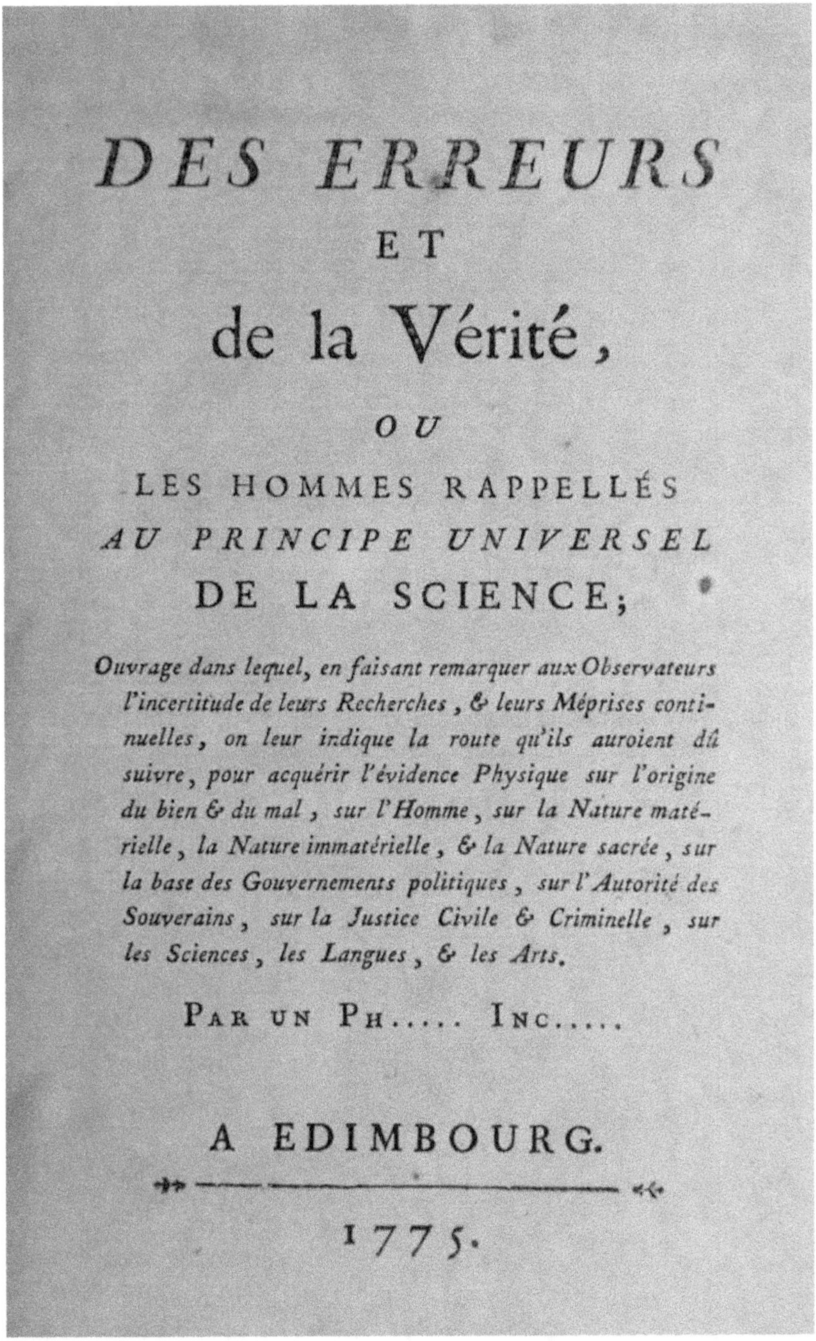

DES ERREURS

ET

de la Vérité,

OU

LES HOMMES RAPPELLÉS
AU PRINCIPE UNIVERSEL
DE LA SCIENCE;

Ouvrage dans lequel, en faisant remarquer aux Observateurs l'incertitude de leurs Recherches, & leurs Méprises continuelles, on leur indique la route qu'ils auroient dû suivre, pour acquérir l'évidence Physique sur l'origine du bien & du mal, sur l'Homme, sur la Nature matérielle, la Nature immatérielle, & la Nature sacrée, sur la base des Gouvernements politiques, sur l'Autorité des Souverains, sur la Justice Civile & Criminelle, sur les Sciences, les Langues, & les Arts.

PAR UN PH..... INC.....

A EDIMBOURG.

1775.

Figure 1 - Image of original Frontispiece

Contents

Contents	5
Note on Illustrations	13
Foreword	15
Translating Conventions	16
Introduction	25
Saint-Martin's 1775 Foreword	37
Chapter 1 – The Philosophy	**41**
The Cause of Errors	41
The Truth	42
Good and Evil	43
The Good and Evil Principles	43
False Doctrine Concerning the Two Principles	45
The Difference between the Two Principles	46
Evil, a Result of Freedom (I)	48
The Origin of Evil	49
Evil, a Result of Freedom (II)	49
Liberty and Free Will	50
Original State of the Evil Principle	55
Present State of the Evil Principle	56
Incompatibility of Good and Evil	56
The Two States of Man	57
The Primitive Estate of Man	59
Man's Degradation	60
Man's Punishment	60
The Path of His Rehabilitation	61
Relief afforded to Man	62
The Works of Man	64
Twofold Result of the Body of Man	65
The Origin of Materialism	65
The Theory of Sensations	66
The Dangers of This Theory	67
Innate Ability in Man	68
Man's Original Envelope	69

Man's New Envelope 69
Two Beings in Man 69
Animals Only Use the Senses 70
The Active Being in Animals 71
The Habits of Animals 71
The Intellectual and the Physical 72
How to Distinguish the Three Kingdoms 72
The Universal Quaternary Progression 74
The Union of the Three Elements 75
Man's Superiority 76
Man's Thought 77
Man's Senses 77
Man's Rights over His Thoughts 78
Man's Greatness 79
Misconceptions About Man 79
The Means to Avoid These Misconceptions 80
The Universality of These Misconceptions 80

Chapter 2 – The Body 83
The Universal Source of Errors 83
The Suffering of Animals 83
Dual Action 84
Research on Nature 85
Matter and its Principle 86
The Divisibility of Matter 88
The Limitations of Mathematics 89
Offspring and Their Principles 89
The Reproduction of Forms 90
The Immutability of Their Principles 91
Emanations from the Unity 92
Secondary Beings 92
The Generation of the Body 93
The Destruction of the Body 96
Digestion 98
The Disintegration of the Body 98
Woman 99
Vegetation 100
Food 101

The Mixing of Bodies 102
Verminous Seeds 104
Unity of Action in the Principles 105
False Theories about Matter 105
The Diversity of Material Essences 106
The Theory of Development 107
Summary 109

Chapter 3 – Nature 111

A Series of Errors 111
The Rights of Intelligent Beings 113
The Principle of Movement 113
Nature's Guide 114
Disorders in Nature 115
The Clear Cause of Matter 116
Temporal Causes 117
The Universal Ternary 119
Air 121
The Divisions of the Human Body 123
Man, the Mirror of Science 126
The Harmony of the Elements 126
The Observers' Misunderstanding 127
The Laws of Nature 128
Paths of Knowledge 129
Mercury 130
Thunder 130
Protection Again Thunderbolts 134
Relationship Between the Elements and Man 135
Principle Errors 136
Weight, Number and Measure 136
The Different Actions in Animals 137
Different Actions in the Intellect 138
Man's Two Natures 139
Two Universal Natures 139
The Seat of the Physical Spirit 140
The Seat of the Intellectual Soul 140
The Connection Between the Intellectual and the Physical 141
Deformities and Ailments 142

8 Of Errors and Truth

The Effects of Amputation 143
The Three Temporal Actions 145
The Source of Ignorance 145
The Need for a Third Cause 146
Chance 146
The Third Cause 149
A Comment on the Two Principles 149
The Chain of Truths 150

Chapter 4 - Religion 153

An Allegorical Scene 153
The Observers' Carelessness 153
The Danger of Errors Concerning Man 154
The Various Institutions 157
Source of False Observations 158
The Religious Institution 159
False Religions 159
Truths Independent of Man 161
The Diversity of Religions 163
Zeal Without Light 164
Man's Motive 165
Unity In Worship 166
Man's Uncertainty 167
The Rule of Man 168
Mysterious Dogmas 169
The Outside of Religions 171
Morals 171
The Antiquity of Religion 172
The Affinity of Thinking Beings 173
The Difference Between Immaterial Beings 175
The Difference Between Thinking Beings 175
The Tribute Imposed on Man 177
Error in the Origin of Religion 178
Man's Intellectual Seed 180
Man's First Religion 181
Man's Second Religion 182
Reading and Writing 183
The Book of Man 183

Errors in the Book of Man 188
The Origin of the Diversity of Religions 190

Chapter 5 – Politics & Law 191

The Uncertainty of Politicians 191
Involuntary Association 192
Voluntary Association 193
False Conclusions of Politicians 195
Man's Sociability 196
The Source of Political Errors 198
Man's First Empire 199
Man's New Empire 200
Sovereign Power 201
The Dignity of Kings 202
The Knowledge of Kings 203
The Legitimacy of Sovereigns 204
Legitimate Governments 204
The Military Institution 205
The Inequality of Men 207
The Light of Governments 208
Submission to Sovereigns 208
The Obligation of Kings 211
The Instability of Governments 211
Stable Governments 212
The Difference Between Governments 213
Government by a Single Person 214
The Rivalry of Governments 215
The Right of War 216
The True Enemies of Man 216
The Three Defects of Government 217
The Administration 218
The Public Right 219
Exchanges and Usurpations 219
Civil Law 220
On Prescription 220
Adultery 221
Types of Irregular Men 223
Modesty 224

The Two Natural Laws 225
Two Adulteries 225
Criminal Administration 226
The Right to Punish 227
The Right of Life and Death 228
Source of the Right to Punish 228
Witnesses 230
Human Power 231
The Right of Execution 234
The Connection Between the Punishment and the Crime 235
Criminal Codes 236
Torture 237
The Blindness of Legislators 237
False Judgements 238
The Rights of True Sovereigns 239
The Healing of Disorders 239
Three Elements, Three Disorders 240
Disorders of the Skin 241
Disorders of the Bone and Blood 241
The Apothecary 242
The Privileges of Sovereigns 243

Chapter 6 – Mathematics & Geometry 245

The Principles of Mathematics 245
Axioms 245
Length 247
The Measurement of Length 247
Nature of the Circumference 248
Two Kinds of Lines 249
Number of Each Kind of Lines 250
Calculating to Infinity 252
Generally Accepted Measurements 252
True Measurement 254
Movement 255
Two Kinds of Movement 256
Immaterial Movement 257
The Number of Movement 258
The Number of Area 259

The Circular Line	260
The Straight Line	261
The Squaring of the Circle	262
Longitude	264
Solar and Lunar Calculation	265
Astronomical Systems	266
The Earth	267
The Plurality of Worlds	268
The Nonary Number	269
The Division of the Circle	271
The Artificial Circle	272
The Natural Circle	273
The Quaternary Number	274
The Square Root	276
Decimals	279
The Intellectual Square	279
Effects of the Circumference	280
The Superiority of the Square	281
The Measurement of the Circumference	282
The Measurement of Time	282
Upheavals in Nature	283
The Temporal Course of Beings	285
The Age of the Universe	287
The Sides of the Square	289
The Temporal Square	293
Man's Resources	294

Chapter 7 – Language & Art 297

Man's Attributes	297
Artificial Languages	297
The Unity of Languages	298
Intellectual Language	299
Physical Language	300
The Origin of Languages	301
Experiments with Children	302
The Language of Physical Beings	303
The Relationship Between Language and Abilities	304
Universal Language	305

Writing and Speech 306
The Uniformity of Languages 308
Grammar...309
The Verb..311
Accessory Parts of Speech 312
Universal Relationships of Grammar 313
The True Language 315
The Works of Man 316
Intellectual Products 316
Poetry...318
Written Characters..321
Painting..322
Coats of Arms...325
Errors Regarding The True Language......................................325
The Means of Recovering the True Language 326
Music 326
The Common Chord 327
The Seventh Chord 330
The Second 331
Dissonance and Consonance 332
Pitch...334
Principles of Harmony...335
Artificial Music 335
Musical Measure or Beat..337
Physical Measure..338
Intellectual Measurement 339
The Works of Man 339
Rights of the True Language 340
Properties of the Universal Number 341
Conclusion...344

Note on Illustrations

All the illustrations in this book are images of my personal copy of the First Edition of *Des Erreurs et de la Vérité*, printed in Lyon in 1775.

All the photographs were taken by myself.

The images include the Frontispiece; Cover, Spine and Inside Cover; a detail of the Printer's insert; one of the pages on the Book of Man; and on the last page, the image which was used at the end of Saint-Martin's original book.

Foreword

It's two hundred and forty-two years since Louis-Claude de Saint-Martin wrote his first book at the young age of thirty-two, while staying in Lyon, France, in 1775.

He was concerned by what he saw as the dangerous intrusion of atheist ideas under the cover of those writing the first Encyclopedia, whom he suspected of using the articles to push their agenda of undermining the Church. He therefore decided to write a book based upon the teachings of his Master, Martines de Pasqually. This would establish a covertly Christian Theosophical model of the creation of the universe, and of Man's privileged origin, his Fall, and the steps he could take to return to his original condition, or what Saint-Martin called his 'primitive estate'.

His readers, who were mostly from the educated classes and, of course, Freemasons, ensured his book was an instant success, and placed this young man, who wrote under the pseudonym of *An Unknown Philosopher*, in the forefront of a counter-movement which wished to defend the idea of a mankind which would reawaken to its glorious origin, and seek to reintegrate with the First Principle, his Theosophical term for God.

As well as providing an interesting view of unusual theological concepts, this book gives us a unique glimpse into the mind of a well-educated aristocrat in 18th Century France, and shows the scope of subjects such a man would have studied in those days. Saint-Martin talks with equal confidence about politics, philosophy, music, mathematics and art. He truly reflects the rounded education of a man who had pursued the Seven Liberal Arts and Sciences, the basis of all university education at that time.

Although Saint-Martin wrote a number of books, two of which were translated in the mid-nineteenth century by Edward Burton Penny, it's surprising that this original work has never seen the light of day in the English language. I hope that this translation adds to our understanding of this extraordinary visionary of Eighteenth Century France.

If I can provide a translation which allows contemporary readers to experience the same sense of interest in his theories, instead of having to struggle to understand his concepts and find themselves buried in archaic language, then I will have accomplished my mission.

Piers A. Vaughan, Corpus Christi 2017

Translating Conventions

There are a number of decisions I've taken in translating this work. For the sake of clarity, I will outline them here.

1. General Comments

Firstly, it was common for books at that time to be written in a continuous style, without subheadings and little more than Chapter numbers, resulting in a text which can be hard to follow.

To make the text and the ideas it contains a little easier for more modern eyes to follow, a common French practice over the past forty or so year has been to take the titles at the top of the pages, which reflected the content of the page below, and to turn them into subheadings. I've adopted that approach, and have also given names to the seven Chapters which, while adding little to the book itself, will at least make it easier to navigate, and hopefully make the Index more helpful. too.

Next, the French language tends to make rather freer use of capital letters at the start of nouns than English. I've therefore removed these in most cases, except in particular cases of commonly-used philosophical terms, in which case I've retained the original. The author italicized a significant number of words for emphasis, and these have been retained in this text, to reflect the writing style of the author.

2. Stylistic Comments

I've taken the approach of translating, rather than transliterating the text. There's a reason why languages differ, and it can be generally agreed that, just as the culture and style of different Nations vary, languages reflect the way in which the members of each Nation view the world. This fact is seen in many ways: in the syntax; whether nouns precede verbs, adjectives precede nouns; the number of tenses; and so forth. The English tend to live far more in the 'present' than other Nations, and therefore I will often use the Present Simple when the French text uses the Imperfect, Perfect. Pluperfect, Subjunctive, and some other tenses.

Secondly, translating a concept – especially a philosophical one – from one language to another can be challenging. Two approaches are normally adopted: either the words of the sentence are changed sufficiently to convey an idea as close to the original as possible, or sometimes a completely different phrase may be substituted, where a simile or idiom exists in both languages. For example, 'a stich in time saves nine' has a French counterpart: 'mieux vaut prévenir que guérir', literally 'it is better to prevent than to cure'. We can see from this that they have the same intent, but to translate either into the other language would be to leave the hearer confused. English has been one of the more forgiving of languages in this context, in that it often takes a foreign phrase wholesale and makes it its own. Consider words and phrases such as *bona fide*, *klutz*, *al dente*, *fin de siècle*, *zeitgeist*, *Glasnost* and *andante* as a few examples which are words used in general, or in a particular field of interest in English.

Another challenge for professional translators is the vocabulary and its particular context. A translator may be bilingual, and capable of producing a near perfect copy of a novel in another language. However, if that person is not an accountant or a chemist, a musician or a Freemason, he or she is not necessarily going to know the vocabulary used in that field. A further difficulty is that some fields use common words with very different meanings. The words 'lodge', 'apron' and 'degree' have a completely different use in Freemasonry than they have in regular speech. Therefore, on occasion, it is actually better for an informed amateur with a strong understanding of the material being presented to attempt a translation, rather than a bilingual translator with no background in the subject matter.

However, having made this observation, I feel I must to some extend prove my credentials as translator of this book, seeing that I am neither bilingual nor a professional translator, by outlining some of my background and the skills I bring to this enterprise.

Firstly, regarding the overall subject matter, I learned French at school from the age of seven, and have been translating French Masonic and esoteric books and rituals into English for over twenty years. My thirty-eight years in Freemasonry and my thirty-five plus years pursuing many esoteric paths have assured me of a sound understanding of the concepts covered in this and similar books, including the rarified vocabulary which goes with such interests, in both English and French.

Saint-Martin's subject areas cover a broad spectrum. Fortunately, I have experience in all of them. As well as sixteen 'O' levels and three 'A' levels from school, which included English, French, mathematics, calculus, geometry and the sciences, I studied Psychology and Philosophy at Oxford

University. While Saint-Martin's treatment of physiology and Nature are not exactly standard, even by Eighteenth Century standards, my background in practical and spiritual alchemy have helped significantly in these fields. Religion is covered by a Master's in Divinity, and Music by an Associateship with Trinity College of Music, London, in addition to which I was Director of Music of a church choir for many years, both conducting, composing and orchestrating settings for it.

While I feel awkward in laying out my credentials in this manner, I wish to avoid the very issue that Saint-Martin faced in 1775, when his book, while eagerly read by some sections of society, was roundly attacked by the Encyclopedists and others. Since he wrote under a *nom de plume*, they had no idea of his credentials to support such a polemic against them; and he was in no position to respond to any criticism without revealing his true name.

There are a few other rules which tends to change from French to English. On occasion, what is singular in one language translates better to the plural on the other, and vice versa. Again, what flows better is normally the best approach.

This means that this translation, rather than being a slavish word-for-word copy of the original text, has been modified to convey as closely as possible the author's intention, given his background as a philosopher, a theurgist, a Christian and a Freemason; all of which he was when he wrote *Of Errors & Truth*.

Finally, there are a lot of 'filler' phrases, the written equivalent of a person saying 'er…,' or 'You know…'. These include 'so to speak', 'I tell you', 'in other words'. Most of these can be safely omitted since they do little but distract from the narrative. However, where it's clear Saint-Martin means to give emphasis to a passage, other ways of accomplishing this are used.

3. Choice of words

As well as the specific words used in a field of study or profession, authors tend to use words idiosyncratically, which can also lead to problems in translation. A final challenge is the fact that a person living and writing over two hundred fifty years ago lived in a very different world, saw things through quite a different pair of eyes, and processed what he saw through a very different set of filters to nowadays. This was a man living in the very heart of the Enlightenment, excited on the one hand by the possibilities, but also horrified at how some of the Encyclopedists and Scientists of the time were using the medium of writing to share beliefs with the man in the street which he found particularly subversive.

As a result, it's possible to some useful extent to determine the meaning which an author might attribute to certain words. Despite the fact that we can read several definitions of a particular word in a dictionary, most people tend to use a particular word in only one way. As an example, Saint-Martin regularly uses the word 'sensible', which normally translates to 'sensitive'. However, in the context of Saint-Martin's book, a more appropriate translation of the word would be 'physical', as in the physical world of Matter; and that is the translation I've adopted that in the vast majority of times this word appears. There are a few instances in which 'sensitive' is more appropriate, and where the latter reads better, I've used that instead.

Another word which can cause a problem is 'science', which in English has become somewhat separated from the word 'knowledge'. Yet this is its Latin root (*scire* – to know), and in French the word 'science' still has both meanings. Therefore, I've translated it as knowledge, unless the context specifically relates it to the Sciences.

A comment on the words 'err', 'error' and 'stray'. This word originates from the Latin *errare*, to wander or stray. We can see from this that the words all have a common source. In the text, therefore, there is an interplay between the physical and intellectual, since the imagery of straying down paths suggests physical removal from the Source; while at a higher level, the concept also suggests a mental straying or erring from right thinking, and allowing negative ones to intrude.

On this topic, it's possible we may find one of Saint-Martins' sources for this first book, besides the obvious influence of Martines de Pasqually's *Treatise on the Reintegration of Beings*, discussed in more depth below. This is the famous English poet, Alexander Pope (1688 – 1744). Now, while I am not aware of any proof that Saint-Martin read Pope, as to my knowledge there isn't a list of the books he had in his library, there would appear to be a considerable amount of evidence pointing this way. Firstly, Pope was a Freemason: not a particularly active one, he attended a short-lived Lodge which met in the Goat Tavern in London, which closed the same year he died. However, his main claim to Masonic history is his *Universal Prayer*, written in 1738, and still often used in Masonic instruction in England. The second and third verses contain the telling words:

> "Thou Great First Cause, least understood:
>   Who all my sense confined
> To know but this – that thou art good,
>   And that myself am blind:
>
> "Yet gave me, in this dark estate,
>   To see the good from ill;
> And binding Nature fast in fate,
>   Left free the human will."

Remember, too, the famous quotation from his first book, *An Essay on Criticism* (1711): "To err is human, to forgive divine." This book also ended with a discussion of the moral qualities which should be exhibited by a critic. In his *Essay on Man*, Pope discusses man's condition as a being who has fallen through his own fault, and sees the universe as a seemingly random and chaotic place. However, man's intelligence can only take in a small portion of the entire Truth, and if he only had the capacity, he would see the divine harmony and order which prevails. Man's happiness would be assured if he saw his place in the 'Great Chain of Being', between the angels and the animals. This last phrase is very similar indeed to Saint-Martin's *Universal Quaternary Progression*, see in Chapter 1 of his book.

Finally, in John Everett Butt's article on Pope in the *Encyclopedia Britannia*, he tells us: "He was the first European poet to enjoy contemporary fame in France and Italy, and throughout the European continent and to see translations of his poems into modern as well as ancient languages." So, his poems were freely available in France in Saint-Martin's time. Pope was a Catholic, a Freemason whose most famous prayer spoke of a 'Great First Cause', who wrote about man's position in the universe and his free will, his position in the 'Chain of Being', and generally ideas not dissimilar to those of Saint-Martin. This is not the place to go into further detail about this, but it may be an interesting starting point for a scholar at a future date.

There are a few instances where I would seem to use a word which is archaic or where there would be a better translation. On occasion, I use 'superior' instead of 'higher', or 'inferior' instead of 'lower'; 'estate' instead of 'state', and 'primitive' instead of 'initial' or 'first'. This stems from the fact that Saint-Martin drew much of his terminology from Martines de Pasqually's *Treatise on the Reintegration of Beings into their Primitive Estate*, and since many of his ideas drew their origin from this important source, this is itself sufficient reason to keep the terminology of the source document. Indeed, many of the terms have been used regularly in English since that time, and have become indelibly linked both to Pasqually and Saint-Martin and to their respective theosophies. So, introducing more modern terms at this point would most likely lead to error than to further enlightenment.

4. Saint-Martin's Style

Surprisingly, for a well-educated man of letters with a background in law, and of undoubted intelligence, who took up German in order to read Jakob Böhme in the original language and even translated this German Mystic's works into French, the style of Saint-Martin's first book is opaque and difficult to follow. In a way, it's not unlike the *Treatise* of his first Master, Martines de Pasqually, although the latter had the excuse that French was not his first language, and from his humble background, had a poor grasp of grammatical structure. However, Saint-Martin could not claim these disadvantages.

In his posthumously published work *Portrait de M. de Saint-Martin fait by lui-même* ('Portrait of Monsieur Saint-Martin made by himself') Saint-Martin himself tells us that he penned the first thirty pages of the book quite precipitously, in reaction to a comment by the Encyclopedist and Philosopher Boulanger, who wrote that the origin of religion was, in his words, "to be sought in the terror occasioned by the catastrophes of Nature." On reading these pages to some friends at Willermoz' house in Lyon, he was encouraged by them to continue, and says he wrote all five hundred fifty pages of his book in four months, therefore averaging four or five pages a day. Given this frantic hand-written speed and the broad scope of his book, it's perhaps not surprising that his grammar is sometimes found wanting. As Waite puts it: "he spoke from the fullness of the heart, as from an unfailing fountain", and this constant outpouring would also have led to unintentionally obscure phrases, and to repetition. His later books are written with greater clarity, which reflect a maturing of style together with a greater amount of time spent composing them.

It also goes without saying, that given the times in which he wrote, the masculine was always used. While no offense is meant, rather than make the entire book gender-neutral, I've left it in its original form.

5. Footnotes

One of the challenges in translating a foreign book on a philosophical subject is that, unless the reader has access to source materials, it can sometimes be difficult to follow the concepts without some background understanding of the author's starting point. Nowadays, we have access to such internet tools as Google and Wikipedia, which, while not always entirely accurate, nevertheless give us an almost infinite source of information to browse.

The issue with Saint-Martin is that, since so little has been translated into English, there are very few resources available to English speakers.

There was little point in creating an erudite and academic book, full of citations and quotes in the original language, since few would be able to read them, and the only people who would appreciate this would be those bilingual experts who could read the book in its original French anyway!

My intention was to create a book which would be accessible to anyone who wanted to understand more about Saint-Martin and his world view, regardless of whether they were going to read it as a Martinist, Freemason, Esotericist, Theosophist, Philosopher, Historian, or simply as a person who thought the cover looked interesting.

Footnotes seemed to be the best approach, since, instead of listing additional materials at the back of the book as Appendices, and thereby placing them at an inconvenient distance from the passages they were meant to clarify, footnotes give the reader instant access to explanations of the concepts being discussed in the body text immediately above. While some of the longer footnotes lead to shorter pages in the book, I believe this approach is the most likely to make the contents of the book more accessible to the general reader.

I'd finally add that even Arthur Edward Waite, in his book on *Saint-Martin, The French Mystic, and the Story of Modern Martinism* (1922) said of Penney's translation of the *Theosophic Correspondence:* "I question whether there could be a better gift than an annotated translation at the present day by one who knows Saint-Martin, his work and his period."

Taking Waite's words to heart, for Saint-Martin's first book at least, I've done my best.

6. Errors in translating

Having said all the above, it goes without saying that any errors in translation, and any mistyped words or sentences are my responsibility alone.

Introduction

This introduction is intended to put this seminal book in its proper context. I realize that not everyone who opens this book will have a deep understanding of the times, the country, Freemasonry, the work of Martines de Pasqually, or the key characters who affect this story. It's to them that I address these opening remarks, in the hope that it will help them to navigate what can be a difficult book to understand.

There would be little point in going into great detail about the man and his life. So much has already been written about Saint-Martin and his works that I could do little but repeat what has already been said. But the problem we face is the fact that, while many pages have been written on this topic, almost invariably they are in French! Indeed, the very English-speaking people who follow the teachings of this man, which were 'codified' by Dr. Gérard Encausse (also known as Papus) towards the end of the Nineteenth Century into an Order known as *Martinism*, have almost no access, not only to the vast amount which has been written on this subject, but even to the original writings of the man himself. Further, although there were three key figures in this story, as we shall see, their contributions to the three diverse fields of Freemasonry, theosophy and theurgy have often become conflated into one movement in Anglo-Saxon minds; though strictly speaking one practiced theurgy, or the active approach to communicating with higher forces, the second practiced what is called the Cardiac Path or Way of the Heart, which is closer to Christian mystical contemplation, and the third was a high-ranking Freemason who wrote Masonic rituals (although it must be confessed he tried to fill these rituals with esoteric ideas).

I'll therefore limit myself to a brief *resumé* of Saint-Martin's life up to the appearance of this book, the main influences which inspired him to write it, and give an outline of the ideas he sets forth in *Of Errors & Truth*.

1. The Man

Louis-Claude de Saint-Martin was born in 1743 in Amboise, France, in the Loire valley, surrounded by many of the famous Châteaux of that region. His mother died shortly after his birth, and he formed a close attachment to his step-mother, who he tells us emphatically, influenced his love of learning, religion and the company of women.

At his father's wish, he entered the legal profession, but finding it not to his taste, sought his father's permission to join the army instead. Remarkably, France was not at war at the time. Having just come out of the Wars of Polish and Austrian succession, the Jacobite Rebellion, and finally the oddly-named Seven Years' War from 1754 – 1763, so Saint-Martin was able to enjoy a period of peace. The next major involvement of the French would not be until the Revolutionary American War in 1775. He was therefore relatively free to enjoy his commission in the Regiment of Foix, then garrisoned in Bordeaux, and to continue to read extensively.

It was during this period of tranquility that he met Martines de Pasqually and, in 1768, at the age of 25, became one of his pupils.

Pasqually was a Freemason who claimed his authority from a Charter signed by Prince Charles Edward Stuart, better known perhaps as Bonnie Prince Charlie, and claimed hereditary Grand Master of all Masonic Orders. As an aside, when King James II was expelled from England and settled in Saint-Germain-en-Laye, just outside of Paris, both he and his successors claimed a right to be hereditary Grand Masters of Freemasonry, no doubt sensing a benefit in having the ability to dispense largesse to the nobility and senior citizens of France, many of whom were enamored of this new Order. This view had certainly been bolstered by Chevalier Ramsay's famous *Oration* in 1737, which further supported the idea of Freemasonry as descending from the early Chivalric Orders (as a matter of fact, he only quoted the Hospitallers, and not the Templars, as commonly quoted). For these reasons, Freemasonry in France, particularly seeing that France was so often at war with England, sought origins other than the Premier Grand Lodge of England, and therefore eagerly embraced a Scottish – *Écossais* in French – origin. Thus, the term 'Scottish Rite' or 'Rite Écossais' tended to mean most Masonic Orders in France in the earliest days.

Pasqually's Order, grandly called the *Order of Elect Cohen of the Universe,* therefore claimed authority from a hereditary Charter issued to his father by Bonnie Prince Charlie. Its Degrees were based on the early Lodge of Perfection, but there the similarity ended, for he had created a series of rituals and educational materials which were distinctly theurgical in nature, requiring its members to pray and undertake regular 'magical; operations including evocations and exorcisms. It's interesting to note that, while he had success in opening a number of Lodges around France, his greatest success was in Bordeaux, the very city where Estienne Morin had established his nascent Scottish Rite only a handful of years earlier; and indeed it's believed that there was some overlap in membership.

Saint-Martin took to this Order, and shortly thereafter resigned his army commission in order to become Pasqually's full-time secretary. He worked with Pasqually on his *Treatise on the Reintegration of Beings into their Primitive Estate*, an extensive handwritten document which was given only to those members who had attained the highest Grade in his Order, that of *Réaux Croix*. There is no doubt that this document played a major part in shaping Saint-Martin's own ideas on theurgy, and this peculiarly gnostic approach to Christianity remained with him throughout his life, even long after Pasqually had gone, and even after Saint-Martin himself had divested himself of Masonry and theurgy in order to pursue the contemplative life. Indeed, as late as 1789 Saint-Martin wrote: "It's to Martines de Pasqually that I owe my introduction to the higher truths." This, despite his once asking his Master, when despairing of the complexity of the work required in the Elus Cohen, "but Master, can all this be needed to find God?"

Yet by 1772 Pasqually was gone, having sailed to St. Domingo in order to take up an inheritance, and where he died soon after, in 1774. Without the guidance of this charismatic leader, the Order quickly fell into abeyance.

It was during his connection with this Order that Saint-Martin met another Freemason, who was to feature much in his life: Jean-Baptiste Willermoz.

Willermoz was a silk merchant who lived in Lyon. Yet his main legacy is that of being a prominent Freemason who was prolific in writing rituals (most of which still exist, and can be read in the *Fonds Willermoz* in the Library of Lyon), as well as establishing many Lodges in his city. He worked alongside Saint-Martin in educating the members of his Elus Cohen Lodge in Lyon, and Saint-Martin stayed with him at his house on more than one occasion. Indeed, it was at Willermoz' house that Saint-Martin first read the early pages of his book, *Of Errors & Truth*, to some of their disciples; and it was another close friend of Willermoz, Jean-André Périsse, who with his brother printed Saint-Martin's book in Lyon in 1775.

Perhaps Willermoz' greatest legacy is his creation of the *Rite Écossais Rectifié*, or Scottish Rectified Rite, following the Convent of Wilhelmsbad in 1782, convened primarily to replace Baron von Hund's *Rite of Strict Observance* with an Order which retained the main concepts, but without carrying on the idea of 'Secret Chiefs', or the potential stigma of adhering to the neo-Templar code of 'vengeance', or revenge against the French monarchy and the Vatican for their persecution of the Order of the Temple many Centuries earlier. This profession was no doubt intended to avoid persecution by the French authorities.

This Order had six Grades, and also two higher, 'hidden' Grades not known to the regular members. It was in these that Willermoz had summarized the teachings of Pasqually's *Treatise*, using this vehicle to perpetuate his doctrines, and quite probably, at least some of the theurgic activities as well.

Just as Saint-Martin was to perpetuate his Master's teachings in a modified format in his mystical approach, so Willermoz was later to codify them in the higher Orders of his Masonic masterpiece; and we should remember, too, that Willermoz has been credited by a number of scholars with creating the Rose Croix Degree in the Ancient Accepted Scottish Rite, which is nonetheless a Rosicrucian Grade, and not based directly on Pasqually's Réaux Croix, which takes its symbolism from quite another source.

2. The Book

We're told that in the winter of 1774 Saint-Martin set out the first thirty pages of this book, and following the encouragement of his circle of friends when he read it aloud at Willermoz' house (which makes it highly probably that both Willermoz and Périsse were present, too), he spent the next four months pouring out his ideas onto paper.

The book itself was published in Lyon by the Brothers Périsse, although the Frontispiece claims it was written in 'Edimbourg' or Edinburgh (see Figure 1). Why the subterfuge? There are two possible reasons. The less probable one is that Saint-Martin was trying to hide his identity: after all, he signed this and other books 'An Unknown Philosopher'. However, this is unlikely since his identity seemed to be an open secret, and following the success of his book he was invited to talk in salons in Lyon, Paris and other intellectual centers, both in France and in England, Italy, Switzerland, Russia and elsewhere. More likely is the fact that the crown imposed high taxes on publishers for printing works in France, which had initially led to many books being printed abroad, then imported; and later to publishers simply *saying* that the works were printed abroad while printing them in France.

Figure 2 - Printer's insert on inside page

There's no doubt the book appealed to those who were tired of the determination of Science to place everything into neatly categorized boxes. He goes to great lengths to appeal to the mysterious by hinting at secret initiations and hidden knowledge he has received which he is nevertheless not at liberty to pass on. Of course, this was grist to the mill in a society full of plots and intrigues, and especially Masons surrounded by 'Secret Chiefs' and 'Hidden Masters'. His description of the 'Spear of Four Metals', and the 'Book of Man of Ten Leaves' evoke powerful images which still float at the edge of our understanding, just out of reach. The book is also liberally peppered with Masonic allusions. For example, he talked of Four Degrees of earthly existence, which spoke loudly to a Masonic Brotherhood based on the idea of three basic Degrees and a fourth Grade of Scottish Master which sat as a degree of Perfection above them; and referred to 'regular steps', which is another term which would have Masons of the time nodding eagerly as they devoured the text. Finally, one can't miss the allusion to the *Seven Liberal Arts and Sciences*, which at the time was the standard curriculum of all Universities, as well as being a key part of the Companion or Fellowcraft Degree in Masonry. It's not by chance that Saint-Martin includes discussions of arithmetic, geometry, astronomy and music, while using the skills of grammar, logic and rhetoric to get his points across.

The book appeared, and was an instant success with its target audience. Many had grown concerned that the Enlightenment had perhaps gone too far in its search to explain everything, and in the process 'de-spiritualized' both man and his world.

Figures 3,4, 5 – Cover, spine and inside page of book

The split between Science and Religion had made itself felt, particularly in the fields which studied Man and Nature for the Cause and Origin of things, which in some eyes was leading to God being ignored, or, worse, denied. And Saint-Martin was a very personable representative of this reaction to creeping atheism. As Matter eloquently put it in his biography of Saint-Martin: "At the age of thirty years M. de Saint-Martin found himself very favorably placed in the world. An expressive countenance and polished manners, marked by great distinction and considerable reserve, presented him to the best advantage. His demeanor announcing not only the desire to please but something to bestow, he soon became known widely and was in request everywhere."

Saint-Martin's book could not expressly be called anti-Enlightenment. After all, it was not an overtly religious book, notwithstanding it was added to the Roman Catholic *Index* of prohibited books. Similarly, his criticism of Governments, and challenging the Establishment, may well have helped to save him during the French Revolution. However, on the other hand the book could be said to be a harbinger of the returning interest in the spiritual and especially the occult, which was shortly to be seen in the inevitable pendulum swing away from the rational thinking which had epitomized the early days of the Enlightenment.

Its success opened doors to him and allowed him to move freely in society, and certainly helped his finances. We know he was not a wealthy man, and indeed he had given up his commission in the army and no doubt worked as Pasqually's secretary for little or no recompense. His own comments tell us he was living in Lyon in very modest accommodation while writing the book, and the fact of his mentioning that he scalded himself while cooking soup one day tells us he had no servants.

However, it should come as no surprise that his work did not please everyone. Indeed, when Voltaire was given a copy of the book, he declared: "I don't believe anyone has ever printed anything more absurd, more obscure, more crazy, and more stupid." This is hardly surprising, given the stern manner in which Saint-Martin constantly takes those he refers to as 'the Observers' to task time and time again.

Indeed, it's perhaps a measure of its success that it inspired a number of parodies in more than one country. And just as exposés of Masonry often give us the clearest idea of a ritual's worth, we can end this section by quoting from John Robison's work *Proofs of a Conspiracy* (1798), a tome which puts much of the blame for the ills of society and the French

Revolution at the door of Freemasonry in general and the Illuminati in particular: "*Des Erreurs et de la Verité* …is a sort of holy scripture, or at least a Talmud among the Free Masons of France. It's intended only for the initiated, and is indeed a mystery to any other reader. But as it was intended for spreading the favorite opinions of some enthusiastic Brethren, every thing (*sic*) is said that does not directly betray the secrets of the Order. It contains a system of Theosophy that has often appeared in the writings of philosophers, both in ancient and modern times."

3. The Ideas

The title, *Of Errors & Truth*, itself gives an indication of Saint-Martin's viewpoint: there is only one Truth, but many ways to err. Indeed, much of the philosophy involves a sense of movement, since to stray – or err – is to move physically away from the true path. And in his work Saint-Martin describes man as being *physically* separated from Truth, rather than just *conceptually*.

Much of the symbolism of the work comes from the *Treatise on the Reintegration of Beings* by his Master, Pasqually. Indeed, Robison's comment about Saint-Martin's first book being a *Talmud* would apply equally to the *Treatise*, although the *Zohar* might be a more apt description, as it's nothing less than a commentary on many of the early stories of the Bible. It's possible that the final work was intended to be a much longer and complete commentary; but it stops dead, almost in mid-sentence, during Saul.

Despite being written in the 1760s it could almost read as a gnostic text, and its description of the spiritual Beings does not sound very dissimilar to the idea of Archons.

Outside of Time, God emanated Spiritual Beings, which formed four distinct categories. However, these Beings sinned against God by wanting to emanate lesser Beings themselves, independent of God, to prove that they were as powerful as Him. God therefore created Time and Materiality in which to imprison them, so that they could exercise their evil intentions in isolation from the rest of creation; for God had given them free will, and they had a right to exercise it. All He could do was to limit their sphere of activity. However, he created Adam to be the Guardian over this Temporal and Physical prison, and He endowed him with the same powers the Spiritual Beings has originally been given. Man possessed a Glorious Body, not being made of matter, and despite being emanated after the Spiritual Beings he was superior to them, being as God in likeness. This, then, was man in his *first* or *primitive estate*.

The power of God was described as 'four-fold', a fact which becomes important in Saint-Martin's teachings. Indeed, all of Pasqually's writing is deeply dependent on numbers. He took his inspiration for this from the *Book of Wisdom*, which states that God has "ordered all things in measure and number and weight." (Wisdom 11:20). Indeed, Saint-Martin pointed out that measure and weight were subordinate to number, since neither could exist without it. In his *Treatise* Pasqually said: "It is this virtue of numbers that brought the wise men to say that no-one can be learned, either in the spiritual divine, or in the celestial, terrestrial and particular, without the science of numbers." He therefore attributes very specific properties to each number. It should be noted he only concerned himself with the numbers 1 through 9, seeing 10 as being a return to 1, or Unity, through Theosophical addition (i.e. $10 = 1 + 0 = 1$). However, his numbering system was not that of the Kabbalah or of any other commonly held system of attributions. Further, it should be noted that when both Pasqually and Saint-Martin use the terms 'root' and 'power' of numbers, they are not referring to simple mathematical calculations, but rather a spiritual outcome. As an example, the essential root of 4 is 10. How is this so? In Theosophical addition $1+2+3+4=10$, and therefore 10 is the root of 4. But 10 can be reduced to 1, as in $1+0=1$. So, 1 is the second essential root of 4. Without going into further detail, it's important to remember that Saint-Martin's use of mathematics isn't therefore traditional in any sense.

Now, when man was originally placed in the center of the Universe and in direct and immediate communication with the mind of God, or the First Principle, he was placed in the abode of perfection. And there he should have remained. However, a fallen Spiritual Being tempted him in its turn, appearing to Adam in his own form as a Glorious Body, and telling him that he himself could be like God, and create on his own. In his hubris, Adam attempted to perform (or *operate* in Pasqually's terminology) an act of creation in order to impress his audience, but being unable to do so without God's cooperation, he both alerted the First Principle to his act, and created a material form. As punishment God enclosed a spirit in the material form Adam had created, and cast him, with this form which Adam named *Heva* or Eve, down into the temporal, physical world he had once ruled.

Man was therefore condemned to live in the material world, in a material body which was subject to pain and decay, separated from the mind of God, yet never able to settle for his new estate. although he was now part of it. His immortal part which was trapped was incompatible with the matter in which he was imprisoned in every way. Being on earth, he was now more than ever surrounded by the very demonic forces which had led him to prevaricate in the first place.

Man's hope therefore lies in the fact the God has never abandoned his creature, and hopes that he will work to reunite with Him in a process Pasqually called *Reintegration*. In man's place God put a second, known as the *Reconciler* (Christ) who supports us in our endeavors to reunite with God.

While Pasqually saw this process of Reintegration as being one of performing regular operations, in this case magical ceremonies, in order to establish contact with a guide which would help him in his efforts, Saint-Martin had moved beyond the need for physical actions, and saw the process as being in a progression which was more internal than external, which he called the *Way of the Heart* or the *Cardiac Path*.

The overriding purpose of *Of Errors & Truth* was to raise man's consciousness above the daily motions of living, a state he later came to call '*Men of the Stream*', and to have them strive towards reunion with God, or the First Principle, through an act of gnosis or recognition, and a way of living which ever recalled to man the fact that he was living in the *Forest of Errors*, and that only by foregoing the pleasures of this dark world and striving to fulfill his potential in living a virtuous life, could he hope to escape and keep his feet on the Path.

Perhaps the most astonishing thing about Saint-Martin's book is its sheer scale. In order to get his point across he moves through philosophy, theosophy, religion, law, politics, the military, astronomy, mathematics and geometry, music, art and poetry. While it might seem that he does this for effect, in order to show off his knowledge, nevertheless we should remember that he always talks to his strengths: after all, he had studied law and had served in the military, was well-acquainted with all the social graces of an aristocratic and genteel life, and was well-read in all manner of subjects.

Indeed, when we find him comparing straight lines to curved lines, or the notes of a musical scale, it can sometimes seem as if he is applying elegant arguments in order to support his theory: whereas, he is in fact demonstrating to us that, despite the Scientists' attempts to expand knowledge into a thousand different areas of study, all these areas are really subject to but one Law which underpins everything, and that everything can be understood if we could only stop seeing the effects, and try to understand the underlying Causes and Principles.

One final comment. On page 321, Saint-Martin says: "All men are C-H-R." What he is saying is that all men are Christs; in other words, that all men are called to become sons of God through grace. Here Saint-Martin is not so much making a statement of Faith, but rather a giving us a reassurance that, however far from the light we have strayed, every man has the potential to set himself back on the Path of Reintegration. My thanks to Serge Caillet and to Dr. Eric Fanjeaux for our discussions on this point.

4. Suggested Reading

For those who wish to learn more about the man and his work, I would refer them to the two translations by Edward Burton Penny of *Theosophic Correspondence Between Louis-Claude de Saint-Martin and Kirchberger, Baron de Liebistorf* (1863), and *The Spiritual Ministry of Man* (1864). More biographical details may be found in *Saint-Martin the French Mystic & The Story of Modern Martinism* (1922), and the substantial work *The Unknown Philosopher* (1901), both by Arthur Edward Waite. However, for the more adventurous, the vast majority of works on this subject may be found in French by such writers as le Comte Joseph de Maistre, Dr. Gérard Encausse (Papus), Jacques Matter, Alice Joly, Robert Amadou, Serge Caillet, and many others.

The basic waypoints which I've provided help the reader understand the book were in no way intended to be an in-depth assessment of the ideas set forth. However, for those who wish to delve more deeply into the concepts outlines, an excellent treatment of the Theosophy contained in the book, and of Saint-Martin's theosophy in general, I would recommend the paper titled *The Mystery of Truth: Louis-Claude de Saint-Martin's Enlightened Mysticism* by David Bates (2000), published by the University of Pennsylvania Press and available on several internet sites, including: https://rhetoric.berkeley.edu/files/saintmartin.pdf.

Saint-Martin's 1775 Foreword

This book I offer to mankind isn't just a series of speculations. It isn't simply an explanation I am offering. I believe I'm giving them a more useful gift. But it isn't Knowledge itself that I'm giving them: I know only too well that man can't expect that from another man. It's only a glimmer from their own torch which I'm giving back to them, so that it can shed light upon the false ideas they have been given about Truth, and on the feeble and dangerous weapons that unsteady hands have used to defend it.

I admit to being greatly affected when I review the present state of *Knowledge*. I've seen how misunderstandings have distorted it. I've seen the hideous veil which covers it, and in the interests of my fellow man I believe it my duty to tear it away.

There's no doubt that I would need more than normal resources for such an undertaking: but, without explaining the ones I'm going to use, suffice it to say that they're connected with man's very nature, that they've always been known by a few men since the beginning of time, and that they will never be forgotten so long as there are thinking Beings.

It's from them that I've drawn the evidence and the certainty of that Truth whose search occupies the entire Universe.

After this admission, if I were still accused of teaching an unknown doctrine, at least I can't be suspected of being its inventor; for if it concerns men's nature, not only did it not come from me, but it would also be impossible to attribute it to any other man.

And truly, if the Reader waits until he has read the whole book and seen its concepts before giving his verdict, and gives himself time to grasp the importance of and connections between the Principles I show him, he will agree that they are the real key to all the mysterious allegories and fables which are common to all Nations, the source of all types of Institutions, and the very model of the Laws which govern the Universe and which constitute all Beings. These Principles serve as a basis for everything that exists and everything that takes place, either in man and by his hand, or outside of man and independently of his will. Finally, he will see that, outside of these Principles, there can be no true Knowledge.

From this he will better understand why we see an endless variety of dogmas and theories proposed by men; why we see a multitude of philosophical, political and religious sects, each of which can barely agree among themselves, let alone with other sects; why, despite the efforts the leaders of these sects endlessly make to create stable doctrines around the key points, and to reconcile specific views, they never manage this; why, as they can't offer anything solid to their disciples, they can't persuade them, and even lead them to mistrust all Knowledge, since they've only known what is imaginary or faulty; and finally, why both the Teachers and the Observers[1] constantly and brazenly show they've neither explanation nor proof of what is really true. Then I believe the Reader will conclude that, if the Principles I set out are the only basis for Truth, it's because they were forgotten that so many errors consume the Earth, and they have clearly been almost totally disregarded, since ignorance and uncertainty of them are widespread.

These are the subjects which the man who seeks to understand can find here, to help him to form ideas which are sounder and more consistent with the nature of the seed he carries within him.

However, although the Light is made for all eyes to see, it's even more certain that not all eyes are created to see it in all its brilliance. This is why the small number of men who are the custodians of the facts which I'm setting out are sworn to prudence and discretion by the most solemn vows.

In addition, I've promised to be very guarded in this book, and to wrap myself frequently in a veil that even the most perceptive Reader won't always be able to pierce, seeing that I will on occasion speak about something entirely different to what I appear to be discussing.

For the same reason, although I'm going to bring a large number of different subjects under one roof, I'll only be able to give a rough outline of the vast panorama that I could offer. Nevertheless, I will say enough to provide food for thought for most, including those who enjoy great fame working in the Sciences.

But since my goal's only to benefit mankind in general, and certainly not wishing to create any discord between individuals, I won't attack any accepted Dogmas or any established Political Institutions directly; and even in my comments about the Sciences and the various types of Government,

---

[1] As mentioned in the *Introduction*, 'the Teachers', and particularly 'the Observers', are the target of Saint-Martin's contempt throughout the book. These people, never named, are portrayed as a unified collective of shadowy presences hovering with sinister intent in the background, as if it is their mission to mislead humanity. In fact, Saint-Martin puts the Encyclopedists, Materialists, and anyone who appears to him to deny the active presence of God's influence on mankind and Nature together in this group, and uses them to good effect as a foil for his arguments throughout the book.

I will refrain from discussing anything which could have the slightest connection with subjects which are too specific.

Also, I decided against using quotations, because firstly, I don't often frequent libraries, and the books I reference aren't to be found there; and secondly, because truths[2] which are only based on testimonies would no longer be truths.

Here, I think it's appropriate to give an outline of the order and layout of this book. To begin with, there will be a few observations on Good and Evil, why modern theories have confused them, and because of this have been forced to deny any difference between them. A brief look at Man will clarify this problem, and educate us about why he's still in such great ignorance, not only about what surrounds him, but also concerning his true nature. The differences between his abilities will be confirmed by those we find between the abilities of lesser Beings; and by this we will show the universality of a two-fold Law in everything that's subject to time. The need for a third temporal Law will then be even more clearly proven, by showing that the two-fold Law's completely dependent upon it.

Understanding the mistakes made about all these subjects will clearly identify the cause of this obscurity, the variety and uncertainty shown in all of man's works, as well as in all Institutions – both civil and sacred – connected with them. This will teach us what the true source of their Sovereign Power, and of all the rights which constitute their different establishments, must be. We will also study the Principles established by the Higher Sciences, and particularly in Mathematics, where the origin and true cause of errors will clearly be seen.

Finally, we'll remind man of that natural attribute which distinguishes him best from the other Beings, and which is the most appropriate to bring him in harmony with all the knowledge which agrees with his nature. All these subjects are contained in seven chapters, which, while based on the same foundation, each discusses a different subject.

If some Readers have issues in accepting the Principles which I am about to recall to mankind, since their issues would only be because they followed their own path instead of that of this book, they should not expect any further explanations from me, since they would be no clearer than the book itself.

---

[2] In the text, the word 'truths' will not be capitalized, and refers to evident or provable facts. Capitalization will be reserved for 'Truth', the one referenced by Saint-Martin in the title of this book.

In reading these thoughts you will easily see that I am not very interested in format, and that I haven't been fastidious about style. But if the Reader's sincere, he will at least acknowledge that I was sufficiently engrossed in my theme, and in any case my subject doesn't really suffer because of it.

Chapter 1 – The Philosophy

The Cause of Errors

It's a distressing sight, when we try to think about man, to see him at the same time tormented by a desire to understand, not seeing the answers to anything, but nevertheless having the audacity and the nerve to want to give answers to everything. Instead of contemplating the darkness which surrounds him and beginning by testing its depth; he goes ahead, not only as if he was sure of dispersing it, but also as if there were no barriers at all between him and *Knowledge*. Very soon, in trying to create a Truth, he dares to set it up in place of the Truth that he ought to respect in silence, and over which today he has barely any right other than to want it and wait for it.

If he's totally separated from the Light how can he light the torch, which should serve to guide him, by himself? How can he produce a Knowledge which takes away all his doubts, through his own abilities? Don't these glimmers and appearances of reality, which he believes he's discovering in the luxury of his imagination, vanish under the simplest examination? And having given birth to lifeless and unstable phantoms, isn't he forced to replace them with new illusions, which soon suffer the same fate, leaving him thrown into the most terrible uncertainty?

Fortunate would he be, however, if his weakness were the only reason for his errors! His situation would be far less deplorable, since being by nature unable to find peace except in Truth, the more painful his trials, the more they would serve to lead him to the one purpose for which he was created.

But his errors still take their origin from his unruly will. We can see that, far from using the few powers that remain to him to his benefit, he almost always uses them against the Law[3] of his Being: indeed, we see that,

---

[3] A brief comment on Laws: Pasqually and Saint-Martin saw the First Principle or God as a Creator but not necessarily as a power which interfered in the daily functioning of His creation. Indeed, the concept of free-will to them meant that not only did intelligent Beings have complete autonomy over their actions, but that the First Principle didn't necessarily know a thought until it came into existence. The first two sentences in Pasqually's *Treatise* (using the translation by Trevor Stewart, pub. 2007 by Septentrione Books) read: "Before Time began God, in the Divine Immensity, emanated superior spiritual Beings for His own glory. They were to function therein according to eternal laws, precepts and commandments which He had fixed for them." We can draw two conclusions from this passage. Firstly, that originally Man was outside of time, so he was originally immortal; and time can therefore be seen as a prison into which Man was placed after his prevarication, or sin. Secondly, while God,

far from being held back by the darkness which surrounds him, he puts his blindfold on with his own hands. Then, no longer glimpsing the slightest spark of light, he's overcome with fear or despair, and propels himself along dangerous roads which distance him forever from his true path.

So, it's because of this mixture of weakness and carelessness that man's ignorance persists. This is the source of his continual indiscretion, so that, giving up his days to pointless and useless efforts, we can hardly be surprised that his work produces no fruit, or only leaves a bitter aftertaste.

However, when I recall the faults and the unthinking direction of my fellow men, in no way do I want to disparage them. My ardent desire, on the contrary, would be for them to never lose sight of the greatness of which they are capable. Let me at least help them by trying to make the problems which stop them disappear, stirring up their courage, and showing them the path that leads to the goal they desire!

If man were to take a long hard look at himself, it wouldn't be hard for him to feel and admit that there must be a Knowledge or a Law for him, because there's one for all Beings, although it's not universally within all Beings; and because, even given our weakness, ignorance and misconceptions, we spend our time seeking peace and light.

Then, although the efforts man makes daily to reach the goal he seeks so rarely meets with any success, we must not believe that this goal's imaginary, but only that man's wrong about the path which leads there, and that he's therefore in the greatest privation, because he doesn't even know which path he should take.

The Truth

So, we can now agree that man's current misfortune doesn't come from he being unaware there's a Truth, but rather from misunderstanding the nature of this Truth; because those very people who intended to deny and destroy it never thought they could succeed without having another Truth to substitute for it. And indeed, they dressed up their fantastic theories with power, immutability and universality – in sum, all the properties of a Being which is both real and exists independently – as they felt that a Truth

---

or the First Principle, created Beings, he established Laws which were to function independently of Him, to perpetuate His creation and keep it in motion. The action of these Laws upon Beings and objects determines their nature, character and manner of evolution.

couldn't be such without existing on its own, invariable and completely independent, containing within itself the source of its existence. For if it had received its existence from another Principle, that Principle could later plunge it back into the nothingness or inertness from which it had drawn it forth.

Also, those who have fought against Truth have proved by their own explanations that they still have an enduring concept of a Truth. To repeat: what torments most of mankind here below[4] is less about knowing whether there *is* a Truth, than knowing what this Truth *is*.

Good and Evil

But what disturbs this feeling in man, and so often hides the brightest rays of this light in him, is the continual mixing of Good and Evil, light and dark, harmony and disorder he sees in the Universe and within himself. This universal contrast makes him uneasy, and spreads confusion in his ideas which he can barely disentangle. As much distressed as surprised by such a strange union, in trying to explain it he gives himself up to the most distressing opinions, and soon, no longer feeling this same Truth, he loses any confidence he had in it. Then, the greatest service we could offer him in his distressing situation would be to convince him that he can learn about the source of this confusion which troubles him, and most importantly to prevent him from deciding anything against that Truth which he acknowledges, which he loves, and which he can't live without.

The Good and Evil Principles

It's certain that in thinking about the cycles and contradictions experienced by all Beings of Nature, men must admit that it's under the influences of Good and Evil, which necessarily leads them to recognize the existence of two opposing Principles. Indeed, nothing is wiser than this observation, and nothing truer than the conclusion they took from it. Why weren't they just as pleased when they tried to explain the nature of these

---

[4] Specifically, here on earth. However, *ici-bas* translates as 'here below'. Since this phrase is so often used by Saint-Martin to contrast with man's former estate, in keeping with the Hermetic axiom 'as above so below' I have retained this phrase throughout the book.

two Principles? Why did they give their knowledge a basis so narrow that they are forced to keep demolishing the very theories they want to use to support it?

It's because, neglecting the real means they had to educate themselves, they were foolish enough to give an opinion on this sacred matter themselves; as if, far as they are from the abode of light, men could still be sure of their good sense. Then, having acknowledged the existence of the two Principles, they were unable to tell the difference between them.

Sometimes they saw them as having the same strength and the same age[5], which made them equal rivals by placing them both at the same level of power and greatness.

Sometimes, they did proclaim Evil to be inferior to Good in all forms; but they contradicted themselves when they wished to go into detail about the nature of Evil and its origin. Sometimes they were not afraid to put Evil and Good together in one and the same Principle, believing they honored this Principle by assigning it an exclusive power that made it the Creator of all things without exception, so that this Principle was father and tyrant at the same time, destroying as it raises up, spiteful and unjust in virtue of its greatness, and as a result having to punish itself in order to maintain its own Justice.

Finally, left to drift through these uncertainties, unable to discover a credible idea, some chose to deny both Principles, and made themselves believe that everything worked without law or order, and unable to explain what Good and Evil were, they said that neither Good or Evil even existed.

When, after making this claim, they were asked about the origin of all those rules spread throughout the earth; and the origin of that one inner voice which seems to compel everyone to adopt them; and which, even when he strays, makes man feel that he has a destination which is truly superior to the things which take up his attention here; these Observers, in their blindness, talked about natural habits and feelings. They attributed the power of thought and all man's abilities to mechanical structures and laws; and then they claimed that, because of his weakness, major physical disasters across the ages had made him fearful and full of dread; that in constantly experiencing the superiority of the elements and the Beings which surrounded this weak individual, he had imagined that some undefinable power governed and disrupted Nature at will; from all of which

---

[5] The reference to 'same age' comes from the fact that, in the military at least in those times, if two people had the same rank, the older person would automatically be considered to be the senior one.

he had developed a series of fantastic rules about subordination and order, punishment and reward which education and example have perpetuated, but with great variations depending on circumstances and region.[6]

False Doctrine Concerning the Two Principles

Then taking for evidence the endless variation in the arbitrary customs and practices of Nations, the dishonesty and rivalry of the Teachers, as well as the war between human opinions, the result of doubt and ignorance, it was easy for them to show that man saw only uncertainty and contradiction around him, and because of this they thought themselves authorized to reaffirm that nothing is true, so nothing really exists since, according to what had already been explained, existence and truth are the same thing.

This, then, was the means these foolhardy Masters used to proclaim their doctrine and justify it. These are the poisoned wells from which all the scourges which afflict man and torment him even more than his natural miseries, were drawn.

How much error and suffering they would have spared us if, instead of seeking the truth in manifestations of material nature, they had decided to go into themselves, if they wanted to explain things through man, and not man through things; then, fortified with courage and patience, in the quiet of their imagination, they had pursued the discovery of that light we all desire so fervently. It might not have been in their power to see it at first glance; but struck by the brightness that surrounds it, and using all their abilities to study it, they wouldn't have thought to comment about its nature, or want to bring it to the attention of their fellow man before being guided by its rays.

When man, takes a courageous stand, and manages to overcome everything which is revolting to his being, he finds he's at peace with himself, and from this he's at peace with all of Nature. But if, through negligence or becoming weary of fighting, he allows the tiniest spark of a

---

[6] Here we see Saint-Martin's immediate reaction to Boulanger's comment about religion coming out of man's fear of natural events, such as thunder, lightning, eclipses and earthquakes, and his clear contempt for 'the Observers'.

fire alien to his own essence to enter him, he suffers and languishes until he's completely rid of it.

Because of this, man recognizes on an even more personal level that there are two different Principles; and since he finds happiness and peace with the one, while the other is always accompanied by hardship and torment, he has distinguished them by calling them the Good Principle, and the Evil Principle.

The Difference between the Two Principles

Since then, if he wanted to study all the Beings of the Universe in the same way, it would have been easy to focus his thoughts on the nature of Good and Evil, and through this to find out what their true origin was. Let's say, then, that for every Being, Good is the fulfilment of its own Law, and Evil is what opposes this. Let's also say that, since each Being has only one Law, since all hold to a First Law which is one, then Good, or the fulfilment of this Law, must be one as well, that is, solely and exclusively true, even though it embraces an infinity of different Beings.

On the other hand, Evil can have no agreement with this Law of Beings, since it fights it; from which it can't be included in a unity since it desires to damage it in wanting to form another unity. In other words, it's false, since it can't exist alone; and despite this Evil, the Law of Beings exists alongside it, and it can never destroy that Law, even though it can impede or disturb its completion.

I've said that when he draws close to the Good Principle, man is filled with joy, and as a result beyond all Evil. Then he's complete in his happiness, and can have neither a sense, nor a notion of any other Being; and therefore, nothing that comes from the Evil Principle can mingle with his joy, which proves that there, man is in his element and his Law of Unity is accomplished.

But if he seeks a support other than this Law of his, his joy is first of all uneasy and nervous. He only obtains pleasure from reproaching himself for his enjoyment, and finding himself divided for a moment between the Evil which is winning him over and the Good that he has left, he experiences emotionally the effect of the two opposing Laws, and he learns by the sense of uneasiness which follows that he no longer possesses unity, because he strayed from his Law. Soon, it's true, this uneasy sense of enjoyment becomes stronger, and can even come to dominate him: but far from making him more unified and more real, it produces confusion in man's abilities which is even more dreadful because, given that the action of Evil is sterile and limiting, the raptures felt by the man who gave himself over to them only lead him all the more quickly to a feeling of emptiness and inevitable depression.

So, this is the infinite difference which is to be found between the two Principles: Good contains all its power and all its value within itself, whereas Evil is nothing when Good reigns. By its presence, Good makes the notion and the least trace of Evil disappear. Evil, even at its most successful, is always fought and beset by the presence of Good. Evil has no strength within itself, nor any powers; while Good has universal powers which are independent, and which extend even over Evil itself.

So, it's clear we can't accept any equality of strength or age between these two Principles, for a Being may not equal another in power if it doesn't also equal it in age, since it would always be a mark of weakness and inferiority in one of the two Beings if it had not come into existence at the same time as the other. Now, if Good had coexisted with Evil originally and throughout time, neither would ever have been able to gain superiority, since in this supposition the Evil Principle would be independent of the Good Principle, and would therefore have the same strength, and they would have no superiority over each other, or would be mutually balanced and contained. Then, because of this equality of power, the two Beings would have been totally inactive and sterile, because their reciprocal powers would be eternally equal and opposite, and it would have been impossible for either to do anything.

We can't say that, to end this inaction, a Principle superior to both would have increased the powers of the Good Principle as it was more like its own nature; because then this Superior Principle would itself become the Good Principle we are discussing. We are therefore compelled, through compelling evidence, to recognize in the Good Principle a superiority without measure, a unity, an indivisibility, with which it has necessarily existed before everything; which is sufficient to clearly demonstrate that Evil could only have come into existence after Good.

Establishing the inferiority of the Evil Principle this way, and showing its opposition to the Good Principle, proves that there has never been and that there will never be the slightest alliance, or the least affinity between them. For how could one think that Evil could ever have been part of the essence and powers of Good to which it's diametrically opposed?

But this conclusion necessarily leads us to another, equally important one, which is to impress us with the fact that this Good, powerful though it may be, can't participate at all in the birth and the effects of Evil. If this were the case, it would have been necessary, before the origin of Evil, for the Good Principle to have contained some evil seed or power; and putting forward this opinion would revive the confusion which man's opinions and carelessness have spread concerning these subjects. Otherwise it would be necessary to claim that following the birth of Evil, Good had had some intercourse and connection with it, which is both impossible and contradictory. Such then, is the inconsistency in the arguments of those who, fearing to limit the powers of the Good Principle, stubbornly continue to teach a doctrine which is so contrary to its nature, and which attributes everything that exists to it – even evil and disorder.

Evil, a Result of Freedom (I)

We no longer need to think about the immeasurable distance between these two Principles, to know the one to which we should give our trust. The concepts I've just outlined should remind men of their natural feelings, and the knowledge which should be found in their hearts. At the same time, it should foster in them the hope of discovering new light on the subject we are studying. Since man is the mirror of Truth, he must see all the rays reflected there within him. Indeed, if we had nothing more to look forward to than what men's theories had promised us, I would not have taken up the pen to fight them.

But recognizing the existence of this Evil Principle, and considering the effects of its power in the Universe and in man, in addition to the false conclusions that the Observers have drawn from it, is not to reveal its origin. Evil exists. All around us we see its hideous traces, regardless of the efforts made to deny its deformity. Now, if this Evil clearly doesn't come from the Good Principle, how could it have been born?

Surely, this is the most important question for man, and the one on which I would like to convince all my Readers. But I am not deluded as to my success, and I am certain that, whatever truths I put forward, I will not be at all surprised to see them rejected or poorly understood by most people.

The Origin of Evil

When man, on being raised up toward Good, acquires the habit of remaining permanently connected to it, he has no concept of Evil. This is a truth which we have established, and which no intelligent Being may reasonably challenge. If he constantly had the courage and desire not to descend from this elevation to which he was born, Evil would never have anything to offer him; and indeed, he would only feel its dangerous influences in proportion to how far he moved away from the Good Principle. We must therefore conclude from our punishment that man then performed an act of free will: for if it's impossible for a Being who doesn't have free will to deviate from the Law imposed upon it through its own actions, it's also impossible for it to be found guilty and punished. We will develop this idea shortly, when speaking about the suffering of animals.

Finally, by considering the power and all the *virtues* which form the essence of the Good Principle, it's clear that Wisdom and Justice are its rule and Law; and from this we can perceive that if man suffers now, he must previously have had the power not to suffer.

Indeed, if the Good Principle is fundamentally just and powerful, our punishment is clear proof of our wrongdoing, and therefore of our liberty. Thus, when we see man subjected to the action of Evil, we can be sure that he exposed himself to it freely, and that it's up to him to defend himself and keep himself away from it. Therefore, don't look for any other cause for his misfortunes other than the fact that he voluntarily removed himself from the Good Principle, with which he could have continually delighted in peace and happiness.

Let us apply the same reasoning to the Evil Principle. If it's clearly opposed to the fulfilment of the Law of Unity of Beings, whether it be the physical Law or the intellectual Law, it must itself be in a state of *disorder*. If it drags along behind it only bitterness and confusion, it's without doubt both the subject and the instrument: which tells us that it should be delivered up without respite to the torment and horror that it spreads around itself.

Evil, a Result of Freedom (II)

However, Evil only suffers because it's estranged from the Good Principle; because it's only from the moment that they are separated that Beings are unhappy. The suffering of the Evil Principle can therefore only be a punishment, since Justice, being universal, must act on it as it acts on man. But, if it's being punished, it must have strayed from the Law which should have perpetuated its happiness by its own free will, and it therefore gave itself over to evil voluntarily. This leads us to say, that if the Author of the evil had made proper use of its freedom, it would never have separated from the Good Principle, and Evil would still be unborn. By the same reasoning, if today it could use its free will to its advantage and direct it towards the Good Principle, it would cease to be bad, and Evil would no longer exist.

It can only ever be through the simple and natural sequence of all these observations that man may focus his thoughts on the origin of Evil; because, if it's as a result of letting his will degenerate that a free and intelligent Being acquires the knowledge and sense of evil, we can be confident that Evil has no other Principle, nor other existence that the very will of this free Being; that it's through this desire alone that the Principle, on becoming bad, originally gave birth to Evil, and that it endures to this day. It's by this same desire that man acquired and daily acquires this disastrous Knowledge of Evil through which he sinks into darkness; whereas he was born for Good and for the Light.

Liberty and Free Will

When people have debated so many questions concerning liberty in vain, and these discussions have so often ended by vaguely deciding that man is not capable of it, this is because they have not observed the dependency and the connection of this ability of man with his free will, and because they didn't know that his will is the only agent which can preserve or destroy liberty. In liberty, we seek a stable and invariable ability which is both universal and endless; which neither diminishes nor increases, and which we can always get to do our bidding, regardless of the use we may make of it. But how can we imagine an ability which belongs to man, yet is independent of his will, when this same will makes up his basic essence? And do we not agree it necessarily follows that, either liberty doesn't belong to man, or he can influence it by the good or evil use he makes of it, by means of adjusting his will more or less towards the good?

And indeed, when the Observers want to study liberty, they tell us that it must belong to man, since they must always follow its tracks and characters within man. But if they continue to study this liberty independently of his will, isn't this exactly as if they wanted to find an ability which was within him, yet which was foreign to him; which was his, but over which he had neither influence nor control? Is there anything more absurd and more contradictory? Is it any wonder that we learn nothing from observing this way, and after pursuing such flimsy research, would we ever be able to give a valid opinion regarding our own nature?

If possessing liberty wasn't at all dependent on the exercise of one's will; if man could never change as a result of his weakness and unruly habits, then I would agree that all his actions would be fixed and uniform; and therefore, that there could not be, as there could never have been, any liberty for him.

But if instead this ability wasn't as the Observers saw it and wished to make it, if its strength could vary at any moment, if it could be rendered null through inaction, or maintained through exercise and the continual and constant practice of the same actions, then one couldn't deny that it belongs to us and it's within us, and as a result, we have the power to strengthen or weaken it, as a result of the sole rights of our Being over it, and by the privilege of our will; that is, according to the good or bad use that we voluntarily make of the Laws that are imposed on us by our nature.

Another error the Observers make to deny liberty, is in trying to prove it through the very action which takes place; so that, in order to satisfy them, it had to be an action which could at the same time be and not be, which obviously being impossible, they concluded that everything that happens must happen out of necessity, and therefore there is no liberty. But they should have noted that the action and the will which conceived it can only agree and can't be opposed; that the power which produced the action could not prevent its outcome; and finally, that liberty, even taken in its usual sense, isn't about being able to do something for and against simultaneously, but being able to do one thing then another thing alternately. Now, when taken in this sense, man could clearly prove what is commonly called his liberty, since he visibly exhibits this for and against in his different successive actions; and he is the only Being in Nature who is capable of not always having to take the same path.

But we would commit a grave mistake if we didn't think up a different example of liberty, because this contradiction in the successive actions of a Being indeed shows that there must have been some disruption and confusion in his abilities, yet no proof at all that he was free; since we still need to know if he gave himself freely or not, both to evil as well as to good; and it's partly by having incorrectly defined liberty that this issue is still veiled by the thickest darkness for most men.

I will therefore say that the true ability of a free Being is to be able to keep itself within the Law prescribed to it, and to maintain its strength and independence, voluntarily resisting obstacles and objects which serve to prevent it from acting in accordance with this Law; which necessarily leads to the fact that it can also succumb to them, because to do so only requires it to stop wishing to oppose them. Then we must judge whether, in the darkness in which we find ourselves, we can claim we can always accomplish our goal with the same ease; or whether we feel, on the contrary, that being the least neglectful increases this task greatly by making the veil that covers us even thicker. If we carry this concept across to man in general for a moment, we will find that if man can debase and weaken his liberty at any time, then the human species is less free now than it was in its first days, and even less so than it was before being born.

So, we can no longer examine the present state of man or his daily actions to come to a decision about his true liberty, because nowadays nothing is more difficult than finding in them those effects of liberty which are pure and completely independent of Causes external to it. But one would be more than foolish to conclude from this that liberty had never been one of our rights. A slave's chains clearly prove that he can no longer act to the full extent of his natural powers, but they don't prove he has never been able to: on the contrary, they tell us that he still could if he hadn't deserved to be in servitude. For, if it wasn't possible for him to recover the use of his powers, his chains would be neither a punishment nor a disgrace to him.[7]

At the same time, since man is so rarely totally free nowadays, wouldn't it be more reasonable to infer from this that his actions are indifferent, and that he is not obliged to fulfil the measure of good which is still required of him in this state of servitude; because the deprivation of his liberty consists of being unable, through his own efforts, to obtain complete possession of the benefits contained in the good for which he was made, and being unable

---

[7] This attitude appears terrible in modern times. However, we must remember that, in the 18th Century, the fact of slavery was either ignored or simply accepted (few people had rights in those days), or even justified, most often by quoting St. Thomas Aquinas who said that, as there should be no punishment without a crime, slavery must be a penalty for sin. This seems to be the line adopted here by Saint-Martin. However, slavery was abolished by France in 1794, twenty years following this book; and although it was hard to stamp out in the colonies, in 1804 a revolt in Haiti (formerly St. Domingue, to which Pasqually traveled in 1772) ended slavery in the West Indies.

to approach Evil without making himself even more guilty; since it can be seen that his material body has only been loaned to him in order for him to make a continual comparison between the false and the true, and that the indifference his neglect of this brings him to every day can't destroy his essence. So, it's sufficient that he once distanced himself from the light on which he should be focused to explain the succession of his inexcusable faults, and he has no right to complain about the suffering this brought down on him.

But, it should be said, if the Observers were so inconclusive about man's liberty, it's because they still haven't the first notion about his will. Nothing proves this better than their continual attempts to understand how it acts. Being unable to realize that its Principle must be within it, they seek it in external Causes, and seeing, that here below it's often driven by apparent or real motives, they conclude that it clearly can't act by itself, and that it always requires a reason to take a decision. But if that were so, how could we talk about *having* a will, since, far from belonging to us, it would always be subject to the various Causes which endlessly acted upon it? Isn't this going round the same circular argument, and reviving the same error that we have already dispelled concerning liberty? To say that there is no will without motive is like saying that liberty is no longer an ability which depends on us, and that we have never been its master. However, to reason this way is be ignorant of what free will is, and that it clearly announces a Being acting by itself, without the aid of any other Being. Consequently, this multitude of alien motives and objects which attract us and lead us so often today doesn't prove that we are unable to exercise will without them, and that we are not capable of liberty, but only that they are able to take over our will and carry it away when we do not oppose them. For we can agree in good faith that these external Causes disturb us and tyrannize us; so how could we feel them and perceive them if we weren't essentially made to act by ourselves, and not by the attraction of these illusions?

As to the manner in which the will makes up its mind independently of the motives and objects external to us, as much as this truth will appear evident to anyone who can ignore everything around him and look within, so its explanation is itself an impenetrable abyss for man and for all Beings, since giving one would require making the incorporeal into Matter. Of all research, this would be the most harmful to man, and the most likely to plunge him into ignorance and degradation, because it leads to falsehood, and uses all the abilities which are within him in vain. Also, the scant success that the Observers have had on this matter, has served only to discourage those who have had been foolish enough to follow them, wanting to get from them that illumination from which their false path had distanced them. The wise man looks for the Cause of things which have one, but he is too prudent and too enlightened to look for those which have none; and the natural will of man is of this number, for it is Cause itself.

For this reason, since free will remains with him forever, and since it can't be corrupted except by the misuse he makes of it, I'll continue to regard man as free, even though he is almost always subservient.

I don't set out these notions for the man who is deluded, frivolous and without desire. Since he only uses his eyes as guides, he judges things by what they are, and not by what they have been. It would therefore be pointless for me to show him truths of this nature, since in comparing them with his dim ideas and with the judgment of his senses, he would only find jarring contradictions there, which would then lead him to deny both what he already believed, and what he would have to conceive anew to save him from the resulting confusion of his emotions, and instead follow the dead and obscure Law of animals without intelligence.

But the man who is sufficiently enlightened to seek to know himself, who has studied his habits, and who has already given his attention to pulling aside the thick veil which envelops him, could draw some benefit from these reflections. To him I say: you may open this book. I gladly entrust it to you, with a view to strengthening the love you already have for Good.

However, regardless of in whose hands these writings may fall, I urge them not to seek the origin of Evil elsewhere than in the source I've indicated; that is, in the corruption of the will of the Being or Principle which became Evil. I can strongly affirm that they would seek another Cause for Evil in vain; since, if it had a basis which was more fixed and solid, it would be eternal and invincible, like Good. If this degraded Being could produce anything other than acts of will, if it could form real and existing Beings, it would have the same power as the Good Principle. It's therefore in the nothingness of its works that we feel its weakness, which totally prevents any comparison between it and the Good Principle from which it's separated.

Original State of the Evil Principle

It would be even more foolish to seek the origin of Good elsewhere than in Good itself; because after all that we have just seen, if degraded Beings, like the Evil Principle and man, still have the right to be the Cause of their actions, how could we refuse this property to Good which is the infinite source of all virtue, the very seed and essential agent of all that is perfect? It would make no sense to seek the Cause and origin of Good outside of it, since they aren't, and could only be within it.

I've said enough to give an understanding of the origin of Evil. However, the statement I made obliges me, firstly, to present a few concepts on the nature and the state of the Evil Principle before its corruption; and secondly, to avoid a problem which could give pause to those very people believed to be the most educated on these subjects; that is, why the Author of Evil doesn't use its liberty to reconcile itself with the Good Principle. I will only dwell for a moment on these two subjects, so as not to interrupt my train of thought, and to avoid straying too far from the boundaries set for me.

By saying that the Evil Principle was made evil by the sole act of its will, I gave it to be understood that it was Good before taking this action. Then was it equal to this Superior Principle we encountered previously? Absolutely not. It was Good, without being its equal; it was inferior, without being bad. It had originated from this Superior Principle, and therefore it could not equal Him in strength or power. But it was Good, because the Being which had produced it was Goodness and Excellence Himself. Finally, it was still inferior to Him, because in not taking on the Superior Principle's Law for itself, it had the ability to do or not do what was imposed on it by its origin; and because of this, it could deviate from this Law and become Evil, while the Superior Principle, containing His Own Law within Himself, must necessarily remain in the Good which constitutes Him, without ever having power to strive for another purpose.

As to the second subject, I explained that if the Author of Evil made use of its liberty to approach the Good Principle, it would cease to be bad and to suffer, and therefore there would no longer be Evil. But we see every day from its works that it's still chained to its criminal will, so that it doesn't produce a single action that doesn't have the intention of perpetuating confusion and disorder.

Present State of the Evil Principle

It's on this point that the fatalists believe they have triumphed, by claiming that Evil carries within itself the reason and necessity for its existence. And so, they throw mankind into discouragement and despair, since, if Evil is necessary, it's impossible for one ever to avoid its attacks, and retain any hope of that peace and light which is the object of all our desires and pursuits. But let us guard against embracing these errors, and demolish the dangerous consequences which result, by exposing the true Cause of the continuation of Evil.

By going into ourselves, it would be easy to sense that one of the first Laws of universal Justice is, that there is always an exact correspondence between the nature of the crime and that of its punishment, which can only subject the prevaricator to powerless actions identical to those it criminally produced, and which were therefore opposed to the Law from which it had strayed. That is why the Author of Evil, being corrupted by the culpable use of its liberty, perseveres in its evil will in the same way it conceived it; so that it never ceases to set itself against the actions and will of the Good Principle, and in these futile efforts, it experiences a continuation of the selfsame suffering, so that, according to the Laws of Justice, it's in the very act of committing the crime that it meets its punishment. But let us add a few more thoughts on such an important subject.

Incompatibility of Good and Evil

If the Good Principle is essential Unity, if it's kindness, purity and perfection itself, it can't itself suffer any division, contradiction or blemish. It's therefore clear that the Author of Evil must be entirely separate from it, and rejected by the single act of opposition of its will to the will of the Good Principle; so that from that time it could only endure as an Evil power and will, with no communication with or participation in the Good. Being the voluntary enemy of the Good Principle, and of the single, eternal and invariable Rule, what Good, what Law could remain of this Rule in the Evil Principle, since it's impossible for one and the same Being to be simultaneously both good and bad, or simultaneously produce both order and disorder, the pure and the impure? It's therefore easy to convince ourselves that by its complete separation from the Good Principle, having necessarily distanced itself from all good, it's no longer in a state to know or to produce anything good, and henceforth it can only bring forth acts without rule or order, and a total opposition to the Good and the True, from its own will.

The Two States of Man

So it is that, buried in its own darkness, the Evil Principle is no longer open to any light or any return to the Good Principle; because, to direct its desires to this true light, it would first be necessary for knowledge to be given to it, and it would be necessary for it to be able to conceive a good thought: and how would this thought find any access if its will and all its abilities are completely impure and corrupt? Since it has absolutely no correspondence with Good, and since isn't in its power to know or feel it, its ability and liberty to return there are always of no effect, and this fact is what makes the privation to which it's condemned so terrible.

The Law of Justice is similarly exercised on man, although by different means; so, it will also provide us with the light to guide us in the study we need to make concerning him.

No sincere person, whose reason isn't clouded or biased, would disagree that man's physical life is one of almost continual privation and suffering. So, applying the ideas that we have explored about Justice, it can't be without reason that we regard the duration of this physical life as a time of chastisement and atonement; but we can't see it like this without thinking that man must have known a prior state which was preferable to the one in which he now finds himself, and we can say, that just as his current state is limited, painful, and strewn with disgust, so his former state must have been limitless and filled with joy. Each of his sufferings points to the happiness he now lacks; each of his privations proves that he was made for enjoyment; each of his subjugations speaks of former authority. In other words, the feeling that he has nothing now is secret evidence that he had everything in the past.

From the painful feeling of the dreadful situation in which we see him today, we can form an idea of the happy state where he previously was. Now, he's no longer master of his thoughts, and it's a torment for him to have to wait for those he desires and push away those which he fears. From this we sense that he was made to dispense these very thoughts, and that he could produce them at will, and it's easy to imagine the invaluable benefits attached to such a power. Nowadays, he can only obtain a little peace and tranquility by means of infinite effort and painful sacrifice, from which we conclude that he was made for perpetual enjoyment and not to work, in a calm and happy state, and that the abode of peace was his true domain. Once he had the ability to see everything and understand everything, yet now he crouches in the darkness, trembling in his ignorance and his blindness. Yet isn't this certain proof that the light is his element? Finally, his body is subject to destruction, and this death – and he is the only Being in Nature to be aware of it – is the most terrible step of his physical career, the most humiliating act for him, which he holds in the greatest horror. Doesn't this Law, so severe and so awful for man, lead us to believe that his body had once been an infinitely more glorious one, and had allowed him to enjoy all the rights of immortality?

Now, where could this sublime state, which made man so great and so happy have come from, if not the intimate knowledge and continual presence of the Good Principle, since it's this Principle alone that is the source of all power and all happiness? And why does this man now languish in ignorance, weakness and misery, if not because he is separated from this very Principle, which is the one light and the sole support of all Beings?

It's here that, recalling what I said above about the Justice of the First Principle and the freedom of the Beings issuing from it, we will understand completely that if, as a result of its crime, the Evil Principle still suffers the pain attached to its rebellious will, so man's current suffering is simply the natural result of an original straying from the path. So, too, this separation could only arise out of man's liberty, when having conceived a thought contrary to the Supreme Law, he gave in to it by his free will.

Following this understanding of the connection we've found between the crime and the suffering of the Evil Principle, I could, following this analogy, guess at the nature of the crime of original man by the nature of his sentence. By this means, I could even calm the murmurings which continue to swell over the fact that we are condemned to participate in his punishment even though we didn't participate in his crime. But these truths would be spurned by the majority, and appreciated by such a small number, that I believe it would be a mistake to expose these to the full light of day. I shall therefore confine myself to setting the Readers on the path with a figurative image of the state of man in his glory, and the penalties to which he is now exposed after he was stripped of his primitive estate.

The Primitive Estate of Man[8]

There is no origin superior to his, for he is more ancient than any Being of Nature. He existed before the appearance of the least of germs, even though, however, he came to the world after them. But what elevated him high above all these Beings, was that they were subject of being born of a father and a mother, whereas man had no mother. Moreover, their function was entirely beneath that of man; man's duty was ever to *fight* to stop disorder and bring everything to *Unity*; while the duty of these beings was to obey man. But as the *fights* that man had to wage could be very dangerous for him, he was clothed in an impenetrable *armor*, the wearing of which he changed at will, and from which he could even *fashion* copies equal to and absolutely consistent with their model.

In addition, he was equipped with a *spear* composed of four *metals* so well amalgamated, that from the existence of the world it has been impossible to separate them. This spear[9] had the property of burning like

---

[8] As mentioned previously, I am retaining some of the archaic wording of Pasqually and Saint-Martin since it features so prominently in Pasqually's *Treatise*, from which many concepts in the early Chapters are drawn; and because in a way it links us to these luminaries. Again, this could be translated more simply as 'Man's original condition'. It is perhaps also worth noting, that sections of this part of the book were used wholesale by Papus in his creation of the Rituals of the *Ordre Martiniste*.

[9] This reference to a spear has puzzled many people, ever since it first appeared in Papus' and Blitz' Martinist rituals. In Letter XIII of *Theosophic Correspondence*, Saint-Martin says: "The 'lance composed of four metals', is nothing else than the great name of God composed of four letters. The extract of this name constitutes the essence of man; it is thus that we are in the image and likeness of God, and this quaternion which we have in us, and which distinguishes us so clearly from all the creatures of nature, is the organ and imprint of that famous cross in which friend Böhme so magnificently describes to us the eternal divine generation…". Although Saint-Martin was unfamiliar with Böhme's writings at the time of writing this book, nevertheless this passage indicates several points. Firstly, Saint-Martin is clearly referring to the Hebrew form of the name of God יהוה. That the passage later goes on to give this spear the 'property of burning like fire' may well be a reference to the Hebrew script, which has been called the 'language of fire', due to its letters looking like tongues of fire, and also because the *Sefer Yetzirah*, or Book of Creation, describes God creating the Universe through the manipulation of the Hebrew alphabet. This, then, would indicate that Saint-Martin was familiar with the teachings of the Kabbalah, the mystical body of writings from the Jewish tradition, which he may have received from Pasqually, himself believed to be of Jewish descent (notwithstanding his documented Catholic marriage), from his own reading, or possibly from the Secret Initiatory Society he hints at throughout his writings. Saint-Martin's comment about the imprint of the cross in his letter is similar to his comment in Chapter 7 of this book, in its Conclusion, concerning the Universal Square, being God's imprint on his creatures, "found written everywhere in indelible characters." It will become apparent in reading this book that, for Saint-Martin, the square is equivalent to the cross, as both have four straight lines, encompass the four cardinal points, and reflect perfection. Man's primitive abode was at the center of the square, and when he fell that

fire; moreover, it was so sharp that there is nothing which was impenetrable to it, and so active that it always struck in *two places* at once. All these benefits joined to an infinity of other gifts that man had received at the same time, made him truly strong and formidable.

The Country where this man had to *fight* was covered in a forest formed of *seven* trees, each of which had *sixteen* roots and *four hundred and ninety* branches. Their fruits regrew without cease, providing man with the most excellent nourishment, and these trees themselves served him as a stronghold, and made his *Post* inaccessible.

Man's Degradation

It's in that place of delight, the abode of man's happiness and the throne of his glory, that he would have been forever happy and invincible; because having received the order to occupy the *center*, from there he could observe without difficulty all that was happening around him, and so had the advantage of seeing all the ruses and movements of his adversaries, without ever being seen by them. Also, during all the time that he guarded this position, he retained his natural superiority, and he enjoyed a peace and felicity indescribable to men of present times. But as soon as he strayed, he ceased to be its master, and another *Agent* was sent to occupy his place; Then man, having been shamefully stripped of all his rights, was precipitated into the realm of fathers and mothers, where he has remained since this time, in the pain and affliction of seeing himself mixed and confused with all the other Beings of Nature.

Man's Punishment

It's not possible to conceive of a state more pitiful and deplorable than that of this unfortunate man at the moment of his fall; for not only did he immediately lose that formidable spear which no obstacle could resist, but the very armor with which he had been clothed disappeared from him, and was replaced, at least for a time, by another armor which, no longer being

---

position was taken by another Agent, called Héli by Pasqually, perhaps a variation of *Elias*, whom he identified with Christ. Incidentally, the only biblical reference to 'Heli' is in the Gospel of Luke, 3:23, where he is identified as Jesus' paternal grandfather.

impenetrable like the first, became a source of continual dangers to him, so that, while having to engage in the same fights, he was infinitely more exposed.

However, in punishing him this way, his Father[10] didn't want to remove all hope, and abandon him entirely to the rage of his enemies. Touched by his repentance and shame, He promised him that, through his own efforts, he could regain his original estate; but that this could only be after he had restored the spear he had lost to his possession, and which had been entrusted to the Agent which had replaced man in the very center he had just abandoned.

It's therefore the search for this incomparable weapon that has occupied men ever since, and in which must occupy them every day; since it's by this alone that they can be restored to their rights, and obtain all the favors which were intended for them.

We must not be surprised at the resources that remained to man following his crime. It was a Father's Hand who punished him, and it was also the tenderness of a Father who watched over him, even when His Justice distanced him from His presence. For the place which man departed is prepared with so much wisdom, that by retracing his steps along the same roads which led him to stray, this man can be sure of returning to the central point of the forest, in which place alone he can enjoy any strength and any rest.

The Path of His Rehabilitation

Indeed, he strayed by going from *four* to *nine*, and he will never be able to return except by going from *nine* to *four*. Moreover, it would be wrong to complain about this subjugation, for such is the Law imposed on all Beings who inhabit the realm of fathers and mothers; and since man descended there voluntarily, he must experience all its misery. This Law is terrible, I know, but it's nothing in comparison with the Law of the number

---

[10] It's perhaps interesting to note that, while Saint-Martin strives for neutrality in this religious theory of man's origin by referring to God as the First Principle, he occasionally slips into a less austere mode, as here where he refers to that Principle as 'Father'; whereas Pasqually's Treatise refers to the First Emanator as 'God', and reserves the title of 'First Father' for Adam.

fifty-six, a frightful Law, terrible for those who face it, since they can't get to *sixty-four* until they have experienced all its severity.[11]

Such is the allegorical history of what man was at his origin, and what he has become in deviating from his First Law. Through this picture I've tried to lead him back to the source of all his hardships, and pointed – mysteriously, it's true – to the means to overcome them. I must add that, although his crime and that of the Evil Principle are both the fruit of their evil will, it should be noted however, that each of these crimes are of a very different nature, and as a result they can't be subject to equal punishment, nor have the same consequences; since besides, Justice even considers the difference between the places where their crimes were committed. Man, and the Evil Principle therefore have their fault continually before their eyes, but the two of them do not receive the same help, nor the same consolations.

I gave it to be understood earlier that the Evil Principle can only persist in its rebellious will until communication with the Good is offered to it. But man, despite his condemnation, can pacify Justice itself, be reconciled with Truth, and occasionally taste *sweetness*, as if, in some manner, he was not separated from it.

Relief afforded to Man

Nevertheless, it's true to say that the crimes of both are punished by privation, and that the only difference is in the extent of this punishment. It's even more certain that this privation is the most terrible penalty, and the only one which can truly subjugate man. For it's very wrong to claim to lead us to Wisdom by means of frightening images of physical suffering in

---

[11] We can gain some idea of these numbers from the book *Theosophic Correspondence*. Firstly, Saint-Martin associates the number '4' with spirit and '9' with matter, so this references man's Fall and his Path of Return. In Chapter 6 of this book, which deals with Mathematics and Geometry, we find another approach, which assigns the straight line or square to '4' and the curved line or circle to '9'. The discussion at that point touches on the great esoteric question of 'Squaring the Circle', and Saint-Martin's take on this subject is truly fascinating. As for '56' and '64', in Letter XIII (*Theosophic Correspondence*) he cryptically refers to receiving instruction on this matter in Lyon around 1772, the year that Pasqually departed from France. However, he mentions that it is associated with the progression of the number '8', which is associated with Christ, or the Repairer. The number is composed of the three Elements which compose Him, being '1' for deity or in this case spirit, '4' for soul, and '3' for his body, which by Theosophical addition (1+4+3) gives us '8'. Now, if the square or *octave* of 8 is 64, and the imperfect square, or 8 x 7 gives 56, this should give the reader enough information to ponder the relevance of these two numbers. Note that I will use a capital letter for Elements when referring to the constitutive Elements of bodies.

a life to come. These images mean nothing when we do not feel them. So, since these blind Masters can only give us an idea of the torments they imagine, they must necessarily have negligible effect on us.

If they had at least taken the care to portray to man the remorse he should feel when he is bad, he would have been easier for them to reach, since it's possible for us here below to feel this pain. But how much happier they would have made us, and would have given us a worthier notion of our Principle too, if they had been magnanimous enough to tell men that, since this Principle is love, it can only punish men through love; but at the same time, since it's only love, when it deprives them of that love it leaves them with nothing.

This is how they could have enlightened and supported men, by making them feel that nothing should frighten them more than to stop having this Principle's love, since from that moment they would be in nothingness; and certainly this nothingness, which man can experience at any moment, had they portrayed it to man in all its horror, would be for him a far more effective and salutary notion than that of eternal torture, in which, despite the doctrine of these Ministers of blood, man always sees an end and never a beginning.

The help granted to man for his rehabilitation, precious though it's, nevertheless comes with very strict conditions. And truly, the more glorious the rights he has lost, the more he must suffer to recover them. Finally, being subjected for his crime to the Law of time, he can't avoid suffering its dire effects, for while he fights all the obstacles that time contains, this Law states that he can only obtain anything in proportion to what he experiences and overcomes.

It's at the instant of his physical birth that the penalties awaiting him begin. Then he bears all the marks of the most shameful rejection. He is born like a vile insect in corruption and degradation. He is born amidst suffering and his mother's cries, as if it was a disgrace for her to bring him to the light of day. However, what lesson it's for him to see that, of all mothers, woman is the one creature whose birth is the most painful and dangerous! But hardly does he begin to breathe when he is covered with tears and tormented by the keenest pains. Thus, the first steps he takes in life tell him that has only come here to suffer, and that he truly is the son of crime and sorrow.

The Works of Man

If, on the contrary, man had not been guilty, his birth would have given him his first feelings of happiness and peace. On seeing the light, he would have celebrated its splendor with keen rapture, and tributes of praise to the Principle of his joy. Untroubled by the legitimacy of his origin, unconcerned about the durability of his fate, he would have tasted every delight, for he would have physically known their benefits. O man, shed bitter tears over the enormity of your crime, which has changed your condition so terribly; shudder at the disastrous decision which has condemned your seed to be born in torment and humiliation, when it could have known only glory and unending happiness.

After the first few years of his youthful career, man's situation becomes far more frightening, since up to now he has only suffered in his body, whereas the place where he will now suffer is in his thoughts. Just as his physical envelope[12] had previously been subjected to the impetuosity of the Elements before acquiring the minimal powers needed to defend itself; so his thoughts will now be haunted at an age where, not yet having exercised his will, error can seduce him more easily, using a thousand ways to carry its attacks to the source, and corrupt the tree at its root.

It's certain that man then begins a career which is so painful and so perilous, that if help does not follow him on the same path, he will inevitably succumb. But the same hand which gave him being neglects nothing to preserve him. In proportion to his advance in years, when obstacles proliferate and oppose him exercising his abilities, so in proportion too, his physical envelope acquires firmness: that is, his new armor will strengthen him and become more powerful against the attacks of his enemies, until finally, when man's intellectual temple is built, this envelope becomes useless and is destroyed, leaving the edifice revealed and beyond any attack.

---

[12] 'Envelope' or 'physical envelope' refers to the external covering of man. While it might seem an odd term to use, I have retained it for two reasons. Firstly, it has become common parlance in esoteric circles, and is often used in translation of French esoteric books into English (e.g. Papus, Lévi, Sédir, etc.). Secondly, it reminds us that this 'envelope', in Pasqually and Saint-Martin's minds, is not an integral part of our bodies, but rather a 'coating of red mud' in which we became enmired, thereby taking on physical form. It is an allegorical term, of course, and does not directly equate to the skin.

Twofold Result of the Body of Man

It's therefore clear that this material body we wear is the organ of all our suffering. Thus, it's this body which forms thick boundaries to our sight and all our abilities, keeping us in deprivation and pain. I can no longer hide the fact that joining man with this coarse envelope is the very penalty to which his crime has temporally subjected him, since we see the horrendous effects he feels from the moment he is clothed thus, to the time when he is finally stripped of it; and it's by means of this body that those trials begin and continue, without which he can't restore the connections he formerly had with the Light.

But despite the darkness that this material body spreads around us, we should also admit that it serves us as a defense and a safeguard against the dangers surrounding us, and without this envelope we would be infinitely more exposed.

These are, without doubt, those ideas which wise men have had in all ages. Their first concern was to protect themselves continually from the illusions that this body showed to them. They despised it because it's despicable by nature. They feared it because of the disastrous consequences of the attacks to which it exposed them; and they knew perfectly well that, for them, it was a way of error and lies.

But experience also taught them that it's the channel by which the knowledge and light of Truth reach man. They felt that, since it serves as an envelope, and man doesn't even have his own thoughts, his ideas must all come from outside of him, necessarily coming through this envelope, and that his physical senses are its principal organs.

The Origin of Materialism

However, it's on this subject that man, through his hasty and shallow opinions, began to engage in disastrous errors which produced the most monstrous ideas in his imagination. It's from this, most certainly, that the Materialists[13] drew that humiliating theory of sensations which reduces man

---

[13] Materialism at that time essentially encompassed a belief that there is only one substance – matter – and that everything else, including thought, will and consciousness, can be explained by means of material interactions. One of the foremost Materialists of Saint-Martin's time was Denis Diderot (1713 – 1784), who played a large part in the publication of the Encyclopedia mentioned earlier. The final edition of 28 volumes was released to its subscribers in 1772, which is why it was so much on

below the level of the beast, since the latter, only ever receiving a single impulse at a time, is not likely to stray; whereas man, being put amidst contradictory impulses would, according to this opinion, calmly give himself up indiscriminately to all the impressions by which he was affected.

But, given the lights of Justice which we have already recognized in him, we certainly won't adopt these demeaning opinions. We have demonstrated that man, being responsible for his conduct, is accountable for all his actions. I will therefore refrain from permitting the Materialists to remove such a sublime privilege, which raises man up so greatly above all other Creatures.

The Theory of Sensations

Nothing will prevent me therefore from assuring my fellow man that this error is the most skillful and dangerous ruse that could be used to stop them in their tracks, and lead them astray. A traveler, coming across two roads leading in different directions, not knowing where either one leads, could experience a discouraging uncertainty. However, by observing the road he had taken up till then, and remembering the place he had departed from and the place he was traveling to, he could perhaps make enough calculations to take a decision and choose correctly. But if somebody appeared and told him that it was totally unnecessary to make the effort of calculating the correct one, since both roads before him led to the same place and he could follow either one, at this point the traveler's situation would become much more troubling and embarrassing than when he was forced to take his own counsel; because now it would be impossible for him to deny the differences he had seen between these two roads, and the first thought he would have would be to distrust the advice given to him, and convince himself that the other person wanted to set a trap.

Yet this is the current position of man regarding the darkness that the inventors of the theory of sensations have thrown across his path. Telling him that there are no other Laws than those of his senses, and that he can have no other guide, is telling him that seeking to choose between the things

---

Saint-Martin's mind. Another reason would have been the fact that most of the subscribers to the Encyclopedia were Freemasons! Ironically, the frontispiece of this 1772 edition featured an image of Truth surrounded by brilliant light, while Reason and Philosophy tear away the veil which covers her. This image alone may well explain the themes and the layout of Saint-Martin's book, even though it clearly inspired him in a very different way!

before him would be pointless, since the senses themselves are subject to vary in their activity, and therefore man can't control them, and would direct their functions and effects in vain.

But, like the traveler, man can't ignore his own convictions. He sees that his senses bring everything to him, yet at the same time he is forced to admit that among the things they bring to him, there are some things he senses are good, and some things he senses are bad.

The Dangers of This Theory

How much, then, should he distrust those who try to prevent him from making a choice, suggesting that all these things are unimportant, or of the same nature? Shouldn't he feel a deep indignation, and guard himself against such dangerous masters?

This is, as I said, the most common attempt made against man's thinking. At the same time, it can be the most attractive, and the one from which the Evil Principle benefits the most; for if it can encourage the conviction in man that there is absolutely no choice to be made between the things which surround him, it can easily succeed in passing on to him that horrible uncertainty and disorder in which it's itself immersed by being deprived of its First Law.

But if Justice always watches over man, he must have within him the means to unravel these plots and confound all his enemy's attempts whenever he wants: otherwise he couldn't be punished for letting himself be taken by surprise. These means must be based on his own nature, which he can no more change than the very nature of the Principle from which he came, and since his own essence is incompatible with lies, sooner or later it lets him know that he is mistaken, and he is naturally brought back to the Truth.

I shall therefore use these same means which I have in common with all men, to show them the danger and the absurdity of this opinion which is the enemy of their happiness, and which would only serve to swamp them in crime and despair. I've sufficiently proved that by observing our suffering we know that we were once free: so, I will address the Materialists, and ask them how they can be so blind as to see man as nothing more than a machine? I would at least hope that they had the good faith to see an acting machine, containing its own Principle of action; for if it were purely passive, it would take everything and give nothing back.

Innate Ability in Man

Then, seeing that it manifests action, it must at least have within it the power to make this manifestation, and I don't believe anyone would claim that this power comes to us through feelings. At the same time, I believe that, without this innate power in man, he would be unable to acquire or retain knowledge of anything, as we have clearly seen in Beings deprived of the ability to differentiate. It's therefore clear that man carries within himself the seeds of the Light and Truth of which he so often gives evidence. And is anything more needed to overthrow these reckless theories by which they are trying to demean him?

I know that on first reflection, one might counter that not only animals, but all physical Beings perform external actions, from which it must be concluded that all these Beings have something in them too, and aren't just simple machines. Then I will be asked what the difference between their Principle of action and the Principle within man might be? This difference will be easily seen by those who wish to observe closely, and my Readers will see it along with me, when we consider for a moment the cause of this misunderstanding.

There are Beings which are only intelligent, and there are Being which are only physical[14]. Man is both. This is the crux of the matter. These different classes of Beings each have a different Principle of action, while man alone unites the two; and whoever takes care not to confuse them will be sure to find the solution to all the difficulties.

---

[14] To reiterate my comment in *Translating Conventions*, some words in French can have two meanings in English. This is unfortunate, since it means the French word will always carry both nuances, while it becomes necessary to select one English word and stick with it as much as possible, because alternating the two alternative words will lose the consistency the author intended. Here, the word in French is *sensible*. This can mean *physical*, as in belonging to the physical realm, and *sensual*, as in belonging to the senses. Now, one can see that they belong to the same idea, since being physical beings we can only interact with our external environment through the five senses. However, since the main thrust of the philosophy outlined in this book concerns the fall of man from an incorporeal state outside of time to a physical state constrained by time, I believe the term *physical* is the better choice, even though it may lead to some phrases which don't flow quite so well. Also, nowadays the word *sensual* in English has a very different meaning to that in 1775. The Merriam-Webster Dictionary defines *sensual* as: "relating to, devoted to, or producing physical or sexual pleasure", which is a far cry from Saint-Martin's intention of reflecting physical existence!

Man's Original Envelope

Because of his origin, man possessed all the rights of an intelligent Being, although he had an envelope; because, in the temporal region, no being could survive otherwise. And here, having already said enough to give you a hint, I will acknowledge that the impenetrable armor I mentioned earlier was none other than this first envelope of man. But why was it impenetrable? It's because, being of one piece and pure due to the superiority of its nature it could not decay, and the Law of elemental combination had absolutely no effect on it.

Man's New Envelope

Since his fall, man has been covered by a corruptible envelope, for as it's composite, it's subject to the different actions of the physical world, which only operate successively, and which as a result destroy one another. But, despite this subjection to the physical, he has not lost his status as an intelligent Being; so that he is both great and small, mortal and immortal, always free intellectually, but bound in the body by Laws beyond his control. Being a composite of two diametrically opposed Natures, he manifests their effects alternately in such a distinctive manner that it would be impossible not to see it. For, if present day man only had senses, as Humanist theories would like to assert, we would always see repetitive behavior in all his actions, and this would be due to his senses: that is, that being equal to the animals, every time he was prompted by his bodily needs he would make every effort to satisfy them, never resisting any of their impulses except to give in to an even stronger impulse, but as a result these impulses should then be considered as acting alone, being born each time in the senses, acting in the senses, and always belonging to the senses.

Two Beings in Man

So why can man turn aside from the Law of the senses? Why can he refuse what they ask of him? Why, when pressed by hunger, is he nevertheless the master who can refuse the most exquisite dishes presented to him, leaving himself tormented, devoured, even destroyed by need, even though that would be the most appropriate way to soothe him? Why does man have a will which he can set against his senses, if there is nothing more than a Being in him? And can two actions which are so contrary, though appearing together, be connected to the same source?

In vain can you object, at this moment, that when his will acts in this way, it's because it's determined by some Cause. I've made it clear enough, when speaking about liberty, that man's will, being a Cause itself, must have the privilege of deciding on its own without an external Cause, for otherwise it couldn't be called 'will'. But even assuming in this instance, his will is indeed determined by a Cause, the existence of man's two Natures would be no less obvious, since we should always look for this Cause elsewhere than in the action of his senses, because his will counteracts it. Even when his body always seeks to exist and to live, man can want to let it suffer, use up all its strength and die. This dual action of man is therefore convincing proof that there is more than one Principle in him.

Animals Only Use the Senses

On the contrary, Beings which are only physical can never give signs of what they are. They must, it's true, have the power to convey and manifest what effect sensations have on them: without this, everything communicated to them would be as naught, and would produce no effect. But I do not fear making an error when I assure you that the most beautiful affections in animals and their best ordered actions never rise above the physical level. Like all Beings of Nature, they have an individual to maintain, and along with life they receive all the powers necessary for this end, depending on their species, because of the dangers to which they will be exposed during their lives, whether in the means of procuring food, or in the circumstances of their reproduction, or in all the other things important to the different classes of these Beings, as well as for each individual Being. But I ask if anyone has ever noticed any activity in animals that was not solely for their physical well-being, and if they have ever demonstrated anything that was a true indication of intelligence.

What deceives the greater part of men in this regard, is seeing that there are several species among the animals which can be taught acts which are not at all natural to them. They learn, they remember, they often act because of what they have learned and what their memory recalls. This observation could indeed stop us in our tracks without those Principles we've already established.

I said that, since animals manifest something externally, they must necessarily have an inner active Principle, without which they wouldn't exist: but I've also said that this Principle only had the physical senses as its guide, and the body's preservation as its goal. It's through these two means that man can train an animal. He beats it, or gives it something to eat, and by this he controls the animal's active Principle by means of his will, which, since it only acts in line with maintaining its Being, is directed with effort to perform acts that it would never have practiced if it had been left to its own devices. Man, by means of fear, or food, pushes it and obliges it to extend and increase its activities. It's therefore obvious that this Principle, being active and physical, is susceptible to receiving impressions. If it can receive impressions, it can also keep them, since for this to happen it's enough for the same impression to be prolonged and continuous. Then, receiving impressions and retaining them is, in fact, proof that the animal can form habits.

The Active Being in Animals

So, we can confidently recognize that the active Principle of animals is capable of acquiring the habit of various actions through man's industry; because both in those actions that the animal naturally performs, or in those it's taught we can see no movement or combination of movements in which the physical senses aren't responsible for everything and the Cause of everything. Then, while I find the few wonders that the animal parades before my eyes certainly very admirable, my admiration will not go so far as to recognize an intelligent Being, when I only see a physical Being; because in the end, being physical is not necessarily being intelligent.

The Habits of Animals

To better understand the difference between the animal and the intelligent Being, should we consider the Kingdoms which are beneath the Animal one, such as the Vegetable and the Mineral? Since these lower Kingdoms operate by means of external actions such as growth, fruition, reproduction and others, we can't doubt that, like the Animal, they possess an active Principle innate within them, and from which all these different actions emanate.

Nevertheless, although we perceive a living Law in them which strongly impels them towards accomplishing their purpose, we have never seen any sign of pain, pleasure, fear, or desire in them. These are all emotions which are peculiar to animals. From this we can say that, just as there is a significant difference in Principles between the animal and the lower Beings, although they both have all the abilities of the Vegetable Kingdom, so Man has an active Principle in common with the animal, susceptible to physical and sensual emotions, but he is fundamentally distinguished by his intellectual Principle, which makes any comparison between him and animals pointless.

The Intellectual and the Physical

It's therefore only in being interested in this universal chain, where a Being is always connected to the one which follows it and the one which precedes it, that people have confused the different links which make up man today, and why they have not thought of him as being different from this inferior, physical Principle to which he is only connected for a time.

What confidence then can we have in the theories which man's imagination has produced on these matters, when we can see they are based on a clearly false foundation? And what stronger proof can we wish for than that of perception and experience?

How to Distinguish the Three Kingdoms

Now I will go into a few details concerning the distinctions and the connections between the three Kingdoms of Nature, to confirm the Principles we've just established regarding the difference between Beings, despite their affinity. However, I warn you that these discussions will be unfamiliar to man, and it's unfortunate that he needs this proof to know himself and believe in his own nature; because it contains far clearer testimony than those he can find in his observations of sensory[15] and physical things.

Human sciences provide no certain rule to classify the three Kingdoms correctly; one can only do this by following an order which conforms to Nature. In this case, one must first assign to the ranks of Animals those physical Beings which carry within themselves the entire extent of the Principle of their reproduction, which therefore only having one, have no need to be attached to the earth to make this happen, but take their physical creation from the warmth of the female of the species, whether they acquire it in the female's womb, or from the external warmth communicated to them after the fertilization of the egg-laying animal takes place, either from the heat of the sun, or from some other source.

Secondly, one must assign to the ranks of Vegetables all Beings which have their incubation in the earth, are germinated by the action of two agents, and manifest a result, either outside, or within this same earth.

Finally, we must regard as Minerals all Beings who also have their incubation in the earth, and take their growth and vegetation from it, but which, arising from the action of three agents, can't give any sign of reproduction, because they are only passive, and the three actions which constitute them do not belong to them exclusively.

Once these rules, in order to know if a Being is Vegetable or Animal, have been established, we need to see if it draws its sustenance from the sap of the earth, or if it feeds itself on earth's products. If it's attached to the earth in such a manner that it dies when it's detached, it's Vegetable. If it's not attached to this same earth, though it's nourished by earth's products, it's Animal, whatever the means of its creation may have been.

It's infinitely more difficult, I know, to show the difference between the Vegetable and the Mineral Kingdoms than between the Vegetable and the Animal Kingdoms, because there is such a great affinity between plants and minerals, and they have so many abilities which are common to them, that it's not always easy to distinguish them.

---

[15] There will be times when a distinction between the word 'physical' and the world of 'sensation' will be needed. The word 'sensory' will be used on these occasions, as it also refers to the action of the senses.

The Universal Quaternary Progression

This difficulty arises from the fact that the difference between the types of all physical Beings is always in a Quaternary geometric proportion. Now, in the true order of things, the greater the degree of the power is raised, the weaker the power becomes, because then it's more distant from the Original Power from which all subsequent powers are emanated.[16] Thus, the first results of the progression, being closer to the Root, have more active properties, which consequently results in more visible effects, and because of this they are easier to distinguish. This strength in abilities diminishes as the results of the progression increase, so it's clear that the properties of the end results can only have almost imperceptible differences.

That's why Mineral is more difficult to distinguish from Vegetable than Vegetable from Animal; because it's in Mineral that we find the end result of the progression of created things.

We should apply the same Principle to all Beings which seem to be intermediate between the various Kingdoms, and which appear to link them, because the progression of number is continuous, without limit and without separation; but, to know precisely the power of any result of the progress on which it acts, one must at least know one of the roots, and this is one of the skills that man lost when he was deprived of his original estate. Indeed, today he doesn't know the root of any number, because he doesn't know the first of all the roots, as we shall see later.[17]

---

[16] In other words, the greatest difference between Beings can be seen in those who are closest to the First Principle (here called the 'Original Power' and 'Root'), and as the creations become proportionally or progressively more distant from the First Principle, the more alike or less differentiated they become. Therefore, it is much easier to see the difference between animal and plant, than plants and minerals. As an example, consider *lithops*, the genus of plants called 'living stones'. The implication is that minerals are at the bottom of the list in terms of Creation.

[17] Much of this is Saint-Martin's development of Pasqually's *Treatise*, since Pasqually focused almost exclusively on cosmology, limiting himself to the creation of spiritual Beings and man: his only mentions of lower kinds are passing references to animals used as sacrifices, and in his commentary on Noah's Ark. Given the number Pasqually and Saint-Martin assign to perfection is '4', towards the end of this book Saint-Martin says: "That (First) Cause, though it is connected to the source of all numbers (*i.e.* '1', or Unity), is nevertheless especially proclaimed by the number of the square (*i.e.* '4'), which is at the same time the number of Man." (*bracketed italics are my addition*). We saw earlier that this association comes from the Tetragrammaton, and Adam, as microcosm, was created in God's image. So, the progression of emanations or acts of creation from the Supreme Cause can be referred to as the 'Quaternary Progression'. In *Les Nombres*, Saint-Martin says: "The powers weaken as they move away from their primitive source, since, there being only one perpendicular line, the more you divide it, the more the parts of that division will shorten." And: "Each number has three powers, its root, its square and its cube…to know all the powers of a number,

It's also important to apply the Principle of the Quaternary Progression to Beings who are above Matter, because it can be seen with equal certainty and even more clearly that they are less distant from the First Term in this progression: but few people would understand me in the practical application I could make to this type of Being, and in any case my intention and my duty prevent me from speaking openly on the subject.

If the man had a Chemistry[18], by which he could know the body's true Principles without having to decompose it, he would see that Fire is the property of the Animal, Water the property of the Vegetable, and Earth the property of the Mineral. Then he would have even more sure signs to recognize the true nature of Beings, and would no longer be at a loss to discern their rank and class.

The Union of the Three Elements

I am not preventing anyone from observing that each of these three Elements, which can serve as signs for distinguishing the various Kingdoms, can't exist separately and independently of the other two. I presume that this concept is sufficiently well-known not to have to mention here that in the Animal, though Fire dominates, Water and Earth must also exist; and similarly, in the two other Kingdoms the dominant Principle is necessarily accompanied by the other two Principles. There is nothing, even Mercury, where this observation does not apply just as appropriately, though some Alchemists find no Fire in it: but they should note that mineral

---

one must first know and own the value of its root, then square and cube it..." Why is this necessary? In *Les Nombres*, Saint-Martin explains: "These three roots suffice to complete any Being, because through the essential root he has life or existence, through the square root he has progress, and through the cube he has the end or the completion." Remember Saint-Martin uses mathematics Theosophically to explain philosophical concepts, so 'root' means 'source'; it isn't a mathematical formula. Finally, in an earlier footnote we saw the number of the Repairer or Christ was '8'. It was composed of three values, '1', '3'' and '4', representing the divine element, the material element or body, and the element which linked them, or soul. While he worked (or 'operated') here on earth, he took on physical form. However, He always knew his powers, or put another way, His roots or numbers, which allowed Him to control all aspects of His body. Therefore, He was in the world but not of the world, since He had the power to release His body and return to spirit. In *Les Nombres*, Saint-Martin conjectures that, after his fall, man was still aware of his divine number, '1' and his physical number, '9'. However, he no longer had knowledge of the number of his soul. Since the soul is the key to our temporal prison, because he no longer knows this power or number, he doesn't possess the key to unlock his prison and follow the Path of Return.

This explanation is long, but I felt it necessary to better understand what Saint-Martin is saying here.

[18] In the original text, Saint-Martin used the term 'Chymie' which is an archaic term for Chemistry.

Mercury has only undergone the second operation, and because of this, although it has – as with all physical Beings – an elemental Fire within it, this Fire however is not perceptible until a superior Fire comes to activate it, and this is the third operation that I will show is necessary to bring anything to physical form. That is why Mercury, though it has an elemental Fire, is nevertheless the coldest body in Nature.

It is, I repeat, only to defend the nature of man that I've allowed myself to go into all these details. I wanted to show that those who degrade him by confusing him with the animals fall into an inexcusable error, even with regard to the very simplest Beings, since we observe no end of differences from one Kingdom to another, even though all of these Kingdoms have parallels and basic similarities.

Man's Superiority

We can see that in every class, the lower members have none of what is manifested in a particular manner in the higher members. So, as we haven't seen any signs of intelligence in physical Beings lower than man in the Animal Kingdom, we can't deny that, here below, man is the only Being favored by this sublime advantage, although in his elemental form, he is subject to the physical world and all the material desires of the animal.

Therefore, those who have tried to strip man of his most precious rights, based on his subjugation and his union with the physical Being which envelops him, have only presented as evidence one truth which indeed we recognize too, since we all know he can only receive light by means of his senses. But, by not developing their observations further they have remained in darkness, and have taken the majority there with them, too.

In man's present unhappy condition, no idea can make itself felt in him unless it has entered through his senses; so, we must again acknowledge that, since he isn't always in command of the objects and Beings that act on his senses, he can't, for this reason, be held responsible for the ideas that are born in him. So, recognizing, as we have done, the existence of a Good Principle and an Evil Principle, and in consequence, a Principle of Good thoughts and a Principle of Evil thoughts, we shouldn't be surprised when man is exposed to both without being able to avoid being conscious of them.

Man's Thought

This is what led the Observers to believe that all our thoughts and all our intellectual abilities have absolutely no other origin than our senses. But firstly, having confused these two Beings which today comprise man into only one, having not perceived the two opposing actions which clearly manifest the different Principles, they only recognize in him one kind of sense, and have vaguely derived all of this from his ability to feel. However, after all we have said, we only need to open our eyes to agree that man today has two different Beings to govern within him, and since he can only know the needs of each through his senses, this ability must be two-fold, since he is two-fold himself: and how could man be so blind not to find within himself a sensory ability relating to the intellectual one, and a sensory ability relating to the physical one? And shouldn't we agree that this distinction, taken from Nature itself, would have clarified any misunderstandings? I should say, however, that in this book I will use the words senses and perception a great deal in the physical meaning of the words, and when I speak of intellectual perception, this will be in such a manner so that the one can't be confused with the other.[19]

Man's Senses

Secondly, from any point of view that the Observers may have used to consider the sensory abilities of man, if they had thought about their explanation more deeply, they would have seen that our senses are really the organs of our thoughts, but they are not their source; which is surely too great a difference for them to be excused for not noticing it.

Yes, such is our punishment, that no thought can reach us directly without the aid of our senses, which are its necessary organs in our present state; but if we have recognized an active and intelligent Principle in man which distinguishes him so perfectly from the other Beings, this Principle must have within itself its own abilities. Now, this sole Principle which remains to us to use in our pitiful situation is our innate will, which man possessed during his glory and which he still possesses after his fall. Since

---

[19] As mentioned earlier, although Saint-Martin uses a word, *sensible*, which doesn't translate too well into English, I will usually refer to the physical as opposed to the intellectual. The senses are physical organs, and intelligence – or the mind – is an incorporeal Principle which is used to process the information received from the physical senses.

it was because of this will that he strayed, so it's by the strength of this will alone that he can hope to be restored to his primitive rights. It's this will which preserves him from the precipice from which the Observers would like to cast him down, and from believing in this nothingness to which they would like to reduce his nature. It's because of his will that, while unable to prevent Good and Evil from communicating with him, he is still responsible for the use he makes of his will regarding them both. He can't do what isn't offered to him, but he can choose and choose well; and, for now I won't give any further evidence of this, other than the fact that he suffers and is punished when he chooses Evil.

The intelligent Reader, for whom I write, can't be unaware of the fact that the pain and suffering I am talking about are of a very different nature to those temporary inconveniences, either physical or social, which are the only ones known to the majority.

All the attacks that have been brought against the dignity of man therefore no longer have any value to us. Otherwise, it would be necessary to discard the Principles and the solid foundations of Justice we have previously established, as well as the invariable notions we know to be common to all men, which no intelligent and reasonable Being would ever call in question.

Man's Rights over His Thoughts

I won't stop to examine whether, in the ordinary conduct of man, his will always waits for a decisive reason to make up its mind, or if it's only guided by inclination or feeling. I think he is susceptible to either motive; and I would say that, in order to function normally, man shouldn't exclude either of these two means, because, just as thinking too much without feeling would make him cold and impassive, similarly feeling without thinking would lead him astray.

But, I repeat, these issues are not relevant to my subject, and I believe they are improper and unproductive avenues of study. So, I leave it to the School of Metaphysics to research how the will decides and how it acts. It's enough for man to recognize that it's always freely, and that this freedom is in any case a misfortune for him, and the reason for all his suffering, when he abandons the Laws which should govern it. Let us return to our subject.

Although we've recognized that all beings necessarily have something in them, without which they would have neither life, nor existence, nor action, we will not accept for all that, that they are all the same thing. Although this Law of an innate Principle is unique and universal, we can't say that these Principles are equal and act uniformly in all Beings, because on the contrary, our observations reveal a fundamental difference between them; and particularly between the Principles innate in the three material Kingdoms and the sacred Principle with which man is the only one favored among all the Beings which make up this Universe.

Man's Greatness

For this superiority of the active and intelligent Principle of man should no longer surprise us, if we remember the concept of the Quaternary Progression which determines the rank and abilities of Beings, and which ennobles their essence according to how close they are to the First Term of the progression. Man is the second Power of this Universal and Generating First Term; and the active Principle of matter is only the third. Is anything more required to recognize that one absolutely can't claim any equality between them?

Misconceptions About Man

The source of the theories offensive to man therefore comes from the fact that their authors were unable to understand the nature of our condition. On the one hand, they attributed to our intellectual Being the movements of the physical Being; and on the other they confused intelligent acts with material impulses, as limited in their Principles as in their effects. It's not surprising that, having so disfigured man, they found a resemblance to the animal in him, and nothing more. It's not surprising, then, that by this means, by stifling any idea or any thought in him, far from enlightening him about Good and Evil, they instead keep him permanently in doubt and ignorance of his own nature, since they obliterate the only differences which could educate him.

The Means to Avoid These Misconceptions

But having taught that man is both intelligent and physical, we must observe that these two different abilities must necessarily manifest themselves in him by different signs and means, and as the conditions which are specific to each aren't in any way the same, they can't present themselves in the same way!

Man's focus, therefore, should be to continually observe the infinite differences between these two abilities and between the conditions unique to each; and as they are joined in almost all his actions, nothing should seem more important to him than to distinguish precisely what belongs to one or the other.

Indeed, during the short interval of man's physical life, the intellectual ability, finding itself joined to the sensory ability, can receive absolutely nothing except through the channels of this sensory ability; and in its turn, the inferior and sensory ability must always be directed by the precision and the regularity of the intelligent ability. We see as a result, that in so intimate a union, if man ceases to pay attention for a moment, he will no longer be able to distinguish his two natures, and then he won't know where to find the proof of order and truth.

In addition, since each of these abilities can receive both good and bad impressions in its own way, man is constantly exposed to the possibility of confusing not only the physical with the intellectual, but also what may be beneficial or harmful to each.

The Universality of These Misconceptions

I'll examine the consequences and effects of this danger associated with man's present situation. I will unveil the misunderstanding where his negligence in discerning his different abilities have led him, regarding both the Principle of things and the works of Nature, and those things that have come from his own hands and imagination: Divine, Intellectual and Physical Sciences, civil and natural duties of man, the Arts, Legislation, Institutions and Abilities of all kinds. These are all part of the subject I am concerned with. I would even boldly state that I regard this examination as an obligation on my part, because, if the ignorance and darkness in which we find ourselves concerning these important points are not of man's essence, but rather the natural effect of his first faults and all the errors which resulted from them, it's his duty to seek to return to the light he has left. And if this knowledge was his prerogative before his fall, it's not completely lost to him, for it flows ceaselessly from that inexhaustible source where he was born. In a word, if despite the state of darkness in which he languishes man can always hope to perceive Truth, and if all he must do for this to happen is to exert himself and to have courage, then to not do everything in our power to bring us closer to this Truth would be to set it at naught.

The continual use I will make in this book of the following words: *abilities, actions, Causes, Principles, Agents, properties, virtues*, will no doubt awaken the contempt and disdain that my Century has for occult qualities. However, it would be unfair to give that name to this doctrine, simply because it offers nothing to the senses. What is occult to the eyes of the body is what they don't see; what is occult to the mind is what it can't conceive: however, in this sense, I ask if there is anything more 'occult' for the eyes and the mind than the generally accepted theories concerning all the things I've just stated? They explain Matter by Matter, they explain man by the senses, they explain the Creator of things by elemental Nature.

Thus, the physical eyes, seeing only composites, look in vain for the elemental Principles they have learned about; and as they can never see them, it's clear they have been deceived.

Man sees in his senses the interplay of his organs, but he doesn't recognize his intelligence there.

Finally, visible Nature presents the eyes with the work of a Great Artist, but since she doesn't offer the mind the reason for things, she leaves us unaware of the Justice of the Master, the tenderness of the Father, and all the counsels of the Sovereign, so that we can't deny that these explanations are absolutely null and without truth, because they always need to be replaced by new explanations.

So, if I only concern myself with removing from all these things the coverings which hide them, if I only lead men's thoughts to the true Principle in each thing, then my steps will be less obscure than that of the Observers; and indeed, if they truly have an aversion to occult qualities, they should begin by changing their path; for most assuredly there is no path more occult and darker than the one along which they wish to lead us.

Chapter 2 – The Body

The Universal Source of Errors

Everything I've said about man regarding his origin and his first splendor, his impure will which led to his fall, and the distressing situation into which he is now plunged, is confirmed by the observations we are going to make of his conduct and about the opinions he has each day.

One can make the same observations about the initial purity, then the degradation and current torments of the Principle which made itself evil. The course of all these digressions is the same: the original errors, the ones which followed and those that will follow them had, and will forever have, the same Causes. It's always ill will to which we should attribute man's missteps, and those of any other Being who has the privilege of liberty; for as I've already said, to show that the Principle of any action is legitimate, we must consider its consequences: if the Being is unhappy then he is surely guilty, because he can't be unhappy if he isn't free.

The Suffering of Animals

No doubt someone could stop me here, and point out that all animals suffer, but that objection has not escaped me; and as I can resolve this issue now without interrupting my subject, I'll comment on this before going into the subject in hand.

I know that animals suffer since they are Beings that can feel, and that to some extent we might regard them as being unhappy; but I beg you to consider whether the title of 'unhappy' doesn't apply more accurately to Beings who, knowing that they could be happy because of their nature, experience an inner sense of despair for not being so. In this sense, this can't be applied to the animal, which has its place here below, and which is not made for any well-being other than that of its senses. So, when this well-being is disturbed, no doubt it suffers like any Being that can feel, but it sees nothing beyond its suffering. It puts up with it, it even strives to make it stop, but only through the actions of its sensory abilities, without being aware that there's another state which it could be in. It has none of what can make man unhappy, that remorse and the need to claim that suffering as his alone. How could it? It doesn't act: it's made to react.

However, it remains to be known why the animal suffers, and why it's so often deprived of that physical well-being which would make it happy in its own way. I could give an answer to this problem, were I allowed to dwell longer on the relationships between things, and to show where evil has won because of man's faults; but it's a point on which I can only hint, and for now it will suffice to say that the Earth is no longer undefiled, which makes both it and all its offspring vulnerable to all the ills which have resulted from the loss of that virginity.

We can therefore say with good reason that there really can't be a truly unhappy Being other than a Being which is free, to which I will add that if man freely immerses himself in his pain and sorrow, liberty imposes a continuing obligation on him to atone for his crime; because the more he neglects to do this the guiltier he becomes, and therefore the unhappier he is. Let us go back to our subject.

To guide us in the important examination we suggest, and which today becomes man's main task, let's note that the principle reason for all our errors in knowledge comes from not observing a Law with two distinct actions, which appears universally in all Beings of Creation, and which often throws man into uncertainty.

Dual Action

However, we shouldn't be surprised to see that every Being here below is subject to a dual action, since we previously saw two very distinct Natures or two opposing Principles whose power we have seen since the beginning of things, and which is felt continuously throughout Creation.

However, of these two principles, there can only be one that is real and truly necessary, seeing that after ONE, we know nothing more. And so the Second Principle, though it requires the action of the First in an act of creation, can certainly have neither weight, or number or measure, since these Laws belong to the very essence of the First Principle. One is stable and permanent, and possesses life within itself and through itself. The other is irregular and without Laws, and has only apparent and illusory effects on the mind, which wants to be deceived by it.

So, as we have just noted, if a dual Cause gave birth and temporal life to the Universe, it's essential that its individual bodies follow the same Law, and can neither reproduce nor exist without the help of a dual action.

However, the dual Cause which controls the body and all of Matter is not the same as that dual Cause which arises out of the opposition of the two Principles. The latter is purely intellectual, and only has its source in the opposing will of these two Beings. For, when either of them acts on the sensory and the physical, it's always with the intellectual in view; that is, with the intention of destroying the intellectual action opposed to it. But it isn't the same with the dual action which controls Nature. This is only associated with physical Beings, serving both in their reproduction and in their maintenance. This dual action is pure in that it's directed by a third action which makes it regular, for this is the means required by the Source of all Powers for the construction of all His material works.

However, although there is nothing impure in this dual action connected with everything physical, and neither of its processes is bad, there is still one which is fixed and imperishable, and another which is only fleeting and momentary, and for this reason not real to the mind, although its effects are real enough to the eyes.

This is to help us proceed in distinguishing between the nature and results of these two different processes, or these two different Laws, which support physical creation; because, if we learn to recognize their action in all temporal things, it will be another way of distinguishing them in ourselves. Indeed, you can't imagine how many errors are made every day regarding our Being, just as there are concerning all physical Beings and Matter; and he who has the mind to judge the body will soon have what he needs to judge the man.

Research on Nature

The first error of this kind to take place was in making material Nature a class and area of study in its own right. Although men saw that this branch was alive and active, they regarded it as being separate from the trunk; and as a result of dwelling on this dangerous view, the trunk now seemed so far from the branch that they no longer saw a need for it to exist, or at least if they did recognize its existence, all they saw in it was an isolated Being whose voice was lost in the distance, and that it was unnecessary to understand it in order to understand and examine the scope and the Laws of this material Nature.

If, like them, we limited ourselves to thinking about Nature by itself, as acting without the mediation of an external Principle, it's true that we could certainly understand its physical and apparent Laws. Yet we couldn't say that our theory was complete, since we would still need to know its true Principle, which is only visible to the intellect, by which everything that exists is necessarily governed, and whose physical and apparent Laws are only the results of this.

On the other hand, if during our time among the Beings of this material Nature, we wished to exclude them completely from our research, and try to reach the invisible Principle, we would have to fear staying too high above the path we ought to follow, and as a result not accomplishing our objective, obtaining only part of the light intended for us.

We must be conscious of the disadvantages of these two excesses. They are such that in dedicating ourselves to either one, we are sure of being unsuccessful, and if we neglect one of the two Laws to study the other, we can only have an incorrect notion of both, since their present connection is essential, even if it isn't always visible. Finally, wishing to rise up to the level of the superior and invisible First Principle without being supported by Matter, is to offend against Him and to tempt Him; yet wanting to understand Matter while excluding this First Principle and the *virtues* He uses to sustain it, would be one of the most absurd impieties.

Matter and its Principle

It's not that men aren't destined, one day, to have perfect knowledge of the First Principle without being obliged to join Him to the study of Matter, just as there was a time following their fall when they were completely subject to the Law of Matter, and were unable to think about the existence of the First Principle. But during this intermediate period given to us, and placed between the two extremes, we mustn't lose sight of either if we do not want to go astray.

The second error is that, since man is bound in the physical Realm he has indeed searched for the Principle of Matter, because he couldn't doubt he has one; but in this search, he confused the two Laws, and wanted the

Principle of Matter to be as tangible as Matter itself. He wanted both to submit to his physical gaze.

However, physical measurement can only apply to extent.[20] Extent is simply a combination, and therefore a composite Being; and if man continues to believe that the Principle of Extent or of Matter is the same thing as Matter, then that Principle would then be extended and composed like it; and then it's true that he'd be able to work out its dimensions with his physical eyes, but only according to the limits of his abilities, and without advancing his knowledge as a result. Because to measure correctly, he'd have to have a basis for his measurements, and he doesn't have one. But indeed, we'd be a long way from having a correct understanding of the Principle of Matter, when compared with the one we have of Principles in general.

All those who wanted to explain what a Principle is, have had to agree that it must be indivisible, immeasurable and completely different from what Matter presents to our sight. Even Mathematicians and Geometricians, even though they only work with their senses and only have extent in mind, support this definition; because as material as the mathematical point on which they base all their work is, they are obliged to dress it up in all the properties of the immaterial Being, for without that, their science would have no beginning.

So, what else is an indivisible and immeasurable Being, as we feel any Principle must be, but a simple[21] Being? And there is surely no doubt that material appearances are, on the contrary, divisible and may be submitted to measurement by the senses. Therefore, Matter is not a simple Being at all; and consequently, it can't be its own Principle. It's therefore absurd to try to confuse Matter with the Principle of Matter.

---

[20] The word *étendue* presents a problem in English. Strictly speaking it means 'extent', or 'length'. However, it can occasionally mean 'area', as in two dimensions, or 'acreage', which, being a country term carries with it a sense of three dimensions, since it is hard to picture a field without thinking of soil and even crops, especially in Eighteenth Century France. Now, strictly speaking the term used for area in Geometry is *superficie*, and not *étendue*. Here, Saint-Martin is comparing extent to matter, and since matter is clearly three-dimensional, I have used the more neutral term 'extent', since neither 'line' nor 'area' seem to fit the context: and this is why I may appear to be tortuously avoiding the term 'area'. However, in Chapter 6, as we shall see, Saint-Martin makes a number of important points about different types of lines; and then I will use the word 'length' for *étendue* far more often, since his argument is based on lines rather than area or mass.

[21] The word *simple*, common to both languages, is meant in this context to say that the Being is not mixed or a composite. Another possible word is 'pure'. However, I have retained the original word 'simple' throughout. Also, note that for Saint-Martin, a key difference between Matter and its Principle is the fact that Principles can't be measured or divided, whereas Matter can.

The Divisibility of Matter

On this subject, I must point out the ignorance into which this incorrect way of thinking about the body has led most people. They think that by mutilating, dividing and subdividing Matter, they are mutilating, dividing and subdividing the Principle and the essence of Matter; and believing that it's only the limitations of their physical organs which prevent them from going as far as their thinking in this process, they imagine that this division can theoretically be possible beyond what they can manage themselves. As a result, they believe Matter to be infinitely divisible; and as a result, they regard it as indestructible, and therefore eternal.

It's precisely in confusing Matter with the Principle of Matter that these errors have been almost universally adopted. Dividing the forms of Matter isn't dividing its essence or, to phrase it more clearly, separating the various parts of which all bodies are composed isn't dividing or decomposing Matter, because each of the material parts coming from this division remains whole in its appearance as Matter, and therefore in its essence, and in the number of Principles which constitute all Matter.

By what strange blindness was man able to believe that, by changing the body's dimensions he was truly dividing up Matter? Isn't it easy to see that all operations of this kind by man simply transpose or separate what was joined together; and for his hands to be able to separate Matter, wouldn't he have to have made it in the first place?

Therefore, I here only see the weakness and limitations of man's abilities, which are halted by the invincible power of the Principles of Matter. For we know it can change physical forms and shapes at will, because these forms are simply composites of different particles, and for this reason these forms have none of the properties of Unity. Finally, there isn't one of these particles that he can destroy, for if the Principle that supports them isn't composite, it can't be divided in its essence; and in this sense, not only is Matter not divisible to infinity, as commonly thought, but it's not even possible for man's hand to begin or work the slightest division of it: further proof which shows that this physical Principle is one and simple, and therefore not Matter.

The Limitations of Mathematics

What I said about the methods of the Mathematicians should have shown us the difference between their path and Nature's. Mathematical Science, by not offering anything more than a misleading copy of true knowledge, has its basis and results in relationships alone, and once they have based their assumptions on these, the results are correct and appropriate for those assumptions. We could say that Mathematicians can't stray because they never leave their ivory tower, and can only go around in circles. All their steps lead them back to the point where they started. Indeed, their tower is built in such a way that we can see it's equal in all its parts, and there is not the slightest distinction between the materials that serve as its foundations and those they use to build the top floors. What can they teach us, then?

Nature, on the contrary, having as its Principle a true and infinite Being, produces things which resemble it, and although these things are the envelope with which it conceals itself from our eyes, even though they are fleeting, they are so numerous, so varied and so active, that we can see quite clearly that their source must be inexhaustible. But we will find further observations on Mathematical Science later on in this book, and the use we should make of them to come to an understanding of Nature, and of that which is above.

Offspring and Their Principles

Here we will add another truth which will support those we've established so far, to prove how Matter is inferior to the Principle which serves as its basis and which produces it.

I pray first for the Observers to consider whether it isn't universally certain for any act of generation, that the product can never be equal to its Generating Principle. This truth is constantly seen throughout material generation, even though when growing, the fruits and the products of any class may equal and even surpass in strength and greatness the individual which gave rise to it; for since the individual in that class is subject to the Law of Time, the generating individual perishes at the same time its fruit advances towards the completion of its growth and perfection.

But at the moment of generation, this fruit was necessarily inferior to the individual from whom it came, since it owes its life and action to that individual.

Whatever class we study, I can confidently assure you that we'll find the same result. From this we can certainly say with good reason that it's universal. We can also conclude that it applies to Matter in relation to its Principle, because if we can see Matter born, we can't deny that it has been generated; and if it has been generated it is, like all other Beings, inferior to its Generating Principle.

We're already made progress in recognizing the superiority of the Principle of Matter over Matter, and in sensing that they can't both be of the same nature; and in this we keep ourselves safe from accepting the dangerous conclusions that some have dared to offer on this subject, and which, due to the reputation of the Masters who have been their spokesmen, have become like Laws for most men. Because of this we can't believe, like them, that Matter is eternal and imperishable. In distinguishing form from Principle, we know that the former can vary endlessly, while the latter always remains the same; and it's not hard to recognize the end and the death of Matter in the succession of Beings and actions which Nature presents to us; while the Principle of this Matter, not being Matter, remains unalterable and indestructible.

The Reproduction of Forms

This succession of actions, and this continual renewal of physical Beings has led the Observers of Nature to other opinions which are just as false as the previous ones, and which expose them to the same inconsistencies. They saw bodies change, decompose and disappear in front of them; but at the same time, they saw that these bodies were continually replaced by other bodies. From this they believed that these were made from the remains of the previous bodies, which having dissolved, the various parts which composed them went into the creation of the new bodies. From this they concluded that bodies experience continual change, while their fundamental Matter always remains the same.

Then, not knowing the real Cause of the existence and action of this Matter, they couldn't see why it wouldn't always have been in motion and why it wouldn't be so forever, which again led them to decide that it was eternal.

But if, raising their eyes a little, they had recognized the true Principles of bodies, and had attributed the stability they believed they saw in their so-called fundamental Matter to those Principles instead, we wouldn't have to blame them for this new misunderstanding. Like them we also see the cycles and the mutations of forms; we also recognize that the Principles of the body are indestructible and imperishable; but having shown, as we have done, that these Principles aren't Matter, to say that they are timeless is certainly not to say that Matter does not perish.

The Immutability of Their Principles

It's by distinguishing bodies from their Principles, that the Observers would have avoided the dangerous mistake which they try in vain to excuse, and they would have avoided attributing eternity and immortality to the material Being they see before them. I agree with them about the daily course of Nature: I see all forms being born and dying, and I see them replaced by other forms; but I avoid concluding from this that this cycle has no beginning and no end; because it only takes place and can be seen in transitory bodies, and not on their Principles, which are never affected by them in the slightest. Once we've accepted the existence and stability of these Principles as independent of and separate from bodies, we must also acknowledge that they can exist before these bodies, and that they can still exist after them.

I won't speak of a proof which is of such a nature that you'd refuse to believe me: but it's of such a kind that I can't doubt what I've just said any more than if I had been present at the Creation.

Besides, the numerical Law of Beings is an irrevocable testimony; ONE exists and comprehends Himself independently of the other numbers; and after bringing them to life during the course of the Decade, He leaves them behind and returns to His Unity.[22]

---

[22] One, or Unity, is of course God or the First Principle. Both Pasqually and Saint-Martin's Theosophical numerical systems attributed the numbers from two to nine to classes of Beings, and therefore Saint-Martin talks about Unity bringing the Decade (1 – 9) to life, before returning to Unity. I have used the 'He' to describe the First Principle, but of course it could also be 'She'. However, this is not to give the Creator a sex, but rather to avoid calling the Creator 'It' which, in the English language at least, suggests something inanimate.

Emanations from the Unity

The Principles of bodies being one, can therefore be conceived as being alone and separate from all forms of Matter, whereas the least particles of this Matter can only survive or be conceived by being supported and animated by their Principle; just as we can picture numerical Unity as being able to exist apart from the other numbers, though none of the numbers following Unity can be understood except as being the emanation and the product of this Unity.

If we want to apply the basic premise we established earlier concerning the inequality that necessarily exists between the generating Being and its product, we will see that, if the Principles of Matter are indestructible and eternal, it's impossible for Matter to possess the same privileges.

However, this assertion about a necessary inequality between the generating Being and its production could lead to some concern about man's nature, who, being born of an indestructible source, and being inferior to his Principle, can't have the same benefits, and he must therefore be susceptible to destruction. But simple reflection will dispel this doubt.

Secondary Beings

Although Matter and man both have their own Generating Principles, it would be very wrong to think they were the same. The Generating Principle of man is Unity. As Unity possesses everything within Himself, and transmits an existence which is complete and independent to His offspring, He can, as their Leader and Principle, expand or contract their abilities; but He can't give them death, because, since His operations are true, what *is* cannot *not* be.

It's not the same for Matter which, as the product of a secondary Principle which is lower and subordinate to another Principle, is always dependent upon both, in that the cooperation of their joint action is essential to the continuation of its existence: because it can be certain that, when one of the two ceases, the body will be extinguished and disappears.

Now, the beginning and end of these different actions manifests itself quite clearly in physical Nature, by showing us that Matter can't endure forever. Besides, as we must recognize that while the action of Unity, or the First Principle, is perpetual and indivisible, we can't attribute the same perpetuity of action to the secondary Principles which create Matter without committing a serious error. That's why the Creator of things can't make the world to be eternal like Him; because the World could only be eternal if all the Worlds were created directly by Him, since this will always be in His power. But because all these Worlds are only the work of a secondary Principle, they are therefore not permanent, and can die.

The Generation of the Body

Let's now examine another theory concerning our subject. It has been taught that, following the dissolution of physical Beings, the remains of these bodies are used to form part of the substance of other bodies. The Observers of Nature are certainly mistaken in this doctrine, as well as the conclusions they have drawn from it. To say that bodies are formed from one another, and that they are merely different successive collections of the same materials, is just as great an error as claiming that Matter is eternal. They would've been more careful about proposing such ideas if they had taken more precautions while marching so confidently towards an understanding of Nature.

The Universal Principles of Matter are simple Beings. Each of them is *one*, as our observations have established, and the notion we've given about a Principle in general: the innate Principles of the least particle of Matter must therefore have the same property. Each of them will therefore be *one* and simple, like the Universal Principles of this Matter. There can be no difference between these two kinds of Principles, other than in the duration and strength of their action, which is longer and more extensive in universal Principles that in specific Principles. However, the personal action of a simple Principle is necessarily simple and unique itself, and therefore can only have a single purpose to fulfill. It contains within it everything it needs for the complete accomplishment of its Law; and finally, it's susceptible neither to combination nor division.

The universal Principle of Matter therefore has the same abilities, and although the results that come from it multiply, extend and are subdivided to infinity, it's certain that this universal Principle only has a single task to fulfill, and a single action to perform, too. When its task is completed, its action must cease, and be withdrawn by the One who had ordered it to perform it. But for the entire length of that time it must perform the same action and manifest the same effects.

It's the same with the innate Principles of the various individual bodies. They are subject to the same Law of single action, and when their time is over, it's also withdrawn from them.

So, if each of these Principles has only one action, and at the end of this action they must all return to their Primitive Source, we can't reasonably expect new forms from them, and we must conclude that the bodies we see successively born derive their origin and their substance from other Principles than those whose action we've seen come to an end following the dissolution of the bodies they'd produced. We therefore need to look elsewhere for the source from which these new bodies must have been born.

But where can we better find this than in the strength and activity of that dual Law which constitutes universal physical Nature, and which shows itself at the same time in a thousand different ways in the production and progression of each body?

Indeed, we know that this earth we inhabit could not exist and be maintained if it didn't have within it a vegetative Principle[23] which was its own; but there must necessarily be an external Cause, which is none other than the Celestial or Planetary Fire, which reacts on this Principle for its action to be manifested.

It's the same with individual bodies. Each of these bodies comes from a seed, in which lies an innate germ or Principle, depositary of all its properties and all the effects it must produce. But this seed would forever remain inactive, and couldn't reveal any of its abilities, if it wasn't activated by an external fiery Cause, whose warmth allows it to react on all the physical Beings around it; which in their turn penetrate its envelope, prodding it, warming it, and preparing it to perform the external action of producing its own fruit and its own *virtues*.

Yet the external fiery Cause, making this reaction take place, would soon overwhelm the action of the individual Principles and destroy their properties, if the aid of alimentary Beings didn't come to renew their strength, and help them to resist the devouring heat of this external Cause. It's for this reason that, if we expose seeds deprived of nourishment to heat,

---

[23] At this time, the functioning of all things was seen to have two parts: mind, or the conscious part and soul, or the vegetative part. The Scientists of the time recognized that the body had functions which did not require a conscious effort to function, such as breathing and the beating of the heart, and they termed these activities 'vegetative', as opposed to conscious actions which were controlled by the mind, or intelligence. Saint-Martin is here extending this concept to the Earth, suggesting that it, too, had vegetative functions which were accomplished without the need for conscious intervention. This will be revisited in more depth during Chapter 3.

they're burned up where they lie, before they can have a chance to grow. It's also for this reason that seeds which have begun to germinate are still consumed and destroyed if they lack the nourishment necessary for them to protect themselves from the continual activity of the fiery reaction, since that reaction, having now penetrated the seed's envelope, can far better deploy its destructive power.

We can see from this that the aliments are themselves a second means of reaction used by Nature to maintain and preserve her works: but this will be seen even more clearly later on.

So, this is the dual universal Law which rules over the birth and development of physical Beings. The cooperation of these two actions is absolutely necessary so that they can live visibly to us: namely, the first action innate within them, or the internal action, and the second or external action which comes to energize and activate the first; and never among material things is a body formed except by this means.

Let us apply what we have said about the Earth to the creation of the Universe. We can regard it as a collection of an infinite multitude of germs and seeds, all of which have in them the innate Principle of their Laws and Properties, according to their class and species, but which, to generate and reproduce outside, wait for some external Cause to come and help them and prepare them for reproduction. Here indeed we find the explanation of a phenomenon which surprises many: namely, why one can find worms in fruit without a puncture, and live animals in the heart of stones. It's because each put there by Nature, or entering these kinds of incubators by filtration, are found there, or received there by the same path of filtration as the sap necessary to perform the necessary Law of reaction on them.[24] But let's not stray from our subject.

We'll now see what role bodies and the remains of bodies can have in the formation and growth of other bodies. They can supplement the strength of physical Beings, and maintain them against the continual reaction of the external fiery Principle. They can, through their own action, even contribute to the manifestation of the abilities of seeds, and make their properties function. But it would go against the Laws of Nature, and disregard the

---

[24] While this comment may seem extraordinary to us in modern times, we should remember that the theory of Spontaneous Generation was not fully discredited until Louis Pasteur's time in the 1850s. Prior to then, Spontaneous Generation was assumed to be a fact. Jan Baptist van Helmont (1580 – 1644) "describes a recipe for mice (a piece of soiled cloth plus wheat for 21 days) and scorpions (basil, placed between two bricks and left in sunlight)." [*From Wikipedia entry on 'Spontaneous Generation'.*]

essence of any Principle, to believe that they could introduce themselves into the substance of these seeds. They can, I repeat, be a support and even spur it into action; but they will never become a part of its essence. The following observations will be proof of this.

The Destruction of the Body

We have previously determined that the Principles of bodies are not Matter, but rather, simple Beings; that in this quality, they must have in them everything that is necessary to their existence, and that they require nothing from other Beings. They wouldn't even accept the assistance of the external reaction we have just discussed if they weren't subject to the dual Law which governs all elemental Beings, because of the inferiority of their nature. For there is indeed a higher Nature where this dual Law is not needed, and where Beings are born without the aid of secondary Beings, and by the sole virtues of their own Generating Principle; as was man in former times. But, to be sure our understanding is all the clearer, we won't rely on theory alone, but look to experience to support it. Firstly, let us look at what takes place when bodies are destroyed.

This destruction can only take place through the cessation of action by the innate Principle which produced these bodies, since this action is their true basis and their main support. However, this Principle can't cease its action until the Law which causes it to work is suspended, since then, being delivered from its chains, the Principle can separate from its products and returns into its Original Source. So long as this Law operates, the envelope can never cease to be in its natural and individual form; and if this form is subject to decomposition, this can only take place because, when the Law of action is removed, the innate Principle within this form, which makes it exist by binding together the three Elements which compose it, separates from these Elements and abandons them to their own Laws. Then, as these elemental Laws are opposed to one another, the Elements finding themselves free, combat one another, divide, and finally destroy themselves utterly in front of our eyes.

This is how bodies gradually die, disappear, and are destroyed. In a corpse, therefore, I only see Matter without life, deprived of the innate Principle which had produced and supported its existence. In these remains, I only see parts which are still sustained by the presence of the secondary actions which the innate Principle had emanated in this body during the time of its own action; for these secondary emanations are spread throughout the smallest physical particles. But after the Principle which produced them abandons the whole body which was formed from their union, they separate themselves successively from the individual's envelope.

So, what could a body deprived of life, during its dissolution, communicate to new bodies to support their formation and growth? Could it be the dominant Principle? Yet it no longer exists in the corpse, since it's because of the withdrawal of this very Principle that the body became a cadaver. Besides, each seed, having its own innate Principle which is the depositary of all its abilities, has no need to join with another Principle. Two simple Beings can never unite or mingle their action. If they were to come together, far from contributing to the life of the new bodies, this would only cause disorder and destruction, since it's not possible to place two centers in a circumference without distorting it.

Could we say that the material parts of the body which have dissolved could reunite and pass into the essence of the seeds? Yet we have just seen that each seed is animated by a Principle which contains within itself everything that needed for its existence. Moreover, don't we see all the parts of the body dissolving successively, not leaving the slightest trace behind? Don't we already know that this specific dissolution only occurs because of the departure of the secondary emanations which resided in the corpse, each of which we can consider as the center of the part it occupied? And then, wouldn't we have to recognize that the body, that the parts of the body, that the entire Universe is but an assembly of Centers, since we see the body dissipate completely over time? Yet if everything is a center, and if all these centers disappear in the dissolution, what would remain of a dissolved body that could become part of the existence and life of new bodies?

It's therefore a mistake to believe that the Principles – be they general or specific – of physical Beings which have dissolved, after separating from their envelope, go on to animate new forms, and that by beginning a new lease of life, they can live several times in succession. If everything is simple, if everything is one in Nature and in the essence of Beings, then it must be the same for their action, and each of them must have its specific task, as simple and as unique as it is itself: otherwise there would be weakness in the Creator of things, and confusion in His Works.

Digestion

But, taking animal digestion as an example, no doubt someone will object that during the dissolution of food through digestion, the greater amount passes into the blood, into the lymph, and into the other liquids in the individual, and from there, being carried to all parts of the body, the animal receives support and sustenance from them. Then they will ask me how this food could strengthen the animal's life and actions without communicating the least part of itself to that animal, and without the fire innate in the food penetrating the Principle and the essence of this individual, uniting with it to increase it.

I'll reply that, most certainly the only use of this food is to support the life and activity of the individual which has eaten it. It can't accept it to be a new Principle nor as an increase of its Being, but simply as the agent of a reaction it requires to make use of its strength and continue its temporal activity. And although no physical Being can survive without this action, there is not one in which it could have such an effect, since it's a given that if the Principle contained in the food could unite with the Principle of the body that feeds on it, the Law of action, which constituted it, would no longer have any effect.

The Disintegration of the Body[25]

We know this through experience and through the havoc that raw food, and undercooked and poorly bled meat, can cause in an animal. We know how too strong a reaction is contrary to physical life; and we can't deny that animals which by their nature are intended to devour other animals are more ferocious and cruel, and have a more voracious and destructive nature than animals which only eat plants. This is because carnivores experience an excessive reaction, because along with the flesh on which they live, they receive a large quantity of animal secondary Principles, and because they use all the efforts of the innate action within them to bring about the dissolution of these Principles' envelopes as quickly as possible; but since these now find themselves outside their natural habitat, they also use all

---

[25] The actual title at the top of this page reads 'Reintegration of the Body' (*De la Réintégration du Corps*). However, given the subject matter of this section and the fact that the term 'Reintegration' was appropriated by both Pasqually and Saint-Martin to refer to the reinstatement of man into his primitive rank and estate, the title has been slightly amended.

their powers to break these foreign chains and return to their Original Source.

During this internal battle, the individual experiences a ferment which agitates it and leads it to confused actions, and it can't be restored to a more tranquil state until the envelope of these secondary Principles has been dissolved, and they have rejoined their Generating Principle.

It's on this subject that we should, in passing, criticize the custom of many Nations, who believe they honor the Dead by preserving their corpses, or by consuming them with fire. Both practices are equally foolish and contrary to Nature. For the true menstruum of bodies is the earth, and since man's hands haven't created these bodies, it should neither attempt to fix nor extend its duration, leaving to each of their Principles the duty of suspending its action in accordance with its Law, and to reunite in its own time with its Source.

Woman

I can no longer excuse myself from stopping for a moment on this proposal, that *the true menstruum of bodies is the earth.*[26] It is indeed in the earth that man's body should decompose. Man's body forms in the woman's body; and when it decomposes, it gives back to the earth what it received from the woman's body. The earth is therefore the true Principle of the woman's body, because things always return to their source, and these two Beings are so similar to each other, it can't be denied that woman's body has a terrestrial origin; and, recalling that she was the first physical origin of man, we will see clearly why woman is universally inferior to him.[27]

---

[26] This is a fascinating concept. In Alchemy the term *menstruum*, which has carried over into modern Chemistry, denoted 'solvent', and particularly a solvent used to extract the essential parts of (preferably living) tissues. This was common practice in Spagyrics, or Plant Alchemy, which used solvents like alcohol to extract the living essences from plants. However, there was also an Animal Alchemy, which used animal and human tissues and fluids (famously, blood, sperm or urine) in their experiments. But the term *menstruum* itself originates in the term 'menstrual', or the monthly discharge of women. This was considered especially powerful, since it was therefore linked with woman, with life, with bodily fluids, and with the cycle of the moon. The analogy here is that, since the womb warms, feeds and grows the man, if the earth warms, extracts and dissolves man's corpse, there must be a connection or correspondence between woman and the earth.

[27] It should be noted that this doesn't contradict Saint-Martin's earlier comment about the product always being inferior to its Generating Principle. This is not talking about women giving birth to men, but rather, to the moment that man was forced into a corporeal body due to his imperfect act of creation: therefore, woman was the reason for man's *first* physical origin.

But you'd be very much mistaken to think you could take this difference beyond form or physical abilities. When speaking of the Intellectual Principle, woman has the same source and the same origin as man, because, since man was only condemned to suffering and not to death, he needed a Being of his nature with him, as unhappy as him who, through her infirmities and deprivation, would recall him to wisdom by continually having before his eyes the bitter consequences of his prevarication. Moreover, man is most certainly not the creator of the intellectual Being of his products, as false and disastrous doctrines based on comparisons taken from Matter, such as the inexhaustible emanations of the elemental Fire, have taught: but in all this there is a Mystery which I will never believe is hidden enough. Let us resume the chain of our observations.[28]

Vegetation

There is a fact that the Naturalists[29] never fail to use to oppose me. This is the use of colored liquids which they pass through certain plants, modifying the color of the flowers, and even totally changing the color which Nature gave them. My answer to this is simple, and abides by everything I said concerning digestion.

All plants have an innate Principle just like any other body. Sap, which takes the place of food, can't add anything to this Principle; but it serves as a defense against the external fiery Cause which, without it, would quickly overcome and consume the forces and the action of the individual Principles

---

[28] This paragraph goes to the very heart of Pasqually's *Treatise*. Adam's act of defiance against God, or the First Principle, was to believe himself capable of an act of creation without God's cooperation. However, he only managed to create a physical form out of the earth. But it's most important to realize that this form did not contain life, and it was only after Adam had confessed to his crime, naming his inferior creation 'Houva' or 'Eve', that the First Principle completed the work by emanating a soul and placing it in the physical form; while He punished Adam by imprisoning him in a similar material form and placed them both in the material temporal prison called Earth, so that, as we read, Houva would be an eternal reminder to Adam of his prevarication. We must therefore note that, while Saint-Martin – and Pasqually – reflect the political and social viewpoint of their time, that material woman was subordinate to man and had a different physical form, this in no way suggests that her spiritual nature is anything but identical to Adam's. Indeed Houva, as the archetype of womankind, has an equal part to play in the Operation of Reconciliation, and an equal chance of finally Reintegrating with the Source. And remember, too, that Saint-Martin counted many women among his disciples.

[29] Naturalism is "is the "idea or belief that only natural (as opposed to supernatural or spiritual) laws and forces operate in the world." (*Oxford English Dictionary*). Many see it as philosophically aligned with Materialism, which was discussed in an earlier footnote.

by its heat. Then we should see, by the infinite number of different substances which can serve as nourishment to tangible Beings, the variety of reactions to which they are exposed. It's true that there is only one that is truly specific to each species: but the nature of perishable things, such as bodies, and the continual cycles to which they are subjected, leaves them capable of receiving foreign substances which weaken them, compromise their abilities, and even destroy them completely, although the Principle of the Being is indestructible.

These reactions are operated, as we know, by secondary Beings, which are also each depositaries of a Principle that is its own. This Principle can't perform an action, either by itself or through the specific Principles emanated from it, unless completely clothed in the physical envelope, since all simple Beings can only exist in this condition here below. It's therefore certain that the envelopes of these secondary Principles pass along with them, through the physical mass of plants and animals to serve as their food, and to help them resist the action of the external fiery Cause. It's certain that they also carry with them their color and all their properties. But, although they pass into these different individuals, we would never suggest that they become joined with them or become part of their substance.

Food

For these alimentary envelopes to succeed in uniting with the substance of the individual who ingests them, it would be necessary for their Principles to be joined together. But we have seen that since these Principles are simple Beings, this union is impossible, and since envelopes can only belong to their Principles, the union of their envelopes is also impossible. Food is therefore always a foreign substance, though necessary for the Being who receives it, for we know that they are only advantageous for him so far as he can accomplish their dissolution.

I think everyone would agree that there can't be any kind of mixing before this dissolution begins. However, if the dissolution can't take place unless preceded by the departure of the innate Principles from the food, and if the process is all about division and destruction, how could the Individual performing this destruction become joined to the very envelope it's destroying?

Indeed, if the food and the Principle it contains could be mixed up with the substance and Principle of the Being with which it reacts, it could also be substituted by it and take its place. If this were possible, it would be easy to change the nature of species and individuals completely. Now if, having changed the class and nature of a Being once, the same could now be done to every class that exists, this would lead to complete confusion, preventing us from ever being sure of the rank and place which Beings should occupy in the order of things.

Therefore, the Law by which Nature has constituted its products is totally resistant to these fantastic attempts; for it has given a unique innate Principle to each physical Being, which can extend – and which often does extend – its action beyond normal measures with the help of forced reactions and a favorable environment; but it can never lose or change its essence. This Principle, being the creator of its envelope, can't separate from it without the envelope quickly dissolving, and gradually being destroyed completely; and it's absolutely impossible for another Principle or another creator to come into and inhabit this envelope, and serve as its support, because in physical Nature there are absolutely no adulterers, or adoptive sons, since nothing is free.

The Mixing of Bodies

Each simple Being or Principle therefore has its own separate existence, and consequently, its own action and individual abilities, which are as incommunicable as its existence.

I don't object to the idea that, when mixing liquids, or bodies capable of being brought together, one can see united and simple effects which neither of these bodies was capable of producing on its own; because I've no problem in assuring you that, in these mixtures, the action and reaction of the various Principles upon one another produce results which only seem to be united and simple, because of the weakness of our senses in perceiving what is actually taking place, and because these results are actually a composite, and produced by the unique and specific action of each of the Principles brought together.

If we have a mixture of various bodies which are not capable of having a physical action on each other, but each has their own particular property of color, flavor or whatever, a third property comes out of their mixing which is really only an apparent product of the first two, since they may be mixed and combined, but are not in fact united and joined together. In this instance, nobody can deny that the Principles and their envelopes remain perfectly distinct and separate, and it's only the weakness of our senses which prevent us from perceiving the individual and specific actions of each of these bodies as being separate. Therefore, we are really only seeing a multitude of bodies of the same kind, piled up or gathered together with a multitude of bodies of a different kind, but always retaining their own individual existence, abilities and action.

If a solid body is thrown into a liquid which is similar in nature, the liquid overcomes its power and properties, separates its parts, divides them, destroys their apparent and visible solidity, dissolves it and appears to take it over. Through this dissolution, the liquid indeed shows us an outcome which is impossible to find in either of the individual substances which created the mixture. But can it be concluded from this that any merging of the Principles has taken place, and isn't it certain that this is only a simple extension of the action of a superior Principle over that of an inferior Principle, an extension which diminishes and even stops when the superior Principle has acted on a sufficient quantity of the body which was exposed to its action, and has consumed all the power which was in it?

If a solid body is given a liquid and absorbs it; or two liquids are mixed together and produce solid bodies or amalgams indissoluble in appearance; or finally, if bodies which previously showed neither particular strength nor special properties, but on being brought together produce surprising effects, such as bright flames, sparks, noises, lively and brilliant colors; could it ever be proved that there is a combining, confusion or communication of a Principle with another Principle in any of these events? If the strength of the dominant Principle only suspends the action of the weaker Principle without destroying its envelope, then it's still possible to separate them and return them both to their original state through industry; which would be infallible proof of the truth I've just established.

If, again without destroying the envelopes, the superior Principle in control divided the combination, and if, in giving the constituent parts of the mass freedom from its natural airiness by driving them off through evaporation, then the individual Principles of the same nature which were previously gathered together would, it's true, be dispersed hither and thither over the earth and in the air, but still without communicating anything, or losing their abilities, their substance or their action.

But if, on the contrary the dominant Principle had, by its power and strength, decomposed the actual envelope of the inferior Principle; if it had dissolved and destroyed it, then the action of the inferior Principle would be destroyed. Yet far from ending its career, this Principle would have been able to unite with or communicate its action to the dominant Principle; and if this were this case, the action of the dominant Principle would nevertheless still find itself still limited to its original activity: that is, if it hadn't been irrevocably altered or exhausted by its own victory.

Verminous Seeds

Finally, the confusion spread about the continuity of action by this same Principle through different successive forms won't be supported by the birth of those worms and other insects which appear when corpses putrefy. The Principle of the existence of these animalcules is again within their own seed; for our bodies, like all those of Creation, are a combination of an infinite multitude of destructive germs and verminous seeds which are only waiting for a reaction and suitable circumstances to be produced and generate.[30]

So long as our bodies remain in the fullness of their lives and their action, the dominant Principle which directs it keeps the whole envelope in balance, preventing its dissolution and containing the action of these destructive seeds. But when this dominant Principle abandons this envelope, then the secondary Principles, no longer having any attachment, separate themselves from the body naturally and leave the field open to all these animalcules. They even aid in their birth and their growth by means of a reaction and warmth capable of helping them to pierce their shells.

Then the remains of the corpse serve as food for these insects, and pass into them as food passes into all living bodies by digestion. In both, we see the same dissolution, the same use of innate Principles; but in neither does the Principle of the dissolved body pass into the living body to animate it; because, as I've established, each Being has life within itself, and needs only an external Cause to activate it and to maintain its own Principle.

---

[30] As was seen earlier, the idea of Spontaneous Generation was prevalent at the time. The idea that a fly might actually come and lay eggs on a corpse was unknown at the time, so the appearance of maggot was assumed to occur spontaneously.

Unity of Action in the Principles

It's therefore clear that, in the most hidden acts of physical Beings, such as conception, birth, growth and dissolution, the Principles never mingle and become fused with other Principles.

Food is therefore only the means of reaction to protect living bodies from an excess of the fiery action which successively devours and dissolves these alimentary Beings, as without them it would dissolve the living body itself. They are not, as the Observers and the multitude which follows them believe, the materials from which the Being, on being formed must be composed, since this Being already has everything within it including life, which the dissolved alimentary Beings no longer have; and what may remain of them is continually lost as their particular Principles separate from their envelope, and go to reunite with their Original Source.

False Theories about Matter

Thus, this apparent mutation of forms should no longer attract us and lead us to believe that the same Principles can begin new lives. We remain confident that the new forms we can see constantly born and reproducing before our eyes are simply the effects, the results and the fruits of new Principles that had not acted before then; and this must surely be an idea appropriate to the Creator of things when we say that, since everything is simple and everything is new in His works, everything must be appearing for the first time.

It's through such truths that we demonstrate once again how the theories about the eternity of Matter is contrary to the Laws of Nature. Not only are they not the same innate Principles which are continually responsible for the successive reproduction of bodies; but it's clear that any Principle can have only a single action, and therefore only a single purpose. Now, it's quite evident that the lives of the specific Beings which comprise Matter are subject to limits, since there is not a moment when we don't perceive their end, and time is only visible by means of their continual destruction.

But we should no longer be surprised by the errors which have prevailed on this subject, but if we were to adopt the theories resulting from them, there would be no end to our ability to stray. The Observers, having barely taken a single step towards distinguishing Matter from the Principle that supports and engenders this Matter, attributes to the one what belongs to the other alone. They regard original Matter as being always and essentially the same, endlessly receiving a multitude of different forms; and so, confusing it with its inner and innate Principle, they tell us that, since there is only one essence in Matter, there can be only one universal action in this Matter; and therefore, Matter is permanent and indestructible.

I urge them to go more deeply into what I said at the beginning of this book about the origin and nature of Good and Evil. I showed that it's repugnant to any man of sense to concede that these different properties could have the same source. Therefore, let's apply this to the different properties that Matter manifests, and see if it's true that there is only one material essence.

The Diversity of Material Essences

I ask you if the action of Fire is like that of Water, if Water acts like Earth, and if we don't see in these Elements properties which are not only different, but even completely opposed. Yet these Elements, though being several, are in fact the basis and foundation of all material envelopes. It's therefore impossible to agree with the Observers that there is only a single essence in bodies, when we see their properties show themselves so differently. Furthermore, since they also claim that Matter is continually used in the successive creation of forms, there are not even two of them in which one can reasonably accept this.

Therefore, I will continue to repeat that the essence of all bodies is definitely not singular, as they believe; that all forms are the result of their innate Principles, which can only manifest their action through the general Law of the three Elements[31] which are fundamentally different in nature; that a result of this kind can't be considered to be a Principle, seeing that, not being *one*, it's able to vary, and depends on the relative strength of action of one or more of these Elements; and therefore Matter can't be stable and permanent, nor pass successively from one body to another; but these bodies all come from the action of a new Principle and are therefore all different.

---

[31] The perceptive reader will have noticed that Air is missing from these Classical Elements. The reason for this is explained in the following Chapter.

This difference between all innate Principles is quite visible, if you observe that all the classes and Kingdoms of physical Nature are marked by strikingly distinctive characters. If you observe the differences existing between most of these classes and species; this should convince anyone that the innate Principles of the various bodies are necessarily different. Because if the innate Principle in bodies was only one, or the same across the whole of Nature, it would have to act everywhere and appear continually and in an identical manner in all the different bodies.

But, having recognized the individual differences between Principles, let us remember the precision and accuracy with which each one operates the particular action imposed upon it, and through this we will support the notion we've already had about these Principles of physical Beings, by saying they clearly can't be a composite like the essences of Matter, but rather that they are simple Beings, custodians of their Law and all their abilities; Beings who are custodians of a single action, like all simple Beings; that is, indestructible Beings, but whose physical actions must come to an end, and end at any moment, because they can only act in time, and compose time.

The Theory of Development

I've a small remark to make to the Observers of Nature concerning a word they use when talking about the body. They talk about birth and growth using the word *development*. We can't accept their use of this expression; because, if it were true that the body does nothing but develop, it would mean that were completely contained within their seeds or within their Principles. However, if these bodies were essentially and truly completely contained in their Principles, this would deny their unique quality as a simple Being. Then they would no longer be indivisible, or clothed with immortality; for to preserve the immortality of the Principles it would also have to be preserved in the physical Beings in which they are enclosed: and that would be to accept what we have refuted till now, and completely contradict what we've established.

If the Observers don't want to expose themselves to the most absurd consequences, they should stop seeing the growth of physical Beings as a development, but instead the work and operation of the innate Principle, the producer of the material essences, which prepares them and makes them conform to the specific Law which it carries within. I know that those I address are a long way from believing in such a doctrine, and that they would be reluctant to accept it; because nothing could be more opposed to their thoughts and to the way they have considered Nature up to now. However, I present them these Truths with confidence, and with the conviction I have that they can put nothing else in its place.

I don't even know how, by accepting the growth of physical Beings as development, they were able to accept even for a moment the idea I fought earlier about the passage and reunion of the various parts of one body in another body. If a seed can only develop, it must therefore be true that it contains absolutely everything necessary within itself. However, if it has all its parts, why would it need parts of another body to form itself?

But, so that someone doesn't think they can turn my argument against me, and say that, if I deny that all the parts required for the physical creation of a material Being must be contained within its seed, I am agreeing that it must receive the materials for its growth from outside. This, of course, would be completely contrary to the truths that I've tried to set forth about Nature. This Nature is alive everywhere, and contains within her the motive for all her actions, without the need for seeds to contain within themselves an abridged collection of all the parts which must one day serve as their envelope. They only need the ability to produce them, and this they have. Therefore, if they have this ability, all the other measures invented to explain the growth and formation of physical Beings become superfluous; because the Observers only needed them after misunderstanding in Matter the Principle innate in its life and action, and only after imagining that it was essentially dead and sterile. One final comment will serve to banish this theory about the development of physical Beings completely; which is, if their theory was correct, there would be no monsters, since everything would have been created to be regular; and if there was only one means of development, the Creator of things would have nothing more to do. However, we are a long way from believing that He, or all that He has produced, can remain inactive.

Summary

Here I'll end my comments about the imperfect way that men have thought about the essence of physical Nature. I dare to believe that if they wished to meditate on what I've told them, they would admit that it's because they didn't distinguish Matter from its Principle that they have so often erred; and after what I've just said about the formation of Beings, the continual mutation of forms, the distinction of essences from their innate Principle, the properties and simplicity of this Principle – both in the specific as in the universal – and on the unity of its action which is only performed for a period of time, they will agree that the Principles of the various physical Beings can't be mingled, nor can they communicate, since they're indivisible. Being indivisible, they can never be dissolved. They are different to each other, both through the specific nature of their action and by the length of their existence, seen in the destruction of the Elements which make up Matter. This results in an infinite number of successive physical combinations, from which the Observers have all too easily concluded that the body endlessly succeeds itself, and that Matter which serves as their basis is imperishable. But far from regarding it as eternal, they should agree with us that there is not one instant when it doesn't destroy itself, since within it one action is takes the place of another. Then they will no longer hope, like the Alchemists, for a continual revivification which preserves them and all bodies from dissolution; because, if the existence of bodies has only a limited duration, once this term has come, it would be impossible to delay their destruction without attaching a new Principle to the one which is ready to separate from it. However, we've seen that this can't happen in the natural Order of things. Do these men then believe that their powers are superior to Nature, and the Laws that constitute all Beings?

Thus, having learned to distinguish Matter from the Principle which gives birth to it, and having recognized the different actions which are manifested in this Matter, they can no longer believe in all these fantastic identities which have led them to confuse everything, even Good and Evil. Let's now fix our view on higher things.

Chapter 3 – Nature

A Series of Errors

If it were possible for an error not to inevitably be the source of an endless number of other errors, I wouldn't be that concerned about the ones I've just combatted on the Principle and the Laws of Matter. Since understanding these things isn't too important, these errors aren't particularly dangerous in themselves. But, as things stand, these errors are held up by the Observers to be true; and just as our proofs against man's false reasoning are mutually supportive, so their theories on bodies and the fragile conclusions they have drawn from them have led to the most terrible consequences, since they are fundamentally linked to things of a Higher Order.

Having confused Matter with the Principle of Matter in every physical body, these men, misguided in every step, were no longer in any condition to discover the true essence of this Matter, or to identify the Principle which sustains it and gives it its action and life. Then, having joined the two natures which constitute the entire elemental realm together as one, they didn't give a moment's thought to discovering if there was another, superior one.

Indeed, we saw that they opened themselves up to the following unpleasant alternatives: either to ascribe Matter's limits and constraints to the Principle, or to give Matter the rights and properties of the Principle. So, to them, the Principle of bodies and the grossest parts which constitute them are one and the same. By similar reasoning, they even found it easy to confuse these bodies and their Principles with Beings of a Nature independent of Matter.

Thus, step by step, they quickly established a universal equality between all Beings, in such a way that we'd have to agree with them that: either Matter itself is the Cause of everything which takes place, or the Cause which makes Matter function is no more intelligent than the Principles we identified in Matter; both of which are really saying the same thing. Giving Matter such sweeping properties, as they do, is saying that it contains everything within it. However, if it contains everything within it, why would we need an intelligent Being to watch over it and direct it, since it can direct itself? Then, what would this intelligent Being be, if men refuse it knowledge of and control over Matter? And by removing its power, wouldn't this remove its intelligence too, since then it would have something inferior to it which it couldn't understand.

This is the narrow circle in which unwise men would like to contain our knowledge and our understanding.

I know that most of them saw the dangerous consequences of their theories, and if they still let themselves be carried along by them, it's less due to their conviction and attachment to them than a lack of precaution; but they are no less to blame for exposing themselves to these inconsistencies. Man can stray at any moment, particularly when a true knowledge of something he wishes to explain has been obscured due to his exile. Nevertheless, despite his privation there are errors which he is guilty of not avoiding. The ones we've just discussed are numbered among these, and with a little good faith and by applying the principles we've established, it would be impossible for the authors of such theories to continue to see anything plausible in them.

In sum, I'm quite happy with what I've already said about the difference between physical Beings and intelligent Beings, and the proof I presented to show that the most refined abilities of a physical Being still can't elevate it above the physical. This I've shown in Animals, which occupy the highest rank among the three Kingdoms of Nature. Then, by comparing the movements and lives of animals, which have abilities of a different order to those we have identified so clearly in man, we can't doubt that man is an intelligent Being; and we can't deny either, that while there are no other Beings endowed with the gift of intelligence, we've also seen that in man's present state he has nothing within him, and he must wait for everything to come to him from outside, even down to the least of his thoughts.

Also, remembering that among the thoughts he receives there are some which are offensive to his nature and others which are in harmony with it, and that he can't therefore reasonably attribute a single Principle to them both, we've already adequately proven the existence of two Principles external to man, and as a result, external to Matter, since Matter is infinitely inferior to him.

The Rights of Intelligent Beings

So again, we can't deny intelligence to these two opposing Principles, since in this state of reprobation we are suffering, they're the only ones by means of which we can be conscious of our intelligence. Now, if they're intelligent, they must know and comprehend everything that is below them; for if they don't they wouldn't possess the slightest ability of intelligence; and if they do indeed know and understand everything below them, it can only be that, as active Beings, the Evil Principle is concerned with destruction, and the Good Principle with preservation.

By this we can easily demonstrate that Matter doesn't function all alone. But it's within Matter that we must seek the proof to dissuade those who have attributed to it an activity which is in fact essential to its Nature.

We have shown that the Principles of Matter, both universal and individual, contain within them the life and physical abilities which must come from them. We added that, despite this incredible property innate within these Principles, they could never produce anything unless they had been activated and warmed by the external fiery Principles required to set their abilities going; and this by means of that dual Law to which all physical Beings are subject, and which governs all the actions and all the generations of Matter.

The Principle of Movement

It's no doubt a mark of weakness and subjugation in the Principle of the physical Being to have life within itself, yet be unable to activate it by itself. However, we can be sure that this Principle of life, innate in the seed of every physical Being, is superior to the external fiery Principles which only use a simple secondary action upon it, without being able to communicate anything of essence to its existence. Now, if these fiery Principles are inferior to the Principle of Life which they've just activated, they would clearly be even less capable than of activating themselves than activating this Principle.

It would be pointless to go around the circle of development of physical Beings to try to discover what Principle initiated this action; and if we conclude by saying these Beings react mutually upon one another, having no need for another Cause to activate what's in them, we'd have to admit that, in the beginning, there must have been an initial external movement communicated to this circle in which they're contained. For if the most active of the physical Principles can do nothing without the action of another Principle, how can those which are inferior to them be unaffected by this reaction? We can see from this that, wherever on this circle we claim the first action began, this action most certainly must have taken place.

I therefore ask the Observers sincerely, if they still imagine that the beginning of activity can be found within Matter, and belongs to its nature; or if on the contrary, this gives them physical proof of its initial dependence on that irrevocable Law which subjects the Principle of its reproduction to the daily support and action of another Principle.

They should be all the most certain about this Truth, for the means they use to try to destroy it's, on the contrary, the very means which serves to prove it. They tell us that if we put such and such materials together, we will shortly see them ferment, putrefy then give rise to a product. Yet if these materials could all come together on their own, would they need a person to bring them together? So, if this particular mixing can't take place without the help of an outside hand, isn't the situation exactly the same in general, since its nature is the same in all parts of Matter, and having nothing more than them, it can't act by a different Law?[32]

Nature's Guide

Thus, I believe I can claim the need for a Cause which is intelligent and active within itself, which communicated the initial action to Matter, as it communicates to it continually in the successive actions of its reproduction and growth, and in all the effects it shows us. Not only is it impossible to imagine that Matter didn't receive its origin from a Cause which is external to it; but we can see that even today, there must be a Cause which constantly directs all this Matter's actions, and that there isn't a single moment that it could live and support itself if it was left to itself, and deprived of its Principles of action.

Finally, if a Cause was required to give Matter its initial action, and if the cooperation of this Cause continues to be needed to maintain Matter, it's no longer possible to think about Matter without simultaneously having an notion of its Cause, which alone makes it what it's, and without which it

---

[32] This is quite an elegant argument. If the Observers claim that fermentation takes place of its own accord, Saint-Martin asks who put the ingredients together in the first place, if not an external Cause.

couldn't exist for an instant. And just as I can't imagine the form of a body without the innate Principle which produced it, so, too, I can't imagine the action of bodies and Matter without a physical – yet immaterial – Cause, which is both active and intelligent, superior to the physical Principles, and which gives them the movement and action I see in them, yet which I know does not fundamentally belong to them.

This should suffice to explain all the regular phenomena of Nature, where by recognizing a superior Cause whose intelligence we can't deny as her leader and guide, we can see that order and precision reign in the Universe as a natural effect and result of the intelligence of this Cause.

Then Nature can surprise us no more, and all her workings and even the destruction of Beings appear to us to be simple and consistent with her Law, for death is not nothingness but an action; and time, of which Nature is composed, is just a collection and succession of actions, sometimes creative and sometimes destructive. In other words, we should expect to find throughout the Universe the character and evidence of the Wisdom that built it and sustains it.

Disorders in Nature

But, as much as this Truth makes itself felt in man's thoughts, so, too he is struck by the disasters and confusion which he so often sees in Nature. What should he put this contrast down to? Could it possibly be to this active and intelligent Cause, which is the true Principle of the perfection of physical things? We can't linger even for a moment on this notion, and it's repugnant to think that this powerful Cause could act both for itself and against itself at the same time.

May this hideous idea never lead us to stop offering tributes or weaken our veneration for this Cause! After what we've seen about the dual intellectual Law, on the opposition of the two Principles, we should know to which we can attribute the evils and disorders in Nature, though this is not yet the place to speak of the reasons which make them operate.

But puerile distrust of these Truths is an obstacle which hinders the progress of our knowledge and wisdom the most. It's the main cause of the errors where men's ideas have led them on these subjects, and of the uncertainty in all the theories they have given to explain Nature.

The Clear Cause of Matter

If they had applied themselves better to thinking about the two different Principles they were compelled to recognize, they would have seen the difference and the opposition of their abilities and actions, and would have seen that Evil is completely alien to the Good Principle; acting through its own power on the temporal creations of this Principle with which it's imprisoned here below, yet having no real action on Good itself, which hovers over all Beings, supporting those which by their nature can't support themselves, and allowing those to which it had given the privilege of liberty to act and defend themselves. They'd have seen that, although Wisdom has ordered all things in such a way that Evil is often an opportunity for Good, this does not preclude the fact that at the moment this Evil acts, it's evil, and therefore nobody can attribute its action to the Good Principle.

This could further help to convince us of the fragility of men's theories, and confirm us in the principles which we are following, that it's only by distinguishing the true nature and properties of different Beings that we can come to a correct idea about them. But it's time to go back to our subject.

If the observations we just made about the Laws which direct the formation of bodies have led us to see the need for a superior and intelligent Cause; if we learned that the two inferior agents – the first Principle contained in seeds, and the secondary Principle bringing about the reaction – are not sufficient to produce physical forms on their own; it's Nature itself and reason which teaches us these truths, and we can no longer doubt this fact.

Nevertheless, I will underline this doctrine with a simple observation which should give it more weight and authority by drawing your attention to the fact that the active, superior, universal, temporal, intelligent Cause, which understands and manages all inferior Beings, has an influence over them which will no doubt increase its importance greatly in our eyes, when we see that it's through its action that all physical Beings originally took their form, and that it's also through its action that they maintain and reproduce themselves, just as they'll maintain and reproduce themselves throughout time.

The abilities of so powerful a Being must surely extend to all the works He directs, and He must be such that He can watch over everything and preside over everything; that is, encompass all the parts of His work.

Temporal Causes

We should therefore accept that it was He who governed the production of the substance which serves as the basis for bodies, as He later governed the creation of the physical form out of this same substance; and that His power and intelligence extend to the essence of all bodies, as well as to the actions which have formed them. Simple in His Nature and in His action, like all simple Beings, His abilities show themselves in the same way in everything, and though there is a distinction between the production of the seeds of Matter and the creation of the physical forms which arise from them, it's a single Law which directs both, however different; otherwise there would be diversity of action, and this would fly in the face of everything we have observed.

For we indicated earlier that the essences or Elements of which bodies are universally composed, number *three*. It's through the number *three* that the Law which directed the production of the Elements was manifested: it must therefore also be true that it's through this number *three* that the Law that directed and still directs the creation of these same Elements in physical form manifests itself. It's the need for a simple action in a simple Being which begins to help us understand this analogy; but when the uniformity of this Law is confirmed by close examination and by the fact itself, then it becomes a reality to us.[33]

We'd indeed demean the notion we should have about the intelligent Cause not to recognize its evident action upon Beings, which can't exist without it for an instant. To confuse this intelligent Cause with the inferior Causes of all physical actions and products is the same as denying it; for

---

[33] The reader should see from this section that Saint-Martin maintains the position of Pasqually that, while the First Principle created everything, and was not above personal intervention on occasion, for example, when He clothed Adam in flesh or gave a soul to Houva, in general His purpose for emanating superior Beings and giving them Laws, Precepts and Commands was so that He needn't be involved in the day-to-day management of His Creation. However, this section also reminds us that this was not a gnostic theology, since there is no mention of demiurges (indeed, Adam is punished for attempting such an act of lesser creation), and he is insistent that it was the First Cause that created all things, even if He then handed over their maintenance to Principles. Incidentally, it is interesting to note a stylistic manner which Saint-Martin often employs: he introduces an idea, builds on it, then later devotes an entire section, even a Chapter, to developing his ideas further. It is quite noticeable in this book that each Chapter begins with a development of what he was talking about in the previous Chapter from a purely philosophical viewpoint. This might suggest he spent some time thinking about what he had written for some time; then, rather than reworking the Chapter he had completed, he put his new ideas into the start of the Chapter he was then beginning to write.

that would really return Matter to the sole control of these inferior Causes or actions.

Now, we've seen that these inferior Causes and actions were reduced to the number *two*, being what is innate in all seeds and what comes from the second agent, which is necessarily used in all acts of physical reproduction. Now, let us reexamine whether I was wrong to say that it was impossible to obtain any product from these two Causes when put together by themselves.

If they're equal, they will be inactive. If one is superior to the other, the superior one will overcome the inferior one and render it null: then there would only be one left which could act.

But, from all the possible evidence, we know that a single Cause isn't sufficient on its own to form a physical Being, and that, as well as the action or Principle innate in all seeds, there must be a secondary action which makes it bring the product into existence, without which nothing can happen; just as this secondary Cause must act on these seeds throughout the course of their existence. We know, then, that without these two Causes or actions coming together, it would be impossible for any physical Being to be born, take form, and sustain life. However, we also see clearly that if these two Causes were left to their own actions nothing would be created, since if one overcame the other, it would remain alone.

Isn't this the very fact which makes us realize the need for this third Cause, whose presence and intelligence serves to direct the two inferior Causes, and to maintain them in equilibrium and mutual support, and on which the Law of physical Nature is founded?

It's enough to remember what I said earlier. I established that there was a Law by which all the Principles of bodies were subject to the reaction of other bodies or secondary Principles. This should've been enough to put the Observers close enough to recognizing the two distinct agents used to bring all Beings with a body to physical form? Then I established that without a superior and intelligent Cause, these two inferior agents could not produce the least physical form, since this would require an initial action, and we were unable to find such a thing in them.

The Universal Ternary

So, the need for a superior Agent in the temporal is therefore proved, and since everything teaches us that there is a physical, immaterial and intelligent Cause which governs all the actions that Matter presents to us, the sum of all this proof should convince us in the strongest manner. Let us return to the *ternary* number by which this Cause has manifested His Law in the Elements.

I know that nobody will initially agree with me on what I said previously about the Elements only being *three* in number, since four are universally recognized. It would've been a surprise to find me talking about *Earth, Water* and *Fire*, while saying nothing about *Air*. I should explain, therefore, why we can acknowledge only three Elements, and why Air is not included.[34]

Nature shows us that there are only three dimensions in bodies; only three divisions possible in the extent of any Being; only three figures in Geometry; only three innate abilities in any Being; only three temporal Worlds; only three degrees of expiation for Man, or three Degrees in true Freemasonry. In other words, however we consider created things, it's impossible to find anything above three in them.

Now, with this Law appearing universally with such precision, why wouldn't it be the same for the number of Elements which are the basis for the body? Why would the Law appear in the products of these Elements if they weren't subject to it? We must explain that it's the fragility of bodies which shows their composition, and proves that their essence isn't composed of four Elements: for if they had been formed from *four Elements* they would be indestructible, and the world would be eternal. Instead, being formed of only *three*, they have no permanent existence because they do not

---

[34] While it may seem odd for Saint-Martin to talk about the Elements as being Earth, Air, Fire and Water (and adding Salt, Sulfur and Mercury later), he is not in fact being mystical at all. These were still the prevailing Elements in 1775! By that time very few new Elements had been discovered, and nobody had yet noticed a clear link between them. Clearly people had been aware of gold, silver, mercury, iron, copper, tin and lead since the earliest times, and these seven metals had been attributed to the seven planets, among other things. But there was no general understanding that these were *Elements*. A Medieval Persian practitioner of Alchemy, Jabir ibn Hayyad, had added Sulfur and Mercury to the Classical list of Four Elements associated with Empedocles and Aristotle, later supplemented with Salt by Paracelsus. It wasn't until 1789, some fourteen years after this book was published that a fellow Frenchman, Antoine Levoisier, attempted a first organization of the Elements as we recognize them (by then there were 33) by classifying them as gases, earths, metals and non-metals. And it wasn't until the 1860s, in fact, that the first recognizable Periodic Tables began to be developed.

have Unity in them; a fact which is very clear to those who understand the true Laws of Numbers.[35]

So, having previously shown the state of imperfection and the frail nature of Matter, we must look for this same frailty in the substances which compose it, and proof that its number can't be perfect, since it's not perfect in itself.

I will permit myself to stop for a moment, to forestall the alarm that my observations may have given rise to in many minds. I speak of the number *three* as fragile and perishable: so now, what becomes of that *Ternary* which is so universally revered that there are some Nations which have never counted beyond this number?

I do declare that nobody respects this sacred *Ternary* more than me. I know that without it, nothing that man sees and knows would exist. I affirm that I believe it has eternally existed and that it will exist forever, and that there is not one thought that I've had which does not prove this to me. It's even from this that I will take my response to the current objection, in daring to say to my fellow men that, despite all the veneration they bring to this *Ternary*, their understanding of it's still less than what they should have; and I invite them to be very careful in their judgements on this point. Finally, it's completely true that there is *three in one*, but there can't be *one in three*, without whatever was of such a nature being subject to death. And so, my Principle destroys nothing, and I can safely recognize the imperfection of Matter, based upon the imperfection of its number.[36]

---

[35] The reader may wish to reread Footnote 5, which discusses the reason for the importance for the number '4' in Saint-Martin's System of Numbers. As a short summary, Pasqually and Saint-Martin used a symbolic system of numbering going from '1' to '10'. '1' is Unity, and therefore represents God, or the First Principle. '2' was called "the number of confusion" by Pasqually, and Saint-Martin said: "It is impossible to produce two from one, and if something issues from it by violence, it can only be illegitimate and a diminution of itself." They are both referring to Adam's attempt to operate an act of creation, and in so doing, doubling himself and being punished as a result. However, the number '3' or the triad, is "The number belonging to the Earth and to humanity" for Pasqually, who goes on to say: "The number 3 arose from the three Elements Sulfur, Salt and Mercury...". In parallel to the *Quaternary Law* we saw earlier, this *Ternary Law* is the Law of temporal Beings, and stresses the importance of a third Cause to balance and activate the other two, as well as reminding us that anything bearing the number '3' is temporal and subject to death. Yet, as a four-legged chair is more stable than a three-legged stool, so the introduction of '1' into '3' to create '4', is for Unity or God to unite with Man to create perfect stability and eternity, which is the point Saint-Martin is making here; as well as being his rather contrived reason for why there are only three Elements in his system.

[36] This is a very brave assertion for 1775, although one might argue the risk associated with stating this heretical doctrine was somewhat abated by a weakening Church in France, and the anonymity of the author. Nevertheless, while explaining that his comments on the Ternary referred to the number three as applied to temporal Beings and not expressly the Holy Trinity, Saint-Martin could not resist

I also urge those who read this to make an absolute distinction between the sacred *Ternary* and the *ternary* of actions used for physical, temporal things. It's clear that the *ternary* used for physical things was born, exists and is sustained solely by the superior *Ternary*; but, since their abilities and their actions are evidently distinct, it would not be possible to comprehend how the superior *Ternary* is indivisible and beyond time by judging it by the one which is within time; and since this is the only one we are permitted to experience here below, I can say next to nothing about the superior one in this book.

This is why it would be contrary to my intention to add anything to my discourse which could be applied in any manner to the most sublime subject of my homage, unless it were to declare all the more the superiority and indivisibility of this sacred *Ternary*. Let us now return to the Elements.

Air

I taught that Air isn't among the number of the Elements, because we can't consider this coarse liquid which we breathe, which inflates or compresses bodies depending on whether it's more or less saturated with Water or Fire, as a specific Element.

There is most certainly a Principle which we should call *Air* in this liquid. But it's incomparably more active and powerful than the gross terrestrial Elements which compose the body; which has been confirmed by a thousand experiments. This Air is a product of Fire: not the material Fire that we know, but the Fire which produced Fire and all physical things. Air, in a word, is necessary for the maintenance and life of all elemental bodies,

---

a dig at the First Council of Nicaea, held in 325, when the dogma of the Trinity was first established. Both Pasqually and Saint-Martin had no issue with the idea of *Three in One*, as he says. However, the idea of *One in Three* both seemed absurd and unnecessary to them, and would also go against the teachings of the *Treatise*, whose cosmology does not include a Father begetting a Son and a Holy Spirit of the kind reflected in Catholic dogma, notwithstanding all are mentioned in various passage individually. According to Serge Caillet's course on *Martinesism*, Pasqually wrote: "These three persons are in God only relative to their divine operations and one can't conceive of them in any other way without degrading the Divinity, which is indivisible and can't in any way have in it different personalities separate from each other." (Cited from Section 182 in the 1995 edition of the *Treatise* in the handwriting of Saint-Martin, published by Diffusion Rosicrucienne, edited by Robert Amadou). There is indeed a distinctly Arian flavor to this comment by Saint-Martin, and one strongly suspects it was this paragraph, rather than his somewhat scathing comments on clergy later in the book, which earned this title its place on the *Index Librorum Prohibitorum* of the Catholic Church's Inquisition!

and it doesn't exist longer than them; but not being Matter, like them, it can't be regarded as an Element, and it's therefore true to say that it can't form part of the composition of these bodies.

What, then is its purpose in Nature? We can confidently state that it's only placed here to communicate to physical Beings the powers and virtues of that Fire which produced them. It's the vehicle of life to the Elements, and it's only by its aid that they can receive support for their existence; for without it all the circumferences would return to the center from whence they came.

But, while it cooperates most in the maintenance of the body, we should note that it's also the principle agent of the body's destruction; and this universal Law of Nature should not surprise us, since the dual action which constitutes the physical Universe teaches us that one action can never dominate except to the detriment of the other.

That is why, when physical Beings aren't in full possession of all their particular virtues, it's very necessary to protect them from Air if one wishes to preserve them. That is why we carefully cover any injuries or wounds which can arise from time to time, since there is no true remedy other than to protect them from the action of Air. It's for this reason, too, that animals of all species take shelter when they sleep, since Air acts more strongly upon them at that time; whereas when they're awake, when they have all their strength to resist its attacks, they can draw from it those benefits essential to their preservation.

Now, as well as these properties of Air, if we wish to see its superiority over the Elements more clearly, it will be enough to observe that, when we succeed as much as we can in keeping it separated from the body, it always keeps its strength and its elasticity, however long and violent the attempts made on it are. From this we should recognize that it's unalterable; a state which the other Elements don't share, since they dissolve as soon as they are separated from one another. It's therefore for all these reasons together that we place Air above the other Elements, and don't mix it up with them.

However, perhaps an objection might be raised at this point. Although I don't place Air among the number of the Elements, I still associate it with the maintenance of bodies, and don't allow it to survive any longer than them. They could argue that this makes it another Principle in the constitution of physical Beings, and so they are no longer *Ternaries*, as I previously said. Then, reviewing the connection I established between the Law of the constitution of bodies and the number of agents involved in the creation of their physical forms, it could be concluded that I also need to increase the number of these agents to four as well.

Certainly, there exists a Cause above the three temporal and elemental Causes I spoke about, since it's this which directs them and communicates their actions to them. But this Cause, which dominates the other three only makes itself known by manifesting the others to our eyes. It conceals itself within an impenetrable sanctuary from all Beings subject to the temporal; and since its domain, like its actions, is completely outside the physical, we can't include it with the three Causes used in the act of creating the physical form of Matter and any other temporal action.

Again, it's this same reason which prevents us from introducing Air into the number of the Elements, although the Elements and the bodies they create couldn't live for a moment without it; for, although its action might be necessary for the sustenance of bodies, it can't be visibly seen, as can the other Elements. Finally, when bodies decompose, we can visibly see Water, Earth and Fire, and although we clearly know that Air is also present, we can never see it because its action is of another order and another class.

And so, we always find a perfect analogy between the three actions necessary for the Existence of bodies and the number of the three constituent Elements. Seeing that Air is of the order of the Elements and the first dominant Cause is of the order of the temporal actions which produce physical forms; and just as this Cause must never be confused with the three Causes on which it acts, even though it controls them; so too Air must never be confused with the three Elements, even though it vivifies them. We are therefore well-founded in accepting the need for these three actions, just as we can accept recognition of only three Elements.

The Divisions of the Human Body

Now I will provide some details about the universal connections between these three Elements with the body and the body's abilities. This will put us on the path of making some discoveries of another nature, and will confirm our correctness concerning all the Principles I've discussed.

The generally accepted viewpoint among Anatomists is the one which divides the human body into three parts: namely the Head, the Chest and the Abdomen. Undoubtedly, it's Nature herself which led them to these divisions, and as if by secret instinct, these divisions also justify what I said about number and the various actions of the three different elemental Principles.

Firstly, we find that it's in the Abdomen that the seminal Principles are contained and function, which serve for the physical reproduction of man. Now, as we know that the action of Mercury is the basis of all material forms, it's easy to see that the Abdomen or lower stomach gives us a true image of the action of the Element of Mercury.

Secondly, the Chest contains the heart, or the seat of the blood, the Principle of life or action in the body. But we also know that Fire or Sulfur is the Principle of all vegetation[37] and physical products; and the connection between the Chest and the Element of Sulfur is clearly indicated by this.

As for the third division, the Head, this contains the source and original substance of the nerves, which in the animal body are the sensory organs. But it's also known that it's the property of Salt to make everything responsive, and therefore it's clear that there is a perfect analogy between their abilities, and that the Head has a clear connection with the third Element or Salt. This corresponds perfectly to what Physiologists have taught us about the site and source of the nervous fluid.

Yet, however accurate these divisions may be, and however certain we are of their connections with the three Elements, we would have to have a very limited focus indeed to see this alone. For beyond this ability of the Head to contain the sensory Principle and agent, we can surely see that it's endowed with all the organs the animal uses to discern the things which are healthy or harmful, so it's particularly concerned with watching over the individual's preservation? Surely, we can see that the Chest, as well as being the seat of the blood, is also the receptacle of water, or the spongy vital organs which collect moisture from the Air, and communicate it to the fire or the blood in order to regulate the temperature?

Then, without needing to resort to the Head to discover our three Elements, we can see all of them clearly in the Chest and Abdomen. As for the Head, though it's elemental too, as much by reason of the organs it contains as the location it occupies, it dominates the other two, and occupies the center of the triangle, keeping them in equilibrium. Through this we can avoid the usual error of confusing the superior with the inferior and the active with the passive, since their distinction is clearly written, even on Matter. But these subjects are too lofty to be completely revealed to the eyes of the majority.

---

[37] As in autonomic or unconscious activity in the body, as we saw earlier.

This is what Anatomy has not examined, for man considers it in isolation, as all the Sciences have, and those who practice it believe they can think about the body and the parts of the body separately, and they've convinced themselves that the divisions they can see have no relationship with Principles of a superior order.

However, it's in that division I've just shown, that they would have discovered a physical image of the *Quaternary*, that is, of that number without which we can't know anything, since, according to what we will see shortly, it's the universal symbol of perfection.

But I will not say any more about this number for now, so as not to stray too far from my subject, and I will content myself with having given a glimpse of it, and I will now lay out other Truths concerning the arrangement of the various elemental Principles in man's body, as in all other bodies.[38]

---

[38] This is a suitable point to consider how Saint-Martin departs from the standard concepts of the elements prevailing at that time, and how he differs from Pasqually on some points. The prevailing hierarchy of the elements was as follows: the four Classical Elements of Earth, Air, Fire and Water were the building blocks of material Nature. However, they were governed by three higher Principles, Salt, Sulfur and Mercury. Mercury resulted from the joining of Water and Air; Sulfur from Air and Fire; and Salt from Fire and Earth. This is not surprising given the physical nature and beliefs of the times. Mercury is a liquid substance associated with Mercury, the airy messenger of the gods, which gives a mix of water and Air; Sulfur burns in Air and gives off fire and pungent smoke; while Salt comes from the earth and burns the tongue. However, while Saint-Martin denies Air the title of Element, it was not so with Pasqually, who says in his Treatise: "(Seth) transmitted every spiritual ceremony of Earth, Air, Water and Fire (to Enos)." And also: "This left Adam, even after his Reconciliation, susceptible as a Being to Error in all of his secular and spiritual labor. This happens to us every time we act only by virtue of the three elements: Air, Earth and Fire." Both Pasqually and Saint-Martin view the three 'Elements' of Salt, Sulfur and Mercury more in line with their contemporaries, that is, as Principles rather than fundamental constitutive elements. Indeed, Pasqually says: "All physical forms have originated from three component elements: Mercury, Sulfur and Salt. The spiritual inhabitants of the Central Axis set these components in motion so that they can cooperate in the formation of all bodies by inserting into each of these elements a particle of their Fire." However, Saint-Martin appears to go in a new direction, which we can see in two things. Firstly, most Philosophers – and Alchemists – followed the teaching of Paracelsus on the *tria prima*, which believed that the body was formed from the four basic Elements, and the three Principles derived from their combinations had the associations: Salt with the Body, Mercury with the Spirit, and Sulfur with the Soul. This was a different Ternary Law which spoke of the three parts of man, the Physical (Body/Salt), the Plastic Envelope (Spirit/Sulfur) and the Soul (Soul/Mercury). We must remember that, at that time, the Soul was seen as being the immortal part which returned to God on death, and the Spirit was in fact the intermediary between the body and the soul, which linked the two together. This led to Salt being associated with the Abdomen, Mercury with the Chest and Sulfur with the Head. Now, while we see that Saint-Martin adheres to the traditional idea that Mercury is the intermediary between Salt and Sulfur, nevertheless he assigns these Elements to different parts of the body, in that he associates Mercury with the Abdomen, Sulfur with the Chest, and Salt with the Head. This was counter to the prevailing view of the time. It is worth noting that Saint-Martin

Man, the Mirror of Science

When the Observers so keenly desired to know the origin of things, it was pointless to look outside of or far from themselves. They should have looked within, and the Laws of their own body would have shown them the Laws which gave birth to everything they'd received. They would have seen that the opposing actions which occurs in the chest between Sulfur and Salt, or Fire and Water, sustains the life of the body, and if either of these agents is absent, the body ceases to live.

Then applying this observation to all that exists in physical form, they would have recognized that these two Principles, through their opposition and combat, have the same effect on life and physical cycles throughout Nature. It's not necessary to study Nature to learn, since man has all the means and therefore all the proofs of Science within him, and he only has to examine himself to know how all things originated.

The Harmony of the Elements

But we have remarked that it's necessary for these two agents, being enemies, to have a mediator which serves as a barrier to their actions, and reciprocally prevents them from overcoming each other, since then everything would end. This mediator is the mercurial Principle, the basis for the creation of all physical forms, with which the two other Principles unite to the same end. It's this Principle which, being distributed everywhere with them, compels them to act according to the prescribed order, which is to create and maintain forms.

That is the harmony through which the bodies of animals experience the action of Water through the lungs and the action of Fire through the blood without suffering, because the Law of which Mercury is the depository governs all these actions, and moderates their strength.

---

uses the image of a triangle to show the interplay between these three Elements, just as Pasqually says: "An inverted triangle with a dot in the center can represent the three elements that together form the Earth. The lower angle represents Mercury; the Southern angle represents Sulfur and the third, remaining Northern angle represents Salt." As a final comment, since Saint-Martin's views on three Elements and the disposition of Salt, Sulfur and Mercury were so at odds with traditional Alchemy and the prevailing scientific viewpoint, by the time Papus came to compose rituals for his newly-formed Ordre Martiniste, he preferred to go back to the traditional Elements and Principles. The traditional attributions of Salt, Mercury and Sulfur reappear, and Air is restored to the four Elements.

Through this same harmony the Earth receives the action of Water on its surface and Fire in its core without experiencing any disturbances, since it's the same Law which governs it.

I don't need to repeat that in these two examples, the real property of the liquid is to control the Fire's intensity, which without it would exceed its limits, as we saw earlier in all excessive reactions in the blood of animals, and in all eruptions of terrestrial fire. We can see that if these different fires were not tempered by a liquid which penetrated to its very core, there would be no limits to their action, and they would successively set all bodies, then the entire earth on fire.

This is why animals respire, and why the Earth is subject to the ebb and flow of its aquatic regions; because by breathing the animal receives a liquid which moistens its blood, independently of what it receives from food and drink; and by ebb and flow of Water the Earth receives moisture in all its parts and the Salt needed to moisten its Sulfur, or its Principle of Vegetation.

The Observers' Misunderstanding

I won't talk about how plants and minerals receive their moisture. Since they are connected to the earth, it's natural for them to be nourished by the nutrients and digestions of their Mother; for even to obtain Water, where would they get it if not from her?

Our Readers can now make comparisons with all they've seen about the active and intelligent Cause. They can observe that, if everything comes from the same hand, we should presume that the intellectual Law and the physical Law both move in the same direction, while each is in its respective class and action. Finally, they can discover that if the *Volatile* is everywhere, so must the *Fixed* be too, in order to contain it. As for us, we can go on to show why such beautiful analogies are almost always forgotten by the Observers.

This is because, far from having seen the difference between the two different classes of agents and Laws, like we have, they haven't even seen the difference between the various agents and Laws of the same class, and it's because they separated everything out, and examined each object on its own that they came to view them as being alone and isolated, and weren't wise or intelligent enough to suspect the relationships they had with other objects.

If, for example, they are still looking for a satisfactory explanation for the ebb and flow of the seas which I mentioned earlier, it's simply because they still have this fatal habit of dividing up the Sciences, and considering each Being separately.

The Laws of Nature

If they hadn't removed Matter from its Principle by confusing the two; if they hadn't stripped this same Principle of the superior, active and intelligent, temporal and physical Law which should direct Matter's every action, they would have seen that no physical Being could exist without it, and that the Earth is subject to it in exactly the same way as are all bodies. They would have seen that it was on this Earth that this dual Law, essential to the existence of all physically created Beings, worked in Nature.

But looking at these two Laws, we saw that one resides within the physical Principle of every Being with a physical form, be it general or particular; and the second comes from outside. It follows that this second law must be external to Earth, as well as external to all other bodies, though it's necessary for Earth's existence, as it's for theirs.

We recognize in this, as in the double beat of the heart of animal man, the presence of two Agents violently linked to each other, controlled by a superior physical Cause, and each manifesting their physical nature in turn. We know that this manifestation exists in the quadratures of the Moon, a time when the Solar action makes itself felt on the universal saline part.[39]

Although we can only know the two Agents through their visible action, as we can only know the Principles of bodies through their physical product or their envelope, it would be inexcusable for us to doubt their power, since their effects demonstrate it so obviously.

Thus, this phenomenon of ebb and flow is simply an effect on a large scale of this dual Law, to which everything which is a body made of matter is necessarily subject.

---

[39] More accurately, the most visible – or violent – tides occur around the equinoxes, when the moon is in conjunction with the sun (between the earth and the sun) or in opposition to the sun (the opposite side of the earth). In both cases the sun and moon's gravitational pulls are combined to create higher tides. When the moon is in quadrature, or at 90° to the sun, it subtracts its effect from the sun, and tides are neap, or lower and gentler. In this instance Saint-Martin appears to be calling all four positions 'quadratures'. Yet given he is talking about 'violent links', thereby referring to the high tides, he may even have his facts wrong in this case.

I will add that, since we see so much regularity in the progression and all the actions of Nature, and at the same time sense that the physical Beings which compose it are not capable of intelligence, it follows that in the temporal there must be a powerful and enlightened hand which directs them, an active hand put over them by a True Principle, as it is itself, which is therefore indestructible, living within itself, and that the Law which emanates from both of them is the rule and measure of all Laws which work in physical Nature.

Paths of Knowledge

I know that however evident these truths are, since they are outside of the senses, they'll be found hard for the Observers of my time to accept, since as they're buried in the physical, they've lost all sense of anything that can't be touched.

Nevertheless, since the path they are taking no doubt enlightens them considerably less than the one I am pointing out to them, I won't stop begging them to look for the reason for physical things in the Principle, instead of looking for the Principle in physical things; for if they are looking for a real, true Principle, how can they find it in appearance? If they are looking for an immaterial Principle, how can they find it in a body? If they are looking for an indestructible Principle, how can they find it in a composite? In other words, if they are looking for a Principle existing within itself, how can they find it in a Being which only has a dependent life, and which dies as soon as its fleeting action is fulfilled?

But I only have one thing to say to those who still insist on undertaking such a ridiculous investigation: if they truly want their senses to understand, they should begin by finding senses which speak, since this is the only means by which they can receive information.

This evidence will later become a fundamental Principle, and it's this which can help men understand the true means of attaining the knowledge which should be the sole object of their desire; but in the meantime, let's not neglect to take a brief look at the various parts of Nature which could best persuade the Observers of the certainty of the various facts we are presenting to them. There they could convince themselves of the Truth of the Causes which are beyond their senses, since they would see its actions written in a tangible manner in physical things.

Mercury

Mercury, as I said above, serves universally as the mediator between Fire and Water, which being irreconcilable enemies, can never act in concert without an intermediary Principle, because this intermediary Principle, sharing in the natures of both, brings them together at the same time it keeps them apart, and in so doing turns all their properties to the advantage of physical Beings.

Also in Nature, as in each individual body, there is an aerial Mercury which separates the fire coming from the terrestrial core from the liquid spread over the Earth, since before this liquid can do so, the aerial Mercury purifies it and prepares it to communicate just its beneficial properties to the Earth, which produces the beneficent quality of morning dew, and its superiority over the evening damp and fog, which are only poorly purified liquids.

It's because of this universal property that Mercury is the mediator between the two opposing Principles of Fire and Water in all bodies; and during the body's formation and composition it does what the active and intelligent Cause does in everything that exists, when it maintains the equilibrium between the dual Laws of action and reaction which constitute the entire Universe.

So long as Mercury occupies this place, the well-being of the individual is assured, because this element tempers the communication between Fire and Water. When on the contrary these two latter Principles overcome or break this barrier and join together, then they fight each other with all the power in their nature, and produce the greatest disorders and disturbances in the individual whose composition they form; since in the violence created by these two agents, one must always overcome the other, thereby destroying the equilibrium.

Thunder

For us, thunder is the most perfect image of this Truth. It's known that it's formed from saline and sulfurous vapors from the Earth, which being drawn from their natural abode by the Sun's action, as well as being pushed out by the terrestrial Fire, rise into the Air, where aerial Mercury seizes and surrounds them rather as carbon combines and envelops sulfur and saltpeter in gunpowder.

Here, this aerial Mercury can't interpose itself between the two Principles which comprise this vapor, because it would be too active to remain there, and being of a superior class to theirs, they can't create a body together. But it envelops and encloses them by its natural tendency towards a spherical and circular form, and by its inherent property of joining and encompassing everything.

At the same time, it exhibits another remarkable ability, which is to divide itself up in an incomprehensible manner, such that there is no droplets of these sulfurous and saline exhalations too small for it to create an envelope to contain them, and it's the accumulation of all these droplets which form the clouds, or the incubators of thunderstorms.

Now, in this formation we can't dispense with recognizing our two very distinct agents, Salt and Sulfur, and moreover the image of the superior agent, or that aerial Mercury which links the two others. So, we already see clearly the need for all these different substances to cooperate in any kind of combination, and it's Matter alone which makes this known to us.

But it's not enough to find in this the true signs of all the Principles which have been established in the universal Laws of Beings. We still need to see them in the various actions, and the diversity of the outcomes which arise from the mixing of these elemental substances.

Consider for a moment the clouds where lightning is created as being the union of two types of vapors: one terrestrial, the other aerial. Now, certainly if no other agent were to heat them and make them ferment, we'd never see an explosion. Therefore, we must add an exterior warmth which is communicated to the two substances enclosed in the mercurial envelope, and which divides all the saline and sulfurous globules contained within these clouds with a sudden burst. This external heat is a physical testament to all the Principles which we have previously put forward, and which our Readers will find easy to apply here.

But to make it even clearer, there is definite value in examining the different properties of Salt and Sulfur with regard to the explosion of lightning, because through this we can establish some notions about the two principle Laws of Nature, since Salt and Sulfur are the organs and instruments of these two Laws.

The external heat acts, as we have seen, on the mass of materials which compose the lightning. It dissolves the mercurial envelope whose nature is capable of considerable division; then it communicates with the two interior substances, and sets the sulfurous part on fire, which pushes away and scatters the saline part with force, and whose direct combination with it was contrary to its true Law, creating a disorder in Nature.

In this explosion, the Mercury finds itself so completely divided that all that it previously contained regains its liberty. As for the Mercury, after suffering this complete dissolution, it falls with the liquid upon Earth's surface, and it's because of this that rainwater has more benefits than other kind of water, because it's more charged with Mercury, and this Mercury is infinitely purer than terrestrial Mercury.

The whole cycle works similarly on the two other substances Sulfur and Salt, that is, on those which in physical Nature are the signs of the two Laws and the two incorporeal Principles. Also, it's from the various combinations of these two substances that all the effects we see happen in a thunderstorm are produced.

We know then, that Fire, being the Principle of all elemental action, gathers together the terrestrial and celestial vapors, from which the thunderstorm is formed. It's this Principle, too, which ferments them, and then beings about their dissolution. So, it is to Fire that we should attribute the origin as well as the explosion of the thunderstorm.

As for the noise which comes from the explosion in the thunderstorm, we can attribute this to the shock of the saline part on the columns of Air, because Fire by itself can't make any noise, which can be easily seen when it acts freely; and, although Fire is the Principle of all elemental action, none of these actions would be physical in Nature without Salt. Color, taste, odor, sound, magnetism, electricity, light, all are manifested and appear because of the Salt. It's for this reason we can't doubt it's also the vehicle for the sound of thunder, since the more a thunderstorm is charged with saline parts, the more violent is its thunder and its explosions.

Nor can we doubt that Salt influences the color of the lightning, which is much whiter when it's predominant than when Sulfur prevails.

Finally, it's so true that Salt is the instrument of all physical effects, and that a thunderstorm is much more dangerous when it abounds in salt, because, since its explosions are proportionally more violent, its impacts are more severe and its ravages more terrifying.

On the other hand, when the thunderstorm abounds in Sulfur, its noise is not as sharp or brusque; its lightning is colored red, and its explosions rarely reach us, because in that case it usually forms much higher up, which may be seen by the weakness of the clouds in this instance, and by the natural property of Fire, which is to rise.

Therefore, it's generally accepted that a lightning bolt falls at every thunderclap, even though we don't always have visible proof of this. This is also why a knowledge of the materials charging a storm will help us predict where on Earth its lightning strikes might fall, because they inevitably tend towards Matter which is analogous to it. However, in spite of this we can't always determine the exact point where it will strike, since we must accurately know the direction it's traveling and, given the impact and the opposition of all these different materials, the direction can change at any moment.

Here we can clearly see the effect of the dual action of Nature. All these various impacts, which appear so confused, when observed close-up actually show us, as do all other physical actions, the fixed Law of a Cause which directs them, and it's in this tendency in the materials of a thunderstorm to be attracted to similar materials that this Cause mainly shows us its power and its properties.

Indeed, if the direction of the lightning bolt was towards a part of the Earth's surface where it could lose contact with the aerial columns charged with the same materials, it would end and would be extinguished at the point of its fall once all its Matter had been consumed. This is the reason a lightning bolt never comes back up when it falls into deep water, because then free communication with the Air is denied to it, and in deep water it can't find any Matter to make use of.

But when its direction leads it to columns of Air charged with similar Matter, it pierces them and follows them, increasing its strength to a greater or lesser extent depending on whether it finds more or less to feed it. In this way, by means of all these atmospheric columns, it can navigate different routes very quickly, and even those most opposed to one another; in which instance, it must swerve away when it encounters materials which are contrary to it, or in order to avoid a place where Air has no chance to escape, since the Air is then impenetrable and offers resistance impossible to cross. It will only stop when it no longer finds any more of the materials it can feed on; and yet, even when it seems to be at the end of its journey, if it encounters more materials it can grow stronger again and produce new effects.

This is what makes its course so irregular in appearance, and generally so incomprehensible. However, we can't deny there is a Law, even in this very irregularity, since we are taught this by all the Principles which we have seen earlier, and all the results prove this. There isn't a moment when

Nature is left to herself, that she can take a step without the Cause appointed to govern her.

I only have one more word to say on this subject. It's commonly believed that a man who sees the lighting flash has nothing to fear from its bolt. How much credit can we give to this idea?

If there were only a single column in the Air and only a single explosion of lightning, it's certain that the man who saw the lightning would have nothing to fear from the bolt which accompanies this flash, because celestial Time is so prompt it can't be seen on the Earth.

But, since the columns of Air charged with materials similar to the lightning are normally large in number in a thunderstorm, you might avoid the explosion of the first, yet not be protected from the explosion of the second, nor all the others which will successively light up following the perceived flash, since as we have seen, the storm can prolong its course so long as it meets columns capable of feeding it.

Protection Again Thunderbolts

Then, the theory says, a man who had time to see the lightning would be wrong to believe that he was safe because of that, until the chain of all the explosions which would occur in the current round were completed.

It's certain that this opinion is based in truth, and that there is a part of it which can't be contested. For, just as there is never a flash of lightning without an explosion, so too, and for good reason, there is never an explosion without lightning. Now, when the interval between the two is almost zero, and whether a man is struck with the first or the last bolt, it's certain that he'd never have seen the flash of the explosions whose bolt hit him.[40]

---

[40] As the reader has no doubt realized, this 18th Century theory of thunderstorms is certainly elegant, if fanciful. It is particularly interesting to note that water isn't mentioned at all, except in the context of 'sulfurous and saline vapors'! However, it does pose problems for translating, since there was clearly no idea of separating the sound from the electrical effect of a storm. Thunder was an integral part of the lightning, rather than a phenomenon of the discharge between clouds; while lightning was the result of the reaction of an external Principle of heat dissolving bubbles of Mercury, igniting the Sulfur they contained, thereby causing a violent reaction between the Sulfur and the Salt. This makes it hard to choose between the words 'thunder', 'lightning' and 'thunderstorm', particularly since, even in contemporary French, the word most often used, *foudre*, can refer to lightning, thunder or thunderbolt! However, in fairness to the earlier theories, there is still no definitive agreement on the mechanics of thunder and lightning.

These are natural observations which, frivolous though they may appear in themselves, seemed useful to me to explain the universality of the Principle behind them to men, if they wish to *know*. I can only add that, after all that I've explained to the Reader, it should be easy for him to see the means of protecting himself from lightning bolts. This would be by retreating from the power of the columns of Air in every sense, that is, those which are horizontal as well as those which are perpendicular, and to search out the direction of the thunderstorm to its far reaches, because then, by standing at the center, he needn't fear the storm approaching him.[41]

I won't explain the reason, as that would be to depart from my duty: I'll leave that discovery to my Readers. But I urge them to reflect on what they've just read about the different properties and actions of the Elements, as well as the Laws which govern them, even during the greatest apparent confusion. Then they'll no doubt conclude that, although they can't identify the Causes and agents of these Laws, it's impossible for them to deny their existence. Let us move on, and identify these superior Causes, or those which are distinct from the physical ones, in man himself.

Relationship Between the Elements and Man

The earlier description, about the analogy of the three Elements with the three different parts of man's body, can be explained in a manner that is far worthier of him, and which should interest him all the more seeing how they are directly connected to his Being, and will show him the difference between his physical abilities and his intellectual abilities, or if you will, between his passive abilities and his active abilities.

The darkness in which man generally find himself on these subjects has contributed in no small manner to all the errors which we've seen him make concerning his true nature; and it's in not having perceived the most striking disparities that he still doesn't have the first notion concerning his Being.

---

[41] Saint-Martin can't resist throwing in another analogy, this time to the point within the circle, which by now we should have come to recognize as a reference to mans' original place of glory, implying that, by understanding, then overcoming the lightning bolts of confusion and danger directed at us, man can regain the still center and recover his former estate.

Principle Errors

For the real reason man believes himself to be like the animals is, without doubt, because he hasn't distinguished between their various abilities. Thus, having confused the abilities of Matter with those of intelligence, he only sees a single Being in man, and from this, only one Principle and the same essence in everything that exists; so that, to him men, animals, stones and the whole of Nature present the same Beings, distinct from one another simply due to their structure and shape.

I won't repeat here what I said at the beginning of this book about the differences between the innate actions of Beings, and the difference between all Matter and its Principle, from which we have clearly seen the error of those who have confused all these things. But I will begin by asking my Readers to observe with attentive eyes what can be seen in the animals which agrees with what we see in animal man, namely the division of the form into three distinct parts, and to see if each of these three divisions don't truly show us different abilities, even though they all belong to the same Being, and even though they have all the materials necessary for their object and purpose.

Weight, Number and Measure

Who doesn't know that everything is constituted by *weight*, by *number* and by *measure*?[42] Now, weight isn't number, number isn't measure, and measure is neither; and, if I can say this, *number* is what gives rise to the action, *measure* is what governs it, and *weight* is what accomplishes it. But these three words, though universally applicable, can't mean the same thing in the animal and in intellectual Man. However, it must be true that if the three parts of the animal body are constituted by these three Principles, then we'd find their application in them.

---

[42] This reference to a passage in the *Book of Wisdom* (Ch. 11 v. 21), is key to both Pasqually and Saint-Martin. The Renaissance view of the Quadrivium, that part of university education which encompassed Arithmetic, Geometry, Astronomy and Music, was that the human mind showed its likeness to the divine mind through Mathematics, and its derivatives, as expressed by the Quadrivium. Since weight and measure feature little in these Arts, we will shortly see Saint-Martin admit in Chapter 4, in the section titled *The Difference Between Thinking Beings*, that *"it is number which distinguishes (Beings)."* Not surprising, given that Saint-Martin, like Pasqually, base their theosophy on numbers.

So, it's by means of the organs of the head that the animal puts into play the Principle of its actions, which means that we should apply the term *number* to this part.

The heart, or the blood, experiences feelings which are stronger or weaker, depending upon their relative strength and the constitution of the individual. However, it's the extent of this sensation which determines the extent of action in the physical, and it's for this reason that *measure* can be attributed to the second division of the animal body.

Finally, the intestines perform the activity which, according to the peaceable Laws of Nature, are confined to the digestion of food in the stomach, and the fermentation of reproductive seeds in the loins. It's for this reason that *weight* must correspond to this third part, which together with the other two constitute the basis of all animals.

Since I'm sure we can't avoid seeing the different nature of these three types of action, we must certainly recognize an essential difference between the abilities which manifest them. However, we can't deny that these different abilities reside in the same Being, and therefore need to accept that although this Being only forms a single individual, it's evident that everything isn't equal in it, that the faculty which vegetates isn't the one which makes it actively sense; that the one which makes it sense isn't the one which makes it function and execute its actions as the result of its senses, and that each of its actions brings with it its own character.

The Different Actions in Animals

Let's apply the same observation to man, and then we can preserve him from the terrible confusion into which some try to bring him. For if we see that in man, weight, number and measure represent not only different abilities, but abilities which are infinitely superior to those which these three Laws have demonstrated in Nature, we can legitimately conclude from this that the Being endowed with these abilities will be very different from the physical Being, and then there is no excuse for confusing one with the other.

We can surely agree on the fact that, regarding physical functions, the three distinctions we have made can be applied to the human body, just like any other animal, because this part of him is animal. He can, like the animal, with the help of the organs of the head, manifest his animal functions and abilities. He experiences, like them, his feelings in the heart, and like them he feels in his abdomen the effect of the physical Laws which subject all animals regarding their maintenance and reproduction.

So, in this sense, weight, number and measure belong to him just as much as they do to all other animals.

But we can't doubt that these three signs also have effects in man in which Matter plays no part.

Different Actions in the Intellect

Firstly, though we agree that all the thoughts of present day man only come to him from outside, we can't deny that the interior action and feeling of this thought only take places inside and independently of his physical senses. Now, it's in these inner actions that we'll surely find the expression of these three signs, *weight*, *number* and *measure*, from which all the physical actions that man decides to perform in consequence of his liberty or free will result.

The first of these signs is *number*, which we apply to thought, being the Principle and subject without which none of the subsequent actions would take place.

After this thought, we find in man a good or evil will, which alone makes the rule of his conduct and his conformity to Justice; therefore, nothing would appear to us to be better suited to this will than the second sign, or *measure*.

Thirdly, from this thought and will arises an action which conforms to them, and it's to this action taken as a result that we should apply the third sign, or *weight*. This action nevertheless belongs to the interior, as do thought and will. It's true that in its turn it gives rise to a physical action, which repeats for the body's eyes the order and course of all which has passed through the mind; but as to the link between this inner action and this physical, outward action which arises from it's the true mystery of man, I can't dwell for long on it without indiscretion or danger; and if I speak of it later, when I discuss Languages, it can never be except in a reserved manner.

Man's Two Natures

This doesn't prevent anyone from recognizing along with me, weight, number and measure in inner man, images of the Laws by which everything is constituted; and although we've also recognized these three signs in animals, we should guard ourselves against making any comparison between them and Man, since in animals they work individually, and can only work on the senses; whereas in Man, they work both on his senses and on his intelligence, but in a manner specific to each of these abilities, and according to their place relative to each other.

If one persists in denying these two abilities in Man, I only ask of those who contest them to look at themselves, and they will see that the various parts of their body where those abilities appear, are a clear indication of the difference between them, as we now see.

Two Universal Natures

When Man wishes to consider some argument, and suggest the solution to some problem, doesn't he do all the work in his head?

When, on the contrary, he experiences feelings of some kind, whether they're about something intellectual or physical, surely all the movements, agitations, sensations of joy, pleasure, pain, fear or love, and all the emotions we can feel make themselves known in the heart?

Don't we feel, too, how many actions which take place in these two places are opposed, and if they weren't brought together by a superior link, they'd be irreconcilable?

Here, then is that clear difference which should convince man yet again that there is more than one nature within him.

Now, if man, despite his state of reprobation, can still find a nature superior to his sensory and physical nature within him, why shouldn't he accept the existence of a similar nature in the physical Universe, but similarly distinct and superior to it, though specially charged with governing it.

The Seat of the Physical Spirit

It's also there that we'll learn what we should think of a question which often worries men; namely, in which part of the body is the active Principle, or the spirit, located, and what is the place identified as the seat of all its activities?

In physical and sensory Beings, the active Principle is in the blood, which, like fire, is the source of physical life. Now, after what has been said about the various abilities of Beings, we can't deny that its principle seat must be in the heart, from where it extends its action through all the parts of the body.

We needn't be concerned by the problems raised by those who have said that, if the physical spirit is in the blood, it's divided and escapes to some extent when an animal loses blood. Its action is only weakened by this, in that it loses some of the means to exercise it; but it doesn't suffer any change, since being simple, it is of necessity indivisible.

What we call the death of the body is therefore nothing other than the complete end of this action which is deprived of its secondary vehicles, as in total exhaustion; or when the parts of the body are too constrained, as in disorders of the humors; or in the opposite case when they are too free, and by that we mean intercepted or interrupted, as with injuries which destroy the critical parts of the body needed for it to sustain life.

The Seat of the Intellectual Soul[43]

Although I said that life, or the physical spirit, resides in the blood, nevertheless I must remark in passing that blood is insensitive; an observation which should reveal the difference between the abilities of Matter and the abilities of the Principle of Matter, and which will prevent anyone from confusing the two completely distinct Beings.

---

[43] In the French, Saint-Martin uses the word *âme* for both the physical and intellectual Principles, which is usually translated as 'soul'. *Esprit* is the word normally used to signify 'spirit'. However, *âme* can also be translated as 'spirit'; so, in this case, two different translations are used for the two titles, even though they use the same word: *âme*. Using the term 'soul' for both would make the argument harder to follow, and although Saint-Martin's explanation is not strictly in accordance with Paracelsus' concept of 'spirit' as a link between the body and the soul, and 'soul' as the immaterial part which reunites with God on death, it is sufficiently close to justify the use of two different English words here, where Saint-Martin used only one.

Since man is like the animals in his physical and sensory life, everything we've just seen about the active animal Principle can apply to him regarding this physical part only. But as to his intellectual Principle, since this was never made to live in Matter, it's one of the greatest mistakes man makes when he seeks its birth in Matter, and wants to give it a permanent home, and a link made with physical composites, as if a piece of impure and perishable Matter could serve to enclose a Being of this nature.

It's more than obvious that in its quality as an immaterial Being, it can only have a link and affinity with another immaterial Being, and we should understand that communication with any other type of Being would be impossible.

The Connection Between the Intellectual and the Physical

Also, it's in this immaterial physical Principle of man, and in no part of his Matter, that his intellectual Principle resides. It's there that it's bound for a time by the Superior Hand which condemned it there; but by its nature it dominates the physical Principle, as the physical Principle dominates the body, and we can be sure that it's in the upper part of the body, or the head as we have shown earlier, that it manifests all its abilities. It uses this Principle for the physical execution of these same abilities; and this is how we can clearly distinguish between the physical locations and the uses of the two different Principles in man.

However, although the physical Principle is inferior due to its Nature and its location, it's because of his connection with it that man experiences so much suffering, so much unrest, so much privation in his intellectual Being, as well as that terrible darkness which makes him commit so many errors. It's through this connection that he's forced to submit to the action of the senses which are so necessary today, in order to make use of the true emotions which are created for him.

But, as this path is variable and uncertain, and since it doesn't always convey the light in all its clarity, man can't draw from it the advantage and satisfaction his nature should allow him to enjoy.

Deformities and Ailments

This results in the upsets, natural or accidental, that the sensory and physical Principle can experience, and which are so harmful to the intellectual Principle, since they weaken man, who is both the instrument of its actions and the organ of its feelings.

These facts seemed to be so favorable to the theories of the Materialists, that they thought they could produce them as solid support. Having founded man's intellectual abilities on his physical constitution, they made his intellect depend entirely on the state in which his body was in; whether it was in good or bad condition as a result of the variable result of Nature.

But following all we've seen about man's liberty, and the difference between the two Beings which compose him, these arguments no longer have any value. Man can never expect to possess completely all the possible abilities which could ever belong to his intellectual nature, since, by their very origin, all men don't receive them to the same extent, and because a thousand events outside their control can affect their physical constitution at any moment. Yet man is guilty when he allows the abilities he is given to waste away through his own fault. All are not born to have the same possessions, but all answer for the use they make of those they are allotted.

Thus, whatever upset or irregularity a man experiences in his physical constitution and in his intellectual abilities, we shouldn't be led to believe this keeps him safe from Justice, because however small the number and value of the abilities he is given might be, he will always have to give account; and it's only a madman from whom Justice can demand nothing, for then Justice would be holding itself under its scourge.

Let us not believe along with our adversaries that these physical upsets and irregularities have no other Principle than the blind Law by which they claim to explain Nature. We will shortly show how man's conduct in his physical life extends to his descendants. Moreover, we will show the immense abilities of this Principle or this temporal Cause which is necessarily connected to the progress of the Universe.

So, reflecting upon the nature of that temporal universal Cause, which must not only govern the body, but should also always be the compass of man's actions, we can easily see if anything in this physical realm can happen without a reason and a goal.

We'd rather believe that all the deformities, all the accidents to which we are exposed, both in our physical Being and in our intellectual Being, undoubtedly have a Principle; but we don't always recognize it, since we look for it in the dead Law of Matter instead of seeking it in the Laws of Justice, the abuse of our will, and the prevarication of our ancestors.

I'll leave the blind and fickle man to complain about that Justice which extends punishment for the fathers' mistakes to their successors. I won't talk to him about that physical Law, where an impure source passes on its impurity to its offspring, as proof: for that well-known Law is false and improper when applied to anything which doesn't concern a physical body. And this is not of the body. He would understand even less that, while this Justice can afflict the Children through the Fathers, it can also whiten and cleanse the Fathers through the Children. And this is enough to suspend all our judgements about it, so long as we are not admitted to its Counsel.

This prudent, just and salutary glance is one of the recompenses of true Wisdom. How could one impart it, then, to those who believe that they can do without its light, and convince themselves they need no other guide than their own senses, and the coarse notions of the majority?

The Effects of Amputation

The question I've just discussed concerning the place the soul occupies in the body, leads me naturally to another interesting question about the physical Principle, and one which also intrigues the Observers: that is why, when a man is deprived of one of his limbs by an accident, he continues to experience feelings for a period of time which seem to be in the limb he no longer has.

If the spirit or the physical Principle were divisible, which we must infer from the opinions of the Materialists, it's certain that, after a limb has been amputated, the man could never suffer in that limb, because the parts of the physical Principle which would have been separated at the same time as the amputated limb, no longer retaining a link with their source would themselves been destroyed, and could no longer give any sense of feeling.

Nor should we seek the Principle of this feeling in this limb, since on the contrary, from the moment of its separation it no longer exists to the body from which it has been separated.

Therefore, it's only in the physical Principle itself that we can find the Cause for the way it acts, and remembering the Truths we've established, we can say that in the composite body of present day man, just as his physical Principle serves as the instrument and organ of the abilities of his intellectual Being, so his body serves as the instrument and organ of the abilities of his physical Principle.

We have seen that if this physical Principle experiences trouble in the principle organs of the body, which are fundamentally necessary to exercise its intellectual abilities, the intellectual Principle can suffer; but we can't believe, I sincerely hope, that this suffering could result in a change in the essence of this intellectual Principle, or to divide it in any way. We know that, because of its nature as a simple Being, it always remains the same. So what it experiences is a disturbance in its abilities, and that's because the organ which should exercise those abilities is no longer complete, so the external intellectual reaction can't take place. Because of this, the action sent to those intellectual abilities either becomes void, or flows back into the intellectual Being itself.

In the first case, when the action of the abilities becomes void, the intellectual Being can only manifest deprivation; which is the beginning of imbecility and insanity; but at least there is no pain, so it's recognized that this madness doesn't make him suffer.

In the second case, when this action flows back into the Principle, it brings about confusion, disorder, and true intellectual suffering, because this Principle, which only knows how to perform actions, finds itself restricted and curtailed in the use of its abilities.

It's exactly the same for actual physical suffering in the case of the deprivation of a limb. The body serves as the organ of the physical Principle which animates it. If the body undergoes significant mutilation, it's clear that when the limb is mutilated, the physical Principle can no longer exercise its abilities to their full extent, as the action of the ability which needs the amputated limb to have its effect can no longer find an agent which corresponds to it, so again the action is void, or flows back into itself. It's then that we see confusion and acute pain in the physical Principle from where it emanated, the more so because the amputation of a limb gives rise to exterior and destructive actions, which repels the action of the physical Principle even faster, and makes it violently return to its center.

Despite this suffering, we therefore can't accept the idea of any kind of dismemberment of the physical Principle, or in any other kind of Principle. We will recognize only that all physical Beings which need limbs to execute their actions must suffer when those limbs are removed, because then they can't carry out their functions.

It's worth pointing out that this can only occur with the four external limbs, or the four connections with the body: for if any of the three principle parts which comprise the trunk were cut away, the body would die.

The Three Temporal Actions

Let's summarize the various things I've just discussed in a few words. By means of the different properties of the Elements I've shown several different actions in the composition of the body. I've shown that in addition to the two opposing actions innate in the body, there is a superior Law by which they are governed, even during their greatest shocks and in their greatest confusion. Next, I showed that this superior Law can be found even today in man, in whom it's distinct from the physical while connected with it. We can't therefore deny that there are three actions necessarily employed in the conduct of temporal things, as there are three Elements composing the body.

Of these three actions ordered by the First Cause to govern the creation of physical Beings, one is the intelligent and active temporal Cause which determines the actions of the Principle innate in seeds by means of the secondary action, or reaction, without which we saw that there would be no reproduction; and everything we've seen allows us to understand clearly enough the existence and necessity of this intelligent Cause, whose superior action must govern the two inferior actions.

The Source of Ignorance

How is it that men have misunderstood this, and believed themselves able to progress in the knowledge of Nature without it? We can now see the reason. It's because they have distorted the numbers which compose those actions, as they distorted those which constitute the Elements; for on the one hand where there are *three*, they only recognize *two*; and on the other hand, they believe they see *four* where there are only *three*. That is, when considering the two passive actions of the body, they have lost sight of the active and intelligent Cause, so that they added and confounded the action and abilities of this Cause with those of the two inferior actions; and they added the passive ability of the three Elements to the active ability of Air, which is one of the strongest Principles in their reactions. From this, having distorted these numbers, the Observers no longer saw the connection between the ternary of the Elements and the ternary of the actions which bring about both the universal and individual creation of the physical form.

Since this relationship has escaped them, and thus become meaningless to them, they no longer sensed the need for and superiority of this action of the intelligent Cause over the two inferior actions which serve as the basis of all physical creation. They mistook one for the other in all these Causes and their various actions, or even made them all into one.

And how could they have saved themselves from this error, when they began by confusing Matter with the Principle of Matter, and by ascribing to Matter all the properties of its Principle. Then it didn't take them any more effort to ascribe to it all the properties and action of the superior Cause, which is indispensably necessary to its existence.

But we should now see that, misunderstanding the power and the need for of a third Cause is to deprive ourselves of the only support remaining to man to explain the course of Nature. This is to give her Laws different to the ones she has received; this is to attribute something to her which isn't in her; in other words, this is to admit what isn't only improbable, but is also beyond all possibility.

The Need for a Third Cause

Besides, who doesn't know what men have put in the place of this indispensable Cause? Who doesn't know the puerile reasoning they used to explain the Laws of Matter and establish the system of the Universe without them? Blind to the origin of things, to the object of Creation, its duration, its action, all the explanations they have given about it are couched in the Language of doubt and uncertainty, and their entire doctrine is less a Science than a continual question.

Chance

When, through the sole power of their reasoning, they had to arrive at these conclusions themselves, perceiving the absolute need for a Principle to serve as a guide to Nature, they sought this Principle in the First Being Himself, and didn't fear debasing Him in our eyes by not separating His action from those of physical things. And when they were compelled to give a fleeting thought to the necessity of an intermediate Agent between this First Being and Matter, and not giving themselves the time to consider what this intermediate Cause might be, they vaguely gave it the name of blind cause, fate, chance and other expressions which, being devoid of life and action, could only ever increase the darkness into which man is already plunged today.

They didn't see that they themselves were the source of all this darkness; that 'chance' had been created by man's will alone, and only existed through his ignorance. For he can't deny that the Laws which constitute all Beings must have invariable effects and a universal influence; but when he refuses its accomplishments in those classes subject to its power, or when he is blinded by his own ideas, he no longer sees these indestructible Laws, and from this he concludes they don't exist.

However, he could never admit that chance plays a role in the acts and works of the First Cause, since this Cause being the sole and inexhaustible source of all Laws and all perfection, the order which reigns around Him must be as invariable as His own essence.

Nor could this concept of chance be found in the works of the temporal intelligent Cause, because being charged especially with the temporal work of the First Cause, it would be impossible for this work not to work ceaselessly towards its goal, and to surmount any obstacle to accomplishing this.

So, it can only be in individual actions in corporeal Nature, and in man's acts of will, that we stop seeing that regularity and those results which should always infallible and always foreseen. But if man only remembered how those specific actions and his will are intimately linked, and if he had always been attentive to the thoughts he had while governing himself and the physical realm, he would agree that in fulfilling his destiny, not only could he discover the universal Laws which govern the superior regions, and which he has so often misunderstood; but he would also have sensed the power of these imperishable Laws extending over his Being, as well as over the all the specific actions of his dark realm. In other words, there would no longer be any need for chance, either in his or in any of Nature's actions.

Then, when he saw disorder in specific actions in Nature, or when he was ignorant of the Causes which made them happen and the rules which governed them, he could now attribute this confusion and ignorance to his own negligence and the false use of his will, which hadn't utilized all its rights, or which had been used with criminal intent.

But to acquire knowledge of these truths, we must have more confidence than the Observers in man's greatness and in the power of his will, and believe that if he is superior to the Beings which surround him, his vices, like his virtues, must have a relationship and a necessary influence over all his Empire.

Let us therefore agree that ignorance and the unruly will of man are the sole causes of these doubts which have him vacillating all the time. So it is that, once he has allowed the notion of an order and a Law which encompasses everything to be expunged within him, he replaces them with the first whim his imagination presents him with; for in his very blindness he still seeks a variable in Nature; and this is why he endlessly resurrects this culpable error, by which, having freely sown uncertainty and chance around him, he is unjust and wretched enough to attribute them to his Principle of chance.

Even those who don't deny that physical things had a beginning, haven't given any other Cause for this than chance. Not knowing that there was a First Reason for their existence, or assuming there wasn't a Cause external to them which might have cared enough about them to bring it about; yet however, convinced that this existence had had a beginning, they enclosed within the single property of bodies both the active and innate virtues which animate them and the superior Law which governed their birth at the same time as well.

They followed the same order of explanation they had given to the Law which supports the existence of these same physical Beings; and this is no surprise. Having established their origin upon an imaginary and false foundation, it was necessary for the rest of their works to conform to this, too. And so, according to them, bodies live by themselves, and they were born by themselves.

As for those who claim that Matter and physical Beings have always existed, their error is infinitely more gross and more outrageous for Truth. These two doctrines have equally misunderstood the Law and the First Reason of things, but at least the first only taught that we could dispense with an active and intelligent Cause to explain their origin, while the other committed the crime of disparaging this Cause by making it equal to the active Principle of physical Beings, believing it to be neither superior nor more ancient than Matter.

The Observers didn't stop there. Having proposed similarly obscure principles concerning the progress and nature of things, and having enclosed themselves in such a narrow circle, they found themselves obliged to explain all the phenomena and events we see taking place in the Universe. According to them, a Being without intelligence and purpose made everything and continually makes everything; and since there are only two Causes which are the instruments of everything which happens, once they had found these two Causes in physical Beings, they believed they were spared the need of seeking a superior Cause.

Fortunately, Nature doesn't submit herself to men's thoughts. Blind as they think her to be, she leaves them to do the reasoning, and she still acts. It's even both an inestimable delight for them, and the most beautiful expression of the greatness of the physical and temporal Being which governs them, that Nature's progress is both firm and intrepid; for being impervious to man's theories, demonstrating their weakness by her constancy in following her Law, she will perhaps force them one day to acknowledge their errors, quit the dark paths they crawl along, and seek the Truth from a more luminous source.

The Third Cause

But to alleviate the concern of my fellow men who might believe that this active and intelligent Cause I am speak about is simply a fantastic and imaginary Being, I can tell them that there are men who have known Him physically, and that everyone could know Him too, if they put their confidence in Him, and made more effort to purify and strengthen their will.

I must however warn you that I'm not using the word *physical* in the usual use of the word, which only attributes reality and existence to tangible objects in the material sense. The least reflection on everything contained in this book will suffice to show you that we're a long way from using the meaning of the word *physical* as it applies to material appearance.

A Comment on the Two Principles

Before moving on to another subject, I'll spend a moment resolving a difficulty which could arise, though I've already resolved it to some extent. At the beginning of this book I set out the existence of two opposing

Principles which fight one another, and although I sufficiently demonstrated the inferiority of the Evil Principle to the Good Principle, it might be that from the observations we've just made about physical nature, someone might think that these two Principles are both necessary to each other's existence, since we saw that the two inferior Causes contained in physical Beings are absolutely necessary for them to be able to create a product.

To avoid this misconception, it should suffice to remember I said that all products, all works, all results in physical Nature as well as in all other classes were always inferior to their Generating Principle. This inferiority means physical Nature can't reproduce herself without the action of these two Causes which we have seen in her, and which shows both her weakness and her dependency.

Now, if this temporal creation draws its origin from the superior and Good Principle, which we can't doubt, this Principle must show its superiority in everything, and one of its principle attributes is to have absolutely everything within it with the exception of Evil, and to need only itself and its own abilities to perform all of its works. Then what's the purpose of the Evil Principle, if it doesn't serve to manifest the greatness and power of the Good Principle, which all the efforts of this Evil Principle can never shake.

So it's no longer possible to say that the Evil Principle has been and is universally necessary to the existence and manifestation of the Good Principle's abilities; though as an influence upon the existence of time, this Evil Principle is required to bring about the birth of all temporal manifestations; since, as there are manifestations which are outside of time, and the Evil Principle can't go outside of time, it's quite clear that the Good Principle acts without it; a fact which we will see in more detail shortly.

May men learn, then, to distinguish again the Laws and abilities of the Unique Principle, which is universally Good and living within itself, from those of the material and inferior Being which has nothing by itself, and which can't even exist except with help from outside.

The Chain of Truths

I believe I've given my fellow men sufficient insight into the weak foundation of human opinions concerning all the points I've discussed up to now. Having placed them on the path to teach them to distinguish the body from the innate Principle within this body; having turned their eyes upon the simplicity, unity and immateriality of this indivisible and incommunicable Principle, which can't suffer any mixing, and which always remains the same – though the form it produces and which envelops it is subject to continual variation – they can clearly see that Matter is undeniably in a state of dependence; and that, while they act by means of regular Laws, the two inferior Causes which bring about its reproduction and all the actions of its existence can't take place at all without the additional action of a superior and intelligent Cause, which commands them to make them act, and directs them to make them act successfully.

As a result, they'll admit that these two inferior Causes must be subject to the Laws of the superior and intelligent Cause, so that time and uniformity can be observed in all their acts, so that the results of all their different actions are not null, formless and uncertain; and so that we can give account of the order which reigns there universally.

Then they'll have no difficulty in agreeing that this superior Cause, not being subject to any of the Laws of Matter while being in charge of governing it, is completely distinct from it; that the means of coming to an understanding of both is to accept each in its own class, by studying their particular abilities, by comparing them in the same body, but unravelling their differences so as not to confuse them; and to make this distinction in all Beings of Nature and in all their least parts, where the eyes of the body and the mind teach us that there are always two Beings together, and that it's violence which has united them; but never to lose sight of the fact that this link only unites them to each other for a time; and not to see this union as having always existed and having to exist forever, since on the contrary we see it ending all the time.

These are all the observations which make man prudent and wise, and which prevent him from wandering foolishly along unknown paths, from which he can only extricate himself by going backwards, or giving himself over to despair when he realizes that he is too far advanced on the path and time is running out. These will help him avoid the pitfalls which most men are drawn to when, alone and in darkness, they dare to express their opinion about their own nature and that of Truth. We'll see in what follows the frequent disaster which have happened, and which happen every day. We'll see that most of their sufferings have taken their origin from this, just as it's because they fell from their primitive estate of splendor that they are exposed here and now to being buried more and more in shame and misery.

Chapter 4 - Religion

An Allegorical Scene

A few men raised in ignorance and idleness, on reaching mature age, attempted to travel through a great Kingdom; but since they were only driven by idle curiosity, they made little effort to learn how this country was really governed. They had neither sufficient courage nor the authority to visit the nobles of that State, though this could have led to their finding out about the hidden abilities of the Government. So, they contented themselves with going from town to town, glancing uncertainly at the squares and public places, and seeing the people assembled in a noisy manner, as if they were left to their own devices, they didn't grasp any concept of the order and wisdom of the Laws which secretly monitored the safety and well-being of the inhabitants. They thought all the citizens were idle, and lived there completely independent of the Law.

And indeed, what they had seen showed no sign of rule or Law to their uninformed minds. by only using their eyes, they were far from knowing that men who were superior in rank and powers were governing this multitude which acted in such an apparently random manner, and they convinced themselves that since there weren't any laws in the country they were passing through, there couldn't be a Leader; or if there was one, he had no authority or took no action.

Deceived by this apparent independence, and not predicting any dangerous consequence to their actions, they soon believed the people behaved in an arbitrary and indifferent manner, and so they thought they could give themselves over to their every whim. But they were soon victims of their error and poor judgement; for the vigilant State Administrators, when told about their disorderly life, locked them up and imprisoned them so restrictively that they languished in the deepest darkness, not knowing if they would ever see the light again.

The Observers' Carelessness

This is exactly what has been the conduct and fate of those who have dared to judge Man and Nature themselves. Forever busy with pointless and frivolous studies, their view has been narrowed by habit, and being unable to take in the full extent of their field of study, they went no further than just the appearance; so that, by limiting their research to this alone, they didn't know or even denied the existence of anything they couldn't physically see. They could only see the envelopes of bodies, and so they transformed them into Principles. They could only see two actions or two inferior Causes in the Laws of these bodies, and they immediately rejected the notion of a superior active and intelligent Cause, whose operations they had confused with those of the two other Causes.

Then, believing themselves to be correct in their conclusions, they made a theoretical material Being out of all this, with which they had the foolhardiness to compare all the Beings of Nature which they had completely distorted; and it's in the image of this mutilated model that they dared to design Man.

Truly, there can be no doubt that in this way they committed the same errors they'd previously made about all of Nature. Not only didn't they distinguish – in their own bodies, as in all other physical Beings – the Principle from its appearance or its envelope, and didn't understand or follow its action and its Laws; but, having misled themselves about this, they further confused man's physical envelope with his intellectual and thinking Being, just as they confused the Principle found in all bodies with the active and intelligent Cause which directs them.

By not first of all separating the superior Cause from the abilities innate in the physical Being, and by next confusing the abilities of the two different Beings which compose man today, it was impossible for them to see this active and intelligent Cause acting in him, which as it communicates all its powers to Nature, also gives man, through his intelligence, all the ideas of the good which he has lost. Yet it's in this state of ignorance that they were not only rash enough to give their opinions about man's essence and Nature, but they even tried to explain all the contrasts which he presents, and explain the basis of his works.

The Danger of Errors Concerning Man

When man was only in error concerning elemental Nature, we saw that his errors only had minimal consequences; for as his opinions can't influence the progress of Beings, their invariable Laws are executed continuously with the same precision, regardless of the fact that man had perverted and misunderstood that Principle. But it will never be thus concerning his mistakes about himself, and these errors will always have terrible consequences, because being the depository of his own Law, he can't be mistaken about it or forget it, without acting directly against himself, and without doing himself visible harm. If it's true that he is happy when he recognizes and follows the Laws of his Principle, his pain and suffering are clear proof of his errors and the missteps which were their result.

So, let us examine the outcome for this Being who is so disfigured, and whether he can survive, now that he has been deprived of his main support?

It's easy for us to guess at the consequences of this examination if we remember what we said about the state of Nature, when it's left to the passive action of the two inferior Beings necessary to all physical reproduction. We know these two Beings, being passive, can produce nothing by themselves if the active and intelligent Cause doesn't give them the order and the power to work on what they have within themselves.

Now, if it were possible to suggest these inferior agents had a will, while leaving them with the same lack of power, it's clear that if they tried to put this will into action without the agreement of the active Cause on which they necessarily depend, their works would be misshapen, and horribly confused.

Now, let's take what we just said about these inferior agents, which in reality have no independent will, and apply it to man who has a will within him, and let's try see more clearly the unhappy effects of the errors we're trying to prevent.

Man is presently composed of two Beings, one physical and the other intelligent. We have let it be understood that at his origin he wasn't subject to this combination, and that possessing the prerogatives of a simple Being, he had everything within him, and had no need of anything to sustain him, since everything was enclosed within the precious gifts that he had from his Principle.

We then showed the severe and irrevocable conditions which Justice attached to man's rehabilitation, after he had become a criminal through the false use of his will. We've seen the awful and innumerable pitfalls which have ceaselessly menaced him while inhabiting this physical realm which is so contrary to his true nature. At the same time, we've recognized that the body he presently wears, being of the same class as physical things, in effect forms a shadowy veil about him which hides the true light from his view, and which is at the same time both the continual source of his illusions and the instrument of his new crimes.

At his origin, man had the order to reign over the physical realms for his Law, as he should still do today, but, since he was then endowed with incomparable power, and had no impediments, every obstacle disappeared before him.

Today, he has almost none of the same powers, nor the same liberty, and yet he is infinitely closer to danger, such that, in the battle he must now undertake, one can't express the disadvantages to which he is exposed.

Indeed, such is the awful situation of present day man. When the terrible judgement was pronounced against him, all he retained of the gifts he had received was a shadow of liberty, that is, a will which is almost always without power or authority. All his other powers were taken away, and his union with a physical Being reduced him to being no more than a combination of two inferior Causes; like those which govern all bodies.

I say like and not equal to, because the purpose of the two natures in man is nobler; and properties of these two natures quite different. But, as for the action and exercise of their abilities, they both most certainly submit to the same Law, and the two inferior Causes which compose man today have no more power in themselves than the two inferior physical Causes.

Because of his intellectual Being, it's true that man will always have an advantage over physical Beings by sensing a need that is unknown to them; but he can't alone obtain relief any better than them. He can no better activate his intellectual abilities by himself than they could animate their Being; that is, he can't do anything without the active and intelligent Cause, without which nothing in time can act effectively, any better than them.

What then can man produce today, if in the powerlessness in which we know him to be, he believes he has no other Law than his own will, and if he tries to walk without being guided by this active and intelligent Cause on which he depends despite himself, and from which he must expect everything, as must all the physical Beings among whom he is so sadly mingled.

We can be sure that his own works would have no value then, nor any power, since they would be deprived of the sole support which could sustain them; and the two inferior Causes which presently compose him would fight one another endlessly within him, which would only serve to agitate him further and throw him into the most depressing uncertainty.

It's like the two lines of any angle which can be moved in opposite directions, moved apart, brought closer together, put side by side, and placed on top of one another, but which can never produce any kind of figure unless a third line is added; for this third line is the means needed to fix the instability of the first two, which determines their position, distinguishes them physically from one another, and finally creates a figure, and indeed without doubt the most powerful of all figures.

These are, however, what the pointless attempts made by man each day are like, working on an impossible task, or trying to form a figure with two lines. It's like focusing on the action of the two inferior Causes which today compose his nature, and continually striving to exclude that active and intelligent superior Cause which he absolutely can't do without. Thus, despite the proof he has of the need for it, he goes and runs far away from it, from illusion to illusion, never being able to find the point which should fix it, because there is no perfect work without the cooperation of this third Principle; and if you want to know the reason it's because, from the moment that one is at *three*, one is at *four*.

The Various Institutions

Then reflecting on this terrible uncertainty, he's surprised by the disorder which follows his steps, and soon he denies the existence of this Principle of order and peace which he misunderstands because of negligence or bad faith.

But sometimes too, driven by the power of Truth, he complains about this same Principle which he had initially rejected, and in that he shows us himself the certainty of everything we've said about the variations and inconsistencies of all Beings whose abilities aren't united and fixed by their natural links.

Far from believing that all man's misunderstandings have the slightest effect on this Cause from which he distances himself, we should now know enough about its nature to know that he alone suffers from straying, since as a free Being he's the only one who can be guilty. We should know that when this Cause, as unalterable in its abilities as in its essence, extends its rays to man, they can only purify him and aren't in any way soiled by him.

We will therefore go on with our journey, and clarify the difficulties which halt the Observers when, alone and without a guide, they wish to examine all the Institutions of the Earth: those which men have created themselves, and those which they attribute to a more elevated origin. Indeed, it's here that these blind men, not knowing how to separate the arbitrary from the real, have made a monstrous union of both, capable of obscuring the most luminous notions. It's also, without a doubt, one of the most interesting subjects for man, and where it's important for him not to make any mistakes, since it's here he must learn to moderate the abilities which compose him.

Source of False Observations

Let's examine why, from the observations man made of the various practices, customs, laws, religions and worship which have differed between Nations in every age, they were led to think that there was nothing real in them, and that since they were all arbitrary and arose from habit, it would be wrong to suggest that there were duties to be fulfilled, and some sort of natural and essential order which should serve to guide them.

If it were true that everything was habit, as they claim, they would be right to draw this conclusion from it, since then, as there'd be no distinction to them between good and evil, any steps they took would be unimportant, and nobody would be justified in reminding them of any rules of conduct. But if the misunderstanding comes from the fact that the Observers haven't distinguished in man the two abilities which constitute him; if they've confused the intelligent and the physical within him, and then applied to the former all the variations and disparities to which the latter is subject; if they've taken these errors further by even confusing the active and intelligent Cause with man's specific abilities, could we give any credence to a doctrine which was so shallow, and false as well?

Nevertheless, this is the path they've followed. That is, they've almost never looked beyond the physical. Now, since this physical ability is limited and lacks the power necessary to direct itself, it will only ever show repeated proofs of variety, dependency and uncertainty; and it's by this alone, and by it being left to its own Law, that all the differences we observe here below are introduced.

Indeed, do all the branches of civil and political order which unite the different Peoples have any goals than material ones? Does even the moral part of all their establishments rise up above this human, visible order?

There is nothing, even their most virtuous institutions, which they haven't reduced to physical rules and external Laws, because in everything the Teachers have walked alone without a guide, and this was the only end point to which they could have directed their steps.

Man's intellectual ability therefore plays no part at all in such facts, and even less in the observations on how it functions. So, we must guard against adopting the judgements arising from this until we've seen how far their consequences extend, and whether they apply to everything. For unless they do it would be impossible to accept them, since a Truth has to be universal.

The Religious Institution

Let's begin by looking at the most respected and the most universally widespread Institution among the Nations, and one which they regard with good reason as not being the work of their hands. It's quite clear, from the zeal with which everyone on Earth concern themselves about this sacred object, that all men have an image and a notion of it within them. We see a complete uniformity across all Nations over the fundamental Principle of Religion. All recognize a superior Being, all recognize the need to pray to Him, and all pray. All feel the need for a form to their prayer, and all have given it one. And man's will has never been able to destroy this Truth, nor put anything else in its place.

False Religions

However, the care that the different Nations take to honor the First Being shows us, as with all other Institutions, a succession of arbitrary differences and alterations, both in theory and practice; so that there aren't two Religions known which honor Him in the same way. Now, I ask you whether this difference could have happened if men had had the same guide, and if they hadn't lost sight of the sole light which could have enlightened and reconciled them? And is that light anything other than the active and superior Cause which must maintain the equilibrium between their physical and intellectual abilities, and without which it's impossible for them to take a single accurate step?

It's this Cause which should nourish in man the original idea of a Single Universal Being, as well as knowledge of the Laws to which this

Being subjects men's conduct towards Him, when He allows them to draw near. Therefore, it's in distancing himself from this light that man remains given over to his own abilities, and then even those abilities weaken, and fade away almost entirely within him. Darkness covers him with a veil so thick that, without the aid of a Beneficent Hand, he could never free himself from it.

And yet, though man is then abandoned to himself, he is always obliged to *travel*. It's this fact that in this terrible ignorance, being forever tormented by the notion and the need of this Being from Whom he senses he is separated, he turns his uncertain eyes towards Him, and honors Him according to his ability. And though he no longer knows if the homage he offers Him is truly what this Being requires, he prefers to offer Him something such as he can conceive it, over the secret concern and regret of not doing anything at all.

This is, in part, the Principle which formed all false Religions, and distorted the one the whole Earth should have followed. So can we be surprised to see so little uniformity in the pious customs of man and in his worship; to see him produce all these contradictions, all these opposing practices, all these rites which fight one another, and which offer nothing true to the mind? Isn't this why, since man's imagination is no longer under control, everything becomes the work of his whim and his blind will? Isn't this why, as a result, everything appears to be contrary to reason, since we can no longer see any connection between the worship and the Being to Whom the Teachers and their partisans want to give it?

But I ask you if most of these differences, and even the obvious contradictions, arise from something other than where man's gaze is fixed, that is, from the physical. So, what can we conclude about the Principle they don't even bother with? Would this Principle remain inalterable and intact when the dark thoughts of man introduce variations into theory and dogma. After all, so long as man isn't enlightened by the true light, and supported by His sole support, he can no longer be any surer of the purity of his doctrine, than in the justice of his actions. Finally, whatever nature his errors, could they actually do anything against Truth?

If this error follows the Observers and makes them blind, it's always because he fails to distinguish the man he has dismembered and who only uses a part of himself, from the man who uses all his faculties. It's because he fails to distinguish between the distorted source from which he draws his misshapen information, and where he ought to have drawn it, that we know he's incapable of knowing anything fixed and certain.

Truths Independent of Man

Let's see anyway how far man's specific power can extend when he is left to himself, only given the rights which belong to him, and see if there's nothing beyond what he does and what he knows.

Firstly, we saw that, despite all their observations about Nature, men must submit to her Laws. We also shown well enough that the Laws of Nature are fixed and invariable, even though as a result of the two actions which are in the Universe, their completion was often disturbed.

Here already is a truth which man in all his confusion hasn't grasped at all. Nobody can object to me about these sensations, these impressions of all kinds which different bodies make on our senses and which vary in each individual, from which the majority believes they are right to deny that there is any rule in creatures. We've refuted this objection by pointing out that Nature can only act in relation.

We can strengthen this concept further, by saying that this Law of relation is no more subject to the arbitrariness of man than to Nature herself, and that we are not the masters who can in any way change her effects; because to deter and prevent them is not to change them, but on the contrary to confirm their stability all the more.

We already clearly know that in physical Nature there's a Power superior to man, and which subjects him to its Laws. We can no longer doubt its existence, though for all the care man has taken to understand and explain this Power, he has rarely been able to obtain any satisfactory information or success.

Secondly, let's remember how we have shown Nature's weakness and infirmity relative to the Principles from which she has drawn her origin, and from which she draws her subsistence and action every day. We can then see that if man is subject to this Nature; how much more is he subject to the superior Principles which direct her and sustain her; and although he has also conceived as little of their power as that of Nature, his own reason would prevent him from denying their existence when his own senses don't support this.

What effect then could everything he can do, imagine, say and institute have against the Laws of these superior Principles? Far from being even remotely changed by them, they can only show their strength and power all the more, by leaving man who distances himself from them given over to his own doubt and the uncertainties of his imagination, and by subjecting him to crawl so long as he wishes to misunderstand them.

It takes nothing more than these observations to prove the inadequacy of the man who takes only the physical to be his rule and guide. If the powerlessness we have seen in physical Nature completely stops us from attributing the things she creates to her alone; if man by his own reasoning can come to sense the necessity of the cooperation of an active Cause, without which physical Beings would not have a single visible action, then he only needs to look at himself to admit the existence of this active and intelligent Cause, and from there to come to the First Unique Cause, which produced outside of Himself all those temporal Causes which were destined to accomplish His works and the execution of His will.

I stated that the active and intelligent Cause has a universal action, both on physical Nature and thinking Nature. It's in effect the first of the temporal Causes, and the one without which none of the Beings existing in time could persist. It acts on them by means of the very Law of its essence, and by the rights that give it its purpose in the Universe. So, whether the Beings inhabiting the Universe understand it or not, there isn't one of them that doesn't receive its aid, and since it's active and intelligent, thinking Beings must participate in its benefits, as do the Beings unable to think.

That's why I said that all the Nations on Earth had necessarily recognized a superior Being. They haven't made all the distinctions I've just identified between the different Causes; they haven't distinguished this active and intelligent Cause from the First Cause, which is absolutely separate from the physical and from time[44]; they have often even confused it with the inferior Causes of the Creation, to which they have sometimes addressed their homage. Also, they haven't received from their worship the

---

[44] In this comment, Saint-Martin is in a way addressing the issue of the demiurge, although this concept was not known to the theological scholars of the time. The only gnostic texts known at that time were the Acts of Thomas and the Acts of John, and while the Bruce Codex was purchased for the British Museum in 1769, it was not translated until the mid-1800s. Therefore, the concept of the demiurge was not known. Nevertheless, it is interesting to note that Pasqually's cosmology could be seen as a form of gnostic exegesis, since, although Man was the only emanated Being who got to try out an act of creation (the others being prevented prior to performing their operations), the fact that they had the power to do so is certainly gnostic in concept.

help they could have expected had their approach been more enlightened. But pursuing this subject would lead us too far off course.

Let's therefore limit ourselves to observing that, since this active and intelligent Cause is universal, finally, through perception and reflection, man had to come to recognize its necessity; and in whatever manner he thought of it, he was only wrong about the true nature of this Cause, but never about its existence.

Once man had made this admission, he couldn't excuse himself from continuing his thought progress. His perception and his own reflections led him to the second step, as they had to the first, although by continuing to walk alone upon this new path, he couldn't find anything further that was certain or which offered clearer illumination.

But finally, whatever his discoveries had been, having recognized a superior Cause in Nature, and having even recognized it was superior to his thoughts, he couldn't stop himself from agreeing that there must be Laws by which it acted on whatever it governed, and that, if the Beings which relied on it for everything didn't fulfil these Laws, they couldn't hope for any light, life, or support.

He was led to these results by his observations on the course of physical Nature herself, to which he's closely connected. He saw, for example, that if he ignored the Laws concerning the time and procedures for cultivation, the earth only provided imperfect and unhealthy produce. He saw that, if he didn't observe the order of the Seasons precisely in all his calculations, the results bore no fruit and were unsuccessful. It's this which taught him that physical Nature is directed by Laws, and that these Laws hold closely to the active and intelligent Cause, for which all men sense the need.

The Diversity of Religions

Then, reflecting similarly upon his own thinking Being, he realized that being unable to do anything without the First Cause, it was in his interest to put all his efforts into making Him favorable towards him. He saw that, since this Cause could watch over him and be interested in his well-being, He must have established the means to preserve him from evil; and as a result, actions which benefitted men should please this Cause, and those which could do them harm didn't conform to His Law, which is to make all

Beings happy, so that they couldn't do better than always acting in accordance with His will and desire.

But since each man couldn't determine on his own whether the worship he had thought up would guarantee a connection between him and the First Being whom he wished to honor, each group adopted at will the approach they believed to be most likely to obtain His favor, and all the Nations, who were only led by themselves in the search of this Institution, established the form of worship which their imagination or some specific circumstance had given rise to in their thinking.

And this is the reason that all the Nations of the Earth have been divided, either in the ceremonies in their form of worship, or in the notion and image they have formed of Him who must be the object of their worship. This is also why, despite their differences concerning the formalities of this worship, they are all in agreement that it needs to be done; and that is because everyone has known the existence of a Superior Being, and everyone has felt the need and desire to have Him as their support.

Zeal Without Light

If men so delivered to themselves had been able to bring as much virtue and good faith as zeal to these establishments, each of them would have followed the worship they had adopted in peace, without repressing those in whom they saw differences. But since zeal without light only leads all the more quickly to error, they soon gave exclusive preference to their own form of worship; and the same driving force which had led them to proceed alone in establishing their form of worship led them to regard this worship as the only true one. They believed they fulfilled their duties all the more by not allowing any other form of worship to exist, and made it a merit in the service of their idol to combat and persecute one another, because in their dark opinions they had joined their own Cause with His, and there has been almost no Nation which hasn't believe they honored the Superior Being by banning worship different to the one it had chosen.

That, as we know, is one of the principle Causes of war, both global and regional, and also the disturbances we see agitating the various classes which compose the Political Bodies every day, and which can even overthrow the strongest Empires, although in that instance there was an infinity of other reasons for the divisions which are well known enough and far too pointless for me to concern myself with listing or examining in this book.

However, all these errors and all these crimes which men have committed in the name of their Religion come from a source other than that established by the Enlightened Hand which should be guiding them; and when they believed themselves to be guided by a true Principle, in reality they were only being guided by themselves.

We must therefore conclude firstly from what we have discussed just now, that all men, by means of their reflections and through the voice of their inner perception, could not stop themselves from recognizing the existence of some Superior Being, as well as the need to establish a form of worship for Him; and this is an idea that man can't erase in himself, although it's often hidden in most people.

And certainly, we should be surprised by this, since there are some men who have allowed themselves to extinguish the very idea of their own Being, and in whom the inner abilities are so feeble that they believe themselves to be mortal and perishable.[45]

Man's Motive

But we should also conclude that if this notion of the existence of a Superior Being and the need for worship is in man's very essence, it's also the last state he can attain on his own here below: these are the only results which can come from his physical and intellectual abilities when left to their own efforts. This feeling is a fundamental seed in man; but if no power comes to activate this seed, it can manifest nothing concrete, and certainly its products will have no consistency, just as the seeds of physical Beings remain inactive and without a result if an active and intelligent Cause

---

[45] Remember that at this time, France had few colonies outside of footholds in the New World and Canada, and a presence in some of the Caribbean islands, having lost what little possessions they had held in India. At that time then, and given how large the Catholic-Protestant wars had featured in the life of France, Saint-Martin would mainly have had their image in mind when he wrote this. He takes no side in this war, and leaves it to the reader to decide which side, if either, have the just cause. It is poignant to read these words in our present times, as so little has apparently changed, and we still live in a world where religious ideology is responsible for so much suffering, both across country borders, and even within countries where groups attempt to impose their narrow interpretation of religious dogma upon the whole of society, either through violence, or the rule of unjust – and very human – laws.

doesn't govern the reaction, and in general all the actions which involve them.

We are even more convinced of the truth of this thought when we reflect on the nature and properties of the intelligent and active Cause. It's distinct from the First Cause. It's its first agent. It doesn't give seeds to physical Beings but it animates them. It doesn't give intellectual and physical abilities to man, but it directs and clarifies them. As the first and sovereign among all the temporal Causes, it alone is charged with leading them, and there is not one which could do without its help that isn't subject to it.

So, if it's by this Cause alone that things are manifested, nothing can become physical without it. However, since we are unable to *know* here below except by means of the physical senses, how can we be successful unless this active and intelligent Cause doesn't itself act with us, and work what it alone can work in the Universe?

Here we see the absolute need for the two abilities of man to be always guided and sustained by this temporal and universal Cause. It can't give man an image of the First Being for which it's the first acting Cause, but it can make known to man the abilities of this First Being, by demonstrating them through physical products. Nor will it will give man the notion of how to worship this First Being, but it will clarify his ideas on the subject, and by making him sensitive to the abilities of this First Being, it will make him equally sensitive to the means to honor Him.

Unity In Worship

It's here that I see all man's doubts, and all the variations which are their result, end. This active and intelligent Cause, being predisposed to activate and direct everything, can't fail to reconcile everything when its power is used. And the one and unique means which man has to avoid being wrong is to not exclude this Cause from any of his actions, any of his Institutions, or any of his Establishments, just as it isn't excluded from the regular actions of Nature. Then man will be sure to know his true relationship with the Object of his search. There will no longer be any difference between the Nations' Religions, since they will all have the same light, and there will no longer be any arguments between them over dogma or the means of worship, since they will understand the original reason for everything. In a word, all will agree because everyone will walk in the ways of the true Law.

We can no longer doubt that the reason for all the differences which the Nations present to us in their dogmas and worship only arise because, in their Institutions, they aren't sustained by this active and intelligent Cause which alone should guide them, and which alone could reunite them. We can no longer doubt, surely, that its Light would be the only rallying point; that outside it there is no hope but only error and suffering, and that it's this Cause which acknowledges in its essence and by its nature that invincible Truth: that outside the center there is nothing fixed.

I hope that after this explanation, I'm not suspected of wanting to establish an equality and a uniformity between the various means of worship in use among the Earth's Nations, much less to want to teach the pointlessness of worship. On the contrary, I tell you that there is not a Nation which hasn't felt the need for it, and I also tell you that this worship has existed so long as there have been men on the earth. But we must also accept that, so long as they weren't sustained by a support which was common to them, it's inevitable they would become divided, and as a result, it will be impossible for them to reach the goal they have in view. So, not only do I stress the need for worship, but I stress even more strongly the need for a single form of worship, since there is but one Leader or one Cause which should direct it.

Nor should you now ask me which of all the established forms of worship is the true one? The views I've just put forward should serve as a response to any questions on this subject. The worship directed by this active and intelligent Cause will of necessity be just and good: the worship over which it does not preside will certainly be pointless or evil: that's the rule. It's for those who, among the different Nations, are charged with instructing men and leading them along the path, to compare their statutes and their progress to the Law which we show them. Our goal is not to judge established forms of worship, but to put their Leaders and Ministers in a position to be able to judge themselves.

Man's Uncertainty

I should expect a perfectly natural objection to this active and intelligent Cause which I've shown to be the Principle and sole Leader of all that should work throughout the Universe. Men may well agree on the need for this Cause's action on physical Beings; they can't even doubt that it happens, from the regularity and uniformity of the results which come from it. But, I'll be asked, even when they agree on the need for this Cause's action to direct men's conduct, how would they to know if it governs it or not? Since their dogmas and their Establishments of this kind aren't the least uniform, they must have a completely different Law to that of human opinion to be certain they are on the right path.

It's here that man shows his weakness and his powerlessness, and at the same time by this he gives more power to what we have just said: for, if man could choose and set up his form of worship by himself, the power of the active and intelligent Cause, which I recognize as indispensable, would then become superfluous for this purpose.

The Rule of Man

If, this active and intelligent Cause can never be physically known by man, he can never be sure of having found the best way, or that he possesses the best form of worship, since it's this Cause which should operate everything and manifest everything. Then man must be certain, and it isn't men who can give him this certainty; it's necessary for this Cause itself to offer clearly to man's mind and his eyes the proof of its approval. Finally, if man can be deceived by men, he must have the means not to deceive himself, and he has in hand the resources from which he can expect clear help.

The Principles I've so often laid out prove the certainty of what I am saying. Haven't we already recognized several times that man is free? As such, isn't he responsible for the good or evil effects which might result from his choice among the good or evil thoughts which come to him? Could he be guilty if he didn't possess the ability to distinguish between them without error? We now see that of all the actions he begins, there are none which he wouldn't be required to hold up against this rule, and, for as long as he doesn't see its conformity or otherwise against this rule, he can be sure of absolutely nothing.

Now what can this rule be, if it isn't an acknowledgement of and attachment to the active and intelligent Cause, which being put in charge of leading all the Beings subject to time, must bring balance visibly to man's various abilities, as it does among the various actions of physical Beings, or Matter as well.

For, if it is put in charge of directing man's abilities, what greater reason could it have to direct their actions? And, among these actions, certainly, the most important is the one where it should faithfully observe the Laws which can let him reconcile with the First Principle, and approach this Being to which it universally senses it owes homage. And, if the active and intelligent Cause is the infallible support which must sustain man in every step, if it's the certain light which must direct all the actions of his thinking Being, this universal guide must come and govern man's worship, as it does for all his other actions, and it should govern in such a way that it keeps its voice and its testimony safe from all uncertainty.

The question is not yet resolved, I know; and to say it's necessary for the active and intelligent Cause itself to establish the Laws of our worship of the First Principle is not to prove that it does so. But, having said where man should get this proof, nobody can expect any further suggestions on my part. I will not even quote my own personal experience, despite the confidence I have in it. There was a time when I wouldn't have had any faith in the truths I could certify today. It would therefore be unjust and inconsistent to want to expect to persuade my Readers by this. No, I don't fear repeating my sincere desire that none of them take me at my word, because, as a man, I've no right to the confidence of my fellow men. But I'd be absolutely delighted if each one of them had a large enough opinion of himself and of the Cause which watches over him, to hope that through his perseverance and efforts, it would seem possible to assure himself of the Truth.

Mysterious Dogmas

I know that, through wise views and beyond the reach of the common people, the Leaders and Ministers of almost all Religions have proclaimed dogmas with caution, and above all with a reserve that we can't praise enough. Doubtless inspired by the sublimity of their office, they felt that the general public should remain at a distance, and it certainly for that reason that, as depositaries of the key of Knowledge, they preferred to encourage the Nations to have a shadowy veneration for it, rather than expose its secrets to profanation.

If it's true that these were their motives, I can't blame them. Shade and silence are the sanctuaries which Truth prefers; and those who possess it can't take too many precautions to preserve it in its purity. But I'd remind them that they should also fear preventing it from being spread, for they are charged with seeing it flourish, ensuring its protection but seeing it buried. Finally, isn't locking it up too carefully perhaps denying its purpose, which is to expand and to triumph.

So, I think they'd be acting very wisely if they thoroughly examined that word *Mystery*, which they've made a barrier to their religions. They could certainly place veils over the important points, by announcing their revelation as the prize for work and constancy, and test their proselytes by this, thereby exercising both their minds and their zeal. But they shouldn't make these discoveries so difficult that everyone becomes discouraged. They shouldn't make the most beautiful abilities of the thinking Being useless. Having been born in the abode of light, he's already unfortunate enough to no longer live there, without also being deprived him of the hope of perceiving it here below. If I were them, I'd declare a Mystery to be a veiled truth, not an impenetrable truth, and I have the good fortune to have proof this definition would have been better.

Nothing then will prevent me from persevering in the concepts I am trying to recall to men, and to assure my fellow men that not only must the active and intelligent Cause direct them in all their actions, including those which relate to worship, but also that in their power to assure themselves of this, and this in a manner which will leave them with no doubts.

Indeed, one only needs to observe the behavior of the different Nations to see that they've all believed their forms of worship to be established on the foundation I've just discussed. Don't we know the ardor with which they've defended their ceremonies and religious dogmas? Hasn't each of them supported their Religion with the same zeal and fearlessness as if they were certain that Truth itself had established it?

What am I trying to say? Isn't this name Truth the mainstay of all Worship and all opinions? Haven't we seen the very Ministers who commit the greatest abominations wrap themselves in this sacred name, knowing full well that by that, they could impose it all the more surely upon the people? Why would this approach be so universal if its Principle wasn't in man? Why, even in his missteps, would he want to rely on a Name forced upon him, if he doesn't know within himself that this Name is powerful, and that he needs it? And at the same time, why would he claim that his steps are directed by truth, if he didn't feel that they can be?

We believe these observations are sufficient to convince our Readers of the necessity and the possibility of the cooperation of an active and intelligent Cause in all of men's actions, and principally in the knowledge and practice of those Laws which should direct their homage to the First Being, which none of them could have misunderstood in good faith.

The Outside of Religions

Thus, because of their nature, the Law is imposed on them never to proceed without that support and, after all the Principles we have just seen we know they can obtain this Law. So, it becomes clear that, when they want to act by themselves, they err constantly and become exposed to all kinds of danger. Now it would be all the more reprehensible to tell other men that they are guided by this true light, when they are not certain of this.

But, whatever their errors or their bad faith on this subject may be, whatever oddities they might introduce into their religious Institutions, we already have enough to recognize what I said earlier, that we can't conclude from this that there is neither rule not truth there for man. We should rather see that man's misconceptions of this kind can't be found in anything but the outside and the physical parts of their Religions, and that being inferior and absolutely subordinate to the First Being, all the opinions and all the contradictions to which they give rise don't harm Him in any way.

Morals

This is the first consequence we should take from everything we've just read about the diversity of Religions and worship. From this the wise man, who is accustomed to piercing the envelope of things, shouldn't let himself be seduced by the variety of Establishments of this kind, nor be disturbed by men's universal contradictions on this subject. He should now see their source, and not doubt that when man carries within him the notion of a First Being, he must also have a fixed and uniform means of showing Him that he knows Him and worships Him, a means which must be as unique and unalterable as this very Being, even though men are mistaken all the time on the nature of both of them.

At the same time, we can see how little confidence is merited by those who claim to prove a Religion through morals, and how they are worthy of the minimal success they usually have. For morals, though being one of the first duties of present day man, weren't always taught by the Masters who were sufficiently enlightened to apply them properly; and they have almost always been limited to being in the physical sense, and therefore had to vary according to place and the different practices from which man had created what he recognized as being virtue. Besides, since morals were never anything more than subordinate to Religion, even when they were the most perfect, to want to see them used as proof of Religion is to say one doesn't have any real proof, and at the same time there must necessarily be some which are therefore genuine proofs.

The Antiquity of Religion

I don't think it pointless to show that this is how modern doctrines transgress when they reduce all man's Laws to morals, and all their Religions to acts of humanity or the relief of the unfortunate in the material order; that is, to that virtue which is so natural and so unremarkable, with which my Century tries to shore up its systems and which focuses man on purely passive works, that it is no more than a veil of ignorance, and loses all its value in the eyes of the wise man. This virtue is undoubtedly one of our obligations, and nobody should neglect it under any pretext; but we wouldn't limit all our duties exclusively to temporal and physical acts if we weren't convinced that physical things and man are of the same rank and the same nature.

After the result we've just seen, we should expect a second, which can help us to combat and reverse another error into which the Observers have let themselves be led on this subject, which naturally comes from the same source.

Indeed, if according to them the knowledge of a Superior Being as the object of worship, as well as the need for this worship was not at all innate in man, it would follow that the origin and birth of Religious Institutions would be completely uncertain. It would then be insurmountably difficult to know how and when they'd been imagined, because if men had no Law other than the continual cycles of Nature or the impulse of their whims and their will, the birth of a new Religion could have taken place at any moment, just as any moment could have seen the annihilation of the oldest ones, and successively destroyed all those previously in favor on Earth.

In this supposition, it would be certain that the Institutions we are discussing, if they were nothing more than the work of frailty or self-interest, would not only be despised by the true man, but he should even devote his efforts to removing the least trace of them both in himself and in his fellow men.

But, being sure of all our concepts by basing them, as we've done, on man's nature, and having recognized the universality of the fundamental basis of all the Religions of Nations, we are convinced this feeling is born inside man, and therefore any concerns about the origin of this notion of a Superior Being and the worship due to Him should end.

The Affinity of Thinking Beings

In the agreement and uniformity of the ideas Nations have concerning these two points, we can see the natural results of that indestructible seed which is innate in all men and which has spoken to them throughout the ages, though we can't deny the bizarre and false uses they has almost inevitably made of them. We can't say the same about the uniform Laws they should all have followed in their worship, since as a terrible result of their liberty, they distance themselves and almost always misunderstand the superior physical Cause in charge of directing this worship, as well as all their other actions. Yet we can see that they never lost the ability to feel and understand it, since from the moment they were linked to time, this active and intelligent Cause which watches over time has never lost sight of them, as they would still have the benefit of this Cause if they hadn't been the first to run away and abandon it.

If we want to be even more convinced about the relationships which are found between man and these luminous truths contained in him, we only need to reflect on the nature of thought. As it's simple, unique and unchangeable, there can only be a single species of Beings which can have thoughts, since nothing can be common to Beings of different natures. We see that if man has within this fundamental notion of a Superior Being, and of an active and intelligent Cause which executes His Will, man must share the same essence as this Superior Being and the Cause which corresponds to both. This leads us to see that they must have thought in common; while any Being which can't receive thought, or understand it at all must necessarily be excluded from the class of thinking Beings.

It's just as well that man has this ability, and can acquire knowledge about himself by learning to see himself as different to all the passive, physical Beings which surround him. For, however hard he tries to make himself understood by any of them with regard to the principles of Justice, the knowledge of a Superior Being, or anything coming from the wellspring of his thinking, he won't see any signs or evidence that he's been understood by these physical and sensory Beings. The only thing he might accomplish, and this only with a few kinds of animal, is making them understand and execute acts of his will, without them necessarily understanding the reason for them. To communicate properly with them, he would also need to remember their natural Language, which he has forgotten; for the unnatural means he uses today to replace it are only proof of his powerlessness, and serve to show him that greatness isn't found in hard work, but rather in power and authority.

When man, instead of focusing his eyes on sensory and physical Beings, turns them inwards on his own Being in order to better understand himself, he makes careful use of his intellectual ability, his view acquires an immense breadth, he understands and touches, as it were, the rays of light which he feels to be around him, but which he also feels to be connected to him. New ideas come into his mind, and while he admires them, he's surprised he doesn't find them strange. Now, would he understand his relationship to them if their source and his weren't the same? Would he find himself so at ease and so delighted by the sight of these glimmers of truth communicated to him, if their Principle and his didn't share the same essence?

This is what makes us recognize that man's thoughts are similar to those of the First Being, and to those of the active and intelligent Cause, and that there must have been a perfect correspondence between them from the moment of man's existence. Then, if it's really out of this necessary affinity between all thinking Beings that all the Laws which must govern man are based, both concerning knowledge of the Superior Being and the worship he should offer Him, we can now see the origin of Religion among men, and that it's as old as them.

The Difference Between Immaterial Beings

However, the similarity we've just glimpsed between all Beings endowed with thought now requires me to remark on an important distinction which escapes most men, keeps them in darkness and opens them up to inexcusable errors.

If they accept that an immaterial Being such as man has thought, and agree with me that the Principle of Matter is immaterial, they would also expect this Principle to think, and couldn't imagine it would be otherwise.

On the other hand, if I say the immaterial Principle of Matter can't think, now they don't know if they should also refuse this ability to the immaterial Principle of man, because they only see one nature in these two different immaterial Beings, and therefore the same properties. But they're always deceived by the same error: they don't want to separate two natures, even though they've clearly different. Let's remind them, then, of the first Principles we've already used to support this.

All immaterial Beings come directly or through an intermediary from the same Source, but they are not all equal. We can be certain about the inequality of these Beings, since man, who is an immaterial Being, knows there are immaterial Beings above him which deserve his homage and close attention, since he's dependent upon them. He sees that, though he's similar to these immaterial Beings because of his immaterial nature and thought, he's infinitely inferior to them, because he can lose the use of his abilities and errs, while the Beings which govern him are protected from this fatal danger.

The Principle of Matter is also immaterial and indestructible like the immaterial Principle of man, but what makes them so different is that one can think while the other can't and, as I've said before, this is because man's immaterial Being of man comes directly from the Source of All Beings, while the immaterial Being of Matter only comes through an intermediary.

The Difference Between Thinking Beings

I don't believe I am committing an indiscretion when I explain that it's *number* which distinguishes them, which will be explained below. At the same time, I think I'm provide an essential service to my fellow man by persuading them that there are immaterial Beings which don't think. Several Observers of my time believed they were no longer Materialists, since they were able to recognize an immaterial Principle in Matter, as I do. But Materialism consists of having an imperfect understanding or view about Matter and its Principle; and isn't a real Materialist always a man who places the immaterial Principle of intellectual man and the immaterial Principle of Matter on the same level?

I can't therefore recommend too strongly that you don't confuse the true concepts we have within us regarding these subjects, and that you accept there are immaterial Beings who can't think at all. This is a distinction and a truth which should resolve any difficulties raised on this subject.

If anyone still has doubts about thought, which I've shown needs to be common and uniform in all Beings separate from Matter and the physical, and if, to support these doubts, one indicates the clear variation in intellectual ability between different men, where each of them seems to be no more identically gifted than in their physical and sensory abilities, I'd agree with those who have this concern that indeed, judging by the differences we see in men's intellectual abilities, it can be hard to believe they can all have an equal idea of the Superior Being, and the form of worship they should offer Him.

But we never claimed that everyone's ideas were identical on this subject. It's enough that they are similar. It isn't necessary, or even possible for all men to sense their Principle equally, but it's an established fact that all do sense it, and there's not one who doesn't have some notion of it. This acknowledgement is all we can hope from them, and it's up to the active and intelligent Cause to do the rest.

It won't take me too far off topic to spend a moment considering the natural difference we perceive in men's intellectual abilities, and useful to consider what they would have been like at his origin if he had retained his glory, and what they are like now that he has fallen.

Even if man had kept all the advantages of his first estate, it's certain that the intellectual abilities of each of his descendants would have shown differences, because these abilities are all signs of the First Principle from which they emanate, and since this Principle is always new, though always the same, the signs that represent Him must make known His continual newness, and through that make His fruitfulness all the better known. But, far from these differences producing imperfections, or causing hardships and humiliation among men, none of them would've even noticed. Too busy enjoying themselves, they wouldn't have had time to compare themselves to the others, and although their abilities wouldn't all have been equal, they would've completely satisfied those to whom they had been given.

In man's present state, on the other hand, as well as those very inequalities which have always existed, he is now subject to those arising from the Laws of the physical realm he now inhabits, which makes exercising his original abilities even more difficult, and multiplies the differences between men tenfold. However, he hasn't been condemned to death, nor has he been permanently deprived of these original abilities, so the elemental realm presents him with this new obstacle, and he has always had the necessary obligation to strive to overcome it. Finally, nowadays, as in his first estate, the extent of his gifts would be enough for him, if he still has a strong resolution to use them to his benefit.

But we know that, far from turning these obstacles to his advantage, and deriving glory from them, man increases them even more by the misuse of his will, through irregular procreation, through that ignorance by means of which he sinks every day into those things which he likes, or which are contrary to his nature, as well as a host of other things which lead to the decline of these same abilities, and pervert them to the point of almost making them unrecognizable.

And so, in this state of degradation into which man allows himself to be dragged, he forgets the privileges which belong to him, and his heart is empty. No longer knowing true happiness, he thinks less of himself, and only rates himself according to human conventions which only exist in his unruly will, but which he is attached to with such great zeal; for since he let go of his only real support, he no longer has anything true to support him.

However, despite these original differences, later further multiplied through the pitfalls of the physical realm and through his defective habits, can we actually say that man has changed his nature, when we've seen that physical Beings can't change, despite the many cycles to which their own Law and the hands of man may subject them?

The Tribute Imposed on Man

Now, if it's in men's nature and essence to recognize a Superior Being, and to feel that, since they are attached to the physical realm, there must be a physical means to bring Him their homage, it's certain that despite all their errors, their Law could never change. They can make their task longer and harder, as in fact they do every day because of their blindness and carelessness: but they never excuse themselves from the obligation to fulfill it. Whether one is more burdened than another by nature, or whether he becomes so because of his own fault, nevertheless each man's tribute must be paid; and man's tribute is nothing other than sensing, acknowledging and making the correct use of the abilities which compose him.

Then, however disfigured man might become, we will always find his first Law within him, since his nature is always the same. We will always find him to be similar to the Being which communicates thought to him, since thought can only take place between Beings of the same nature. We must recognize him as being inseparably linked to the notion of his Principle, and to the notion of his duties which connect him to Him, since having agreed that these ideas are universal among men, we can't deny that they're born with them, and that they've always lived with them. That's why we identified the time of Religion's birth as being the time of man's very origin.

Error in the Origin of Religion

What, then, should we make of the imprudent and insane theory which claims this sacred institution was born out of men's fear and timidity? How could such weaknesses have given them the sublime idea of a Guide who could enlighten them and support them in all their steps, if His seed wasn't already in their breast? And since they carry this seed within them, why seek another origin for it?

No. With absolutely no doubt, nobody can say that Nature's terrifying upheavals gave birth to this idea in man. At most, they may have been an appropriate means to stir up within him those precious abilities which are so often suppressed; but they could never have communicated to him the seed of those abilities, since it's only through them that he is man.

Still less would they have given him all the light and knowledge needed to accomplish all his duties relating to his Religion and worship, because just when man senses that this light is lacking, he feels he can only obtain it from an intelligent Cause, which being above him, is for even more reason above material Nature. Now, if man, despite his misery and privation is nevertheless above material Nature because of his essence, what is the help and the enlightenment he might expect from this material Nature?

From this we can see the mediocre results which all the upheavals of the elemental Realm have been able to produce in man, and how unreasonable it would be to seek the source of his virtues and greatness there.

We're not saying that the terrible happenings which elemental Nature can show us haven't often served to reawaken the dulled intelligent abilities in man, by reminding him about the notion of a First Being and the need to honor Him.

I'll even admit that in the miserable situations in which he so often found himself, that must have been all the more frightening because of his ignorance, he selected from the objects scattered around him those which seemed to be the most powerful, and addressed them with his desire to receive aid against the misfortunes which menaced him. I admit that, having made his choice of Gods, he then offered them physical worship and sacrifices. I admit that the same errors took place in various places in different regions of the Earth, depending on how afraid man was there; and this is one of the reasons for the variety we find in all Religions.

What can be concluded from all this which is contrary to the notion I'm defending? Can't they see what the true motivation for these Institutions has been? Can't they see what its futile purpose is? And can't they see that the very people who established them, unable to conceal the weakness of their Idols, sought to shore them up by increasing their number, often discarding them only to replace them by others at will, demonstrating a similar inconsistency in the choice of means they used to appease them? Now, if it had been a fixed light that directed them, they would have been safe from all these contradictions.

It's clear that those who observed these facts took their conclusions too far. Although fear and superstition have given birth to Religious Institutions in various places or, which is even more true, introduced variations into previously established Religions, it's incorrect to conclude that this was therefore the source of all Religions, and that it was from fear and superstition that man drew the basis and the ideas which are common to all men. But it's not possible to show the cause of this error even more clearly, and reveal it completely.

Haven't I shown man to be a composite of physical and intellectual abilities? Couldn't we deduce from this that, since his physical abilities are common to all animals, he become susceptible to habits like them; and also, that since these habits are physical, they could only arise by the aid of physical Causes and means?

We should realize, on the other hand that, since man's intellectual abilities are of a higher order than the physical Causes, they can't be commanded by these physical Causes, and to move and animate them, they needed the action of an agent of another order, that is, one which was of the name nature as man's intellectual Being.

Here, then, is where the solution to the problem can be found. We must distinguish between the physical works of man and his original notions which only belong to his intellectual Being. We must see that climate, temperature and all the more or less large mishaps in physical Nature could indeed affect the customs, habits and external actions of man, and through man's link to the physical, could even work passively on his intellectual abilities. But the support of all the elemental upheavals of whatever kind could never give him the least idea of a superior Cause, nor the fundamental points we've discovered in him. In other words, all the Causes we are currently looking at, since they are of the physical order by nature, they could only actively work on the physical, and never on the intellectual.

Then, in all these results of man's weakness and fear we certainly see a misuse and an insane application of his intellectual abilities; but this would never be the source of their origin. For even though these intellectual abilities act upon the physical, they can only make it move. They don't create it, even if they are superior to it. And this is all the more reason why, since the physical abilities are inferior to them, the intellectual abilities may be affected by them when they act on them, but they will never receive birth or life from them.

Man's Intellectual Seed

We return once more to our subject, which has been to situate the existence of Religion at the first moment of man's existence.

If, after these demonstrations, those who advanced the opposite theory still persist in maintaining it, and claim that man discovered the source of his ideas and enlightenment, whose seed we've said he carries within him, in inferior and physical Causes; we only have one question to ask them to completely overturn their theory: that is, if they say that the upheavals of material Nature gave men Religion, why don't animals have a Religion too, since, like man, they've been present at all these upheavals?

Let's stop thinking about this theory, and instead concentrate on recognizing the immense value of the seed which has been placed within us. Let us concentrate on sensing that if this precious seed gives us innumerable fruits when it has received its natural *cultivation*; it can only show confusion and disorder when it receives a strange *cultivation*. Finally, let us attribute to this false *cultivation* alone the uncertainties which man has shown in all the steps he's taken without his guide.

Man's First Religion

But I anticipate my Readers' curiosity concerning this natural *cultivation*, and the invariable effects of the active and intelligent Cause which I've recognized as the indispensable light of man; in a word, concerning that Religion and that unique worship which, according to the concepts I've outlined, would lead all worship back to the same Law.

Although I declared that man shouldn't expect the proofs and certain witness of these truths from his fellow men; he can at least receive an image of it from them, and I intend to outline this.

I won't hide from him the effort I must myself make to do this. I won't talk about knowledge, so I won't be covered in shame to see all that man has lost, and I truly wish that I didn't know what I know, for I find nothing in me which is worthy of that knowledge. It's for this reason that I can never express myself on these subjects except through symbols.

Man's Religion in his first estate required a form of worship, as it still is today, though its form was different. This man's principle Law was to continually cast his eyes from *East* to *West*, and from *North* to *South*; that is, to determine the *latitudes* and the *longitudes* of all the parts of the Universe.

It's by means of this that he had a perfect knowledge of everything that took place there. He expelled wrongdoers from his entire empire, he guaranteed passage to well-intentioned travelers, and established order and peace in all the Estates under his dominion. By this he clearly manifested the power and glory of the First Cause Who had entrusted him with these sublime functions, and it was his duty to offer a homage most worthy of Him, and the only one capable of honoring and pleasing Him; for being *One* in essence, He never had any other object than to reign in His *Unity*, that is, to ensure the happiness of all Beings.

However, if man hadn't been assisted in fulfilling the immense task confided to him, he couldn't have embraced all its duties on his own. So he also had faithful Ministers around him who executed his orders with precision and speed. He thought, his Ministers read his will, and wrote them down in characters so clear and expressive that they were free from any equivocation.

Since man's first Religion was invariable, despite his fall, man is still subject to the same duties. But as he has changed country, he must also change the Law to direct him in the exercise of his Religion.

Man's Second Religion

Now, this change is that of being subjected to the need to employ physical means for a worship which had never known this before. Nevertheless, as these means come naturally to him, it requires little effort to find them, but much more effort, it's true, to give them value and use them successfully.

Firstly, he can't take a step without encountering his *Altar*; and this *Altar* is always adorned with *Lamps* which never go out, and which will exist so long as the *Altar* itself does.

Secondly, he always carries *incense* with him, so that at any moment he can give himself over to Religious acts.

But with all these advantages, it's frightening to think how far man still is from his goal, how many more attempts he has to make to reach the point where he can completely fulfill his original duties. Yet even when he gets there, he'll still remain in irrevocable subjection, whose severity he'll be made to endure until the completion of his sentence.

This subjection is that of being unable to anything at all by himself, and always being dependent on that active and intelligent Cause which alone can set him back on the path when he strays; which alone can support him on that path, and which must today direct all his steps, so that without it he can know nothing, and can't even draw the smallest conclusion from his own knowledge and abilities.

Reading and Writing

Moreover, it's no longer like the time of his glory, when he could read the most intimate thoughts of his Superiors and his Subjects, and as a result, interact with them as he wished. But in this terrible atonement which he endures, he can only hope to reestablish this communication by beginning to learn to *write*. Then he is happy to find himself in the situation of learning to *read*, for there are many men, even the most famous for their knowledge, who spend their lives without ever having *read*.

Some have indeed *read* without ever having *written*; but these are specific privileges, and the general Law begins by *writing*; whereas man, in his first estate, could continually occupy himself by *reading* at will. Now, as man's atonement must take place in time, it's this Law of time which subjects him to a slow and difficult process in order to recover his rights and knowledge, whereas in his first origin, he had to wait for nothing, and each of his abilities always responded to his needs, acting immediately according to his desire.

The Book of Man

These inexpressible privileges related to the possession and understanding of a Book beyond price, which was among the gifts that man had received at his birth. Though this Book only contained ten pages, it contained all the light and all the knowledge of what was, what is and what will be. And man's power was then so extensive that he had the ability to read the ten pages of the Book at the same time, and to embrace it all at a glance.

At the time of his degradation, this Book remained with him, but he was deprived of the ability of being able to read it so easily, and he could only understand its pages one after the other. However, he'll never be completely restored to his rights until he has studied them all; for, although each of these ten pages contains particular knowledge which is its own, they are nevertheless linked in such a way that it's impossible to possess one of them perfectly without understanding them all; and although I said that man can only read them in order, none of his steps will be certain if he hasn't gone through them all, and principally the fourth, which serves as a rallying point for all the others.

This one contains a truth to which men have paid little attention. However, it's this truth which is absolutely necessary for them to follow and understand; for they're all born with the Book in their hands, and if the study and knowledge of this Book are precisely the tasks they need to complete, we can judge that it's in their best interest to make no error in this.

But their negligence on this subject has been carried to an extreme, and almost none of them have noticed the fundamental unity among the ten pages of the Book, for which reason they are inseparable. Some have stopped halfway through this Book, others on the third page, others on the first. This is what produced the Atheists, the Materialists and the Deists. Some even saw their connection, but didn't understand the important distinctions existing between each of these pages, and on finding them connected with each other, supposed them all to be equal and of the same nature.

What was the result of this? Well, by limiting themselves to the point in the Book past which they didn't have the courage to read, yet relying on what they could say about what they had actually read in the Book, they claimed they'd read it all, and believing themselves to be infallible in their doctrine, they made every effort to convince themselves that they were. But these isolated truths, receiving no nourishment, soon perished at the hands of those who had separated them in this way, and all that was left to those unwise men was the vaguest ghost of Knowledge, to which they could give neither a solid body nor a true Being, without having to rely on deception.

This is precisely the reason for all the errors which we'll examine in the rest of this Treatise, as well as all those we have already identified concerning the two opposing Principles, the nature and Laws of physical Beings, the varying abilities of man, and the principles and origin of his Religion and forms of worship.

We'll see below where in the Book these misunderstanding have arisen; but before we do that, we'll finish the notion we should have about this incomparable Book, by giving details about the different knowledge and different properties about which each of its pages contains an understanding.

The first is concerned with the Universal Principle or Center, from which all Centers continually emanate.

The second, the occasional Cause of the Universe; the dual physical Law which supports it; the dual intellectual Law acting in time; the dual nature of man; and generally, all that is composed and formed from two actions.

The third, the basis of bodies; all the results and products of all the Species, and it's here that the *number* of immaterial Beings which don't think is to be found.

The fourth, all that is active; the Principle of all Languages, whether temporal or outside of time; Religion and man's worship, and it's here that is found the *number* of immaterial Being which think.

The fifth, Idolatry and putrefaction.

The sixth, the Laws of the formation of the temporal World, and the natural division of the Circle by the radius.

The seventh, the Cause of the Winds and Tides; the geographic Scale of man; his true Science and the source of his intellectual or physical products.

The eighth, the temporal *number* of Him who is the only support, the only power and the only hope of man, that is, of this real and physical Being which has two *names* and four *numbers*, as He is both active and intelligent, and His action extends over the four Worlds. It also deals with Justice and all legislative powers, which include the rights of Sovereigns and the authority of Generals and Judges.

The ninth, the formation of physical man in the womb of woman, and an analysis of the universal and particular triangle.

Finally, the tenth is the way and the complement of the nine preceding pages. It's without doubt the most essential, and the one without which all the others can't be understood, since by arranging all ten of them in a circumference according to their numerical order, it's found to have the greatest affinity with the first, from which they all emanate; and if we wish to judge its importance, we can know that is by this that the Creator of things is invincible, because there is a barrier which defends Him on all sides, and through which no Being can pass.

Thus, as we see enclosed in this enumeration all the knowledge to which man can aspire, and the Laws which are imposed upon him, it's clear that he will never possess any knowledge, or ever fulfill any of his true duties without drawing from that source. We also know now which hand should lead him there, and if he can't take a step towards this fertile source by himself, he can be sure of getting there by forgetting his will, and allowing that active and intelligent Cause to act, which alone should act for him.

> *Du Livre de l'Homme.* 255
>
> qu'un vain phantôme de Science, qu'ils ne pouvoient donner comme un corps solide, ni comme un Etre vrai, sans avoir recours à l'imposture.
>
> C'est de-là précisément d'où sont sorties toutes les erreurs que nous aurons à examiner dans la suite de ce Traité, ainsi que toutes celles que nous avons déja relevées sur les deux Principes opposés, sur la nature & les Loix des Etres corporels, sur les différentes facultés de l'homme, sur les principes & l'origine de sa Religion & de son culte.
>
> On verra ci-après sur quelle partie du Livre sont tombées principalement les méprises ; mais, avant d'en venir là, nous compléterons l'idée qu'on doit avoir de ce Livre incomparable, en donnant le détail des différentes Sciences & des différentes propriétés, dont chacune de ses feuilles renfermoit la connoissance.
>
> La premiere traitoit du Principe universel, ou du Centre, d'où émanent continuellement tous les Centres.
>
> La seconde, de la Cause occasionnelle de l'Univers ; de la double Loi corporelle qui le soutient ; de la double Loi intellectuelle, agissant dans le temps ; de la double nature de l'homme, & généralement de tout ce qui est composé & formé de deux actions.
>
> La troisieme, de la base des Corps ; de tous les résultats & des productions de tous les Genres,

Figure 6 – First page on The Book of Man

Let's therefore congratulate him for still being able to find such a support in his wretchedness. May his heart be filled with hope, seeing that even today he can discover without error in this precious Book, the essence and properties of Beings, the reason for things, the certain and invariable Laws of his Religion and the worship he must necessarily offer to the First Being. That is, being at the same time both intellectual and physical, and having nothing which is not either one or the other, he must know the relationships between himself and everything that exists.

For, if the Book only has ten pages, and yet it contains everything, nothing can exist without belonging by its Nature to one of these ten pages. Now, there isn't a single Being which doesn't indicate its class and to which of the ten pages it belongs. By this, each Being offers us the means to instruct ourselves on everything which concerns it. But to direct oneself in this knowledge, one must first know how to distinguish the true and simple Laws which constitute the nature of Beings, from those which men presume and substitute for them every day.[46]

---

[46] This extraordinary and powerful passage should be a reminder of the importance both Pasqually and Saint-Martin attributed to numbers. It should be clear that the power of the Book of Man lies in the fact that it is associated with the first ten numbers, rather than the content of the individual pages. Thus, this allegory reminds us that the ten numbers are the basis on which they established their theosophies, and when arranged around a circle, like the face of a watch, we see that '1' and '10' necessarily occupy the same place, since in Theosophical addition, '10 = 1+0 = 1'. In his *Treatise*, Pasqually gives the following attributions to the numbers:

1 – Unity, the origin of all existence (God).
2 – The number of confusion.
3 – The number belonging to Earth and all humanity.
4 – The Quatriple Divine Essence.
5 – Evil Powers.
6 – Daily conduct; the days of creation.
7 – The Holy Spirit; 7 spiritual powers.
8 – The doubly powerful Spirit (Christ).
9 – The Evil number (of Matter).
10 – The Divine number (God).

It is worth comparing this to Saint-Martin's attributions to fully understand the Book of Man:

1 – Unity, the First Principle, the point.
2 – Duality, Man's Act of creation, the line, dual Laws.
3 – Nature and Man; the Elements; the triangle.
4 – Quaternary; the square; straight line; Man's primitive abode.
5 – Evil, Idolatry, death.
6 – Hexagon marking the 6 days of Creation on the circle.
7 – The Holy Spirit; its manifestation in The temporal
8 – The number of Christ.
9 – The number of Matter, curved line; circle; Man's place after his fall.
10 – Point within the circle; God; the Creator surrounded by creation.

The reader may compare these systems with the Book of Man to advantage. Later, Saint-Martin will go into great detail about most of these numbers.

Errors in the Book of Man

Let's come to the part of the Book which I said has been the most abused. It's that fourth page which has been recognized as having the closest connection to man, in that it's there that his duties and the true Laws of his thinking Being were written, as well as the doctrines of his Religion and his worship.

Indeed, by following all the points clearly enunciated there with exactness, constancy and a pure intent, he could obtain the help of the very Hand which had punished him, raise himself up above this corrupt Realm to which he has been relegated by condemnation, and rediscover traces of his former authority, by virtue of which he formerly determined the *latitudes* and *longitudes* for the maintenance of universal order.

But, since such powerful resources are connected with this fourth page, as we said, it's also with regard to this part of the Book that his errors have the greatest effect; and indeed, if man hadn't neglected any of its benefits, all would still be happy and at peace on Earth.

The first of these errors was to transpose this fourth page and substitute it by the fifth, or the one which discusses Idolatry; because then, by disfiguring the Laws of his Religion, man couldn't get the same results from them, nor the same help he'd have received if he'd persevered in the true worship. On the contrary, now he only received darkness in recompense, and was swallowed up to the point of no longer even desiring the light.

Such was the course of this Principle we spoke about at the beginning of this book, which was made Evil through its own will. Such was the course of the first man, and such has been the course of many of his descendants, above all among those Nations who take their *East* at the *South* of the Earth.

This is the error or crime which can't be overlooked, and which on the contrary, must submit entirely to the most rigorous punishments; but the majority are protected from taking these false steps, because it's only by walking that one falls, and the majority don't walk at all. Yet how can one advance without walking?

The second error is obtaining the vaguest notion of the properties associated with this fourth page, and then believing one could apply them to everything; for, by attributing them to objects they have no connection with, it's impossible to find anything out.

Also, who doesn't know about the lack of success of those who found Matter on four Elements, who daren't refuse to attribute thought to animals, who strive to square the Solar with the Lunar calculation, who seek the Earth's longitude[47] and the quadrature of the circle; in a word, who daily attempt to make an infinity of discoveries of this nature, and in which they never have satisfactory results, as we'll continue to show in the next part of this Treatise? But since this error wasn't aimed directly against the Universal Principle, those who follow it are only punished by ignorance, and that doesn't require atonement.

There is a third, in which, with the same ignorance, man stupidly believed himself to be in possession of the sacred advantages that this fourth page could indeed communicate to him. In this notion, he spread the uncertain ideas he had developed concerning Truth among his fellow men, and turned the Nations' gaze towards him, when they should have only fixed their gaze upon the First Being, upon the active and intelligent physical Cause, and upon those who through their works and their *virtues* had earned the right to represent Him on Earth.

This error, without being as disastrous as the first, is nevertheless infinitely more dangerous than the second, because it gives men a false and puerile notion of the Creator of things and the paths which lead to Him; because in the end, all of those who've had the impudence and audacity to proclaim themselves in this manner have, as it were, established so many theories, so many dogmas and so many Religions. Now, those Establishments which were already impermanent in themselves, couldn't avoid undergoing more and more changes due to the imperfection of their creation, so that being obscure and dark from the moment of their origin, they clearly revealed their distortion over the passage of time.

---

[47] The problem of longitude had been a vexing one for centuries. While the measurement of latitude was accomplished with relative ease, any miscalculation of longitude could put a ship many miles off course. In the early to mid-1700s, one country after another offered increasingly attractive financial prizes to anyone who could solve this problem. Eight years prior to the appearance of this book, Nevil Maskelyne, the British Astronomer Royal, and a member of the Longitude Board, based at the Royal Observatory at Greenwich, published the first *Nautical Almanac*, showing the exact position of the moon during 1767, together with the *Tables Requisite*, a complicated series of calculations to correct for the effects of refraction, parallax, and other arcane issues. These Tables worked, and for the next 80 years this laborious series of calculation enabled ships to navigate the Earth with great accuracy, before the introduction of the chronometer, which was then used in navigation up to the invention of radar, and then the Global Positioning System. Incidentally, Maskelyne's work also helped Greenwich to become the Prime Meridian a century later.

The Origin of the Diversity of Religions

Therefore, let's add the enormous abuse made of the knowledge contained in the fourth page of this Book whose guardians we are born to be, and the confusion which has arisen from this, to all we've observed of the ignorance, fear and weakness of men; and leaving the symbols there, we now have the reason for and the origin of this multitude of Religions and forms of worship in use across the Nations.

When we see this variety which perverts them, and this mutual opposition which demonstrates their falsehood, we can only despise them. But, when we don't lose sight of the fact that these differences and oddities have only taken place in the physical side; and when we remember that man bring all his Laws with him, through his thought and being in the image and likeness of the First Being, we recognize that his Religion was born along with him; that far from being the result of example, whim, ignorance, and fear which the catastrophes of Nature had inspired in him, it's on the contrary all these Causes which have so often disfigured him, and even led man to the point of mistrusting the only remedy he had for his ills. We recognize still more that he is the only one who suffers because of his vacillations and his weaknesses; that the source of his Existence and the path given him to return there will never be any less pure; and that he'll always be sure of finding a place in common with his fellow men when he turns his eyes towards that source, and towards the one Light which can lead him there.

Such are the notions we should have concerning the true Religion of man, and about all those which have usurped this name on earth. Now let's look for the cause of the errors the Observers have made concerning Politics. Having considered man in himself, and in relation to his Principle, it becomes very important to consider him in relation to his fellow men.

End of Book 1

Chapter 5 – Politics & Law

The Uncertainty of Politicians

When considering man in his political relationships, two points of view will be presented as in the preceding observations: firstly, what he could and should be in the state of society; secondly, what he really is in this state. Now, it's by carefully studying what he should be in the estate of society that we can learn to judge more clearly what he is today. This comparison is surely the only way to clearly unravel the mysteries which still veil the origin of societies, establish the rights of Sovereigns, and lay down the rules of administration by which Empires could and should sustain and govern themselves.

The greatest embarrassment those Politicians who've best sought to follow the course of Nature have experienced, has been in trying to reconcile all the social Institutions with the Principles of Justice and Equality which they should be able to see in them. As soon as they were shown that man is free, they believed he was made for independence, and deduced that all subjection was contrary to his true nature.

Thus, they truly believed any kind of Government would be imperfect, and man shouldn't have any leader but himself.

However, they couldn't resist being curious about finding an origin and Cause for this supposed defect regarding man's dependence for and the authority which subjugates him being found everywhere in their view; and it's here their imagination, by taking the thing itself to be the Principle, began to make so many mistakes, and where the Observers showed as much inadequacy as when they wanted to explain the origin of Evil.

They claimed it was cleverness and power which had put authority into the hands of those who control men; and that Sovereign power was simply founded on the weakness of those who allowed themselves to be subjugated. From there, since this invalid right had no firm foundation, we see it's vulnerable to faltering and falling into every successive pair of hands which have the power and talent necessary to grab it.

Others delighted in detailing the violent or skillful means which, according to them, held sway over the birth of Nations; and in this they simply retold the same theory, but applied more broadly. This is the shallow reasoning given by those who said the needs and the ferociousness of the first men were the motivations behind these Establishments, and said that, living as hunters in the forests, these wild men made raids on those who focused on agriculture and the care of herds, with the intention of turning all these advantages to their profit. Next, to maintain that state of authority which violence had created, and was turning into true oppression, the usurpers were forced to establish laws and penalties. This is how the most skillful, the most audacious and the most inventive managed to remain master, and ensure his despotism.

But we see that the first society couldn't have been like that, since it assumes farmers and shepherds already existed. However, this is pretty much the prevailing opinion of those Politicians who've decided Governments have never been founded on Principles of Justice and Equity, and they've made all their theories and all their observations support this conclusion.

Some thought they could remedy this injustice by basing all societies on the common agreement and unanimous will of the individuals which compose it. However, since each individual couldn't withstand the dangerous consequences of the natural freedom and independence of their fellow men, they found themselves forced to place the rights of their natural estate into the hands of an individual or a small number of people, and by so joining together their powers, enter into an agreement among themselves to maintain the authority of those who they had chosen as leaders.

Involuntary Association

Then, since the transfer of power was voluntary, there's no injustice in the authority which comes out of it. Next, determining the powers of the Sovereign, as well as the privileges of the Subjects, through the same voluntary act of agreement, we see the Political Bodies all emerge fully formed, and there won't be any difference between them, such are seen in particular types of Administration which can vary according to time and case.

This opinion would seem the most judicious, and which would best fulfill the natural notion which they wish to give us about the Justice of Governments, where the people and property are under the protection of the Sovereign, and where this Sovereign, having no goal but that of the common good, is solely concerned with maintaining the Law which should accomplish this.

In a forced association, on the other hand, we only see an image of shocking atrocity, in which the Subjects are so many victims, and the Tyrant takes sole ownership of all the advantages of the society over which he has made himself master. Therefore, I won't dwell further on this kind of Government, even though it's not without its examples; but seeing neither trace of Justice nor reason there, we can't reconcile it with any of man's true and natural Principles. Otherwise, we'd have say a band of thieves also forms a political body.

Voluntary Association

However, it's not enough to present us with the notion of voluntary association. It's not even enough for us to see more legality in this kind of Government than in all those born out of violence. We still need to carefully examine whether this kind of voluntary association is possible, and if this structure isn't just as imaginary as forced association. We must also examine whether, if this kind of agreement were possible, man can lawfully to take it upon himself to create it.

It's only from this examination that Politicians can judge the validity of the Rights which founded such Societies; and if we find them evidently defective, by examining in what way they're deficient we can soon see which ones should be replaced.

We don't need to think long to realize how hard it's to imagine the voluntary association of a whole Nation. For the votes[48] to be unanimous, the means of considering the motives and conditions the new agreement must be unanimous, too. This has never happened and will never happen in a region, or when it concerns matters which only have a physical basis, because we can be sure that everything will be relate to the physical, and there is nothing permanent in that.

Besides the fact that every one of its members would need to suppress any ambition to be leader or to be a part of the leadership, each would also have to reach agreement on an infinity of opinions, which never happens among men, either when considering the most advantageous form of

---

[48] *Voix* can also mean 'voices'. However, it is clear the context is discussing a utopian democracy, though it is difficult to be sure how far Saint-Martin's vision extended. At the time, only the clergy, aristocracy and landowners could vote, and only men.

Government, or in the general and specific interests and the multitude of point which would have to be included in the Articles of the Contract.

Moreover, observations over a long period of time would be pointless to show us that a social State, voluntarily formed by all its individuals, is a completely beyond all likelihood, and that we should not only accept that it's impossible, but also, that there has never been anything like it.

But even if we were to allow such a possibility – and here let's assume an unanimous agreement of all the votes, and that the form of Government, as well as the Laws belonging to it, had been decided on by general accord – we still need to ask whether man has the right to take on such a commitment, and whether it would be wise for him to put his trust in those such an agreement would create.

From the knowledge we must have acquired about man from everything we've seen, it's easy to predict that such a right could never have been granted, and that this action would be null and void. Firstly, let's remember that invariable compass that we've recognized to be his guide, remembering that every step which he takes without it's uncertain, since without it man has no light, and by its very nature it's in charge of leading him and governing all his actions.

So, if man took on an obligation of as great importance as submitting himself to another man without the agreement of this Cause which watches over him, we must doubt whether his approach conformed with his own Law, and, as a result, whether it was appropriate to make him happy; which alone should be sufficient to stop him if he only listened to prudence.

Then reflecting more carefully on his conduct, wouldn't he recognize that not only had he made a mistake, but he was directly attacking all the principles of Justice by transferring rights he couldn't legitimately assign to another man, and which he knows truly rest in the hand which must do everything for him?

Secondly, this obligation would be vague and senseless, for if it's true that this Cause must be man's guide in everything, and has all the powers needed to be so, it's completely pointless to seek another guide. All the more reason, then, to say the same thing of man, in the manner of Politicians: that according to them, it's man's helplessness the difficulty he experiences surviving Nature's realm, which leads him to giving up his powers to Leaders and Protectors. Indeed, if this man had the strength to support himself, he'd have no need of foreign support; but ultimately, if he no longer has this strength, if it's after losing it that he now wishes to give it to another man, what is it that he's actually giving him, and where can we find what the Politicians call the consideration of this Contract?

Voluntary association isn't really any more just and sensible than it's practical, since by this action a man must give another man a right which isn't his to give, the right to dispose of himself; and because if he transfers a right he doesn't have, he enters into a contract which is completely unenforceable, which neither the Leader nor the Subjects can enforce it, since it can't bind either party.

So, given everything we've just said, if forced association is clearly an atrocity, and voluntary association is impossible and also opposed to Justice and Reason, where might we find the true Principles of Governments? For after all, there are Nations which have known them and follow them.

As I've said, Politicians expend all their efforts on this search, and if what we've just seen is everything they've discovered so far, we can rest assured that they have still not taken the first step towards that knowledge.

False Conclusions of Politicians

In many of them there's a secret voice which inclines them to agree that whatever may have been the reason behind the association of a Political Body, the Leader is basically the repository of a supreme authority and a power which in itself should subordinate all his subjects to him. Indeed, they recognize a superior power in Sovereigns which naturally inspires respect and obedience in them.[49]

This is what I, too, delight in professing loudly along with the Politicians. But, since they haven't been able to identify the source of this superiority, they haven't formed a clear idea about it, and as a result the use they want to make of it only presents them with falsehoods and contradictions.

---

[49] Saint-Martin is referring to the doctrine of the 'Divine Right of Kings'. This was particularly popular with both King James I of England (VI of Scotland) and Louis XIV in France, and stated that God gave earthly power to monarchs, just as he gave spiritual authority to the Church, and that the King was therefore only answerable to God for the use he made of his absolute powers. This stems from 1 Samuel, where the prophet anoints Saul, and then David as King of Israel, from which stems the tradition of anointing the monarch to designate 'God's anointed'. The motto of the English Royal Family, 'Dieu et mon droit' or 'God and my Right', comes from Richard I, or Richard the Lionheart.

And the majority of them, dissatisfied with their discoveries, and finding no means of explaining why man comes together in societies, went back to their original idea, and were reduced to saying that he shouldn't be in society at all. But we can certainly see that this conjecture is no more strongly based than the ones they'd formed about the means of association, and that really just gives clear proof of their uncertainty and the hastiness of their judgements.

Man's Sociability

We only need to look at man for a moment to decide on this question. Isn't his life a chain of continual dependencies? Doesn't the very act of his entry into physical life bring with it the nature of subjugation to which he will be condemned for the rest of his life? In order to be born, doesn't he need an external Cause to fertilize his seed, and provide a reaction without which he wouldn't be alive? And isn't it that humiliating subjection which he has in common with all Beings of Nature?

As soon as he receives the light of day, this dependence becomes even more physical for now his physical eyes must bear witness to everything. Then, in a state of complete powerlessness and truly ignominious weakness, to keep him from dying, man needs help and limitless care from the Beings of his species until, when he reaches an age when he can look after the needs of his body himself, he comes into his own and enjoys all the advantages and all the strength of his physical Being.

But such is man's nature and the wisdom of the eye which watches over him, that before he reaches this period of physical independence, he senses a need of another kind, which links him even more closely to the hands which sustained him during his infancy. It's the need of his intellectual Being, which beginning to sense its deprivation, becomes agitated and surrenders itself blindly to anything which can give it peace.

At this age, still weak, he naturally appeals to everything that surrounds him, and especially to those who caring for his bodily needs every day, seem to be rightfully the first recipients of his confidence. It's from them he seeks knowledge of himself at every step, and indeed it's only from them that he should expect it, for it's their duty to direct him, support him and enlighten him appropriately to his age, to arm him in advance against *error* and to prepare him for *combat*. In other words, they must do for his intellectual

Being what they did for his body during the time he experienced pain, without having the strength to endure it or avoid it. This, no doubt, is the true source of society among men, and at the same time the image where man can learn the first of his duties when he himself becomes a father.

The reason we can't find anything similar among the animals is because they don't have the nature to know these kinds of needs. It's because animals are only governed by the physical, and when this need is fulfilled, there's nothing more to care about. Since physical feeling is the only ability it has, when this feeling is satisfied, there's no longer any feeling or desire; and for the animal there is absolutely no social bond.

There's no need to point out the attachment that some animals have to each other or to man. At this point we're only considering how Beings normally walk and move; and any example which could be given in opposition would surely be the result of habit which, as we said earlier, can be found in animals since they are physical Beings.

Nor should anyone cite how certain animals live and travel together in groups on earth, in water or in the air. It's only specific and physical needs which bring them together and there is little real attachment between them, since one can die or go missing without the others even noticing.

We can now see, from these observations about the earliest times of our material existence, that man was not born to live alone.

We can see that even after the physical dependence of his childhood has ceased, there remain a link which is infinitely stronger, as it relates to his own Being. We can clearly see that, because of the inseparable need of his present condition, he will always seek out his fellow men, and that if they never deceived him, or if he wasn't already corrupted, he'd never dream of being separate from them even when his body no longer had any need of their assistance.

So, it's wrong for anyone to look for the reason for sociability in physical needs alone, and in the potent way that Nature brings man and the Beings of his species together for the purpose of reproduction. Although man is similar to animals in this need to reproduce, animals have never lived in any form of society, so this reason isn't enough to explain sociability in man. Also, I'm only concerned about the abilities which make him different, and lead him to join with his fellow men in agreeing on moral actions, which must be the basis of any association if it's going to be just.

When, in his advancing years, man's intellectual abilities begin to rise above what he sees, and he begins to perceive some glimmers amidst the darkness in which we find ourselves, he sees everything in a new light. Not only does everything interest him, but how this interest should grow in those who helped him experience the happiness of being a man, just as he can help others to experience this in his turn?

As he continues through the passage of life, this social link is strengthened even more by this increase in what he can see and think. Finally, in his declining years, with his powers degenerating, he falls into the same weak physical state of his childhood. For a second time, he becomes an object of pity to other men, and returns to being dependent upon them, until the Law common to all bodies comes to do its work on him, and ends his term. What more do we need to agree that man wasn't destined to spend his days alone, without any social link?

We see, too, that in this simple and natural society, there are always Beings who give and others who receive; that we always find superiority and dependence, and this is the true model of what a political society should be.

The Source of Political Errors

This is, however, what those who've talked about such things didn't consider when they said that the idea of society was contrary to Nature, and finding no way to justify society, or to make it agree with their principles of natural Law, they decided to proscribe it.

For us who feel an absolute necessity to connect with others and keep company with men, we won't be stopped by the falsehood and injustice of those bonds which have often put them into a social body. We'll even accept that men would not have been born like this, with these reciprocal needs and these abilities which promise them so many advantages, if there wasn't also a legitimate means of developing them, and reaping all the benefits they can give us.

Now, since the use of these means can only happen during interactions between individuals, and since these interactions are imperfect given man's current state of subjection to so many disadvantages, we won't reject political bodies because of that, but we will suggest a foundation which is more solid and with more satisfying principles to those they've proposed so far.

But we must see now that the darkness which envelops the Politicians is same as that which shrouds the Observers of Nature; and because, like them, they've confused the Principle with its envelope, and man's established[50] power with his true power, they've obscured and perverted everything.

Man's First Empire

We've also seen just how unproductive all these observations on Nature, where they tried to separate it from an active and intelligent Cause whose support and power were shown to be absolutely necessity, have been.

From this, we know that since Politics is similar, such observations must be just as unproductive. They looked for the principles of Government in individual man, and they couldn't find them there, any more than the Observers could find in Matter the source of its effects and results.

Thus, just as we can't imagine a circumference without a center, so none of these Sciences can work without its support. That is why all these explanations can't support themselves, and fall apart with no other cause than that of their own stupidity.

If at his origin man was destined to be the leader and to command, as we have clearly established, what notion should we form of his Empire in this first estate, and over which Beings should we believe he had authority? Would it be over his equals? Yet in all that exists and in everything that we can understand, we can find no example of such a Law. Indeed, everything tells us that, on the contrary, he's only familiar with having authority over inferior Beings, and also, that this word authority necessarily carries with it the idea of superiority.

Without taking long to examine over which Beings man's rights originally extended, it's enough to recognize it couldn't be over his fellow men. If man had remained in his first estate, we can be sure that he'd never have reigned over men, and political Society wouldn't have existed, because there wouldn't have been any physical connections or intellectual

---

[50] *Conventionnel*, the word used here by Saint-Martin, can indeed translate as 'conventional'. Nowadays the word is normally used to convey 'traditional' Here, Saint-Martin is contrasting the power exercised by humans in a political society, with that found innately in man because of his intellectual abilities. Therefore, the word has been translated as 'established' or occasionally 'man-made', and this will be used to indicate authority which comes from man, in contrast to the innate power which he received from a Superior Cause.

deprivation, and his sole purpose would have been to fully exercise his abilities, and not like today, where he must laboriously work on his rehabilitation.

When man found himself stripped of this splendor, and condemned to the unfortunate condition to which he is presently reduced, his first rights weren't abolished: they were only suspended, and he still has the power to work and succeed in restoring them to their original value through his own efforts.

So, even today man might govern as at his origin, without having his fellow men as subjects. But man can only recover and enjoy this empire of which we speak, by means of the same abilities which made him its master in former times, and it's only by carrying his former Scepter[51] that he will succeed in assuming once more and forever the title of King. This was his primitive estate, and it's the one he can still claim because of the invariable essence of his nature. Such is his former authority in which, we repeat, the rights of one man over another were unknown, because it's not possible for them to exist between equal Beings in their state of glory and perfection.

Man's New Empire

Now, in the estate of atonement which man suffers today, not only is he within reach of recovering the former powers which all men would have enjoyed without being given their own species to rule; but he can also acquire another right which he know nothing about in his first estate. That's the right of exercising true authority over other men. And this is where this power has come from.

In this estate of reprobation in which man is condemned to crawl, and where he can only perceive the veil and shadow of the true light, he preserves to some extent the memory of his former glory. He nourishes to some extent a desire to return there, all because of the free use of his intellectual abilities as a result of the tasks prepared for him by Justice, and the function he must perform in the *Work*.

Some remain in a state of subjugation, and succumb to the innumerable pitfalls in this elemental cesspool; while others have the courage and the good fortune to avoid them.

---

[51] As we saw in Chapter 1, this 'scepter' is in fact the spear of four metals, the visible symbol of primitive man's authority.

It should therefore be said that the man who best preserves himself from them will have the least distorted idea of his Principle, and will be closest to his first estate. Now, if other men haven't made the same effort, they won't have the same success or the same talents, so it's clear that the man who has all these advantages over them must be their superior, and govern them.

Sovereign Power

Firstly, he'll be superior to them for this very reason, because there will be a real difference between him and them based on the clear superiority of his abilities and powers. Moreover, he'll be superior out of necessity: because other men worked less hard and therefore didn't obtain skills to the same level, given the poverty and obscurity of their own abilities they'll have real need him.

If the latter is a man in whom this darkness goes as far as *corruption*, the man who is safe from both will become his master, not only out of fact and need, but also out of duty. He must make himself his master and leave him no freedom of action, as much to satisfy the Laws of his Principle as for Society's security and example, and he must exercise all the rights of slavery and servitude over him: rights as just and real in this case as inexplicable and void in all other circumstances.

Now this is the true origin of man's temporal sovereignty over his fellow men, just as the bonds of his physical nature were society's origin.

This sovereignty, however, far from contradicting and hindering natural society, should be seen as being its strongest support, and the surest means by which it can sustain itself, either against the crimes of its members or against the attacks of all its *enemies*.

He who finds himself so vested with authority, since he can only be truly fortunate when he is exercising the *virtues* granted to him, finds it's therefore in his own interest to ensure the happiness of his subjects. And we shouldn't believe this occupation would be pointless and without value; for this man could only be such if he had within him every means to act with certainty, and whose actions would give him clear results.

The Dignity of Kings

Indeed, the light which enlightened man in his first estate, being an inextinguishable source of abilities and *virtues*, the more he can come closer to it, the more he should extend his sovereignty over men who distance themselves from it; and the more he should know how to maintain order among them and assure the Nation's stability.

With the aid of this light, he must be able to embrace and manage all parts of Government successfully, clearly understand the true Principles of the Laws and Justice, the rules of military discipline, his rights and those of the individual, as well as the multitude of resources which comprise the bodies of the Administration.

He must also be able to set his sights and extend his authority over those parts of the Administration which aren't currently the main objects of most Governments, but which, in those we are considering should be their strongest link: namely Religion and healing the sick. Finally, even in the arts, whether for pleasure or profit, he should direct their path and indicate good taste. The torch he is fortunate enough to hold in his hand, spreading universal light, should enlighten him about all these things and help him see their connection.

This image, fanciful as it may appear, nevertheless contains nothing which doesn't agree with the notion we have of Kings, when we care to think deeply about it.

Reflecting on the respect which we have for them, can't we see that we regard them as needing to be the image and representatives of a Superior Hand, and therefore capable of more *virtue*, strength, light and wisdom than other men? Isn't it with a kind of regret that we see them exposed to the weaknesses of humanity? And don't we seem to wish they were only ever made themselves known by grand and sublime acts, like the Hand which is supposed to have placed them all on the Throne?

Isn't it by that sacred authority that they present themselves and claim all their rights? Although we can't be certain they act by this right, isn't it our sense of this possibility that gives rise to the kind of terror which comes from their power and the veneration which they inspire in us?

All of this shows us that their first origin is superior to the powers and will of men, and should confirm the notion I've outlined that their source is superior to that which the Politicians have sought for them.

The Knowledge of Kings

Regarding these abilities and the countless *virtues* which we've shown to be necessary in Kings who've rediscovered their former light, these abilities and *virtues* are also demonstrates by the Leaders of man-made Societies, because they act as if they possess everything we feel should be in them.

Isn't their name the seal of all the powers they pour out into their Empire? Don't the Generals, Magistrates, Princes, and all the Orders of State take their authority from them, and when that same authority is transmitted from hand to hand down to the lowest branches of the social tree, isn't it always by virtue of the first emanation? Isn't their seal always needed to accomplish useful things, and sometimes to accomplish things which are simply pleasant?

In all these cases, the Sovereigns themselves give us a clear sign that they are like the center and the source from which all privilege and power communicated by them must come? The very act of this communication and the formalities which accompany it, always show that they are or that they can be directed in their choices by a sure light, and that they are enlightened about the abilities of those subjects to whom they entrust a part of their rights. And even these precautions they take, as well as the decisions which result, not only assume their personal capability, but are like so much evidence of it.

Now, all the information which the Sovereigns obtain from the various cases which come before them, and the approval they bring to the wisdom and decisions of their various Tribunals, shouldn't be seen as the result of their ignorance on the different matters submitted to their Legislation. It's certainly not because they can't know everything themselves: on the contrary, it was them who created these jurisdictions in the first place. The reason is because, in performing the functions of a true and infinite Being in the temporal, like Him they are responsible for all-encompassing and infinite action and, like Him, have the absolute requirement to only perform limited and specific actions through their attributes and by means of the agents of their abilities.

The Legitimacy of Sovereigns

If we went into detail about all the resources which act and support Political Governments, we apply the same comments to the abilities of the Leaders who govern them; the exercise of Justice, both Civil and Criminal, while carried out by hands other than theirs, yet always under their authority, would clearly show that they could have the means to find out the rights and the faults of their Subjects, and determine with certainty the extent and support of the former, and at the same time atonement for the latter. The care they take to watch over the preservation of the Governmental Laws, moral purity, support for the dogmas and practices of Religion, perfection of the Arts and Sciences, all of this surely reminds us that there must be within them a bright light which is shed over everything, and knows everything as a result.

We aren't straying from the Truth when we attribute to the man reinvested in all the privileges of his first estate those advantages which Kings so clearly show us, and we can say with good reason that they teach us what man could and should be, even in the impure Realm he inhabits today.

However, I'm not ignoring the many objections which this point of view concerning Kings – and Leaders of Society in general – must give rise to. Accustomed as men are to explaining things through themselves and not by means of their Principles, it must be new for them to see a source for all their rights and powers which isn't theirs, but which nevertheless is so similar to them.

Legitimate Governments

Being uninstructed in these Principles, they'll begin by asking me what proof Nations could have of their Leaders' legitimacy, and how they can judge if those who occupy those position abuse them.

I don't feel I'm going too far by saying that the proof of this will be evident, both for the Leaders, and for those Subjects who know how to make fair and beneficial use of their intellectual abilities; and on this subject, I'll return to what I previously said about the proof of a real Religion. The same reply can serve against the present objection, because Sacred and Political Institutions should have the same objective, the same guide and the same Law. Additionally, they should always be in the same hands, and when they're separated, they both lose sight of their true spirit, which consists of perfect understanding and union.[52]

The second question they could ask me is to know whether, in accepting the possibility of a Government such as the one I've just described, examples of it might be found on Earth.

No doubt I wouldn't be believed if I tried to convince you that all man-made Governments conform to the model we've just seen, because in reality most of them are very far from it. But I ask my fellow men to believe that true Sovereigns, as well as legitimate Governments, are not imaginary Beings, and that they have existed throughout time, that some exist now, and that there'll always be some, because that enters into the universal Order, because ultimately, it's a part of the *Great Work* which is however different to the Philosopher's Stone.

A third difficulty which presents itself naturally according to the Principles which have been established, is to conclude that every man, because of his nature, can hope to rediscover the light he has lost, and yet I recognize Sovereigns among men; but, if every man reaches the end of his rehabilitation, who, then will be the Leaders? Won't all men be equal? Won't all of them be Kings?

This problem can be discounted following what I've said about the obstacles which stop almost all men on their journey, and which, multiplied still further by carelessness and the misuse of the will, are but rarely and unequally overcome.

The Military Institution

You might even remember what I said about the natural differences in men's intellectual abilities, where we commented that in only comparing

---

[52] Although it may seem strange to Americans, given the First Amendment in the Bill of Rights to maintain a separation between Church and State, which was adopted in 1791, only 16 years after the publication of this book, to read Saint-Martin's strong support of such a union, even going so far as suggesting that both should be in the same hands, it should be remembered that this separation didn't – and in many cases still doesn't – exist in many European countries. For example, in Great Britain the Church of England is the State Religion, though not financially supported by the Government (unlike Germany, Austria, Denmark, Finland, Sweden, Italy, Iceland and some other countries where there is a religious tax on income for practitioners of certain denominations. The tax in Germany is 8 – 9% of income); and even now the Upper House of the English Parliament is a mix of Lords Temporal & Spiritual (albeit with somewhat reduced powers), the Lords Spiritual exercising the right to sit in Parliament attached to certain Bishoprics.

them from this point of view, while there would always be an inequality between them, but an inequality which didn't bother them and didn't humiliate them, because their greatness would be real in each of them, and not relative, like greatness which is only man-made and arbitrary.

This is what we find to some extent in the laws of the Military Institution, which of all man's works paints the most faithful image of his original estate, and which because of this, is the noblest of all his Establishments, albeit with a basis no more real or solid than his other works, so that it can only occupy the first rank in the order of precedence in the eyes of an intelligent man. But I repeat, it's so noble and encourages so many virtues, that one can almost forget it's not actually based on a true foundation.

Thus, regarding this Institution as the one which best applies to man's Principle, we will notice that all the members which compose a Military Corps are all expected to be invested and endowed with the specific abilities proper to their rank. Each is expected to have achieved and fulfilled the purpose assigned to his within his class.

However, although these members are all unequal, there is no distortion in their union, nor humiliation for the individuals, because each person's duty is fixed, and from that it's not shameful to be inferior to other members of the same Corps, but only if he's unworthy of his rank.

At the same time, these Military Corps, being composed of unequal members, couldn't survive for a moment without a Leader, since there will always be one member who is superior to the others.

If these Corps were not the work of man, the differences between and the superiority of their members would be fixed, and it would be the true quality and value of the person which served as the Law. But, when the Legislator is not led by his true light, yet must always act, he makes up for it by establishing a value and merit system which is easier to understand, and which only needs the eyes to be determined. This is age, which, after differences in rank, establishes rights in the Military Corps; and where there are two soldiers in a Post, the Law requires that the elder commands the other.[53]

---

[53] This is an interesting insight into Eighteenth Century French military etiquette, in that, for those of a given rank, it appears seniority was determined by age rather than by length of service or ability. It must be remembered that Saint-Martin's chosen profession was as a commissioned officer in the Regiment of Foix, and given the peaceable times, he had much time to contemplate how the military functioned.

The Inequality of Men

Isn't this law, artificial though it may be, an indication of the correctness of the Principle I've described, and assuming all men to be in possession of their prerogatives, since there could never be complete equality between them, surely one couldn't believe they'd all be Kings?

Nevertheless, it'd be completely absurd to take this comparison to the letter. As the Military Corps is only the work of man, it can only have man-made differences, and the superior and inferior in rank are by their nature of the same species, so despite these clear distinctions they all generally resemble each other, since they are all men in privation.

But in the natural Order of things, if all men reached the final degree of their power, they'd all be Kings. Now, just as Kings on Earth don't recognize other Kings to be their Masters, and therefore aren't subject to one another; so, in this instance, if all men were completely rehabilitated into their rights, none of them could be Subjects, and they'd all be Sovereigns in their Empire.

Yet I repeat, this isn't the current state of affairs, and men don't all reach this degree of greatness and perfection and become independent from one another. And so, since this state of reprobation continues, if they've always had Leaders selected from among them, we must assume that it'll always be so, and that this is essential until the period of punishment has ended.

It's therefore with confidence that I've established the origin of the authority of a man restored to his Principle over his fellow men, his power, and all the rights of Political Sovereignty.

I'd even go so far as to say that this is the only way of explaining all the rights, and reconcile the multitude of different theories Politicians have put forward on this subject; because, in order to recognize superiority in a Being who is over Beings of the same class, one shouldn't consider what he has in common with them, but rather what distinguishes him from them.

Now, since because of their current nature all men are condemned to privation, they resemble one another completely, with a few minor differences; and it's only by striving to make this privation disappear that they can hope to establish true differences between one another.

The Light of Governments

I also believe I can't offer my Readers a more satisfying image than that of the Society we've previously seen based on man's physical needs, and on the desire he has to be able to understand; and to give him the kind of Leader I've just described, which completes and confirms the natural notion we all secretly carry within us of social man and the concept of Governments.

Indeed, there we'd see order and universal activity reign, which would form a texture of delights and joy for all members of the Political Bodies; and we'd see that their very physical ills would find consolation there; because, as I've shown, the light which would have guided this association would have embraced and enlightened all its parts. Then it would be that amidst perishable things, we'd be shown the greatest image and the most just idea of perfection. This would recall that happy age which has been said only to exist in the imagination of the Poets, since, being distanced from it and no longer knowing its sweetness, in our weakness we'd believe that, since it had passed for us, it must no longer exist.

At the same time, if this is the Law which must join men together and govern them, if this is the sole light which can reunite them into a body without injustice, we can be sure that if they abandon it, they can only hope for ignorance, and all the inevitable wretchedness awaiting those who wander in the darkness.

Submission to Sovereigns

Then, if in the examination that we're going to make of recognized Governments, we find defects in them, we can conclude with good reason that they only survive by removing this very light, and because those who founded the Political Bodies didn't know the Principles, or because their successors allowed their purity to be altered.

But, before undertaking this important examination, I must reassure suspicious Governments which might become alarmed by my thoughts, and fear that, by revealing their shortcomings, I might destroy the respect which is their due. Although in some parts of this subject which currently occupies me, I've already shown my veneration for the person of Sovereigns, as well as for their character, it's useful to reemphasize this protest here, the better to convince all who read this book that I express only order and peace, that

I make it the indispensable duty of all Subjects to submit to their Leaders, and that I unreservedly condemn all subordination and revolt as being diametrically contrary to the Principles I'm trying to establish.

One can't avoid adding loyalty to this authentic declaration, when we recall what I previously established about the Law which should direct man here below in all his activities. Didn't I show that the series of sufferings was a result of the misuse of his will; that the use of this will was only abused when man abandoned his guide, and as a result, if he's still equally careless today, he'd only perpetuate his crimes and increase his misfortunes in proportion?

I totally condemn rebellion, even when the injustice of the Leader and the Government are at its height, and where neither one retain any trace of the powers which established them; because, however iniquitous or revolting such an Administration might be, I've shown that it's never the Subject who establishes his political Laws and his Leaders, and therefore it's never his task to overthrow them.[54]

But we must give more sensible reasons for this. If the issue is only with the Administration, and the Leader maintains the power and incontestable rights we assume him to have, being the outcome of his work and the use he's made of them, he himself has all the abilities needed to untangle the fault of the Government and resolve the situation without the Subject having to lend a hand.

If the fault lies with both the Government and the Leader, but the Subject was able to safeguard himself by fulfilling the obligation common to all men never to stray from the invariable Law which should guide them, he'll know how to protect himself against these annoyances without having to resort to violence; or he will know how to recognize if the scourge has

---

[54] This section is interesting as a reflection of France shortly before the Revolution. It is apparent that Saint-Martin was something of a political reactionary – at least then. While nobody in 1775 could have foreseen the Revolution, which began in 1789 – and the American Revolutionary War only began in April 1775 – the French establishment must have seemed quite stable at the time. However, many scholars believe the French Revolution was strongly influenced by Freemasonry, in that most of the original Revolutionaries were Freemasons, and the motto 'Liberty, Equality, Fraternity' was indeed a common theme in the Higher Degrees of the period. His earlier comment about the Sovereign and the Court being the arbiters of good taste is particularly telling, since this was certainly the case a century earlier; but by 1752 – 1754, during the bizarre debate known as the *Querelle des Bouffons*, or 'Quarrel of the Comic Actors', where the relative merits of Italian and French Light Opera were being hotly debated in Paris, nobody looked to the Crown for arbitration, and it was the public who voiced their opinions. Indeed, by 1782, Louis-Sébastien Mercier wrote: "…the court…no longer decides on reputations of any sort." But his opinion was to undergo a sea change in the next fifteen years, as will be seen in the next footnote.

come from a Superior Hand, and then he will be careful not to complain or oppose Justice.

Finally, if the fault is in the Government, the Leader and the Subject, there would no longer be any reason to ask me what should be done; for it would no longer be a Government but a brigandage, and there are no Laws for brigands.

There wouldn't even be any point in telling men in such a disorder that the more they indulge in it, the more they'll attract suffering and affliction; that the interest of their true happiness will always forbid them from meeting injustice with injustice, and that hardship will pursue them so long as they don't try to bend their thought and their will to their natural rule. Such speeches would find no audience in this tumultuous confusion, since they are the Language of reason, and a Being given over to his own desires never reasons.

Don't bring up the objection again about the difficulty of knowing how anyone can tell if things are in order or not, and when one should act or stop. I've made it clear enough that all men were born to be certain of the legitimacy of his actions, that he has a duty to determine the morality of his conduct, and that so long as he lacks that proof, he exposes himself to the consequences if he takes a single step.

From that, you can judge whether I permit man the slightest carelessness, and with greater reason the slightest act of violence or personal authority.

I therefore believe that this statement of mine can reassure the Sovereigns as to the Principles which guide me. They'll only ever see in them an inviolable affection for their person, and only the most sublime respect for the sacred rank they occupy. They'll also see from this that if there were usurpers and tyrants among them, their Subjects would still have no legitimate pretext for supporting the slightest attack.[55]

---

[55] Saint-Martin was imprisoned for a short time during the Revolution, after being questioned both about the fact that he was an aristocrat, and the confusion which his two published books put in the minds of the Revolutionaries: for it was difficult to tell whether he was for or against unjust government, although his views appear to have changed drastically between 1775 and 1789, for in his *Lettre à un ami, ou Considérations politiques, philosophiques et religieuses sur la Révolution française*, written during the Revolution, he vindicates the Revolutionaries for having eliminated the "gangrene" of aristocrats and priests. In the same *Lettre à un ami*, he described the French Revolution as being a religious war of a kind not seen since the war of the Hebrews, which he says lasted from Moses until Emperor Titus' destruction of the Temple and Jerusalem; and if the Revolution brought destruction, it also built anew. This is a far cry from his comments of 1774 – 1775 in this book.

The Obligation of Kings

If Kings ever read this book, I don't think they could convince themselves that by this unquestioning submission to them, I'm increasing their powers in any way, and exempting them from the obligation they have as men to submit their own lives to the common rule which should guide us all.

On the contrary, it's only through the intimate knowledge they must have of this rule, and through their faithfulness in observing it that they bear the title of Kings; and giving them the right to deviate from it would be to favor deception, and insult the very name which makes us honor them.

Thus, if the Subject doesn't have the right to avenge an injustice done to him, they should know they've even less right to commit an injustice themselves; because as men, the Sovereign and the Subject both have the same Law. The political State changes nothing of their nature as thinking Beings; so it's just an additional responsibility for them both, and neither can or should do anything on their own.

I thought it appropriate to make this formal declaration before entering into an examination of Political Bodies, and I believe I can now follow my plan without fear, because however defective Governments may appear, I can no longer be suspected of working to their ruin; because on the contrary, all that I've tried to do has been to give them a sense of the only means appropriate to their happiness and their perfection.

The Instability of Governments

In the first place, what must lead us to presume that the majority of Governments indeed haven't based themselves on the Principle I've just established, which is the restoration of the Sovereigns to their primitive light, is that almost all Political Bodies which have existed have passed away.

This simple observation doesn't exactly convince us that they had a true foundation, and that the Law which had created them was the true Law; for since this Law I speak of has, by its very nature, a living and invincible power, all that was linked to it should have been indissoluble, so long as those appointed to be its minsters hadn't forsaken it.

Therefore, either the Law was misunderstood at the creation of those Governments, or it was neglected following their institution, for if this weren't the case, they would still exist.

And certainly, this in no way goes against the notion we all have within us of the stabilizing effects of such a Law. According to man's concept of Truth, what is true never passes away, and its endurance is proof of the reality of things. So, when men are used to seeing Governments as fleeting and subject to vicissitudes, it's because they've put them at the same level as all human institutions, which having only whim and unruly imagination for support, can falter at their hands and be destroyed on yet another whim.

Nevertheless, and this is an intolerable contradiction, they've demanded our respect for these types of establishment, which they themselves recognize to be decrepit.

But doesn't this show us, in fact, that in their very blindness the Principle still speaks to them; and that they sense that however defective and fragile their Social Institutions may be, they represent one which doesn't have any of these defects.

This should be enough to support my proposal regarding the fixed Law which should govern all Associations; but no doubt, despite the notion we all have of such a Law, we'll always hesitate to put our faith in it, because, having seen all the Empires fade away, it seems evident that they can't endure, and we'd find it hard to believe that there were ever any which hadn't passed away.

Stable Governments

But this is one of the truths which I can actually affirm, and I can't insist strongly enough to my Readers that there are indeed Governments which have stood firm since the time man was first on the earth, and which will exist till the end of time; and this so for the same reasons which made me say that here below there've always been and there always will be legitimate Governments.

So, I wasn't wrong when I said that, if the Political Bodies which have disappeared from the Earth had been founded on a true Principle, they would still exist; and that those which exist today will undoubtedly pass away if they aren't based on a similar Principle, and if they have strayed from it, the best means for them to endure would be to return to it.

By duration when I speak about Governments, it's clear I only mean to speak of temporal duration, since they're only established in time. But though they must end along with all things, this should still enjoy the ability to act in every way up to this end, and they can hope to do this if they know how to rely on their Principle.

I won't stop citing as proof the pride with which Governments boast of their antiquity, and the care they take to claim an even older origin. Nor will I remind you of the steps they take to preserve them and ensure their longevity, or all those establishments which they endlessly create with long-range objectives, and whose results can only be seen after centuries. We can see these as secrets indications of their conviction that they should be permanent.

So, I repeat, once we see a Nation die out, we can assume that either its birth wasn't legitimate, or that the Sovereigns who successively governed it didn't all seek to be guided by the light of that natural torch which we've reminded them should be both their guide and that of all mankind.

For the opposite reason, we wouldn't be able to judge current Governments if we only had this one reason to evaluate them because, so long as we see them survive, we must presume they conform to the Principle which should constitute them all, and it would only be in their destruction that we'd learn if they'd been defective.

But there are other angles from which we still need to consider them, which can help us learn about their faults and irregularities.

The Difference Between Governments

The second fault we can't hide from ourselves regarding accepted Governments is that they differ from one another. Now, if they had bene formed by a true Principle, as this Principle is unique and always the same, it would manifest in the same manner everywhere, and all the Governments it produced would be similar. So, once we see any disparity between them, we can no longer accept they have the same Principle, and almost certainly there must be some among them which were established illegally.

I will not labor these local differences, which having come about by circumstance and the continuous course of things, must make themselves felt daily in the Administration. As the course of this Administration should itself be governed by the universal constitutive Principle, far from the differences it permits depending on time and place altering this Principle, these differences will instead show us its wisdom and fruitfulness.

At this time, I must therefore only consider the basic differences arising from the Nation's constitution.

One of these are the different forms of Government, of which I will only consider the two principle ones, since the others adhere to one of these forms to a greater or lesser extent. These are: when the supreme power is in the hands of an individual; and when it's in several hands at the same time.

If we assume that only one of these two types of Government conforms to the Principle, then we may assume that the other is opposed to it, for since the two are so different, they can't reasonably have the same basis or the same origin.

Consequently, I can't accept the generally accepted opinion which determines the form of Government depending on its location, its extent and other considerations of this kind, by which we are told one may determine the most suitable type of Legislation for each Nation or each Country.

According to this rule, we would have to find the reason for constituting a Nation in local, secondary Causes, and this is totally against everything I've already said about this constituting Cause or Principle. For, being a Principle, it must rule everywhere and direct everything. Being bright, it's true it can adapt to the circumstances I've just quoted, but it must never bend under them to the extent of denaturing itself and producing contradictory effects. In other words, that would be to repeat the error we saw when talking about Religion: that we would be seeking the source of a Principle in the action and Laws of physical things, whereas it's these very things which distance it and distort it. And so, I persist in saying that of the two forms of Government I've just discussed, there must necessarily be one which is at fault.

Government by a Single Person

If you were to press me to decide which one should be preferred, although my approach is to establish Principles rather than give an opinion, I can't avoid acknowledging that Government by a single person is definitely the most natural, the simplest and the most similar to the true Laws I put forward earlier as being essential to man.

It's indeed from himself and from the light which accompanies him, that man should draw his counsel and all his illumination. If this man is King, his duties as a man do no change, but only become broader. Thus, in this elevated rank, still having the same work to do, he also has the same help to hope for.

It's not, therefore, from among other members of his Nation that he should seek his guides, and if he is a man, he should know how to be self-sufficient. All the people who will necessarily be employed in the Administration, although being the image of the Leader, each in their class, their purpose is only to assist him and never to instruct or enlighten him, since we've recognized in him the source of the immense powers which spread across his entire Empire.

Thus, if we can see that a man might unite these privileges within himself, there'd be no point in having several men at the head of a Government, since one alone can do the same thing as all the others.

So, despite the few advantages we might expect to find in Government by several people, I can't regard this form as the most perfect, because this would have the defect of superfluity, and in the notion of true Government we have within us, there should be no defects.

However, even though I give preference to Government by a single person, this is not to say I'm totally convinced all of these are proper, according to the regularity of the Principle. For ultimately, even among Governments of a single person, there are still many differences.

In some, the Leader has almost no authority; in others he has absolute authority; in yet others, he balances dependency and despotism. Nothing is fixed, nothing is stable in this kind of Government. It's because of this that it's unlikely we'll find our invariable Law leading all the Governments where power resides with a single person, and so we should not accept all of them.

The Rivalry of Governments

But the third, and at the same time the most powerful reason which should keep us guessing about the legitimacy of all Social Institutions on Earth, whether they only have one Leader or several, is that they are inevitably enemies of one another. Now, clearly this hostility couldn't take place if the same Principle presided over all these Associations and constantly directed their path. For the object of this Principle is order, both general and individual, so all the Establishments over which it presided would undoubtedly have the same goal; and far from this aim being to invade each other, on the contrary it'd be to mutually support one another again that natural and common vice which ceaselessly prepares their destruction.

Thus, when I see them both using their powers against one another, and straying too far from their purpose, I must then assume that among these Governments there may be some which are irregular and defective.

The Right of War

Politicians, I know, use all their efforts to excuse this distortion. They consider Social Instruction to be formed according to the works of Nature. Then, forgetting that especially in their hands, the copy can never equal the model, they carry over and attribute to these artificial bodies the same life, abilities and powers as those by which the physical Beings of Nature are invested, and in consequence they then bestow on them the same activity, power, right of self-preservation, and therefore the right to rebuff attacks and fight their enemies.

This is how they justify war between Nations, and the large number of Laws established for both the internal and external security of Nations.

But even the Legislators themselves can't hide the weakness and imperfection of the Laws they employ to maintain these rights and to preserve the Political Bodies. They clearly see that if the active Principle which they claim to be in their work were truly living, it would animate without violence and preserve without destroying, like the active Principle of natural bodies.

The True Enemies of Man

So, when the exact opposite occurs, when any Laws of Governments have only the power to destroy, and don't create anything, the Leader no longer finds any real power in the instrument he's using, and he can't deny to himself that the Principle which led him to create his Law deceived him.

Then I ask what this error could be, if it isn't that of being mistaken about the type of combat in which he had to engage; of having been weak enough to believe that his enemies were men, and formed the Political Bodies; and it was therefore against these Bodies that he should turn all his powers and all his vigilance. Now, since this notion is one of the deadliest consequences of the darkness in which man is plunged, it isn't surprising that the rights it caused to be founded are also false, since they can't produce anything.

You shouldn't be at all surprised to see me say that man can't have men as his true enemies; and that because of the Law of his nature, he really has nothing to fear from them; because in fact, since we've recognized they couldn't become each other's superior by themselves, and they're all in the same state of weakness and privation, we can be sure that in this state they have no real advantage over their fellow men; and if they were to try to make use of any physical advantages they might have against one another, such as skill, agility or strength, the one being attacked would no doubt succeed in protecting himself by allowing himself to be guided by the first and universal Law, which I've constantly presented in this book, as being the indispensable guide of man.

If, on the contrary, it was by virtue of the abilities of this same Law and through the power of the Principle which ordered it that there truly were Superior men; since anyone who had these powers would only use them for his own good and for his true happiness, it's clear that man would have nothing to fear from them, and that he'd be wrong to regard them as his enemies.

The Three Defects of Government

So, it's because of weakness and ignorance that man is scared of his fellow men. It's because he has poorly understood the purpose of his origin, and the reason for his being placed on Earth. And if, as we have observed, we can find jealousy and voracious hostility between different Governments, we should realize that this error has no other source or other Principle but this, and as a result, the light which governed their association doesn't deserve our confidence, as it should if it had been as pure as it ought to have been.

Independently of the defects in the Administration which we will consider next, here we'll observe three basic issues, namely instability, disparity and hatred, which we see clearly enough among accepted

Governments, when considered in themselves and in their respective relationships. On that point alone I'd be right to assure you that these associations are formed by man's hand, and without the aid of the superior Law which should give them their approval; and as this approval has been neglected, any Government which can be sustained by it alone, must have degenerated from their original state.

But as I've said that I won't judge any of them, I won't give an opinion here either, especially since each of these Governments could raise objections to defend themselves from blame. If those which died out were false, those which survived may not be. If among these I've noted almost universal differences, from which I concluded that there clearly had to be some bad ones, I've only spoken against Government by many people, and even then, only in general terms; so Government by a single person wasn't included in this judgement.

The Administration

Finally, if I find a marked hatred even among Governments by a single person, or to speak more decently, a general rivalry, each of them could argue that he was the depository of these true rights which should preside over all Societies, and it was then his duty be on guard against other Nations.

It's all of these reasons together which still stop me from giving my opinion about any of these current Political Bodies; but as it's also my intention to place them all in a position to be able to judge themselves, I'll offer them some other observations which will help them to direct their judgements regarding what they are, and what they should be.

I am now going to focus on their Administration, because for a Government to conform to the true Principle, its Administration must conduct itself by Laws which are sure and dictated by true Justice. If on the contrary, they are found to be unjust and false, it will be for the Governments which make use of them to draw their own conclusions on the legitimacy of the Principle and the motivation to which they owe their origin.

The Public Right

The Administration of Political Bodies has two main things to moderate: firstly, the rights of the Nation and each of its members, which is the purpose of Public Law and Civil Justice; and secondly to watch over the security of Society both general and specific, which is the object of War, the Police and Criminal Justice. Each of these branches has Laws to govern them, and to be certain of their fairness we've only to examine whether these Laws emanate directly from the true Principle, or if they are established by man alone and deprived of his guide. Let's begin with Public Law.

I'll only examine one part of it, as that will suffice to indicate the darkness in which this part of the Administration is still plunged, and that is the exchanges which Sovereigns often make between themselves of parts of their Nations, according to their convenience.

Exchanges and Usurpations

Indeed, I ask whether, after a Subject has taken or is deemed to have taken an oath of fidelity to a Sovereign, whether the Sovereign has the right to release him from it, even despite all the advantages which may result from this for the State. The custom by which Sovereigns don't take oaths from the Inhabitants of regions they've exchanged suggests that the former oath hasn't been freed, and that a new one couldn't therefore be taken. Now, can this conduct ever be consistent with the notions which the Legislators themselves want to give us of a legitimate Government?

In the kind of Government which I claimed demonstrated Truth and an indestructible Existence, these exchanges are also the custom, and those who practice this custom among accepted Governments are but their image, since man can invent nothing. However, in this case the formalities are different and dictated by motives which make all the actions just; that is, the exchange is free and voluntary on both sides, and men are not seen as being attached to the soil, and part of the region. In other words, their nature is not confused with that of temporal possessions.

I daren't speak here of those infamous usurpations where various Governments claim to acquire a right of ownership over peaceful and unknown Nations, or even over defenseless neighboring Countries, simply by exhibiting to them their strength and greed. It's true that everything happens by reaction in the Universe, so that Justice has often armed a Nation in order to punish a criminal Nation, but in serving as Ministers of its vengeance against one another, they have only increased their own crimes and their own stain, and those terrible invasions of which we have so many horrible examples, have perhaps been less fatal to those who have been its victims than to those who have engaged in them. Now let's study Civil Law.

Civil Law

I assume that all property rights have been established, I assume that the division of the Earth was made lawfully between men, as happened at the beginning, by methods which ignorance would regard as imaginary today. Then, when greed, dishonesty, even uncertainty cause disputes, who can resolve them? Who can insure rights threatened by injustice, and restore those which have expired? Who can follow lines of inheritance and changes from the first sharing out up to the moment of the dispute? And yet how can so many difficulties be resolved without having clear knowledge of the legitimacy of these rights, and without the power to be able to identify the true owner with confidence? How can anyone judge without having this certainty, and how can anyone dare to decide without being sure that the decision doesn't reward a usurper?

On Prescription

Now, nobody will dare to deny that this uncertainty seems to be universal, from which we will boldly conclude that Civil Justice is often imprudent in its decisions.

Yet this is where it's even more culpable, and where it reveals its audacity. This is when, suffering complete confusion while trying to determine the source of various rights and properties, it determines a limit to its investigation by assigning a time period after which all unencumbered possession becomes legitimate, which is called *Prescription*: for I ask in the case where the possession is wrongly acquired, if there is a period of time which can erase an injustice.[56]

---

[56] 'Prescription' is the legal recourse where a person enjoying a certain right over someone else's property, such as driving across a corner of their land for a period of time – usually 10 or 20 years –

It's evident that Civil Law is acting by itself here, and it's clear that it's creating Justice when it should be carrying Justice out, and therefore repeats the widespread error where man always confuses things with their Principle.

Perhaps it would suffice to limit myself to that one example of Civil Justice, although it could offer me many others which would also provide witness against it, such as the variety and contradictions to which it's exposed at every step, which oblige it to issue retractions on so many occasions.

Adultery

I'll only add that there is a circumstance where Civil Law totally reveals its carelessness and blindness, and where the Principle of Justice which should always direct its steps is far more grievously compromised than when it delivers random judgements on simple possessions. This is when it passes a verdict on separating people joined by marriage for reasons other than adultery. Indeed, adultery is the only grounds on which it can legitimately disunite spouses, since this is the only infraction which directly harms the union, and it can only be broken by that, since it was founded on an undivided union. Thus, when Civil Law allows itself to be guided by other considerations, it shows without a shadow of a doubt that it hasn't the first idea of such a commitment.

I can't therefore excuse myself from admitting how much the process of Civil Law is defective, both in its regard for the person of Society's members, and in its regard for all their property rights; which totally prevents me from seeing this Law as conforming to the Principle which should have directed the association, and forces me to recognize the hands of man in this, instead of that superior and enlightened hand which should do everything in his place.

I will stop here regarding the first part of the Administration of Political Bodies, but before moving on to the second part, I believe it's appropriate

---

can claim the right to continue, even if the true owner then tries to stop them. That is called an 'easement' rather than outright 'ownership'. However, in this case Saint-Martin is talking about the more rigorous version, for example practiced in Scotland, where uninterrupted and unchallenged use of land over a period of 10 years allows the user to claim good title to the land. A similar law was in force in France at that time. While this was meant to tidy up the legal books by reassigning unclaimed land, the time period is certainly short enough for injustices to occur.

to say a few words about *adultery*, which we've said is the only legitimate reason to dissolve a marriage.

Adultery is the crime of the first man, though before he committed it there were no women. Since there are now women, the danger which led him to his first crime still exists, and moreover men are exposed to adultery of the flesh. This means that this latter adultery can't happen unless preceded by the former.

What I'm saying will become clearer if you consider that the first adultery was only committed because man strayed from the Law which had been set down for him, and followed one which was quite the opposite. Now, physical adultery absolutely repeats the same thing, since marriage, being directed by a pure Law, can no more be the work of man than his other actions; because this man, who shouldn't have formed his bond himself, doesn't have the right within him to break it, because to deliver himself over to adultery is to revoke by his own authority the will of the universal temporal Cause, which should have concluded the commitment, and to listen instead to one it had not approved of. Thus, since man's will always precedes his actions, he can't forget himself in his physical acts without having previously forgotten himself in his will, so that in giving himself over to adultery of the flesh now, instead of committing one crime, he commits two.

If he who reads this is intelligent, he may well unravel in the adultery of the flesh some clearer clues concerning the adultery committed by man before he was subjected to the Law of the Elements. But as much as I would like him to succeed, my obligations forbid me from providing the least clarification on this point; and besides for my own well-being, I would sooner blush over this crime of man than talk about it.

All I've to say is that if there are a few men to whom adultery seems unimportant, it's surely those blind enough to be Materialists. For indeed, if man only had senses, adultery would have no meaning for him, since the Law of the senses isn't fixed but relative, so everything should be the same to them. But, as he has another ability which can measure even the actions of his senses, an ability which makes itself known even through the choice and refinement with which he seasons his corrupt pleasures, we can see if man may in good faith persuade himself of the unimportance of such acts.

So, far from adopting this depraved opinion, I will use all my efforts to fight against it. I'll declare out loud that the first adultery was the cause of the privation and ignorance in which man is still engulfed, and that this is what changed his state of light and splendor into a state of darkness and shame.

The second adultery, besides making the first Judgement harsher, exposes man temporally to inexpressible disorders, cruel suffering, and misfortunes whose principle source he often doesn't know, and which he's a long way from suspecting to be so close to him; which however doesn't prevent the fact that that they could have a multitude of other Causes.

It's also in this physical adultery that man can easily form an idea of the ills which he is preparing as the fruits of his crime by reflecting that this universal temporal Cause, or this superior will doesn't preside over unions of which it hasn't approved, nor with even greater reason over those it condemns. So given that its presence is necessary to everything which exists in the temporal, be it physical or intellectual, man deprives his posterity of this support when he engenders them by means of an illegitimate will; and in consequence he exposes his illegitimate offspring to unprecedented suffering, and to the terrible decay of all the abilities of his Being.

Types of Irregular Men

But it would be in the various original adulteries that keen men of Science would find an explanation for all the degenerate tribes, all the Nations of which our species is so bizarrely comprised, and all those monstrous and oddly-colored peoples by which the Earth is covered, and for whom the Observers seek in vain a class in the orders of the regular Works of Nature.

Don't object by quoting those arbitrary beautiful things, made beautiful as a result of familiarity, which are acknowledged in various countries. They're only judged by the senses, and the senses can become accustomed to anything. For the human species, there is most certainly a fixed regularity which is independent of human opinion and the arbitrary whims of Nations, because man's body was constituted by *number*. There is also a Law for his color, and this is quite clearly indicated to us by the arrangement and order of the Elements in the composition of all bodies, where one always sees salt on the surface. It's for this reason that differences in climate and lifestyle often act both on the body's form and color without destroying the Principle which has just been established; for the regularity of men's stature doesn't consist of equality of height, but in the correct proportion of all their parts.

Similarly, although there are nuances in their true color, there is a degree beyond which they can never pass, because the Elements can't change place without an action contrary to what is natural to them.

Modesty

So, let's confidently attribute all these physical signs to the dissoluteness of the Nations' ancestors, which are a striking indication of an original stain. Let's attribute to the same source that degradation into which entire Nations have plunged so completely that they've lost all sense of modesty and shame, so that not only don't they forbid adultery, but they're also not shocked by nudity, so that for some of them the act of physical generation has become a public and religious ceremony. Those who judged from these observations that the sense of modesty isn't natural to mankind haven't paid attention to the fact that they obtained their examples from among degenerate Peoples. They haven't seen that those who demonstrate the least distaste and delicacy are also those most given over to a life of sensuality, and so little advanced in possession and use of their intellectual abilities, that they are almost no different from animals except for having some vestiges of Laws which have been transmitted to them, and which they preserve through habit and imitation.

When the Observers tried, on the contrary, to take their examples from among civilized Societies, where respect for marriage and for modesty are almost always just the result of education, they are again incorrect in their assessment, because these Societies don't educate men about the rights of his true nature, but replacing them with artificial instructions and sentiments which time, place, and lifestyle erase. Then, by removing the outward appearance of accepted decency, or an indifferent attachment to the principles of primary education from these refined Societies, perhaps we wouldn't actually find any more modesty than among the coarsest Nations. But that doesn't prove anything against the true Law of man, because in both these examples, the Peoples in question are similarly distanced from it, some by a defect in their culture and the rest by depravity, so that neither of them are in their natural state.

The Two Natural Laws

To resolve the difficulty, they should have gone back to man's natural state; and then they'd have seen that the physical form was the most disproportionate Being to intellectual man, so it offered him the most humiliating spectacle; and that if he know the Principle of that form, he couldn't even think about it without being ashamed, though since each part of that body had a different purpose and use, they couldn't all inspire the same level of horror in him. They'd have indeed seen that this man would have shuddered at the very idea of adultery, since would have made him remember the hideous and distressing memory of that first adultery from which all his misfortunes arose. But how could the Observers have considered man in his Principle? They don't know that he has one, so what confidence could we have in their theories?

So, let's never forget that all the deformities and all the vices which the various Nations exhibit, either in their bodies or in their thinking Being, derive from the fact that their ancestors didn't follow their natural Law, or because they strayed from it; and that the Materialists don't believe me when I say I now agree with them when they hear me speaking of a natural Law for man. Like them I say he follows his natural Law, but we differ in that they require him to follow the natural Law of the animal, and I require him to follow that Law which distinguishes him from them, that is, the one which lights and assures all his steps; in a word, the one which holds the very flame of Truth.

Two Adulteries

Let's not forget, I repeat, that man's second crime, or physical adultery, only took its source from the first adultery or that of the will, by which man followed a corrupt Law in his work, instead of the pure Law which had been given to him. For, if man can now commit adultery with a woman, he can also, as in the beginning, commit adultery without a woman, that is, perform intellectual adultery; because after the first temporal Cause, nothing in time is more powerful than man's will, and because it has powers, even though it's impure and criminal, like the Principle which became Evil.

Let's examine next whether man, on discovering that he was the author of all the disorders which we have just established, should ever be happy and at peace, and whether he could conceal from himself that he owes even more tribute to Justice than his unfortunate descendants.

Those who thought they could correct all these ills by rendering the results of their crimes null and void can never claim in good faith to have this depraved opinion accepted, and they can't doubt, on the contrary, that this would only turn the full force of the scourge against them alone, whereas their posterity would have shared it with them. Moreover, it would give this same scourge an extension without measure, since by joining this criminal act to his physical and intellectual adultery, there is not one of the Laws which compose man's essence which has not been violated.

I can't expand on this subject further without committing an indiscretion: profound Truths are not appropriate for all eyes. But, although I haven't explained the original reason for all the Laws of Wisdom, they are no less obliged to observe them, because they are physical, and man can understand everything which is physical. Moreover, although it's also understood among them that the act of generation is a mystery, it's no less true that in man it has a Law and an order unknown to the animal, and that the rights which are attached to it are the most beautiful witness to his greatness, as well as being the source of his condemnation and his distress.

Criminal Administration

I leave our Readers to meditate on this point, and pass on to the second part of Social Administration, namely that which looks after the Nation's external and internal security.

We've seen that this second part having two objectives, also has two kinds of Laws to direct it. The first is responsible for keeping an eye on the outside, creating the Laws of warfare and the political rights of Nations. But as I've shown that the manner of being of the Nations and the tradition they have of considering each other as enemies to be false, I can't have much confidence in the Laws they've made on these subjects.

You'll find it easy to agree with me if you examine those constant uncertainties in which we see the Politicians get it wrong when they try to find a basis for their Establishments among human things. As the only establishing principles for Governments they know of are strength or tradition; as they make a point of dispensing with their one true support; as they want to open up their understanding, yet persist in not wanting to use the only key with which they could do this; their investigations remain completely fruitless. This is the reason I won't go further than what I've already said on this subject.

The Right to Punish

It's therefore only on the second type of Laws, or those which are concerned with the internal security of the State, to which I'll direct my observations; that is, on that part of the Administration concerned with the Police and with Criminal Laws. I'll even combine these two branches under one point of view, because, despite the difference in the subjects they cover, they each has the objective of maintaining order, and the redress of offences; which gives both the same origin, and makes them both derive from the right to punish.

But, in the examination I'm going to make, my intention will always be the same as in the entire course of this book, and I'll continue to seek in everything whether things conform or not to their Principle, so that everyone may draw his own conclusions, and be instructed by himself rather than by my own judgements.

Therefore, I'll now examine in whose hands the right to punish should principally reside, then how he who is vested in that right should legitimately proceed; for without these clarifications it would be very foolhardy to take up the sword, since it could fall as often on the innocent as on the guilty, and although nobody should have to fear this injustice, and even if it were possible to ensure that punishment only ever fell upon criminals, it still remains uncertain whether the person who issues the punishment has the right to do so.

If there is a superior Principle, unique and universally Good, as all my efforts have up to now have attempted to establish; and if there is an Evil Principle whose existence I've also demonstrated which constantly works to oppose the action of this Good Principle, it's inevitable that in this intellectual class there would be crimes.

However, as Justice is one of the essential attributes of this Good Principle, crimes can't bear its presence for a moment, and its punishment is as quick as it's unavoidable. It's this which proves the absolute necessity to punish in this Good Principle.

Man, in his primitive origin, experienced this Truth physically, and was solemnly invested with this right to punish; that is what made him resemble his Principle; and it's also by virtue of this resemblance that his Justice was exact and certain; that his rights were real, enlightened, and would never have changed had he wanted to keep them. This was then, as I said, that he truly had the right of life and death over the evil-doers of his Empire.

But let's remember clearly that it was not over his fellow man that he had to exercise this power, because, in the Region he then inhabited, there couldn't be any Subjects among fellow Beings.

The Right of Life and Death

When, in falling from this glorious estate, he fell into Nature, from which the state of Society came about, and soon that of corruption, he found himself in a new order of things where he had to fear and punish new crimes. But just as no man in our present state can have rightful authority over his fellow man without first regaining the abilities he had lost, through his own efforts; so, whatever this authority might be, it can't give him the right to physically punish his fellow men, nor to have the right of life and death over men; for even during his glory he didn't have this right of physical life and death over the Subjects under his dominion.

For that to happen his empire would have had to be expanded through his fall, and he'd have had to acquire new Subjects. But, far from increasing their number, we see on the contrary that he lost the authority he had over the former Subjects. We even see that the only kind of superiority he can have over his fellow men is that of setting them right when they stray; to *stop* them when they give themselves over to *crime*, or rather to support them by bringing them back, by means of his example and his virtues, to the state which they no longer enjoy; and not that of himself being able to exercise over them an authority which their own nature refuses to accept.

Source of the Right to Punish

It would therefore be pointless to try to find the titles of Legislator and Judge in him today. However, according to the Laws of Truth, nothing should remain unpunished, and it's inevitable that Justice universally runs its course with the greatest precision, both in the physical and the intellectual state. Then if man through his fall, instead of acquiring new rights, is left stripped of those he had, he must necessarily find outside of himself other rights he needs to conduct himself in this social state to which he is presently tied.

And, where better to find these than in that very temporal and physical Cause which has taken the place of man, by order of the First Principle? Isn't it this Cause, in fact, which was replaced in the rank which man lost through his fault, and isn't it this Cause whose object and function have been to prevent the enemy from becoming master of the Empire from which man had been chased? In a word, isn't it this Cause which has been charged with serving as a beacon to man, and to illuminate him in all his steps?[57]

So, it's this Cause alone that must now accomplish both the work man had to do in former times, and also that which he has imposed upon himself by coming to inhabit a place which hadn't been created for him.

This alone can explain and justify the course of man's Criminal Laws. The society in which he must live and for which he is intended gave birth to crime; he has neither the right nor the power to stop them; so it's absolutely necessary that some other Cause does this for him, for the rights of Justice are irrevocable.

However, since Cause is above physical things, though is directs them and governs them, and since man's punishments in Society need to be as physical as his crimes, it must use physical means to manifest its decisions, as well as to have its judgements executed.

It's man's voice which it uses for this function, when, however, he has made himself worthy of it; it's he who the Cause charges with communicating Justice to his fellow man and having them seeing it observed. Thus, far from man being by his essence the depository of the

---

[57] This late revelation by Saint-Martin, that the temporal physical Cause is man's replacement at the center, while being a wonderful 'Aha!' moment, actually creates problems. If one compares this idea with Pasqually's *Treatise*, one would be led to believe the new guardian equates with Heli, and therefore Christ. The problem with Saint-Martin's assignment of duties is that it doesn't explain how temporal Causes could also exist in the divine world of no time. This is explained in a most complex manner in the Treatise, and no doubt Saint-Martin and Pasqually had many fascinating conversations on the interrelationships of the many classes of spiritual Beings while Saint-Martin was drawing the extraordinary diagram called the *Universal Table*. Clearly Saint-Martin couldn't go into great depth on this topic, but we should also remember that Pasqually's Treatise was only available to the highest-ranking members of the *Order of Elus Cohen* at the time, the *Réaux-Croix*, so there were no other materials the reader could access to flesh out an understanding of how man – or Christ – could move between the worlds temporal and eternal. Perhaps a clue comes from Pasqually's comment about the spiritual temporal spirits "having to act, diversely according to their vocation and rank, in the world of time to which they are alien. However, contrary to men who are now...*limited by time, the divine spirits are only limited by the temporal.*" (*Course on Martinesism*, 5:27, by Serge Caillet).

sword which avenges crimes, his very functions show that this right to punish resides in other hands, and he is only its organ.

We can also see what immense advantages the Judge who could be the true organ of this intelligent, temporal and universal Cause would have. In this Cause, he'd find a sure light which would make him inevitably distinguish the innocent from the guilty. Through this he would be protected from injustice, he'd be certain to fit the punishment to the crime, and not bring crime upon himself in working to rectify those of other men.

This invaluable advantage, unknown though it may be to men in general, offers nothing which should surprise or surpass any I've already shown man to be capable of; they all come from the abilities of this active and intelligent Cause, destined to establish order in the Universe among all Beings of two natures; and if through it man can be sure of the need for and the truth of his Religion and his worship; if he can acquire the undeniable rights which elevate him and establish his legitimacy over his fellow men; he can certainly hope for the same assistance for the careful administration of Civil or Criminal Justice in the Society entrusted to his care.

Besides, everything I've suggested is shown by what is commonly observed in Criminal Justice. Isn't the Judge supposed to forget himself, to become the simple agent and organ of the Law? Isn't this Law, though human, sacred to him? Doesn't he take every means he knows to enlighten his conduct and his Judgements, and to fit, so far as the Law allows it, the punishment to the crime; or rather, isn't it more often this very Law which is its measure; and when the Judge observes it, doesn't he convince himself that he's acted according to Justice?

Witnesses

It's therefore man himself who instructs us on the reality of this Principle, when otherwise we don't have a close conviction about it.

But at the same time, it appears even clearer that the Criminal Justice system in use among Nations only has the appearance of belonging to the Principle we discussed; and since it doesn't use it as its support, it walks in darkness, like all other human institutions, which results in its terrible chain of iniquities and veritable assassinations.

Indeed, the obligation imposed on the Judge to forget himself and his own testimony and to hear only the witnesses' testimonies, demonstrates that in truth there are witnesses who don't lie, and it's their depositions which should guide him. But also, while such witnesses aren't susceptible to corruption, it's clear that the Law is wrong to seek them only from among men, for most are ignorant and have bad faith, and then the Law opens itself up to hearing lies given as proof and this makes it completely unacceptable, since the Judge should only forget himself, and transform himself into a simple instrument in the face of sure and true testimony; for ultimately the false Law on which he thinks he can rely will never be responsible for his errors or offences.

Human Power

It's therefore for this reason that for the Judge, the most important duty is to try to unravel the truth in the witness's deposition. Now, how can he succeed in that without the help of that light which I showed him is the only guide in his quality as a man, which should be with him at every instant?

Isn't it therefore already a huge fault in Criminal Law not to have this light as its Principle; and doesn't this expose the Judge to the greatest abuse? But let us examine those abuses which arise from the very power that human Law claims for itself.

When men say that Political Law is tasked with the vengeance of individuals, after it prohibited them from taking the law into their own hands, we can be sure that by this they gave it privileges which can't be right so long as it works on its own.

Nevertheless, I concede that Political Law, which can to some extent codify its punishments, contains some advantage in that its vengeance won't always be limitless, as that of individuals could be.

But firstly, it can be wrong about the guilty, and a man is not as easily mistaken about his own adversary.

Secondly, if this individual vengeance, however acceptable it may be if man only had a physical nature, is however completely alien to his intellectual nature; and if this intellectual nature not only never had the right to administer corporal punishment, but still finds itself stripped of any kind of authority and can't administer Justice until it has recovered its original estate, we can be certain that Political Law, which will never be guided by another light, would commit the same injustices, only under another name.

For, if a man hurts me in some way, he's guilty according to the Laws of any form of Justice. If I retaliate by beating him and spilling his blood or even killing him, then I, like him lack the Laws of my true nature, and those of the intelligent and physical Laws which should guide me. Thus, when Political Law alone takes my place to punish my enemy, it takes the place of a man of blood.

In vain it may be objected that nowadays, by social convention, each citizen on committing a crime is subject to the penalties set out in the various Criminal Laws; for as we've seen, if men haven't been able to establish their Political Bodies legitimately by human convention alone, a citizen can't transfer the right to be punished to his co-citizens; because his true nature hasn't given him that right, and because the contract he's supposed to have made with them can't extend man's essence.

Can we say that this act of Political vengeance no longer sees itself as being performed by man, but by the Law? I'll still reply that this political Law, separated from its light, is nothing more than pure human will, and even unanimous approbation doesn't give it any more legitimacy. Therefore, if it's a crime for man to act through violence and by his own hand; if it's a crime for him to spill blood, the united will of all the men on earth could never erase this.

To avoid this pitfall, Politicians thought they couldn't do better than to view a criminal as being a traitor, and as such, the enemy of the Social Body. Then, situating him as if in a state of war, his death would seem to be legitimate; for since Political Bodies are created in man's image, according to them, like man they must also see to their own preservation. Thus, according to these Principles, Sovereign Authority has the right to use all its powers against evil-doers who threaten the Nation, either directly or through its individual members.

But firstly, we can easily see the fault in this comparison, by observing that when two men fight it really is the men who fight, whereas in a war between Nations one can't say that it's the Governments which fight, seeing that they are theoretical Beings, for whom Physical action is impossible.

Secondly, besides my showing that war between Nations doesn't fulfill its true purpose, the very purpose of war isn't to destroy men but indeed rather to prevent them from doing harm. An enemy should only be killed when it's impossible to subdue him; and among warriors it's always more glorious to conquer a Nation than to annihilate it.

However, clearly the advantage of an entire Realm again a guilty party is shown clearly enough that the right and glory of killing him disappear.

Besides, what proves that this assumed right in no way resembles the right of War, is that each soldier's life is in danger, and each enemy's death isn't certain; whereas here an iniquitous apparatus is used in the executions. One hundred men arm themselves, assemble and go to exterminate one of their fellow men in cold blood, whom they deny the ability to defend himself.[58] And yet we want to claim that human power is legitimate on its own, that human power which can be deceived all the time, which so often passes unjust sentences, and finally, which a corrupt will can pervert into an instrument of assassination.

No, man undoubtedly has other rules within him. If he sometimes serves as the organ of the superior Law to allow it to pronounce oracles and dispose of a man's life, it's through a right which is worthy of his respect, and which can also teach him to direct his steps towards Justice and Equity.

If we wish to judge his present incompetence still more, we only need to reflect on his former rights. During his glory, he had full rights over incorporeal life and death, because possessing life itself, he could communicate it to his subjects at will, or withdraw it from them when prudence made him judge it necessary; and as it was only through his presence that they could live, simply by separating himself from them he had the power to make them die.

Today he has but a spark of this first life, and now it's no longer over his former subjects but over his fellow men that he can make use of it.

---

[58] This comment may reflect Saint-Martin's military background. At that time, the penalties of the *Ancien Régime* were still in force. These required the aristocracy to be executed by beheading, at that time by sword. This was general practice across Europe, and had the advantage of being quick and painless. While hanging was the most usual form of execution for the common people, there was still a colorful attitude to the punishment fitting the crime. Thus, heretics and arsonists were burned at the stake; murderers were broken on the wheel; counterfeiters were boiled; and High Treason was punished by dismemberment. We can only assume that the firing squad clearly referred to here was only common in military circles. With the introduction of the Penal Code in 1791, the guillotine became the standard method of execution, adopted to give all citizens the former right of the aristocrat to be executed quickly, cleanly and humanely. The Penal Code also codified punishments so that everyone, including the judge, knew what penalties were associated with each crime. Interestingly, Article 13 of the Penal Code stated: "when the death penalty is handed down for crimes against the safety of the State, execution shall take place by firing squad." So, it appears Saint-Martin was anticipating the Penal Code when he set death by firing squad as the penalty for crimes against the State, and also in his comment about the impartiality of judges when hearing cases brought before them.

As for his right over physical life and death, which is the subject of the present question, we can be certain that it belongs even less to man in his present state. For, can he be said to possess and bestow that physical life which is given to him, and which he shares with all his species? Do his fellow men need his help to breathe and live corporeally? Are his will and even all his powers sufficient to keep them alive, and doesn't he constantly see the Law of Nature act so cruelly upon them, without being able to do a thing about it?

Similarly, does he contain a power and an inherent force which can take their lives away at will? When his corrupt will brings this thought to mind, what distance is there between this thought and the crime which should result? What trepidation, what hindrances are there between the plan and its execution? And don't we see that the care he takes to prepare his attacks almost never corresponds entirely with his views?

The Right of Execution

And so, we can truly say that by the simple Laws of his physical Being, man encounters resistance throughout, which proves that this physical Being doesn't give him a single right.

And indeed, haven't we seen clearly enough that the physical Being only has a secondary life which is dependent upon another Principle; and as a result, isn't it evident that every Being which doesn't have anything more is similarly dependent, and therefore has the same powerlessness?

Therefore, it wouldn't be in physical man taken by himself, that we'd identify that essential right over life and death which constitutes true authority, and all this only serves to confirm what we've established about the source, from which man should draw a similar right today.

Even less would we find the right to execute within him, since unless he used violence and external forces, it'd be unusual for him to be able to kill a malefactor without having recourse to treachery or subterfuge, and these means would be a long way from suggesting a true power in man.

However, the execution of Criminal Laws is necessary for Justice not to be pointless; and even further, I claim it's unavoidable. Now, since this right can't belong to us, this right, as well as the right to judge, must be put in the hands which should serve as our guide. It's the Cause which gives true power to the *natural arm* of man, and puts him in the position of executing the Decrees of Justice without attracting condemnation to himself.

Such are at least the means which true Legislators have used, though they're only made known to us through symbols and allegories. Perhaps they even used the hands of their fellow men to bring about the apparent punishment of criminals in order to provide physical symbols to the unsophisticated eyes of the Nations they governed; to cover with a veil the secret jurisdiction which actually directed the execution.

I speak this way with even more confidence, since we've seen these Legislators make use of this same veil in their simple explanations of their Civil and Social Laws. Although they were the work of a sure and superior hand, they made sure they only addressed the senses, so as never to profane their knowledge.

But as for their Criminal Laws, they painted their physical image with extreme severity, to impress upon the People under them the full severity of true Justice, and to make them realize that the smallest action contrary to the Law won't remain unpunished. It's with this viewpoint that some of them even inflicted punishments on animals.

The Connection Between the Punishment and the Crime

All these observations teach us once again that man can't find within him either the right to convict his fellow men, nor the right to carry out the penalty.

But when this right truly becomes the essence of men who govern, or those employed to support Criminal Justice in Governments, as they all believe, there still remains an even more difficult question to answer. How will they find a guaranteed rule to direct their Judgements and apply the penalties with Justice, precisely proportional to the extent and nature of the crimes; all things about which Criminal Justice is blind, uncertain, and almost only ever guided by prevailing prejudice, genius, or the Legislator's will.

There are Governments which, sensing their profound ignorance, have had the good faith to acknowledge this, and to solicit the counsel of men enlightened on such matters. I praise their zeal for having taken such steps; but I should warn them that they can hope for satisfactory wisdom in vain so long as they only seek it men's opinions and thoughts, and don't have the courage nor resolution to go themselves to get it at its true source.

For the most famous Politicians and Legal Experts still haven't answered this problem. They took Governments at face value; they claimed, like the common people, that its foundation was real and that the knowledge and right to punish were man's. Then they wore themselves out trying to place a solid structure on this foundation; but, as nobody can doubt they were building on a supposition, it's clear that Governments which truly want to educate themselves should address themselves to other Masters.

It's not my intention to decide what penalties are appropriate to each crime. On the contrary, I'm saying it isn't possible for man ever to rule definitively on these things, because no two crimes are the same, and if the same sentence is handed out, it will certainly result in an injustice.

Criminal Codes

But man's simple judgement should at least teach him only to seek to punish the guilty to the extent that the object and order have been hurt, and not to take the punishment from another class of crime, which having no connection to the offense, would itself be harmed without the offense being atoned.

Human Justice is so weak and so horribly defective, for sometimes its power has no effect, for example in suicides and crimes it doesn't find out about. Sometimes this power even violates the connection between crime and punishment which should guide it, for example, in all corporal punishments meted out for crimes in which nobody was attacked, and which are only concerned with possessions.

Even when it appears to observe this connection most closely, thereby seeming to retain a kind of wisdom, this human Justice is still infinitely faulty in that it only has a very small number of punishments to inflict in each class, whereas in each class the crimes are innumerable and always different.

That is also why written Criminal Laws are one of the greatest faults of Nations, because this makes them dead Laws which always remain the same, whereas crime grows and reinvents itself at every instant. Retaliation is almost always banned, and indeed these Laws can almost never fulfill all the clauses humanely, because they don't know all the circumstances of the crimes, or because even when they know them, they aren't sufficiently inventive to always come up with the appropriate remedy for all these wrongs.

So, what are these Criminal codes if we don't find retaliation there, the one penal Law which is just, the only one which could certainly set man on the right path, and which can't therefore come from him, but is rather the work of a powerful hand, whose intelligence knows how to mete out punishments, and extend or constrain them according to need?

Torture

I won't spend time on this barbaric custom where Nations do not content themselves with blindly condemning a man, but also use torture on him to extract the truth. Nothing indicates more clearly the weakness and obscurity in which the Legislator languishes, since, if he was in possession of his true rights, he would have no need of the false and cruel means used to guide his Judgements; since the same light which would authorize him to judge his fellow man and have him execute its sentences, and which would instruct him in the kind of punishments he should inflict, would no longer leave him in error concerning the types of crimes, nor the names of the guilty parties and their accomplices.

The Blindness of Legislators

But what shows us the powerlessness and blindness of Legislators most clearly is seeing that they only inflict capital punishment for crimes which fall in the realm of the physical and the temporal, while a multitude are committed around them which concern much more important things which escape their sight day after day. I'm talking about those monstrous notions which make of man a Material Being; those corrupt and worrying doctrines which deprive him of all sense of order and happiness; in a word, those infected theories which bring putrefaction into his very seed, kill it or render it completely pestilential, and make the Sovereign reigns over nothing more than vile instruments of torture or brigands.

False Judgements

We've dwelt on the defective Administration long enough. Let's limit ourselves now to reminding those who command and those who judge of the injustices they might be committing when they act with uncertainty and without being convinced of the legitimacy of their conduct.

The first concern is running the risk of convicting an innocent man. Now, the misfortune resulting from this is of a nature which man can never assess, since it depends to a great extent on the wrong the condemned man must suffer as compared to the fruits he could have harvested from his intellectual abilities had he remained longer on Earth, and the disheartening effect of an ignominious, cruel and unexpected punishment. How can a Judge ever gauge the extent of all these problems, if he doesn't one day feel the bitter sensation of remorse for his mistakes? Yet how could he satisfy Justice if he didn't suffer atonement for it?

The second concern is that of inflicting on a guilty party a punishment other than what is appropriate to his crime. In this case, here is the succession of misfortunes which the imprudent Judge sets up, either for his victim, or for himself.

Firstly, the sentence to which he condemns him doesn't exempt the criminal at all from what true Justice has assigned to him. Moreover, it only makes it even more certain, for without this hasty condemnation, perhaps true Justice would have given the criminal time to make reparation for his fault through remorse; but now, depending on the harshness of the punishment, his need to feel repentant would have been lessened.

Secondly, if man's blind and hasty Judgement deprives the criminal of time to repent, the atrocity of the sentence loses its force, and the despairing criminal may well lose a precious life in which a more just employment and the sacrifice made to time could perhaps have effaced all his crimes, as if he suffered two penalties instead of one. But this approach, far from giving him an opportunity to reflect, may instead lead him to continue with his life of crime, and make a second penalty all the more inevitable.

So, when the Judge wishes to examine himself carefully, he can't avoid giving himself the first of these punishments, which only differs from murder in form. Then he'll have to take responsibility for all the deadly consequences which we've just seen arising from his temerity and injustice. Then, let him reflect on his situation, and see if he can still be at peace with himself.

The Rights of True Sovereigns

Let's leave these scenes of horror, and instead use every effort to remind all the Sovereigns and Judges to know their true Law, and to have confidence in this light destined to be men's guide. Let's convince them that if they were pure, they'd cause evildoers to tremble far more by their presence and their name than by gibbets and scaffolds. Let's convince them that this is the only way to lift the clouds we see obscuring the origin of their Sovereignty, the association of Political Nations, and the Laws of Civil and Criminal Administration of their Governments. Finally, let's make them promise to constantly fix their gaze the Principle we've offered them as the sole compass for their conduct, and the sole measure of all their powers.

The Healing of Disorders[59]

To add to the idea that the Sovereigns should take from this, let's now show them that this same Principle from which they should expect so much help, could also give them that powerful gift I previously listed among the number of their privileges: that of healing the sick.

If this universal temporal Cause, charged with directing man and all the Being which inhabit time, is both active and intelligent, it's certain that there is no part of science and knowledge which it doesn't know; and this will suffice to show what the man who is led by it can expect.

Thus, it would be correct to say that a Sovereign having this light as his guide would understand the true Principles of bodies, or those three fundamental Elements which we discussed earlier in this book; that he'd be able to determine in what proportion their action is shown in various bodies, depending on age, sex, climate and other natural considerations; that he'd understand the specific properties of each of these Elements, and the relationship between them; and that, when this relationship is disturbed or destroyed and the individual Principles would tend to overcome one another or separate, he'd soon see the correct means to reestablish order.

That's why medicine must be reduced to the following simple rule, singular and as a result universal: *bring together that which is divided and*

---

[59] While the French word used, *maladies*, means 'disease' or 'sickness', it is important to select a word which doesn't carry any modern connotations., since disease, other than its basic meaning of not being at ease, carries a rather different connotation now. Therefore, the word 'disorder' is used throughout, which would have had the same sense in the 18th Century.

divide that which is reassembled. But this rule, which comes from the very nature of things, experiences so much disorder and profanation passing through men's hands; because the slightest degree of difference in the way it's used, or in the action of the remedies, produces effects so contrary to those which they should expect; because the mixing of these fundamental Principles, although there are only three, nevertheless produces changes and multiplies in so many ways that ordinary eyes could never follow all of its variations; and because, in these types of mixtures, the same Principle often has different properties, depending on the kind of reaction it experiences.

Three Elements, Three Disorders

For while we recognize that Fire is universally widespread, like the two other Elements, we know that the inner Fire creates, the superior Fire matures, and the inferior Fire consumes. We can say the same about the salts, that the inner one brings about fermentation, the superior one preserves, and the inferior one corrodes. Mercury, even though its usual property is to occupy an intermediary level between the two opposing Principles we've just discussed, and by this means to establish peace between them; yet, Mercury, in fact, also assembles them in a thousand occurrences and contains them in the same circle, thus becoming the source of the great elemental disorders, and at the same time offers the image of *universal disorder*.

What care, what precautions are therefore necessary to unravel the nature and effects of these different Principles, which when mixed are so much more diverse than their natural properties? But despite this infinite multitude of differences to be observed in the cycles of physical Beings, an enlightened eye, such as a Sovereign should possess, will never lose sight of its rule. He can restore all these differences to three types, by reason of the three fundamental Principles from which they emanate, and as a result, he'll only recognize the existence of three disorders; and he'll even know that these three disorders will have symptoms which are as marked and as distinct as the three fundamental Principles themselves have in their actions, and in their original property.

These three kinds of disorders are each associated with one of the principle substances composing the animal body; that is, blood, bone and flesh, three parts which each relate to one of the three Elements from which they come from. It'll therefore be by means of the same Elements that they can be cured. Thus, the flesh will be healed by Salt, the blood by Sulfur and the bones by Mercury: all with the appropriate *preparations* and *constitutions*.[60]

Disorders of the Skin

We know, for example, that disorders of the flesh and skin arise from the thickening and corruption of saline secretions in the capillary vessels, where they can be stuck because of a rapid and too sudden action of Air, and also by the too feeble flow of blood. It's therefore natural to introduce a Salt to combat these stagnant and corrupt liquids, in order to separate them without having consequences, to corrodes and consume them where they are without letting them re-enter the body of blood, to which they'd communicate their putrefaction. But although this Salt is the most common one produced by Nature, we should note however that it's still, as it were, unknown to human Medicine, which shows how little advanced it's in the healing of these types of disorders.

Disorders of the Bone and Blood

Secondly, in disorders of the bone, Mercury should be used in great moderation, since it links and binds together the other two Principles which support life in all bodies too much, and it's by these impediments given principally to sulfur, that makes it the destroyer of all vegetative processes both terrestrial and animal. Prudence therefore requires one simply to leave the Mercury innate within the body to act, since the action of this Mercury being reconciled with the action of the blood, doesn't grow more than the latter, and contains it sufficiently not to weaken or evaporate it, yet also not

---

[60] Another translation of the word used in the text, *tempérament*, is 'temperament'. This brings us to the fact that, in the 18th Century, the concept of the four humors was still around, although by the latter end of the Century, it was being applied less to bodily functions and more to personality. The four humors originally applied to the for fluid commonly thought to be found in the human body: blood, phlegm, black bile, yellow bile. These led to the idea of four personality traits stimulated by an excess of one of these four humors, which were sanguine, phlegmatic, choleric and melancholic respectively. In Chapter 3 Saint-Martin mentioned "disorders of the humors." However, the translation used here, 'constitutions', is more in keeping with the tone of this section, which is talking about the preparation and mixing of medicines.

to stifle or extinguish it. Thus, on this matter Nature gives us a very clear and instructive lesson by repairing bone fractures on its own, without the aid of any external Mercury.

As for disorders of the blood, sulfur should be used with even greater care, for as the bodies are far more volatile than fixed, it will increase their sulfurous and igneous action further, making it vulnerable to becoming even more volatile. A properly educated man would therefore never apply this remedy except with the greatest sobriety, since he'd know that when the radical humidity is altered, the general humidity can't repair it on its own, and it's because of this that he'd add radical humidity itself, by drawing it from its source, which is not entirely in the bone marrow.

The Apothecary[61]

And, incidentally, this is the reason for the frequent insufficiency and danger of the Apothecary who, searching so eagerly for the volatile Principles of medicinal bodies, too often neglects the use of the fixed Principles whose need is so universal it'd be exclusive, if man were wise. Also, who doesn't know that this Apothecary destroys more than he preserves; that he agitates and burns rather than reviving, and that when on the other hand, he intends to calm, he only knows how to proceed by using absorbents and poisons?

So, we can see what Medicine would be limited to in the hands of a man who had been restored to his primitive rights: he would himself bring a healing action to every remedy, and through this create infallible cures, at least when the active Cause, whose agent he is, hadn't been given orders to act otherwise.

In this worthy and useful science, he'd have stayed away from the material calculations of human Mathematics, which in only working on results, are useless or even dangerous in Medicine, where the object is to work on the very Principles which act in the body.

---

[61] Saint-Martin talks of *la Pharmacie*, which strictly speaking is the Pharmacy itself, rather than the person working in it. However, the text seemed to flow better if it talks about the person performing these tasks rather than use the third person. Hence the use of the term Apothecary instead of Pharmacy.

The Privileges of Sovereigns

By this same reason, he wouldn't become too attached to formulas, which in the Art of Healing are the same thing as Criminal Codes in the Administration of Nations, since among all disorders there are never two which present themselves with exactly the same symptoms, so it's impossible for the same remedy to destroy both.

But as a *Sovereign*, this man would know the properties of physical Beings, and also about their disorders, so he'd avoid being wrong when he applied the remedy. However, we shouldn't forget that in order to get to this, man shouldn't take Matter for the Principle of Matter, for we have seen that this was the main cause of his ignorance.

Let's not believe either that this invaluable power is beyond the reach of ordinary man. On the contrary, it figures among the number of Laws given to him, in relation to the task which he must fulfill during his time on earth, for if it's by means of his physical envelope that attacks are made on him, it's necessary for him not to be completely deprived of the means to sense them and repel them. So, since the use of this privilege can be common to all men, the more reason it should be more especially the province of Sovereigns, who true destiny is, so far as they can, to preserve their Subjects from ills of all kinds and to defend them in the physical, as well as in the intellectual.

So, if this privilege isn't known to them any more than their other rights, it's another reason for them to sense whether they've been put in charge of men by the Principle whose power I've shown them, and which is necessary for the regularity of all their proceedings. This is, I say, one more means which I offer them to judge themselves.

Let them therefore add the observations I've made on the art of healing to all those which I've made about the flaws in the Political, Civil and Criminal Administration of Nations; on the flaws in Governments themselves, which have revealed those of their Association; as well as on the source from which Leaders should draw their various rights. Then let them decide if they can see within themselves the traces of that light which is supposed to have created all of them, and not have left any of them for an instant; for it's only through this light that they can be assured of the legitimacy of their power, and the Justice of the Institutions over which they preside.

Nevertheless, let's repeat at this moment with as much firmness as candor, that any Subject who perceives all these defects in a Nation, and who sees the Sovereigns themselves far below the level they should be, and believes because of that he's excused from the smallest duty towards them, and from submitting to their decrees, would be straying physically from his Law, and working directly against the Principles we've established.

May every man, on the contrary, be convinced that Justice only ever attributes his own faults to him; and as a result, a Subject can only increase disharmony by claiming to oppose and combat them, since this would be to work by man's will, and man's will only leads to crime.

Therefore, I'll believe that despite all the applications that Sovereigns could make to themselves of everything I'm putting before their eyes, they could never accuse me of having established principles contrary to their authority, and my only desire would be to convince them that they could indeed have invincible and unwavering authority.

So, following the sequence of our observations, we'll proceed to an examination of the errors which have been made in the High Sciences, because the Principles of these Sciences are related to the same source as Political and Religious Laws, so knowledge of them should also enter into the number of rights of man.

Chapter 6 – Mathematics & Geometry

The Principles of Mathematics

I'll principally examine the Science of Mathematics here, as being that to which all the High Sciences are linked, and as holding the first rank among the objects of reasoning or man's intellectual ability; and firstly, to assure those to whom the word Mathematics might give pause, I'll reassure them that not only is it unnecessary to be expert in this subject to follow my observations on this subject, but also that it's barely necessary to have the slightest concept of it, since the way I'll discuss it can accommodate any Reader.

This Science will no doubt offer us still more striking proof of the Principles which have previously been advanced, as well as the errors which result when men give themselves up blindly to their senses.

And this must see natural, because mathematical Principles, while not being material but nevertheless the true Law of the physical, Geometricians truly are always masters of reasoning concerning the nature of these Principles in their own manner, but when they come to apply the notions they've formed, they should admit their mistakes, because then the Principle will lead them, instead of the other way around. Thus, nothing is more appropriate to discern truth from falsehood, than a precise examination of the path they've followed, and the consequences which would result were we to follow them there.

Axioms

I'll begin by observing that nothing is demonstrated in Mathematics unless it leads back to an axiom, because only an axiom can be true. I pray at the same time we note that the reason axioms are true is because they are independent from the physical or from Matter, and that they are purely intellectual, which already confirms all I've said about the path they must take to come to the Truth, and at the same time reassure the Observers about something they can't physically see.

It's therefore clear that if Geometricians hadn't lost sight of axioms, they'd never have strayed in their reasoning, since axioms are connected to the very essence of intellectual Principles, and because of this rest upon the clearest certainty.

The physical and sensory product which agrees with these intellectual Laws is no doubt perfectly regular, taken within its class, in that it conforms precisely with the order of this intellectual Principle, or to axioms which direct it during its existence and execution. However, as the perfection of this physical product is dependent upon, or relative to the Principle which engendered it, it's not in this product that its rule and source can reside.

It would therefore only be by continually comparing this physical product with axioms, or with the Laws of the intellectual Principle, that one might judge its regularity, and I emphasize that it'd only be by this means that one could come to demonstrate its accuracy.

But this rule is the only true one, and if at the same time it's purely intellectual, how can men hope to make up for it with a rule taken from the physical? How can they flatter themselves that they can replace a real Being by a man-made and imaginary Being?

Yet how can we doubt that all the Geometricians' work is going in this direction, since we'll see that, having established the axioms which are the foundation of all the Truths they want to teach us, in order to teach us to estimate length[62], they only offer us a measurement taken from this very length, or arbitrary numbers which also need physical measurement to be seen by our physical eyes.

Then should we stay with such a demonstration, and regard similar proofs as evidence? Since measurement always resides in the Principle where physical production has taken place, can this physical and passive production itself serve as its measure and proof? And are there other Beings than those which haven't been created, or real Beings, which can substantiate themselves by themselves?

Far from challenging the evidence of mathematical intellectual Principles or the axioms, we should already recognize the weak ideas which

---

[62] In French, *étendue* can refer both to *length* and *extent, expanse* or *area*. This makes it very difficult to translate this word. The reader can surely appreciate that it encompasses a single idea in French, whereas in English these can be two very different ideas. In a way, we can see the thinking through the English word 'extent', so the French word *étendue* can refer to the extent of a line (one dimension) or the extent of an area (two dimensions). It is also clear that Saint-Martin is not consistent in his use of the word, since he sometimes compares the *étendue* of a 'straight line' to a 'curved line'; and in another section, he discusses the *étendue* of a 'circular line' or 'circle', which clearly introduces an element of area or expanse. I've therefore used the word 'length' when he refers to a line, and 'extent', when he refers to a circle or enclosed space. I've avoided the term 'area' since the philosophical tone of the passages indicate sweeping concepts rather than simply length times breadth.

Geometricians have taken from this evidence, and the poor use they have made of them to arrive at the knowledge of length and the other properties of Matter. We should say that, if they know nothing about this topic, it's because they fell into the same error that the Observers made regarding all the other subjects I've considered; that is, that they have separated length from its true Principle, or rather that they sought the Principle within it, that they confused the Principle with it, and that they haven't seen that they're two distinct things, yet indispensably brought together to constitute the existence of Matter.

Length

To make this clearer, it's appropriate to establish our notions of the nature of length. Length, like all the other properties of the body, is a product of the Generating Principle of Matter, according to the Laws and order which are given to this inferior Principle by the superior Principle which governs it. In this sense, as length is only a secondary product, it can't have the same advantages as the Beings included in the class of original products. These have their own fixed Laws; all their properties are invariable since they are linked to their essence; and it's there that weight, number and measure are so regulated that they can no more be changed than the Being itself can be destroyed.

But, as for the properties of bodies, or secondary Beings, we've seen clearly enough that this can't be the case, since having absolutely no fixed property according to our senses, they can never have any value to our eyes except by comparison with other Beings of their own class.

The Measurement of Length

If this is true, then the length of bodies can't be determined with any more certainty than their other properties. Therefore, when, we try to discover the value of this length, we use a measurement which is taken from this same length, and then this measurement we're now using will be subject to the same drawback as the object we wish to measure, that is, its length will be no more clearly determined. Then we must find a measurement of this measurement; for whatever means we want to use, we can clearly see that it'll never be in this length that we'll find its true measure, and as a result, we'll always have go back to the Principle which engendered length and all the properties of Matter.

This is what shows the absolute insufficiency of the Geometricians' approach, when they claim to establish the true measurement of physical Beings. It's true, I agree, that they attach numbers to this physical measurement of length. But not only are the numbers they use only relative and man-made, not only is man free to change their proportions and use any scale he judges fitting, but also this scale, while perhaps useful to measure all the dimensions of one kind of species, doesn't work at all to measure the dimensions of other species, and men have yet to find a fixed, invariable and universal basis by which they can correlate the measurements of all kinds of lengths.

Nature of the Circumference

This is the source of the difficulty Geometricians experience when they try to measure curves, because the measurement they use is made for straight lines, so it doesn't accommodate itself to this kind of line, and offers insurmountable difficulties when applied to a circular line, as well as to any curve which derives from it.

I said this measurement offers insurmountable difficulties; for although Geometricians have cut the Gordian knot[63] by presenting a circular line as being a collection of straight lines which are infinitesimally small, they'd be wrong to believe they had solved the issue by this means, since a falsehood never resolved anything.

Now, I can't avoid considering this definition as false, since it directly conflicts with the notion both they themselves and Nature give us of a circumference, which is nothing more than a line whose points are all equidistant from a common center; and I don't even know how Geometricians can reasonably rely on two such contradictory propositions; for ultimately, if the circumference is simply a collection of straight lines, as infinitely small as one might suppose them to be, all the points of this

---

[63] The Gordian Knot refers to a legend set in Phrygia. There are many variations, but basically Alexander the Great arrived in that country, and was told there was a complex knot named after Gordias, a former king, and a prophecy foretold that whoever untied the knot would become King of Asia. Many had tried and failed, for the knot was extremely convoluted. Alexander decided it didn't matter how the knot was united, so he cut it apart with his sword. Therefore, the Gordian Knot has become the symbol of an extremely difficult problem to be solved.

circumference will never be equally distant from the center, since these straight lines will themselves be composed of several points, among which those at the ends and those in the middle surely can't be the same distance from the center; so they can't all have a common center, and the circumference will no longer be a circumference.

Two Kinds of Lines

Thus, they want to unite these two opposites, to treat two things with contrary natures as having the same nature, which is really saying they want to make two Brings conform to the same number. But, seeing as they're so different from one another, their numbers should clearly be different.

We should therefore admit that we see here how men clearly have a natural inclination to get everything confused, for they see a false uniformity in Beings of different classes, and then go on to try to compare things which are completely unlike each other. For it's impossible to think what could be more opposite, more contrary or contradictory to one another, than a straight line and a circular line.

Aside from the moral proofs to be found in contrasting the properties of a straight line, with its regularity and perfect unity, with those of the circular line, with its impotence and confusion attached to the multiplicity which this circular line represents, I can give still more convincing reasons that they came from intellectual Principles, the only ones which can be accepted as real, and as Law in the search for the nature of things; the only ones which are truly as unshakeable as axioms.

I'll nevertheless advise you that these truths won't be clear to most men, and still less to those who till now have accepted those false principles I'm contesting. The first step a man needs to take to understand me would be to study everything at its source, and not accept the ideas which imagination and hasty judgement have given them.

But I know how few would have the courage; and even if I were to presume a great many would, I'd also guess that few of them would have any success, since so many original sources of Knowledge have been infected by error and poison.

If it makes sense that everything has its own *number* in Nature, and if it's because of this that all Beings find it easy to distinguish one another, since all their properties could only result from conforming to the Laws contained within their *number*, then it's certain that the straight line and curved line have difference natures, as I've already indicated, and must therefore each have their own specific *number* to indicate their different natures, and to prevent us from thinking of them as being equal and confusing the two.

When we reflect only for a moment on the functions and properties of these two kinds of lines, this should suffice for us to convince ourselves of the reality of what I've just said. What's the function of a straight line, if not to continue to infinity the products of the point from which it emanates? When it's perpendicular, doesn't it govern the foundation and bearing of all Beings, and to delineate for each one its Laws?

On the contrary, doesn't the circular line limit at all its points the products of the straight line[64]? As a result, doesn't it constantly try to destroy it, and can't it be regarded in this manner as its enemy? Then, how would it be possible for two things which are so opposed in their function, and which have such different properties, not to be distinguished by their *number*, just as they are by their action?

If this important observation had been made instead, those who work in Mathematical Science would have been spared endless pain and effort, for they'd have been stopped from seeking, as they do, a common measurement for two types of lines which will never have anything in common.

Number of Each Kind of Lines

It's therefore after accepting this essential difference which distinguishes them in their form, their use and their properties, that I can confidently affirm that their *number* is also different.

If you press me to explain more clearly, and to indicate what *number* I attribute to each of these lines, I would state without issue that the straight

---

[64] In case this appear a little obtuse, we must remember that Saint-Martin is talking Theosophically about numbers. He doesn't see the point as being on its own, but as always being surrounded by the circle, as in the diagram known to all Freemasons of the point within the circle. The point is unity, or God, and the circle is His creation. The central point expands in two opposite directions to form a straight line (a diameter), but when it reaches the circumference or boundary, it is prevented from continuing its expansion by the limiting circle. Therefore, since straight and curved lines are not only different in nature but even in opposition, they must possess different qualities, and one of these is number (the others being weight and measure).

line carries the number *four*, and the circular line the number *nine*: and I'd dare to assure you that there is no other way to come to this knowledge; since however long or short lines are, the *number* I attribute to them each never changes, and they always preserve the same *number* in their respective class, however long we make them.

Again, I realize this could well be misunderstood, since Matter has made much progress in the minds of my fellow men. There are some, then, who despite the clarity of my proposal, could wrongly infer from this that if a large and small line have the same *number*, according to me, they must be equal as a result.

But, to avoid this apparent paradox, I'll add that both a large and a small line are the result of their Law and their *number*; so although both always belong to the same class, the same Law and the same *number*, that Law and that *number* always act differently in each of them; that is, with more or less force, activity or duration. By this we can see that the resulting line will show all these physical differences, although the Principle which varies its action is itself unchangeable.

It's this, we can be sure, that can alone explain the universal difference of all Beings of two natures, both those where each nature occupies a different class, and those which are of the same class and the same type. This can help us understand how all individuals of the same class are different, even though they have the same Law, the same origin and the same *number*.

It's because of this as well, that the arbitrary, man-made numbers which Geometricians use in their physical measurements come to nothing, and indeed the disadvantages of this kind of measurement make us clearly see their inadequacy. For trying to select the measurement of length from length itself, is to open oneself up to having to reduce or increase that measurement when the length on which it's based changes; and as these changes don't always come to exact multiples or divisions of the given measurement; they can give us parts of numbers which aren't whole, compared to the principle number, and the chosen measurement itself must undergo the same distortion; then finally what calculators call fractions must be accepted – as if a simple Being or a unity could divide itself this way.

Calculating to Infinity

If Mathematicians had focused on this last reflection, they'd have obtained a more accurate notion of a scholarly calculation that they'd invented: that is, *infinity*. They'd have seen that they could never find something *infinitely large* in Matter which is limited to *three* Elements, but certainly in *numbers* which are the powers of all that exists, and which truly have no limits, in our thoughts or in their essence. On the contrary, they'd have realized they could only find the calculation of the *infinitely small* in Matter, whose indefinite division of molecules[65] is conceived as being possible, though our senses still can't do this. But they should never have sought this type of infinity among numbers, for, as unity is indivisible, it's the first term of Beings and accepts no number before it.

Generally Accepted Measurements

Nothing therefore conforms less to the true Principle than this generally accepted measurement which man has established in his Geometrical processes, and as a result, nothing is less suited to advance him in the knowledge he absolutely needs.

The help of such a measurement is, I know, of the greatest assistance in the material details of transacting man's social and physical life, so I'm not claiming it's wrong to put it to such a use. All I'd ask of man is not to be careless enough to use it in his research into natural Truths, because in this field it can only mislead him; for errors, even the simplest ones, are of the greatest consequence here, and since all Truths are connected, there isn't one which can be even slightly affected without passing this on to all the others.

The numbers *four* and *nine*, which I presented as essentially belonging to the straight line and the curved line respectively, don't have the problem we've just seen in the arbitrary method of assigning numbers; because these

---

[65] While the idea of the four Classical Elements still prevailed, people generally knew that metals and salts could be combined to form other substances, which they knew as molecules. They had no idea how large or small these were, other than they were too small for the senses to detect. However, this idea of elemental substances was curious. Prevailing theories suggested that heat was composed of small, round atoms, while water was made of slippery atoms, and cold was composed of tiny pyramids which pricked the skin; while salt was also made of tiny pointy atoms which pricked the tongue. Atoms were held together as molecules by hooks or joints, or even a form of glue.

numbers always remain intact, though their ability extends or contracts in all the variations to which length is susceptible. Also, in the real world, there are never fractions in a Being, and if we remember what we said previously about the nature of the Principle of physical Beings, we'll see that as they're indivisible in their quality as simple Beings, the numbers which can only represent them and render them physical must possess the same property

But, I repeat again, all this is outside the physical and Matter, so I don't flatter myself that many people will understand me. It's for this reason that I expect some to object again, and ask me how it'd be possible to evaluate different lengths of the same order, if I give the number *four* to all straight lines, and the number *nine* to all circular and curved lines without exception. They'll ask me by what sign we can know for certain the different ways the same number can act on unequal lengths, and how we could accurately determine a line's length.

It's useless to seek a different response to the one I've already made. So, I'll say that if the person asking me this question only needs to understand length for his own personal use, and for his needs or tastes, since there is nothing of this sort which isn't relative, then man-made and relative measurements will suffice; because with the aid of the senses alone, regularity can be used to the point of making the error undetectable to the senses.

But, if we want to know more than this relative and approximate value, if we ask for the fixed and true value of a length; since this value exists through the action of its *number*, and this *number* isn't Matter, it's easy to see if we can find the desired rule in material length, and if we were wrong to say that true measurement of length can't be known to the physical senses. Then, if this measurement can't be found in the physical senses, we don't need to reflect long to determine where it must be, since we haven't stopped explaining that in everything that exists there is only the physical and the intellectual

Thus, we see what the Geometricians have to teach us, and what the errors with which they delude our mind are, when they only offer measurements taken from the physical, and therefore relative ones, whereas our minds conceive that there are true measurements, and that they were made to know them.

True Measurement

At the same time, we see that universal Truth which is the subject of this book reappearing here, that it's only in the Principle of things that it's possible to evaluate their properties correctly, and that however difficult it's to know how to read it, it's undeniable that this Principle governs all and measures all, and when we move away from it, we find nothing.

Nevertheless, I must add that, although it's possible to accurately determine the measurement of length with the help of this Principle, since it's this Principle itself which governs it, it'd be a true profanation to use it for material measurements, for it can help us uncover far more important Truths than those which are only associated with Matter; and the senses, as we've already said, are sufficient to direct man in physical things. We also see that Beings below man have no other Law, and their senses are sufficient to their needs. So, for this purely relative purpose, true and correct Mathematics – or intellectual Mathematics – would not only be superfluous, but wouldn't even be understood.

What greater inconsistency could there be than to try to subject and subordinate this invariable and enlightened Mathematics to the Mathematics of the senses, which are so limited and modest; to want this to replace the former; and finally, to want the physical to serve as the rule and guide of the intellectual?

Here we show again the disadvantage to which the Geometricians are exposed; for, in seeking a physical measurement for length and presenting it to us as real, they haven't seen that it's as variable as length itself, and that far from directing Matter, it's actually dependent upon Matter, since it has to follow its course and all the results arising from this connection.

Then, since the numbers *four* and *nine*, which I've claimed are the measures of the two possible types of lines, are completely protected from this subjection, I know I'm correct in giving them my every confidence, and stating, as I did before, that they're the true measures of their respective classes.

I'll admit it's hard for me not to be able to outline these Truths without sensing how humiliating they are for the Geometricians, since, seeing the efforts they make each day to confuse these two measures, I'm obliged to say that even the most famous of them still doesn't know the difference between a straight line and a curved line, as we'll now see in more detail.

Movement

But the error we've just perceived isn't the only one that they've made concerning length. Not only is it in length that they've sought its measurement, as we've seen, but they've also sought the source of movement there. Never daring to raise themselves above this dark matter which surrounds them, they believed they could establish a space and a limit to this Principle of movement, so that, according to this theory, nothing could be imagined as being active and able to move beyond this limit.

If they still don't have an accurate notion of movement, isn't it always because they make the same mistake of confusing two distinct things, which leads them to seek movement in length, instead of seeking it in its Principle?

For as this length only has relative properties, or abstractions, it's impossible for it to offer anything fixed and stable enough for man's mind to focus on in a satisfactory manner; and to try to find in it the source of its movement is to repeat all these inadequate attempts which have already been rebutted, and to try to submit the Principle to its product, when according to the natural, real order of things, the work is always inferior to its Generating Principle.

So, it's within the immaterial Principle of all Beings, whether intellectual or physical, that the source of movement found in each of them basically resides. It's by means of the action of this Principle that all their abilities are manifested according to their rank and their personal use, that is, intellectual in the intellectual order, and physical in the physical order.

Now, if the only action of the Principle of physical Beings is movement, if it's through this alone that they grow and feed themselves, and finally that they manifest and render all their properties physically, and consequently their very size, how can one see movement as being dependent on length or Matter, since on the contrary it's length or Matter which comes from movement? How can one say that movement clearly belongs to Matter, when it's Matter which clearly belongs to movement?

It cannot be denied that Matter only exists through movement; for we see that when bodies are deprived of what's given to them for a time, they dissolve and gradually disappear. It's also very clear through this same observation that the movement which gives life to bodies clearly doesn't belong to them, since we see it stop in them before they cease to be alive to our eyes; just as we can't doubt they're completely dependent on it, since the end of movement is the first action of their destruction.

Besides, let's remember the Law of universal reaction to which all physical Beings are subject, and recognize that if the immaterial Principles of physical Beings are themselves subject to the action of another Principle, that's all more reason the physical results of these Principles, such as length, must necessarily prove this subordination.

So, let's conclude that if everything disappears at the rate that movement withdraws, it's clear that length only exists because of movement, which is very different from saying that movement is from length and in length.

However, from this assertion that it's movement which creates length, it could be inferred that since movement is the essence of immaterial Principles, we must now recognize it to be indestructible, for it's impossible for this movement not to have existed forever, and as a result, for length or Matter not to be eternal; which plunges us back into the precipitous darkness from which I've taken so much care to protect my Readers; for I know the objection could be raised that one can't conceive movement without length.

This last proposition is true in the physical order of things, where one can't conceive movement which doesn't produce length, or which couldn't be made of length; but although the Principles which give rise to movement in the physical order are immaterial, it would be wrong to claim their action is necessary and eternal, since we've seen that these physical Principles are only secondary Beings, having only one particular action and not an infinity of them, and that they're absolutely dependent upon an active and intelligent Cause, which communicates this action to them for a time, as it also withdraws it from them according to the Order and the Law of the First Cause.

Two Kinds of Movement

Besides, it's in this very physical order that we can find the proof of movement without length; although in this physical region it's always done in length. For this result, let's note that, because of the dual universal Law which rules physical Nature, there are two kinds of movements in all bodies.

Firstly, their growth, or the very action which manifests and sustains their physical Existence.

Secondly, their tendency towards the Earth, which is their common Center; a tendency which we see as much in how bodies fall as in the pressure their own weight makes on them or on the terrestrial surface.

These two movements are in direct opposition to one another. Also, the second of these movements, or the tendency of bodies towards their terrestrial Center, although it can only be done by length, nevertheless doesn't produce length like the first movement, or that of growth and existence in these same bodies.

On the contrary, one tends to destroy what the other produces; since, if physical Beings were to reunite in their *Center*, from that time on they'd be inactive, with no physical manifestation, in other words without movement, and consequently without length; since it's certain that all these effects can only happen because the Beings which produce them were separated from their *Center*.

Now, if from these two movements, of which one produces length, as we have said, there's one which destroys it, and that at least can't be seen as belonging to length, although it can only exist in length; then it'd be this which could answer the objection that one can't conceive movement without length, and not believing that movement belongs to the classes of immaterial Beings; since the Beings of the physical class are only its depository for a time.

Immaterial Movement

Let's further underscore the fact that it can indeed have movement without length. We've agreed that movement can only exist in physical Beings and intellectual Beings; if it's the latter class which rules the former, and can make it give this productive movement to physical things, it must be this intellectual Being which, by means of its essence, is the true source of movement; as such, it's of another order than the class of immaterial physical Principles which are subordinate to it. Therefore, in this class it must have an action and results which are also distinct and independent from the physical, that is, in which the physical doesn't act.

So, since the physical does nothing in all the actions which belong to the First Cause, and in all the immaterial results which come from this; if it does nothing but receive passive life which supports it for the duration of time; if finally all the physical effects, during the actual time of their existence have absolutely no influence over the purely intellectual class, all the more reason that this class could act before the existence of physical things, and can act after they've disappeared, since from the moment that these physical things lived, they haven't affected the action of the First Cause for a moment.

Then, although movement and length would be necessarily linked to one another in the physical, this would certainly not prevent there from being an eternal movement or action in the superior class, even when nothing physical would exist, and in this sense, we can say with confidence that, although we couldn't imagine length without movement, it's undeniable that we could imagine movement without length, since the Principle of movement, be it physical or intellectual, is outside of length.

Then, bringing all these observations together, we should see if it's possible to correctly attribute any movement to length, as the necessary essence does, and whether man errs when he seeks its Principle and knowledge of it there.

The Number of Movement

I've said in general that movement is nothing more than the effect of action, or rather action itself, since they are inseparable. I recognized moreover, that in physical things there are two types of opposing movements or actions: that is growth and diminution, or the force which distances the bodies from their Center and their own Law which leads them back to it. But, as the second of these two movements can only return in the tracks of the other, at the same time, and in accordance with the same Law but in the reverse direction, we aren't wrong when we say that both come from the same *number*; and the least of the Geometricians knows that this number is *four*.

Who doesn't know, indeed, that all the possible movements and cycles of bodies are made in Quaternary geometrical progression, either ascending or descending? Who doesn't know that this number *four* is the universal Law of the course of the stars, of mechanics, of pyrotechnics, in a word, the number of everything which moves in the physical Realm either naturally or by man's hand?

And truly, if life acts without interruption, and its action is always new; that is, if it grows or diminishes without cease in physical Beings which are subject to destruction, what other Law than that of ascending or descending geometrical progression would suit Nature?

Indeed, arithmetical progression is entirely excluded from it, because it's sterile and can only include limited facts or results which are always equal and always uniform. So, men should only ever apply it to dead things, fixed divisions, or invariable assemblages; and when they tried to use it to designate the simple living actions of Nature, such as those of Air, those which produce heat and cold, and all the other Causes of changes in the atmosphere, their results or their divisions were very faulty, in that they gave the masses a false idea of the Principle of life or of physical action, whose measure not being physical, can't be indicated in Matter without making a grave error.

We won't, therefore, encourage anyone to err by saying that the Quaternary geometric progression is the Principle of life in Beings, or asserting that the *number* of all actions is *four*, however strange this Language may seem.

The Number of Area

But what we still haven't determined is knowing what the *number* of area is. It should therefore be said that it's the same number *nine* which was applied earlier to the circular line. Yes, the circular line and area have such a connection, and they're so inseparable that they definitely have the same number, which is *nine*.[66]

If they have the same number, they are necessarily the same measure and the same weight; for these three Principles always work together, and one can't be determined without equally determining the other two.

---

[66] In this instance, where Saint-Martin discusses circles, the word *étendue* needs to be translated as 'area' rather than 'length', since he's referring to the circular line which encloses the area of the circle, as opposed to the straight line. Therefore, a straight line has the number *four*, while the circle and the area enclosed by this circle has the number *nine*. Note that in this instance Saint-Martin refers only to *la ligne circulaire*, or 'circular line', and expressly not to *la ligne courbe*, or 'curved line', which of course cannot contain an area. This could indicate he also saw the problem with the use of the word *étendue*.

The Circular Line

In fact, however new this may appear, I can't hold back from asserting that area and the circular line are the same thing; that is, that there can be no area without the circular line, and reciprocally that it's only the circular line which is physical or sensory; or put another way, that material Nature and length can only be formed from lines which aren't straight, or which is the same thing, that there is not a single straight line in Nature, as we will see below.[67]

I've only one thing to say before coming to this, which is that, if the Observers had examined this more closely, they would have long since resolved a question whose answer still isn't clear to them, which is: whether generation and reproduction is performed through eggs, or through worms or spermatic animals. They'd have seen that, since everything here below has an envelope, and since all envelopes or areas are circular, everything is a worm in Nature because everything is an egg; and also, everything is an egg because everything is a worm. I'll return to my subject.

I know it's not enough simply to exclude the straight line from Nature. I should explain the reasons which have led me to decide this.

Firstly, if we follow the origin of everything physical and material, we can't deny that the Principle of physical Beings is Fire, but that their corporisation comes from Water, and that bodies therefore begin in liquid.

Secondly, we can't deny either, that this liquid is the Principle which also works the dissolution of bodies, and that then Fire works their reintegration, since one of the most beautiful Laws of Truth is that direct order and inverse order have a uniform order in the contrary sense.

But all liquid is only an assemblage of spherical particles; and it's the spherical form of these particles which gives liquid the property it has of

---

[67] It could be said that the entire book revolves around this notion, that *four* went to *nine*, and now *nine* must try to return to *four*. As we have frequently seen, particularly in the footnotes expanding on Pasqually's and Saint-Martin's Theosophy of Numbers, *four* is the state of perfection and *nine* refers to the material world. So, going from *four* to *nine* represents man's loss of his primitive state and becoming a temporal and physical being. Immaterial to physical; eternal to temporal; perfect to imperfect; superior to inferior. *Four*, being eternal perfection, is represented by the straight line and the square, while *nine*, being material and temporal imperfection, is represented by the curved line and especially the circle and the area of the circle. Here Saint-Martin reinforces his view by telling us that there is no such thing as a straight line in nature, and if we believe we are seeing one, we are only seeing an imperfect reflection of the perfection contained in the superior Physical or Intellectual Principle. Again, we must remember he is talking in theosophical and allegorical terms. Finally, *One* is God or the First Cause, or *Unity*, represented by a central dot or period, from which everything was emanated.

spreading out and circulating. So, if bodies are born in it, it's therefore certain that they must preserve in their perfect state the same form which they received at their origin, as they continue to show it in their dissolution into liquid and spherical particles. For this reason, bodies should be considered to be an assemblage of these same spherical globules, but which have taken on stability in proportion to the extent that Fire has dried out the grosser part of their moisture. To whatever degree this assemblage of spherical globules is taken, it's therefore evident that the result will always be spherical and circular like its Principle.

Would we like to convince ourselves materially about what I'm proposing? Let's turn our attention to bodies whose dimensions appear to us to be straight, and closely observe the smooth surfaces. Everyone knows that we can find unevenness, ridges and hollows in them; everyone clearly knows, or should know, that the surfaces of bodies, when viewed close up, present a multitude of furrows to the eyes.

But these furrows are themselves composed of furrows, and so on *ad infinitum*, and however much our sight or those instruments which help us extend it tries, we will never see, either in the surfaces of bodies, or in the furrows they show us, anything but an assemblage of many spherical particles which only touch one another at one point of their surface. Now let's see if it's possible to accept there's a straight line in them.

The Straight Line

Let nobody object about that interval which exists between two given points, between which we can assume a straight line which connects one to the other.

Firstly, these two points, being separated, are no longer assumed to make a single body together. Thus, the straight line we believe to be between them would be purely in the mind, and couldn't be conceived as physical and sensory.

Secondly, this interval which separates them is itself filled with aerial mercurial particles, which being spherical, like those of other bodies, can never touch each other except at the surface; so this gap would be a body, and for this reason subject to the same inequalities as bodies; which agrees completely with what we previously said about the Principles of Matter, which, despite their union, can never become fused together.

There being therefore no continuity in bodies, everything in them being successive and interrupted, it's impossible in any sense to presume or recognize straight lines in them.

As well as the reasons we've just seen, there are others which can support them, and which confirm the proof of this Principle. I acknowledged that the number *four* was the number of the straight line; I've since seen, in common with all the Observers, that the number *four* is also the number which governs all types of movement. There is therefore a close connection between the Principle of movement and the straight line, since we see they have the same number, and besides we've accepted that in this movement resided the source and action of physical and sensory things, and that at the same time we've seen that the straight line was the symbol of the infinity and the continuity of products from the point from which it emanates.

Now, I've sufficiently shown that movement, although producing physical and sensory things, or extent, can however never truly belong to that same extent or depend on it; so if the straight line has the same number as this movement, it must have the same Law and the same property; that is, although it directs physical things and extent, it could never be mixed with them, nor mingle itself and become physical, since the Principle can't be mingled with its product.

These are all the reasons together which should stop us from ever including the straight line in physical Nature.

The Squaring of the Circle

So, let's review all our Principles. The number *four* is that of movement, and that of the straight line. In a word, it's the number of all which is not physical or sensory. The number *nine* is that of area and the circular line, which universally constitute extent; that is, that it's the number of the body and of all parts of the body; for we must absolutely regard the circular line as the necessary result of movement made in time.

These are the only two unique Laws which we should recognize, and which surely embrace everything that exists, since there is nothing in existence, within or outside of extent, which isn't passive or active, a result or a Principle, fleeting or unchangeable, physical or incorporeal, perishable or indestructible.

Taking then these two Laws as guides, we'll return to the manner in which we have seen that the Geometricians have considered the two only types of line which are possible, the straight and the curved; and we will judge if it's true that the circle is, as they claim it to be, a collection of straight lines, since on the contrary, there are no straight lines in the physical world which aren't an assemblage of curved lines.

However, it's because he hadn't discovered the different numbers of these two different lines, that since his exile man has sought to reconcile them, or which is the same thing, tried to discover what is called the Squaring of the Circle; for before his fall, knowing the nature of Beings, he wouldn't have been bothered with pointless efforts, and wouldn't have given himself over to investigating a discovery whose impossibility he clearly knew. He wouldn't have been blind enough nor stupid enough to try to unite Principles as different as those of the straight line and the curved line. In other words, it'd never have crossed his mind to consider how he could change the nature of Beings, and to make *nine* equal *four* or *four* equal *nine*; which is the very object of study and the work of the Geometricians.

If one in fact tried to reconcile these two numbers, how could one go about this? How does one apply *nine* to *four*, how does one divide *nine* by *four*, or which is the same thing, divide nine into four parts without using fractions which, as we have seen, can't be found in the natural Principles of things, even though they can work on their results, which are only assemblages? For, having found *two* as a quotient, wouldn't there always remain a Unity, which it would be necessary to divide by this same number *four*?[68]

Therefore, we see that this Squaring is impractical in a body, or in the physical and the sensory, and that it can never happen except in number and immaterially; that is, by accepting the Center which is physical or Quaternary, as we shall see shortly. So, I will leave you now to consider whether this Squaring is acceptable in the manner that men try to understand it; if its impossibility hasn't been clearly demonstrated, and if we should therefore be surprised that nothing more has been found concerning this

---

[68] A classic example of theosophical arithmetic: 9 / 4 = 2 + 1 rather than 2.5 (as there are no fractions in Saint-Martin's theosophy), since we obtain two 4's, with a '1' remaining. Incidentally, in Mathematics a 'quotient' is the result of a division, in this case '2'. However, there is another level at work here, since going from 9 to 4 in this manner requires there to be two '4's, which means we are still in the realms of confusion, indeed a sense of man and his creation Heva, indicated by the number '2', though '1', Unity or the First Cause is present and surveying the attempt.

subject; for as a fact of Truth, an approximation or nothing is really the same thing.[69]

Longitude

We can say the same about longitude, which so many men are trying to find on the terrestrial surface with so much rivalry; and from the looks of it, it'll be sufficient to observe the difference which exists between longitude and latitude.

Latitude is horizontal and goes from South to North. Now, as this South isn't indicated by any of the imaginary points invented by the Astronomers to explain the Universe to us, but clearly by the Sun, whose vertical Midday varies by being higher or lower in comparison with the preceding day, means it follows that this latitude is necessarily circular and variable, and as such, bears the number *nine* according to all the Principles which have just been established.

On the other hand, longitude is perpendicular, and comes from the East which is always at the same point of elevation, notwithstanding this East appears at different points on the horizon every day. Thus, longitude being fixed and always the same, it's the true image of the straight line, and in consequence bears the number *four*. Now, we've just seen the incompatibility of these two numbers *four* and *nine*; so how is it possible to find the perpendicular in the horizontal? How can the superior be compared to the inferior? Finally, how can we discover the East on the terrestrial surface, since it isn't in its Realm?

---

[69] As an aside, it is perhaps interesting to note that the Mathematical problem of squaring the circle, in the terms of how to create a square with the same area as a given circle using only a compass and ruler, was originally set in ancient times; but it wasn't until 1882 that it was proved to be impossible by the Lindemann-Weierstraß Theorem, which proved once and for all that pi (π) was 'transcendental' (the root of any regular number, in simple terms) and therefore unable to deliver a rational number which could be used to do the calculation. However, in Esoteric Philosophy the term Squaring the Circle is normally used with regard to reconciling Heaven (depicted as a circle or sphere) with Earth (a square or cube) from the old Hermetic axiom 'as above so below'. However, once again it's interesting to note that Saint-Martin turns the notion of the circle representing perfection, and the angular square as imperfection on its head, by aligning the line or square with perfection, and the curve and circle with imperfection. In Freemasonry, the image is often depicted as a circle with a central point, between two vertical lines (sometimes shown as St. John the Baptist and St. John the Evangelist), surmounted by the Holy Bible. The explanation given is allegorically profound, but touches neither on the mathematical nor the Hermetic conundrums.

When I said the East was fixed, it was clearly understood that I wasn't speaking about where the Sun rises, since it changes every day. Besides, the kind of longitude that the Sun gives in this way is only even horizontal in relation to us, like latitude, and by that alone it's very inaccurate.

I was speaking rather of the true East of which the rising of the Sun is only an indicative sign, and which manifests visibly and more appropriately in the plumb and the perpendicular.[70] This East, which by its number *four* can alone embrace all of space, since in joining itself with the number *nine* or that of expanse, that is, uniting the active and the passive, forms the number *thirteen*, which is the number of Nature.

It's therefore no more possible to find this longitude on Earth than to reconcile the straight line with the curved line, and to find the measurement of extent and movement in extent; new proof of the truth of the Principles we have set forth.

Solar and Lunar Calculation

We should apply this Law further to another observation, and say that it's because of this same difference between the number *four* and the number *nine* that nobody has been able to – and will never be able to – correctly square Lunar calculations with Solar calculations. For the Moon is *nonary*, since it's attached to the Earth which only has curves as latitudes; and the Sun, on the contrary, though designating latitude by the South, is nevertheless, when it's in the terrestrial East or in the place of its rising, the image of the Principle of longitude or the straight line, and as such it's *Quaternary*. Besides, it's clearly distinct from the region of Earth, to which it communicates the reaction necessary for its vegetative ability, another indication of its Quaternary activity. In a word, its Quaternary manifests on the Moon itself by means of the four phases which we see on it, and which are determined by its different positions relative to the Sun from which it receives light.

---

[70] This, as in the comment about Degrees or Grades, is an extraordinarily overt comment about Freemasonry. The Plumb isn't only the symbol of and also the jewel worn by the Junior Warden in Lodge, who represents the 'Sun at meridian', and whose comment at the closing of the Lodge states that Masons should act 'by the plumb', meaning that they should be upright and fair in all their dealings with their fellow men; but it is also the key sign in the Installation of the Worshipful Master in most jurisdictions of the world, who, sitting in the East, represents the rising sun as a symbol of enlightenment, and who creates 'upright men and Masons'.

Thus, applying to this example the Principle which concerns us at present, we can clearly see why the Solar calculation and the Lunar calculation are incompatible, and that the true means of coming to an understanding of things is to begin by not confusing them, but by following them and examining each according to the *number* and Laws which are specific to them.

Astronomical Systems

Might I expand further on this number *nine* which I attribute to the moon, and as a consequence to the Earth whose satellite it is? I'd like to show by the number of this Earth what its use and its purpose in the Universe are; and this could even give us a true indication of the real form it has, and shed even more light on the current theory which doesn't see it as immobile, but on the contrary, as travelling along a very large orbit.

For the Astronomers were perhaps a little too hasty in their judgements; and before giving all their confidence to their observations, they should have examined which among the physical Beings should move the most: the one which gives the reaction or the one which receives it; whether Fire isn't the most mobile of the Elements, and blood more agile than the body in which it circulates. They should have considered that the Earth, though not occupying the middle of the stars' orbits, could nevertheless serve as their *recipient*, and therefore receive and expect their influences, without being forced to add a second physical action to the vegetative action which is normal to it, and of which these stars are deprived.

Finally, the simplest experiments on the Cone[71] would have proved to them the true form of the Earth; and we could show them, in the purpose of this same Earth, in the rank which it occupies among created Beings, and in the properties of the perpendicular or the straight line, the insurmountable difficulties which their explanations can't resolve.

It could also be that these difficulties weren't understood, since Astronomy is isolated like all the Sciences where man has taken control, so

---

[71] The 'Cone of Darkness' is essentially when the Earth covers the Sun and thereby causes an eclipse of the moon. However, this was the subject of Pasqually's rituals which Saint-Martin knew, which also had a symbolic interpretation concerning the presence of evil spirits which lived in this dark region. Suffice it to say, without going into detail, that Saint-Martin must have been subtly referencing this by using the term 'Cone', and hence the hint that 'simple experiments' couldn't resolve their explanations.

it considers Earth, like all the celestial bodies, as being distinct Beings, without any connection between one another. In other words, because man has acted in this as thoughtlessly as he has elsewhere, by not looking at the Principle of existence in all these bodies, or their Laws and purpose, that's the reason he still doesn't know what its first purpose is.

The Earth

What's more, it's from an apparently praiseworthy motive that he's sought to disparage the Earth by comparing it to the immensity and grandeur of the Stars. He had the weakness to believe that this Earth, being but a dot in the Universe, merited little attention from the First Cause. He thought it went against probability that this Earth was, on the contrary, the most precious thing in creation, and that everything existing around or above it could come to do it homage, as if the Creator of things would evaluate His Works merely by physical measurement. But their worth wasn't in their great size and the expanse they occupied, but rather in the nobility of their use and in their properties.

Perhaps it's this false idea which led man to another, even falser scheme, in which he pretends not to be worthy of his Creator's regard, believing he was merely being humble by refusing to admit this Earth and all that the Universe contains were made only for him. He pretended to be afraid that he was showing too much pride in allowing himself this thought.

But he certainly didn't fear the indolence and cowardliness which necessarily come out of this pretend modesty; and if man avoids seeing himself now as before as the King of the Universe, it's because he doesn't have the courage to work towards recovering his *Titles*, whose duties appear to be too taxing to him, and because he fears less renouncing his estate and all his rights than having to work to restore them to their true value. However, if he were to observe himself for a moment, he'd soon see that he should use this humility to admit that he is rightly beneath his rank, but not to believe his nature to be such that he had never occupied it, nor that he could never return there.

The Plurality of Worlds

How, then, could I relieve myself of all that I have to tell you about these things? How can I avoid showing you the relationships between this Earth and the human body, which is formed from the same substance since it comes from it? If my plan permits, I'll draw the evidence for the uniformity of their Laws and their proportions from their undeniable connection, from which it'd be easy to see that they both have the same goal to accomplish.

It'd be here, too, that we'd learn why, at the beginning of this book, I taught that man was so strongly interested in maintaining his body in good condition; for if he's made in Earth's image, and the Earth is the foundation of physical creation, he can only preserve his similarity to it by resisting, as does the Earth, the powers which continually fight against it. We see here, too, that this Earth must be as respected by him as his mother, and since after the intelligent Cause and man, it's the most powerful of all Beings of temporal Nature, Earth's its own proof that no other physical World exists other than the one we can see.

For the theory about the Plurality of Worlds[72] is taken from the same source as all other human errors. It's out of the same desire to separate everything and dismember everything, that man imagines a multitude of other Universes, whose Stars are Suns, and which have no more connection with one another than with the World we inhabit; as if this separated existence were compatible with the idea we have of Unity; and as if, as an intellectual Being, if these theoretical Worlds existed, man wouldn't know about them.

---

[72] Saint-Martin's evident distaste for the theory of the Plurality of Worlds is evident throughout this Chapter, and one is led to believe he'd have much preferred it if the old model of earth being in the center, with the rest of creation encircling, it was still in place, for his arguments would be easier to make. But he lived in post-Copernican times, and the genie couldn't be put back in the bottle. Indeed, by this time the Astronomers has fairly well mapped out most of the solar system, and were now looking further afield for new discoveries. However, part of Saint-Martin's distaste may well have come from the fact that some scientists were now explicitly using these models to counter Christian teachings. The power of the Church had diminished from the time that they'd burned Giordano Bruno at the stake in 1600 for heresy, among which reasons was his statement that: "innumerable celestial bodies, stars, globes, suns and earths may be sensibly perceived therein by us…". Indeed, twenty years after Saint-Martin's book appeared, in 1794, Thomas Paine published his popular *Age of Reason*, in which he argued that in accepting the plurality of worlds and the possibility of them being inhabited, one could find a strong argument against Christianity and its central doctrine of divine incarnation, pointing out that this would require Jesus to go and die continually on multiple worlds, which would surely be absurd.

So, if he can and should know of everything which exists, it must be that nothing is isolated, and that everything is interconnected; since it's with one same Principle that man understands everything, and he couldn't do this with one same Principle if all the other physically created Being weren't similar to one another and of the same nature.

Yes, without doubt there are many Worlds, since the smallest of Beings is one, but they all belong to the same chain and as man has the right to reach up his hand to the first link of this chain, he can't do this without touching all the other Worlds at the same time.

Moreover, we see in the image of Earth's properties that for man's well-being, both physical and intellectual, it's a fertile and inexhaustible source; that it brings together all the proportions, both numerical and shape; that it's the first point of support that man encountered after his fall, and as such he can't value it too highly, since without it he'd have fallen far lower.

The Nonary Number

What, then, if I dared to speak about the Principle which animates it, and in which resides all the powers of vegetation and other *virtues* I could explain? It's certain that men would then learn to have veneration for it, that they'd be more concerned with its *cultivation*, and would regard it as the entrance to the path which they must follow in order to return to the place which gave them birth.

But perhaps I've already said too much about these things, and if I were to go further, I fear I'd infringe on rights which aren't mine. So, I'll return to the numbers *four* and *nine*, which I've said belong to the straight line and the curved line, and also the number of movement or action, and the number of length or extent respectively; for these numbers might appear to be fictitious and imaginary.

It's appropriate for me to show why I use them and why I claim they each naturally suit the lines I've attributed to them. Let's begin with the number *nine*, or that of the circular line and area.

Surely nobody will find it hard to think of a circumference as zero; for what figure could more closely resemble a circumference than a zero? It'll be even less of a problem to regard the center as a Unity[73], since it's

---

[73] The word *unité* can mean 'unit' or 'unity'. Here the argument focuses strongly on the fact that '1' equates with Divinity, and this aspect is far more important than straightforward geometrical

impossible for a circumference to have more than one center. Everyone knows, too, that a Unity joined to a zero gives *ten*, like this: 10. Thus we can envisage the complete image of the circle as making *ten*, or 10, that is, the center with the circumference.

But we can also see the entire circle as a physical Being whose circumference is the form or body, and whose center is the immaterial Principle. Now, we have seen with sufficient detail that we should never confuse the immaterial Principle with the physical form and extent; that although it's in their union that the existence of Matter is founded, it's nevertheless an unpardonable error to take them to be the same Being, and that man's mind is always able to separate them.

Now, isn't separating this Principle from its physical form the same thing as separating the central point from its circumference, and as a result the same thing as removing the unity 1 from the denary 10? But, if one removed a unity from the denary 10, we know that only the number *nine* would remain. However, the zero, 0, or the circular line, or again the circumference, still remains. Now, let's see if the number *nine* and the circumference don't match one another, and if we're wrong to give this number nine to all areas, since we have proved that all areas are circular.

Let's see too, given the connection which exists between zero, which is nothing in itself, and the number *nine* or area, whether we should've been so quick to blame those who claimed that Matter was only apparent.

I know that most of the Geometricians, seeing the number of Arithmetical characters as being man made, would have little confidence in our current demonstration; and I know too, that there are those among them who have attempted to increase the number of those characters to twenty, in order to facilitate calculations.[74]

But firstly, if several Nations have Arithmetical characters which are only man made, the Arab characters should be excepted because they are

---

arguments. Again, one language offers us two related meanings, while English requires two. Therefore, I have kept the word 'unity' throughout, which the reader can interpret as being 'one' or 'unit' as desired. In this section Saint-Martin capitalizes the word whenever it refers to the First Cause. Incidentally, theologically the French word mean 'Unitive', or in Catholicism the final way of perfection (following the Purgative and Illuminative ways), where the Soul, having come through its Long Dark Night, and stripped of its pride and its ego, now fixes its thought on God and turns away from temporal things; which is a particularly pertinent interpretation for this book.

[74] Indeed, a vestige of the so-called 'vigesimal 'system (named after *viginti*, Latin for 20) can be found in old, pre-1971 British currency, when there were 20 shillings in a pound. Another example of using base 20 in counting is in French itself, where 80 is *quatre-vingts*, and 90 is *quatre-vingt-dix*, or four-twenties, and four-twenties-and-ten respectively.

founded on the Laws of nature of physical things, which as well as intellectual things have numerical signs which are specific to them.

Secondly, as Geometricians are completely ignorant of the Laws and properties of *Numbers*, they haven't seen that by multiplying them beyond ten they were perverting everything, and trying to give Beings a Principle which wasn't simple, and which didn't offer Unity. They hadn't seen that since Unity is universal, the sum of all the *Numbers* should show us His image, so that in revealing Himself as real and as unalterable in His products as in His essence, this Unity would have absolute rights to our homage, and that man couldn't be forgiven if he misunderstood this. They haven't seen, I tell you, that the number *ten* is that which bore this imprint most perfectly, and that therefore man's will could never extend the signs of *Numbers* or the Laws of Unity beyond ten.

Thus, experience has plainly confirmed this Principle, and the means used to fight it have met with no success. I will not therefore attempt to defend it, and while attributing the number *one* or Unity to the center, will attribute the number *nine* to the circumference or to area.

The Division of the Circle

I won't repeat here what I've said about the union of the three fundamental Elements, which are always found together in each of the three parts of the body; by which we'll easily find a clear connection of the number *nine* to Matter and to the circular area. I'll say nothing further about the formation of the cube, either algebraic or arithmetic which, when the factors only have two terms, can only take place through nine steps, since among the ten, which should be carefully counted, the second and third are only a repetition of each other, and from this must be considered as making only one.

But I'll support the Principle I've established with some observations on the nature and division of the circle; for it's wrong to say that it's the Geometricians who divided it up into three hundred sixty degrees, as being the most convenient division, and which would lend itself most easily to calculations.

This division of the circle into three hundred sixty degrees isn't at all arbitrary; it's Nature herself which give it to us, since the circle is only made up of triangles, and there are six of these equilateral triangles in the overall area of this circle.

Let's therefore follow with our eyes the natural order of these numbers, and let's add the product which is the circumference or the zero, and then let's see if it's indeed man who's established these divisions.

Need I set out the natural order of these numbers? All products of any kind are ternary, *three*. There are six of these perfect products in a circle, or six equilateral triangles, *six*. Finally, the circumference itself completes the work, and gives *nine* or zero, 0. If we wish to reduce all these Numbers to figures, we'll firstly have 3, secondly 6, and finally 0, which together will give 360.

Then do whatever multiplications you wish with the Numbers we've just recognized as constituting the circle; then, as all the results will be nonary[75], nobody can doubt further the universality of the number *nine* in Matter.

We can't then doubt the powerlessness of this number, when we reflect that whatever number we join to it, it'll never alter its nature; which, for those who have the key, will be evident proof of what we've said: that the form or envelope can vary without its immaterial Principle ceasing to be unchangeable and indestructible.

The Artificial Circle

It's through these simple and natural observations that we can come to see the proof of the Principle I'm explaining. It's at the same time, one of the means which can show men how we should proceed to read the nature of Beings; for all their Laws are written on their envelope, in their gait, and in the different cycles to which their life subjects them.

For example, it's in not having distinguished the natural circumference from the artificial circumference that the error arose which I mentioned above about the way the circumference has been considered till now, that is, as an assemblage of an infinite number of points joined by straight lines.

---

[75] These rather odd terms all came from Pasqually's *Treatise*. In finding terms to refer to numbers while trying to indicate that he wasn't using them for purely mathematical purposes, he invented adjectives and nouns which don't exist in the French language. Therefore, in his and Saint-Martin's work you'll find the words denary (10), nonary (9), octenary (8), septenary (7), sesenary (6), quinary (5), quaternary (4), ternary (3) and binary (2). The strange word 'quatriple' meaning 'fourfold', can also be found frequently in Pasqually's writing, always in reference to the 'quatriple divine essence'.

It's true that the circumference which man draws with the aid of a compass can only be formed by successive movements, and in this sense we can regard it as being an assemblage of several points, which only being drawn in successive arcs are assumed not to have connectivity or continuity between them; which means that the imagination has assumed straight lines in order to join them.

The Natural Circle

But beyond my having shown that, even here, the line which we agree unites them couldn't be straight, since physically there's no way it could be, we've only to study the formation of the natural circle to recognize how false the definitions we're usually given about the circular line really are.

The natural circle expands in all directions at the same time. It occupies and fills all the parts of its circumference, for it's only in the physical order and through the eyes of our Matter that we perceive the inequalities there must be in physical forms, because they are only assemblages; whereas through the eyes of our intellectual ability we see the same force and the same power everywhere. And we no longer see these inequalities because we sense that the Principle's action must be full and uniform; for if this weren't the case it would itself be in danger: and we should say in passing that it's that which makes all these scholastic and puerile disputes pointless. The restricted eyes of man's body must find them at every step, because they can only comprehend area. On the other hand, his intelligence can't see any of this, for it reads in the Principle, and sees that this Principle acts everywhere, that it necessarily fills everything, since *resistance* must be universal like *pressure*.

We can't therefore compare the natural circle with the artificial circle in any way, since the natural circle is created all at once, solely by means of the explosion of its center; whereas the artificial circle is only begun by the end which is the triangle; for everyone knows or should know, that the compass which has one of its points immobile, can't make a single movement with the other without creating a triangle.

The Quaternary Number

We now come to the reasons why the Number *four* is that of the straight line.

I will say first that I'm not using the term *straight line* here in the sense that it has in daily Language, by which we express that length which seems to our eyes to have a common alignment; and indeed, having demonstrated that there are no straight lines at all in physical Nature, I can't adopt the common opinion in this regard without going in the opposite direction to all I've established. I'll therefore regard the straight line solely as a Principle, and as such, being distinct from length.

Haven't we seen that the natural circle grows in all directions at the same time, and that the center throws out an innumerable and inexhaustible multitude of its radii? Aren't each of these radii considered to be a straight line in the material sense? And truly, by its apparent rectitude and by the ability which it has of extending itself to infinity, it's the true image of the Generating Principle, which ceaselessly produces outside of itself, and which never strays from its Law.

Moreover, we've seen that the circle being itself but an assemblage of triangles, since we only recognize three Principles in all bodies, and the circle is a body. Now, if this radius, if this apparently straight line, in other words, if the action of the Generating Principle can only manifest itself through a ternary product, we only have to join the number of unity or the center, or the number of this Generating Principle, to the ternary number of its product to which it's linked during the lifetime of the physical Being, and we'll already begin to see the Quaternary we are looking for in the straight line, according to the notion of it we've given.

But so nobody thinks that we're confusing what we've distinguished with so much care, which is the center which is immaterial, with its product or the triangle which is material and physical, we should remember what was said about the Principles of Matter. I showed clearly enough that although they produce Matter, they are however themselves immaterial. Then, taken as such, it's easy to see a close link between the center, or Generating Principle, with the secondary Principles; and as the three sides of a triangle, as well as the three dimensions of forms, have physically shown us that these secondary Principles only number *three*, their union with the center offers the most perfect idea of our immaterial *Quaternary*.

Moreover, as this Quaternary manifestation only takes place by means of the emanation of a radius from its center; as this radius, which is always a straight line, is the agent and action of the central Principle; as the curved line, on the contrary, produces nothing, and always limits the action and the product of the straight line or the radius; we can't deny this proof, and we can therefore confidently apply the number *four* to the straight line or to the radius which it represents, since it's the straight line and the radius alone which can give us knowledge of this Number.

This is how man can come to distinguish the form and physical envelope of Beings from their immaterial Principles, and by this obtain a true enough idea of their different *numbers*, to avoid confusion and to walk with assurance on the path of observations. This, I say, is the way to discover the Squaring we've talked about, and which can only be discovered by means of the *number* of the center.

It's so true, indeed, that this straight line or this Quaternary is the source and agent of all that's physical and sensory, that it's to the number *four* and the square that Geometry returns everything it wishes to measure; for it only considers the triangles it creates from this point of view as a division, and a half of this square. Now, isn't this square formed by four lines, and by four lines regarded as straight, or like the radius, and as a result Quaternary like it?

Do we need anything more to show that by their very method the Geometricians prove what I am proposing to them? That is, that the *Number* which produces Beings is the same which serves as their measurement; and thus, the true measurement of Beings can only be found in their Principle, and not in their envelope and their extent; since on the contrary, all that the envelope is, all that their extent is, can only the evaluated with precision by approaching the center, and to this Quaternary Number we call the Generating Principle.

I hope nobody would dream of objecting that all figures which are called rectilinear in Geometry, since they are bounded by four supposedly straight lines, also bear the Quaternary, and that therefore I shouldn't limit myself to the square to indicate the Quaternary measurement, which would appear to contradict the simplicity and unity of the Principle just stated.

Regardless of all these facts, and even if it was incorrect that the Geometricians, as I just said, brought everything they wanted to measure back to the square, it would be sufficient from what we've just said about the immaterial Quaternary to agree that all physical things which come from it must physically preserve the mark of this Quaternary origin upon them. Now, since this Quaternary is definitely the only Generating Principle of physical things, being the sole *Number* which possesses this property of production, we may be certain that among all physical things there is only one figure which shows this to us, and this figure, as we've said, is the square.

The Square Root

And how would this truth not reveal itself to us among physical things, since we find it clearly indicated and in an indisputable manner in numerical Law, that is to say, in the most intellectual and certain thing that man possesses here below? How, indeed, could we find more than one Quaternary measure, or in other words, more than one square in the sensory and physical figures which are the subject of Geometry, since in this numerical Law or Law of calculation we just mentioned, it's impossible to find more than one square number?

I know this must be surprising, and however undeniable this proposal is, no doubt it'll appear to be new; for it's generally accepted that a numerical square is the product of any number multiplied by itself, and there's no question that all Numbers have this property.

But, since the connection we've discovered in all classes between the Principles and their products still isn't enough to clarify this point for us; and since, despite the fact that the square is always drawn the same way by men, Geometricians have convinced themselves that there can be more than one numerical square. I'm going to go into other details which will confirm the truth of what I've just proposed.

The shape of a square is most certainly the quadruple of its base; and if it's the physical image of the intellectual and numerical square from which it's derived, this intellectual and numerical square must be the archetype and model of the physical square; that is, that just as the square figure is the quadruple of its base, so the intellectual and numerical square must be the quadruple of its root.

Now, I can certify to all men, and they can know as do I, that there's only one Number which is the quadruple of its root. I will even excuse myself, so far as I can, from giving them a clear indication of this, both because it's so easy to find, and because these are Truths which I can only explain with reluctance.

But, you may ask me, if I only allow for one numerical square, how should we consider the products of all the other numbers multiplied by themselves? For if there's only one numerical square, then there can only be one square root among all numbers; and yet there's not a single number which can't be multiplied by itself. So, since all numbers can be multiplied by themselves, what will they be if they're not square roots?

I agree that any number can be multiplied by itself, and therefore there are none which couldn't be regarded as a root; and moreover, with the smallest calculation I know that there isn't a root which doesn't have a proportional average between its product and unity; but for all these numbers to be square roots, they must all be in a ratio of *four* to unity. Now, among the multitude of different roots whose quantity can never be determined, seeing that there's no limit to numbers, there is only one number or one single root which has this connection of *four* to unity. It's therefore clear that the Number found to have this ratio is the only one which actually merits the name of square root; and since all the other roots have different ratios to unity, could have names taken from these different ratios, but they should never take the name of square roots, since their ratio to unity will never be Quaternary.

For the same reason, although all the roots when multiplied by themselves give a product; since all roots are a proportional average between its product and unity, this product must itself necessarily be to its root what its root is to unity; then if there's only one root which can be in a ratio of *four* to unity, or which makes a square, it's undeniable that there can only be a single product which has a ratio of four to its root, and as a result it can only have one square.[76]

As all the other products don't have this Quaternary ratio with their root, they therefore can't be considered to be squares, but they'll bear the names of their different ratios with their root, as roots which aren't squares bear the names of their different ratios with unity.

---

[76] After experimenting with traditional mathematics for a long time, looking at both arithmetic and geometric means, the Translator has come to the conclusion that this is simply an argument based upon theosophical addition, squaring and roots. See the Introduction to this book, section 3. The Ideas to recall how this works for the number 4. This also helps with the next section, where the connection between the Quaternary and the Decimal (i.e. 4 and 10) are discussed, since 10 is the theosophical root of 4 (obtained by adding 4+3+2+1 = 10).

In other words, if it's true that all roots were square roots, all roots correctly doubled would certainly have squares which would be their doubles, and we know that with numbers that's completely impossible; and that's why we only allow one square, and one square root. It's therefore by not having correct notion of a square root that the Geometricians have attributed their properties to all numbers, whereas they only work properly for one number.

We should nevertheless remark that the difference found between this single square root and all the other roots, as well as that between the only admissible squared product and all other numerical products, is only due to the quality of its factors, which are communicated to the results which come from it. In truth, it's always the Quaternary which directs all these operations; or, to speak more clearly, in all kinds of multiplication, we will always find firstly the unity, secondly the first factor, thirdly the second factor, and finally the result, or the product which arises from the mutual action of the two factors.

And when I say in all kinds of multiplication, it's because this is found to be true, not only in all the products where we know two roots or two factors, as in the multiplication of two different numbers with one another; but also in all the products where we only know one root, because this root being multiplied by itself, always offers us our two distinct factors.

It's therefore this which presents us with new evidence of the true power of the number *four*, the Principle of all products and the Universal generator, as well as the virtues of that straight line which is its image and action.

It's here, too, that we find new proof of the distinction between physical and intellectual things, as well as everything that's been said about their different *number*, since in all numerical multiplications, we know three things physically, being the two factors and the product, whereas intellectually we only know the unity to which they are related, and that this unity never enters into the workings of composite things.

We therefore see why we've recognized this Quaternary as being both the Principle and the fixed measurement of all Beings, and why all products are generated and governed by this Quaternary, both in extent and in all the different properties of this extent.

Decimals

The Geometricians themselves confirm all the benefits which have been attributed so far to the Quaternary by the divisions they use on the radius to determine its relationship with the circumference. They're careful to divide it into the greatest number of parts possible, to make the approximation less defective. But in all the divisions they use, it's important to observe that they always use decimals. Now, by a calculation we won't go into here, though it's known well enough, we can't deny that the decimal and the Quaternary have an undeniable relationship, since they both have the privilege of corresponding to and belonging to unity. By using decimals, the Geometricians therefore still work by means of the Quaternary.

I know that strictly speaking one could divide the radius by Numbers other than decimals; I also know that these decimals never give correct results, like the division of the circle into three hundred sixty degrees, from which one might infer that neither decimals nor the Quaternary, with which they're inseparably united, are the true measurement.

But we should note that the division of the circle into three hundred sixty degrees is perfectly accurate, because it falls on the true *number* of all forms; whereas the decimal division, in expressing the *number* of the immaterial Principle of these forms, can't be exact in physical Nature, both on the physical radius or on any kind of Matter.

This doesn't prevent the fact that, of all the divisions which man could choose, decimals are those which bring him closest to what he wants to do. We can even say that in this, as in many other circumstances, he's been led without knowing it by the Law and Principle of things; that his choice is a result of the natural light which is within him, and which always offers to lead him towards the Truth, and that the means he's used, pointless and useless as it may be to him as he wants to make it agree with extent and Matter, is still the best he had to take of this type.

The Intellectual Square

And so, despite the lack of success that man has obtained from his efforts, we'll always have to agree that the division he's made of the radius into decimal parts confirms what I've said about the universality of the Quaternary measurement.

Whatever reservation I've tried to maintain, following all I've revealed about the number *four* and about the square root, all my Readers will realize that both are the same. Therefore, it's no longer the time to hide it, and even having advanced so far, I find myself obliged to assert that it's in vain that they would seek the source of knowledge and illumination outside of this square root, and in the one square which is its result.

And in truth, if it's possible for those who read this book to grasp the connection between everything I'm placing before their eyes on their own, and to obtain an acceptable idea about the numeric and intellectual square which I'm showing them, I'm in a way obliged to accept the truth and can no longer refuse them the admission they wish to extract from me.

I'm therefore going to begin by presenting, so far as prudence and discretion will permit, some of the properties of this *Quaternary*, and to make myself more understandable, I will consider it as the sensory and physical square which is its figure and product, that is, as having four visible and distinct sides.

By examining each of these four sides separately, we can convince ourselves that the square we're talking about is truly the only way which could lead men to the knowledge of everything contained in the Universe, and that it's the sole support which should sustain him against all the tempests which he's obliged to endure during his journey in time.

But to better sense the infinite advantages attached to this square, let's remember what has been said when comparing it with the circumference. There we learned that the circumference is made to limit and oppose the action of the center or the square, and that they react mutually upon one another, and that as a result the circumference stops the rays of light; whereas the square being itself the Principle of this light, its true object is to enlighten; in other words, the circumference keeps man in bonds and imprisoned, whereas the square is given to him to deliver himself from it.

Effects of the Circumference

It's truly the inferiority of this circumference which causes all of man's misfortunes, because he can only go through all its points successively, which makes him feel at every extent the misery of time for which he wasn't made; whereas the *square*, corresponding with unity, doesn't subject him at all to this Law, since in the image of its Principle, its action is complete and uninterrupted.

However, we must admit that Justice itself has favored man down to the punishments which it has inflicted upon him, and that this circumference which had been given him to limit him and make him expiate for his first errors, doesn't leave him without hope and consolation; for by means of this circumference man can go through the entire Universe and return to the point from which he departed without being obliged to turn around; that is, without losing sight of the center. This is even for him the most useful and beneficial exercise, as we see that when we want to magnetize a strip of iron, after rubbing it each time, we must return it to the magnet by making it go around a circle, otherwise it'd lose the virtue it had just received.

The Superiority of the Square

Nevertheless, despite this property of the circumference, there's absolutely no comparison to be made with the square, since the square teaches man directly about the *virtues* of the center, and that without leaving his place man can understand and encompass the same things he's only learn with the aid of the circumference by going through all its points.

Finally, he who has fallen into the circumference turns around the center, because he strayed from the action of the center or from the radius which is straight and he turns forever because proper action is universal, and because he finds it everywhere on his path and in opposition; instead of he who stays at the *center*, or on the *square* which is its image and *number*, which is always fixed and always the same.

It's no doubt pointless to press this allegorical comparison any further, because I've no doubt that wise eyes will make many discoveries in what I've just said.

This is therefore the reason I've been able to speak about the square as being superior to everything, since there are absolutely only two kinds of lines, the straight and the curved, and everything that's not connected with the straight line or the square must be circular, and as a result temporal and perishable.

It's therefore because of this universal superiority that I've been able to show man the infinite advantages which he can find in the square, or this

Quaternary number, about which I now intend to give some basic details to my Readers.

The Measurement of the Circumference

We pray them to remember that the square which is generally known is only an image and shape of the numerical and intellectual square. They'll no doubt also understand that we only intend to talk about the numerical and intellectual square which acts on time and governs time; and that this itself is proof that there exists another *square* outside of time, but complete knowledge of this square is forbidden to us until we ourselves are outside of the temporal prison; and it's for this reason I shouldn't have spoken about the terms of Quaternary Progression, which is elevated above the Causes acting in time.

According to this, to show how this square contains everything and leads to a knowledge of everything, let's observe that in Mathematics it's the four right angles which measure the whole circumference; and since these four angles each define a specific Region, it's clear that the square includes the East, West, North and South. Now, if in everything that exists, whether physical or intellectual, we can only find these four Regions, what could we conceive of beyond that? And when we've considered them as a class, shouldn't we consider ourselves to be sure that there'd be nothing further in that class for us to know?

The Measurement of Time

That's why the man who carefully observed the four Cardinal points of physical Creation with perseverance would have nothing further to learn in Astronomy, and he could claim to possess an understanding the foundation of the System of the Universe, as well as the true order of the Celestial bodies. In other words, he'd have an understanding of the property of fixed Stars, of Saturn's Ring, of the Times and Seasons favorable to *Agriculture*, and of the two Causes for eclipses; for it's in only ever wanting to see a single material and visible Law in these eclipses, that the Observers have denied any others arising from another source, and in a different time from the time indicated by the physical order.

As for the order of the movements of the Stars, man could equally have a sure knowledge of this by closely examining the four divisions which comprise their temporal course; for Time is the physical measurement which is least subject to error. For this reason, Time is the true measure of the course of the Stars, and one can sense that it's easier for a person to estimate correctly their periodic returns using Time, than to estimate the precise length of their arms using established measures determined by length; since those have no fixed basis determined by physical Nature; and that's why a great many Nations actually measure space and distance traveled by duration or time.

Upheavals in Nature

By the aid of that same square, man can succeed in delivering himself from the thick darkness which still obscures all eyes as to the age, origin and formation of things. It could even resolve all the disputes concerning when our Earth was born, and all the upheavals written upon its surface, and whose traces can also give witness to the results and effects of the first explosion, as well as those of later and successive upheavals which the Universe has continually experienced since its origin.

And indeed, these upheavals are always produced by physical forces, although they've been permitted by the First Cause, and executed under the eyes of the Superior Temporal Cause, by the continual *counteraction* of the Evil Principle, to which immense powers have often been given over physical things for the purification of the intellectual part. For, if it needs to be said, this purification of the intellectual part is the only path which leads to the true *Great Work*, or to the reestablishment of *Unity*. Now, how can this purification take place without its opposite or without its reaction, since it must happen in time, and in time nothing can happen without the aid of a reaction?

What will enlighten man on this is that, in observing the four Regions we spoke about, he'd see that there's one which directs, one which receives, and two which react. From this he'd see that the disasters whose traces the Earth shows everywhere necessarily belong to the action of the two active and opposed Regions, being those where Fire reigns and Water reigns. Then he'd no longer attribute the effects which his eyes witness daily to the one Element which appears to produce them, because he'd realize these upheavals are the result of a continual war between these two enemies, in which the advantage sometimes rests with the one and sometimes with the other, but also in which neither can be victorious without the place on Earth where the combat took place suffering in proportion, and being altered and changed.

That's why nothing we see on Earth should surprise us, because even if the daily upheavals, which we can't deny, hadn't taken place, these two Elements nevertheless began to act in opposition to one another from the moment of the origin of temporal things.

That's why, too, we can be sure that every moment produces new upheavals, because the action of these two Elements upon each other happens and will continually happen until the general dissolution. Thus, all these marvels which surprise the Naturalists so much disappear; all those irregularities, those devastations which happen before our eyes, like those whose remains and debris tell us happened in olden times, are no longer difficult to explain, and agree perfectly with all that we've seen of the innate Principles of Beings, their differing and opposed actions on each other, and finally on the deadly results of universal *counteraction*.

But all these phenomena appear even less surprising when we remember that these two opposing Elements, or two agents, or dual universal Law of Matter, are always controlled by the active and intelligent Cause which is their center and their link, and which can activate one or the other of these two Agents which are subject to it at will, and can even give them over to an inferior and evil action.

We therefore have another means to know where in the great upheavals, these prodigious excesses of Water over Fire or Fire over Water came from; for one simply needs to think of the active and intelligent Cause and recognize that, when the Principles of these Elements are no longer within their natural limits, it's because it abandons or activates one of them more than the other by means of its own *virtue*, to fulfill the decrees and Justice of the First Cause, and to allow the overly great *counteraction* of the Evil Principle which is oppose to it to act, or to stop.

We therefore see through this that, in order to know the reason for the actions this Cause takes in the Universe, we must seek it in its intelligent Nature and in everything which resembles it; for, since it's both active and intelligent at the same time, it brings about its physical effects by communicating its various actions and reactions to all temporal Beings; but it's through its intelligent ability alone that it can explain this, seeing that it's only by this right that it's admitted to the *Council*; and so there will never be a satisfying answer for those who only look for its explanation in Matter.

Let's apply this to everything that's been said about the manner of seeking the Truth in everything, and we'll see if the Principles which lead us aren't universal.

The Temporal Course of Beings

Besides the enlightenment that an understanding of the square can give us about the constitution of physical Beings, the harmony established between them, and the Causes of their destruction; it also includes the four distinct Degrees to which their individual lives subject them, and which we are clearly shown by the four Seasons; for who doesn't know the different properties of each of these Seasons? Who doesn't know that all physical Beings, since they are only born through the joining of two inferior actions, these two actions must above all be suited to one another and be mutually in accord; which can be called *Adoption*.

Now, this act of Adoption is attributed to Fall, because then Beings, by the Law of their immaterial Principle, cast outside of themselves the seeds which must be used for their reproduction; and this Law only begins to act when these seeds come to be in their natural womb. This is the First Degree of their cycle, a Degree on which reflection and thought will easily discover an infinity of things about which I mustn't speak.[77]

---

[77] We must be careful not to confuse the more common Four Ages of Man, which associate Spring with Childhood, Summer with Youth, Fall with Maturity and Winter with Old Age, with Saint-Martin's four Seasons here. In this instance, he begins the cycle with Fall, and the shedding of seeds into the soil (*Adoption*), remaining dormant through Winter (*Conception*) until warmth brings them to life in Spring (*Corporisation*), and finally achieving completion in Summer (*Maturity*). He does largely exclude animals (and man) from this cycle, accepting that most do not follow a yearly cycle, and indeed some animals procreate regardless of the time of year. However, the main point is his emphasis of the four-sided square, therefore basing the Seasons on its image, and thereby suggesting the perfection of this process. But this analogy goes much farther than this, which is why the term 'Degrees' was retained in this section, when a more fitting translation might have been 'stages'. Saint-Martin was a member of the Masonic Order of the Elect Cohens of the Universe, whose rituals focused on the monthly lunar periods (the Neomenies) and the biannual Equinoxes. In addition, the Rituals for the Degrees or Grades strongly emphasized a hierarchy of associations with the four quarters, so that, North, East, South and West were each associated with Ages of Man, Seasons, Angels, Archangels, Parts of the Body, Herbs, Incenses, and a host of other connections. This is almost certainly what Saint-Martin is referring to when he says: "an infinity of things about which I mustn't speak." As a final observation, note that he considers *Adoption* to be the First Degree (a

When the seeds are thus adopted by their womb, the two concurrent actions coming together form what we must call *conception*, which according to the Law of this very physical nature, is indispensable for the generation of Being of matter. This Second Degree of their cycle takes place during Winter, whose influence manages their strength by keeping them in repose, and collecting all their fire in the same hearth, operates a violent reaction on them which forces them to exert themselves, and makes them more able to combine and communicate their properties to one another.

The Third Degree of their cycle takes place during Spring, and we can regard this act as that of *vegetation* or corporisation; firstly, because it's the Third, and we have already shown that the number three is devoted to all outcomes, be they physical or incorporeal; and secondly, because the saline influences of Winter cease after fulfilling their Law, which was to activate not only the Principles of the generating seeds, but also those of their products, and they all make use of their ability and natural property by manifesting externally what they had within them. It's also during this season of Spring that the fruits of this vegetative property begin to appear, and see them come out of the womb in which they were born.

Finally, Sumer completes the work. Then it is that all the products, coming out of the womb where they had been formed, fully receive the action of the Sun which brings them to maturity, and that's the Fourth Degree of the cycle of all physical terrestrial Beings.

It seems however that we should exclude most animals, who although they're subject to the Four Degrees which I've just identified in the individual cycle of all physical Beings, nevertheless they don't always follow the Law and the duration of the seasons in their generation and growth; and this exception shouldn't be surprising, for since they're not inherent within the Earth, although they come from it, it's certain that their Law shouldn't be similar to that of the Beings of the Vegetable Kingdom attached to this same Earth.

---

common term in Freemasonry as the Lodge is known as the *Mother*), *Conception* (or Conceptualizing) the Second Degree, and speaks openly about *Corporisation* being the Third Degree (a Degree which focuses upon the body), completing the period of growth; while the Fourth Degree is a process of reaching *Maturity* with the implication, perhaps, of giving back. This fits well with the Three Blue Degrees and the Red Degree in Freemasonry. And perhaps this latter reminds us both of the heat of the sun, and of the red clay in which Adam was traditionally imprisoned.

The Age of the Universe

We shouldn't reject the Principle of Quaternary universality just because we see that, even among Beings of the Vegetable Kingdom, some don't wait for the entire cycle of the four seasons to complete its course, and others only complete it after several annual solar cycles. This difference comes from the fact that the former need a lesser reaction and the others a more considerable one to effect and operate their specific work. But these Four Degrees or four actions I've just outlined aren't any less appropriate, and are always accomplished with a perfect exactness in the most precocious Beings, as well as in those Beings which are the slowest; because from what we've seen about the number *four* in relation to length, it's what measures everything and maintains its action everywhere, though it doesn't work an equal action on all, and modifies its action according to the individual nature of the Being in question.

Would what we have just seen regarding the properties attached to the four seasons shed any light on the time that the Universe was born? This could only concern those who believe the Universe had a beginning, since for those who are either blind or dishonest enough not to recognize such a possibility, this research becomes superfluous. However, being certain that even they might profit from what I could say about this, I will, so far as I am permitted, raise a corner of the veil before their eyes.

If, thinking about the Earth's origin, we only take onto account the first moment of the appearance of its physical form, it's certain that being guided by the order of the seasons, we'd have to attribute it to Spring, because in effect that's the time of growth.

But if we were to think a little harder, and examined all the actions which must have preceded this visible appearance, we'd have to put the origin of the seed of the world in a season other than Spring. For we'd have to agree that since the present cycle of universal Nature is the same as it was at its birth, the Adoption of its constituent Principles must have taken place in the same circumstances and at the same time that we see the Adoption which perpetuates its cycle and existence takes place today; that is, the initial Adoption must have begun in Fall.

This is indeed, when Beings lose the warmth of the *Sun*, when this Star removes itself from them, that they come together and seek each other out, in order to replace it by communicating their own warmth; and this, as we've seen, is the first act which must take place physically between the particular Beings of Nature. It must therefore be the same with the Universe; and it's when the *Sun* has ceased to be physical to those whom it has warmed till then that physical things take the first step towards existence, and that Nature began.

By the same analogy we can guess the season in which Nature must decompose and cease to exist; that is, that by following the Law of her current cycle, we must believe that it'll be in Summer that this Universe will complete the four acts of its universal cycle, and with this completion done, it'll end its career, and detach itself from the branch, to use the image of fruits. It'll cease to be, and will disappear completely, whilst the tree to which it was attached will remain stable forever.

What I've just said has its basis in a generally recognized Law which is, that things always end where they began. However, I repeat, although the four actions of the temporal cycle are completed in every Being, it doesn't mean that this Law takes the same length of time to be accomplished.

So, if the cycle varies from plant to animal, and even within each of these two classes it can occur so diversely, both in the different species as in different individuals, all the more reason it should be even harder to determine the Law and its length by comparing the individual to the universal. Thus, nothing is further from my mind than wanting to establish a specific period for these great ages. And in truth, these questions are totally unnecessary for man, seeing that by means of the spark he carries within he can acquire more useful light on these things which is far more certain and more important than that which only falls on the periods of transient Beings.

I also pray that no one will accuse me of contradiction or inadvertency if they understood me to be speaking about the Sun before the existence of physical things, for I haven't forgotten that the Sun we see was born just like everything else, and at the same time. But I know too, that there is another very physical Sun of which it's but the image, and beneath whose gaze all the acts of Nature's birth and creation took place, just as the daily and annual cycles of individual Beings occur beneath the gaze and by means of the Laws of our physical and sensory Sun.

Thus, in the interest of those who read this, I urge them not to judge me before they have understood me; and if they wish to understand me, they should always set their view beyond what I say; for, whether through duty or prudence I've left much to be desired.

The Sides of the Square

After describing many of the properties of the square in general, which I always show to be one and unique, I'll briefly outline some of those properties attached to each of its sides, and allow myself to talk about this universal emblem in a more extended manner in the next section.

The first of these sides is its base, the foundation or root of the three other sides, and it's the image of the First Being, unique and universal, Who's manifested in time and in all physical products, but which being His Own Cause and the Source of all Principles, has His dwelling outside of time and physical space; and to recognize what I've already said several times, that although physical products come from Him, they're unnecessary for His existence, we've only to observe the *number* which is His, and everybody knows that this is Unity.

Whatever calculation we make on this number taken in itself; that is, whether we multiply it, raise it to whatever power the imagination might conceive, or successively seek the root of all these powers, this same number of Unity will be the result every time, so that this number *one* being at the same time its own root, its own square and all of its powers, necessarily exists within itself and independently of all other Beings.

I won't talk at all about division, because this calculation can only be done on multiples, and never on a simple number like Unity, which confirms what I said about the nullity of fractions.[78]

I won't talk about addition either, because it's clear that it, too, only has a role in multiples, and a Being Who is everything in Himself can't be added to any other Being, which serves to prove everything we said before about Matter, where nothing used in the growth and nutrition of physical Beings can be mixed with their Principles.

But I can talk about multiplication, or the raising of powers, as well as the extraction of roots, because one is the image of the reproductive property innate in all simple Beings, and the other is the image of the correspondence

---

[78] Incidentally, in *Les Nombres*, Saint-Martin uses Theosophical Mathematics to make a point about the powerlessness of the number '2', which it should be remembered is the number of confusion, representing both the separation of the Evil Principle from the Good Principle, and man's attempted act of creation independent from the First Cause's cooperation. He points out that 1 divided by 2 makes ½, which "is spiritually the true root of 2." Yet this number ½ cannot be multiplied by itself to return to '1'. Instead it makes ¼. In other words, having created confusion, the number '2' cannot simply return to Unity, or 1 by the act of squaring itself, but now, without an act of grace, it's doomed to continually subdivide itself into null.

of all simple Beings with their products, since it's through this correspondence that reintegration takes place.

It's this which should help us to confirm that this first side of the square, this number One, or the First Cause of which it's the characteristic, produces everything through itself, and receives nothing except itself, and nothing which is not of itself.

The second side of the square is what belongs to this active and intelligent Cause which I've presented during the course of this Work as being preeminent among the temporal Causes, and which, by means of its active ability, directs the course of Nature and of physical Beings, just as by its intellectual ability it directs all man's steps, since man is connected to it in his quality as an intellectual Being.

We attribute the second side of the square to this Cause, because just as this second side is the closest to the root, so the active and intelligent Cause appears immediately after the First Being Who exists outside of temporal things. Then, if we put it in parallel with the second side of the square, we must also give it a double number; and we see that we couldn't apply this double number to any Being with more correctness than to this Cause, since it shows us both in its second rank and in its dual property that it possesses it.[79]

And indeed, it's true that this active and intelligent Cause is the first Agent of all that is temporal and physical, that nothing would have ever existed here without its help, and so to speak, without having been begun by it.

Doesn't the square itself give us the proof? Isn't the second of its sides, which we're now considering, the first degree and the first step towards the manifestation of the powers of its root? In other words, isn't it the image of that straight line which is the first product of the point, and without which there could never have been either surface or solid?

---

[79] It's, perhaps, worth pointing out that, while Pasqually and Saint-Martin use the first ten numbers for Theosophical philosophy, they are not above using the numbers in a more straightforward way as well. As well as attributing the number '1' or Unity to God, or the First Cause, Pasqually had no difficulty attributing the number '2' to the Son, and it is hoped that the Reader will have worked out the true nature of what Saint-Martin calls the active and intelligent Cause, which replaced man after his fall, and which is placed on the Chain of Being between the First Cause and man, and which is responsible for working on man's intelligent part to enlighten him and cause him to seek to path to Reintegration. In this instance, one only needs think of the first verses of the Gospel of St. John, which categorically state that the Word was present at Creation; as Creation was brought about by an utterance, or the Word, as implied in the next paragraph.

In the image of the square, therefore, we already find two points which are most important to man: that is, the knowledge of the First Universal Cause, and knowledge of the secondary Cause which represents Him in physical things, and which is His first temporal agent.

I've already expanded on the immense attributes of this secondary active and intelligent Cause, to dispense with recalling them here; and if you want to have an appropriate idea of them, it will be sufficient to never forget that it's the image of the First Cause, and charged with all His powers concerning everything which happens within Time. This is how you can most clearly understand this subject; and it's also what teaches man if there's any other Being in Time in which he can better place his trust.

The third side of the square is that which signifies all results, that is, both those which are physical and sensory, and those which are immaterial and outside of Time. Just as there's one Square affected by Time, and one Square independent of Time, so there are outcomes connected with both of these two Squares, because both have the power to manifest products; and as the products which are manifested either Class always have the number *three*, it's for this reason that we apply them to the third side of the square.

This agrees perfectly with what we've seen regarding physical products, all of which are composed of the three Elements. All that there is to see is the considerable distinction which, despite the similarity in *Number*, is found between temporal products and those which aren't. Those which issue directly from the First Cause are simple Beings like Him, and as a result have an absolute existence which nothing can destroy. The rest, being born out of a secondary Cause can't have the same privileges as the former, but must necessarily sense the inferiority of their Principle. Their existence is only fleeting, too, and they can't exist by themselves, unlike the Beings who have reality.

This is how the third side of the square clearly presents itself to us; for if the second gave us the line, the third gives us the surface, and since the number three is at the same time the number of the surface and the number of bodies, it's evident that bodies are only composed of surfaces, that is, of substances which are only the envelope or the outward appearance of Beings, but which have neither solidity nor life.

And indeed, the final step to create the solid in human Geometry is only a repetition of those which preceded it; that is, those which formed the line and the surface; for depth which this third and last operation creates is nothing more than the vertical direction of several lines combined, and the only difference is that, in the preceding steps the direction of the lines was only horizontal. Thus, this depth is always the product of the line, and as such, it can't be anything more than an assemblage of surfaces.

Since the opportunity presents itself, do we wish to learn more about evaluating more accurately what bodies are? To do this, we only have to follow the reverse order of their formation. Solids are composed of surfaces, surfaces of lines, and lines of points, that is, the Principles which have neither length, nor breadth, nor depth; in other words, which have none of the dimensions of Matter, as I've amply shown when I spoke about this.

Let's therefore bring bodies back to their source and their original Essence, and let's see from this what notion we should have about Matter.

Finally, the fourth side of the square, as it reflects the Quaternary Number by which everything took its origin, offers us the *Number* of everything that's a Center or Principle, regardless of its class; but, as we've spoken enough about the Universal Principle which is outside of Time, and the square we're currently discussing is only temporal, we should only understand the various Principles acting in the temporal class by its fourth side, that is, both those which possess intellectual abilities and those which are limited to physical and physical abilities; and even where the immaterial Principles of physical Beings which we've examined as much as we're allowed to do, we won't recall here either their various properties or their innate action, nor the need for a second action to make the first take place, nor all those observations which we've made concerning the Laws and the cycle of material Nature.

We'll content ourselves with noting that the relationship which can be found between these physical Principles and the fourth side of the square is additional proof that, as Quaternaries or centers, they're simple Beings, distinct from Matter and therefore indestructible, although their physical products, which are only assemblages, are subject by nature to decomposition.

So, we should now focus solely on the immaterial intellectual Principles, and among these Principles there is none we should examine more closely now than man; since it's he who has been the principle subject of this book; since it's in him that all the virtues enclosed in this important square we're discussing should reside; and finally, since this square has only ever been drawn for man, and it's the true source of knowledge and illumination of which this man has unfortunately been deprived.

Therefore, it's by carefully thinking about the fourth side of this square that man will truly learn to evaluate its value and advantages. It would also be in doing this that he'd see exposed the Errors by which men have obscured the foundation and the very purpose of Mathematics; how much they deceive themselves when they replace the simple Laws of this sublime Science with their faulty and uncertain decisions; and how much they hinder their advancement when they limit themselves to examining the material facts of Nature, whereas by using it in another way, they could have obtained so many precious teachings from it.

But we know man can no longer observe this square from the same point of view that he did in former times, and that among the four different classes it contains, he only occupies the darkest and the most mediocre one, whereas in his origin he occupied the first and most luminous.

It was then that, drawing knowledge from its very source, and drawing close without fatigue or work to the Principle which had given him being, he enjoyed a peace and a felicity without limit, because he was in his Element. It's by this same means that he could direct his path through the whole of Nature with advantage and certainty, for having dominion over the three inferior classes of the temporal square, he could direct them at will, without being afraid of or prevented by any obstacle. It is, I say, by the properties connected to this eminent place, that he had a sure understanding of all the Beings which compose this physical Nature, and at that time he wasn't exposed to the danger of confusing his own essence with theirs.

The Temporal Square

Now on the contrary, relegated to the last of the classes of the temporal Square, he finds himself at the extremity of that same physical Nature over which he'd previously ruled, and from which he should never have felt any resistance nor harshness. He no longer has this invaluable advantage, which he possessed to its full extent when, placed between the temporal Square and the Square outside of Time, he could study both at the same time. Instead of that light from which he should never have been separated, he now only sees terrifying darkness around him, which exposes him to all the suffering to which he is subject in his body, and to all the errors to which he is led in his thoughts by the false use of his will and the misuse of all his intellectual abilities.

So, it's only too true it's impossible for man to gain the knowledge contained in the Square we're discussing without help, since it no longer shows him the one side which could make it understandable to him.

Man's Resources

But, as I've promised, I don't want to discourage man. On the contrary, I'd like to kindle a hope within him which can never be extinguished. I'd like to pour consolations over his misery by having him compare it with the means he has he has near at hand to deliver himself from it.

I'll therefore point out an incorruptible attribute which he fully possessed at his origin, and whose possession is not only not completely forbidden today, but which is moreover a right he can claim, which offers him the one path and the one means to rediscover that important place we just spoke about.

Nothing will seem less imaginary than what I'm proposing, when you reflect that even in his privation, man still possesses the abilities of desire and will; and by having these abilities he must have the attributes to manifest them, since the First Cause itself, like everything which comes from its essence, is subject to the need to manifest nothing without the assistance of its attributes.

It's true that this First Principle's abilities being as infinite as Numbers, the attributes which correspond to them must equally be limitless; for not only does this First Principle manifest products outside of Time, to do which He uses the attributes inherent within Himself, which are only distinct from one another by their different properties; but He also manifests products inside of Time, which being outside the help of these attributes which are inseparable from Him, needed to use attributes outside of Him, coming from Him, acting through Him, yet which were not Him; which constitutes the Law of temporal Beings, and explains the dual action of the Universe.

But, although the manifestations which man has to make aren't remotely comparable to those of the First Cause, we can still challenge the abilities we see in him, as well as the indispensable need for attributes connected to these abilities, in order to improve them; and since these attributes are the same as those by which he formerly proved his greatness, we'll see he should expect the same help from them today if he only had a steady will to use them, and had full confidence in them.[80]

---

[80] The question of what man has to *do* to restore himself to his primitive estate is a complex one for Saint-Martin. While he was later far more confident of pursuing a more purely mystical path, at this time he was still influenced enough by Pasqually to believe broadly in his approach, which was one of near constant prayer, and long, elaborate rituals lasting for hours, involving consecrating robes and implements, drawing magic circles and arcs, lighting enormous numbers of candles accompanied by incenses, and utilizing weird sigils and drawings and even occasionally the body parts of animals; though he did on at least one occasion ask: "But Master, is all this really necessary to know God?" Pasqually's view was unequivocal: man attained forgiveness by means of 'operations', which essentially meant magical ceremonies, and the *Treatise* is full of Adam, Abel, Moses and others performing these. It's interesting to note that, in this book, Saint-Martin uses the term *opérer*, which really means 'to operate', far more than *travailler*, which is a far more common word for 'to work'.

Chapter 7 – Language & Art

Man's Attributes

These priceless attributes, in which are found man's sole resource, are contained in the knowledge of Languages, that is, in this ability common to all humankind for communicating his thoughts; an ability which all Nations have indeed cultivated, but in a manner which is of little benefit to them, because they haven't applied it to its true purpose.

We see evidently that the advantages connected with the ability of speech are the true rights of man, since it's by their means he communicates with his fellow man, and he makes all his thoughts and moods clear to them. It's this alone which truly responds to his needs in this situation; for all the physical signs we see used to replace speech by those who can't communicate verbally, either because of nature or accident, can only fulfil this role imperfectly.

Artificial Languages

In those, communication is normally limited to negations and affirmations, those things which can only follow a question; and if we ask them a question, they usually can't make us understand their thought unless, and which comes to the same thing, it's about an object in front of them, and then through touch or another visible sign they can make us understand what they want to do with it.

Those who've gone into this more deeply can only be understood by the Masters who taught them, or by other people who've been instructed in the conventions; but then, though we've a kind of Language here, we could never say that it's a true Language, since firstly it isn't common to all men, and secondly, while it uses expressions, it lacks the crucial advantage of pronunciation.

So, man's true attributes will never be found in this, or in any other artificial Language for, since everything is man-made, arbitrary and constantly changing, it doesn't manifest the characteristics of a true Language.

The Unity of Languages

According to this account, we can already see what the nature of Languages should be; for I've said that they should be common to all men. Now, how can they be common to all men if they don't all use the same symbols; which is really to say that there should only be one Language. I won't seek to proof what I'm advancing by pointing to the enthusiasm with which men seek to acquire several different Languages, and the kind of admiration we have for those who know a good number of them, although this enthusiasm and this admiration, false though they may be, do give an indication of our tendency towards universality or Unity.

I won't say anything further about the partiality in which different Nations hold their particular Language, and how each Nation is jealous of its own.

I'll speak even less about the custom established between some Sovereigns of only writing to one another in a dead Language, and which is common between them for communications of State, because not only is this practice not general, but also it comes from a motive too frivolous to give any weight to the matter of which I am discussing.[81]

It's therefore in man himself that the reason and proof that he's made only to have one Language must be found, and from this we can recognize by what Error we've come to deny this Truth and say that, since Languages are simply the result of habit and convention, it's inevitable that they'll vary like everything else on Earth; which led the Observers to believe that there

---

[81] There is, surely, a certain irony in what Saint-Martin says, given the fact that French has been the language of that artificial and mannered practice called 'diplomacy' among Nations for centuries. That said, he is clearly referring to Latin and Greek in this instance, and the comment is all the more poignant as this was also the language of the Roman Church at that time. Now, one of the indicators of a 'dead' language is the need to establish a Committee to invent words in that language which didn't exist when it was spoken: for example, when the pope wishes to issue a encyclical in Latin and include the word 'computer' or 'space shuttle', the Committee has to create it. One wonders what Saint-Martin would have made of the *Académie Française*, which is tasked with inventing French words to replace those words from other languages – particularly English – which have crept into the French language. While most language evolve naturally, official human intervention is normally only used when a language is 'dead' and new words are needed. Incidentally, as this footnote is being written, many French are up in arms over the fact that a new French Dictionary coming out in September 2017 will contain thousands of simplified French words, in an attempt to make it easier for French schoolchildren to learn how to spell. The beloved circumflex accent will be removed from most words, making *coût* into *cout* (cost), and some letters will be dropped *oignon*, the word for 'onion' will become *ognon*, in a move alarmingly reminiscent of George Orwell's 'Newspeak' in *1984*.

can be many different ones at the same time which are all equally valid, though they're different from one another.

Intellectual Language

In order for them to continue with certainty along this path, I'll ask them to consider whether they wouldn't discern two kinds of Language in themselves: one physical and demonstrative, through which they communicate with their fellow men; and the other internal and mute, which however always precedes everything they manifest outside of themselves, and which is truly the mother of the first kind.

I'd next ask them to think about the nature of this internal and secret Language; to see if it's anything other than the voice and expression of a Principle which is external to them, but which engraves its thought on them, and which brings about what happens there.

Now, according to the knowledge we've received about this Principle, we know that everyone must be led by it, so we should only always find everyone on the same path, with the same goal and the same Law, despite the endless variety of good thoughts which may be communicated to them by this voice.

But, since this path should be so uniform, since this secret expression should be the same everywhere, surely men who had not allowed the traces of this inner Language to become distorted would all understand it perfectly, since they'd find a conformity in it to what they felt inside. They'd see the similarity and the representation of their own ideas, and they'd learn that, apart from those which came from the Evil Principle, there'd be none which would be strange to them. Finally, they'd be strongly convinced about the universal equality of the intellectual Being which constituted them.

It's by means of this that they'd clearly understand that the true intellectual Language of man, being the same everywhere, is essentially one; that it can never vary, and that it's not possible for two to exist without one being fought and destroyed by the other.

So, as we've seen, since external and physical Language is the product of the inner and secret Language; if this Language always conformed to the Principle which must direct it; if it were always one and always the same; then it'd produce the same physical and external expression everywhere. As a result, although we are obliged to use the material organ of the mouth nowadays, we'd still have a common Language which would be understandable to all men.

Physical Language

So, when did physical Languages start to vary among them? When did they notice the disparity in how they communicated their ideas? Isn't it when this secret and inner expression itself began to vary? Isn't it when the intellectual Language of man was tarnished, and was no longer the work of pure hands? Then, no longer having his light beside him, he received the first idea offered to his intellectual Being without question, and no longer sensed either the connection or the relationship of what he was receiving with the true Principle from which he should obtain everything. Then finally, left to himself, his will and imagination were his only resources; and out of necessity and in his ignorance, he followed everything these false guides presented to him.

It's for this reason that physical expression was completely changed, because man no longer saw the true nature of things, and gave them names which came from him, which no longer being connected to the things themselves, could no longer designate them as their natural names had done unambiguously.

If even only a few men had pursued this mistaken path which isn't capable of uniformity, each of them would certainly have given different names to the same things, which, repeated in great numbers and perpetuated more and more over time, would indeed present us with the most variable and bizarre spectacle. We cannot doubt that this is the origin of the differences between and divisions of Languages, and after all I've said, were I to offer no further proofs, this would be more than sufficient to convince us that men have strayed greatly from their Principle. For I repeat, if they had all been guided by that Principle, their intellectual Language would be the same, and then their physical and external Languages would have the same signs and idioms.

Nobody can disagree, I hope, with what I've just said about the natural and identifying names of Beings. Even though names show us no uniformity among the various Languages used on Earth, nevertheless we must believe that they should only use names which indicate things clearly and universally. For this reason, these Languages which are so different from one another can't reasonably pass for true Languages; and besides, each of these Languages considered alone, false thought it may be, clearly offers us proof of what I am saying.

Won't the words that each of these Languages uses, although being subject to man-made conventions, be a sure sign of the Beings they represent to those who understand those conventions? Don't we see in this the natural desire we all have, to express things by signs or words which appear to us to be the most analogous? Don't we sense a secret pleasure mixed with admiration when we're given signs, expressions and characters which bring us closest to the Nature of the objects we're shown, and which help us understand them best?

What are we doing here, other than repeating the path of Truth itself, which has established a common Language between all its products, and which, having given them all their own names which are linked to their essence, preserved them from any ambiguity? Wouldn't it protect men, whose task it's always been to reestablish their connection with its works, from this by the same means; and shouldn't he have known that he should work towards knowing their true names?

The Origin of Languages

We can't therefore deny that in our very deformity and privation, we only draw expressive emblems of the Law of Beings, and that the misuse we make of Language doesn't show us the more satisfying and correct use we could make of it, without needing to go outside of Nature to do it, and only by not forgetting the source from which this Language should take its origin.

It's therefore true that if the Observers had gone back to this secret, inner expression that the intellectual Principle made within us before manifesting externally, there they'd have found the origin of physical Language coming from the true Principle, and not in the fragile and powerless Causes which are restricted to operating their individual Law, and which can never produce anything more. They wouldn't have tried to explain the details of a superior Order which existed before time, and which will exist without interruption after time beyond Matter, by means of the simple Laws of Nature. It's not an organization, nor a discovery made by the first men which, in passing from age to age, continued up till now among the human species through example and instruction: instead, as we've seen, it's man's true attribute, and although he's been deprived of it since he rose up against his Law, vestiges of it remain to him which can lead him back to its source, if he had the courage to follow them step by step and strongly apply himself to them.

Experiments with Children

I know that among my fellow man this point is one of the most argued about. Not only are they uncertain as to which man's first Language might have been; but also, because of going away from this thought completely, they even came to believe that man didn't have the source of Language within him, since they didn't see him speak normally when he is left to himself in infancy.

Yet, don't they see that they always get their observations wrong? Don't they know that in the state of privation in which man finds himself today, he's condemned to do nothing, even use his intellectual abilities, without the help of an external action which beings them into play and into action; and that as a result, to deprive man of this Law is to deprive him completely of all the resources which Justice had given him, and to put him in the position of stifling his abilities, without which he can't produce anything.

However, it can't be denied that this was the approach of the Observers, with the repeated experiments they did with children in order to discover, by not speaking in front of them, what their natural Language would be. When they then saw that these children didn't use speech, or that they only emitted confused sounds, they interpreted this as they wanted, and built theories based on facts which they'd created themselves. But isn't it evident that physical Nature and the intellectual Law also require men to live in a society? Now, why is man placed among his fellow men who are supposed to have been redeemed, if it isn't to receive all the help he needs from there, to reanimate his hidden abilities in turn, and be able to use them to his advantage?

It's therefore acting directly contrary to these two Laws and against man which deprives him of the help he could expect from them. It doesn't seem very intelligent to remove every means to acquire the use of the abilities we're discussing, and then seek to believe him incapable of them.

It's like putting a seed on a stone, then denying that the seed's capable of bearing fruit.

But, without going too far down this path, if it's clear that when man is deprived of the help he needs, he can't produce a permanent Language; yet men nevertheless have Languages, where can we find the origin of that universal Language; and shouldn't we agree that the man who first had to teach it must have received it other than from the hands of men?

The Language of Physical Beings

There is, I know, a kind of Language which is natural and uniform, which the Observers are in general agreement about acknowledging in man, and this is the one by which he indicates his emotions of pleasure and pain; which is shown by him in kinds of sound appropriate for this use.

But it's very clear that this Language, if it is one, only has physical sensations as its guide and object; and the most convincing proof we have of it is that it's also found in animals, in which the majority manifest their feelings externally through movement and even through characteristic sounds.

But this kind of Language shouldn't really surprise us in animals, if we remember the Principles established earlier. Isn't the physical Principle of animals immaterial, since there can't be any Principle which isn't? As such, shouldn't it have abilities, and if it has abilities, shouldn't it have the means to express them? But also, the means each specific Being can use should always be proportional to its abilities; for it there were no limit to this, as in everything else, there would be an irregularity, and in the Laws of Beings this isn't possible.

So, it's through this measure that we can evaluate the kind of Language by which animals show their abilities; since being limited in their ability to feel, they only need a way to make known what they are feeling, and they have them.

Beings who have no other abilities than those of vegetation show this ability very clearly in the same way, but that of course is all they show.

Thus, though animals have feelings, and express them; though in the current state of things these sensations are of two types, one good and the other bad, and although animals indicate both by showing when they are happy or when they're suffering, we can't avoid limiting its Language and all the demonstrative signs it can make to that one purpose; and we could never regard this manner of expression as being real Language, since the purpose of Language is to express thoughts, and thoughts are the characteristic of intellectual Principles, and I've shown clearly enough that the Principle of the animal is not intellectual, though it's immaterial.

If we're justified in not seeing the way animals make their feelings known as being anything like a real Language, then though man, as an animal, also has these feelings and the means to make them known, we'll never accept the slightest comparison between this limited and obscure Language to that of which man's intellectual Nature makes him capable.

The Relationship Between Language and Abilities

It would no doubt be an interesting and instructive study to observe the connection which exists between the abilities of Beings and the way they express them across all of Nature. We would see that relative to their distance because of their nature from the first ring of the chain their abilities are less extensive. We'd also see that the means they have to express them precisely follows this progression, and in this sense, we could assign a kind of Language to the least of created Beings, since this Language would be nothing more than expressing their abilities, with a uniformity without which they couldn't communicate or correspond, or have an affinity with other Beings of the same class.

Nevertheless, in this examination it would be necessary to pay great attention to observing each Being according to its class, and to not attribute to the one anything which could only belong to the other. We shouldn't attribute a plant's abilities to a mineral, nor the same manner of manifesting them; any more we should attribute what we observe in an animal to a plant. Even less should we attribute to these inferior Beings, who only have a fleeting action, to everything that we've just discovered in man. Without this, we'd fall back into this horrible confusion of Languages, which is the reason for all our Errors and the true cause of our ignorance, in that it's from this that the nature of all Beings would be distorted for us.

But, as this point would perhaps be a little too far outside the scope of my Work, I will content myself with pointing this out, and I leave it to those who have the modesty to limit themselves to isolated subjects, less vast than the one I am presenting, to consider writing on this matter,

Universal Language

I now return to this true and original Language, man's most precious resource. I say again, that as an immaterial and intellectual Being, in his first existence he must have received abilities of a superior order, and in consequence the attributes necessary to manifest them. These attributes are nothing other than knowledge of a Language common to all thinking Beings, and this universal Language must have been dictated to them by a unique, single Principle which is its true sign. Now, man no longer possesses these original abilities completely, for we've seen he no longer even has thought remaining in him, the attributes which accompany thought have also been removed from him, and it's for this reason that we no longer see that fixed and invariable Language in him.

But we should repeat also that he hasn't lost all hope of recovering it, and that, with courage and effort, he can still claim to come into his first rights once more.

If I was allowed to quote some proofs, I'd show that the earth is filled with them, and that since the world came into existence, there has been a Language which has never been lost, and which will never be lost even after the end of the world, although then it must be simplified. I'd show that men of every Nation have known it, and that some who were separated by centuries, and even contemporaries, though separated by considerable distances, still understood one another by means of this universal and imperishable Language.

Through this Language we'd learn how true Legislators were instructed in those Laws and Principles by which men who possessed Justice behaved in all ages, and how by directing their course in light of these models they could be certain that their steps were regular. We'd also see the true military Principles of which the great general had knowledge, which they used with so much success in *combat*.

It'd provide the key to all *calculations*, knowledge of the construction and decomposition of Beings, as well as their Reintegration. It'd make known the *properties* of the North, the Cause of the deviation of the compass, *virgin territory*, the object of desire of aspirants to occult

Philosophy.[82] Finally, without entering into greater details of its advantages here, I don't fear assuring you that those it can procure are without number, and that there isn't a Being over which its power and its light doesn't extend.

But, aside from the fact that I can't talk further on this subject without breaking my promise and my duties, there'd be no point my speaking more clearly, because my words would be lost on those who have not turned their eyes towards this, and their number is infinite.

As for those who are on the path of knowledge, what I've said will suffice, without the need to raise another corner of the veil for them.

All I can do, therefore, to show the universal relationship between the Principles I've established, is to pray my Readers to remember that Book of *Ten Pages* given to man at his first origin, and which he has kept even since his second birth, but knowledge of which and the true *Key* to its understanding have been taken from him. I pray them to investigate again the relationships they can perceive between the properties of that book and those of the fixed and unique Language, to see if there isn't a great affinity between them, and to try to explain each one by means of the other. For it's truly there that we'd find the *key* to knowledge, and if the book in question contains all knowledge, as we've seen earlier, the Language we're speaking about is its true *Alphabet*.

Writing and Speech

It's with the same precaution that I must speak of another point which is basically connected to what I've just covered, that is, the means by which this Language manifests itself. This is certainly in only two ways, like all Languages; that is, by verbal expression and by written characters, the

---

[82] This last sentence appears to return to the problems with navigation. The term *virtue* has been translated here as 'properties', since, given the reference to the compass, it's probably concerned with magnetic variation, which is the difference between magnetic North and true North. He also refers to magnetic deviation, which is the effect local magnetic effect can have on a compass. This was especially prevalent on ships, where the assortment of canons and other ferrous objects on board could significantly affect the accuracy of the ship's compass. Both affect the ability to circumnavigate the world and discover new countries (and sources of wealth). As for the reference to 'occult Philosophy', this could perhaps simply be read as 'hidden knowledge'. It appears that Saint-Martin is making his universal Language more attractive by pointing out that, not only would it help man to pool his resources in a spiritual sense, and work together on his reintegration; but such a Language would also help him on Earth by facilitating advances in science by solving problems currently facing mankind with respect to navigation and no doubt other conundrums of the time.

former coming to our knowledge through the sense of hearing, and the latter through the sense of sight, the only senses connected with intellectual actions. But this is in man alone, for although animals also have these two senses, they can only be used to material and physical ends, as they have no intelligence. Also, hearing and sight in animals, like all the other senses, are only used to preserve the physical individual; which is why animals have neither speech nor writing.

It's therefore true that by these two means, man receives knowledge of many higher things, and this Language truly uses man's senses to comprehend its precision, power and accuracy.

And how could it be otherwise, since he can't receive anything except through the senses? Even in his first estate man had senses by means of which everything worked as it does today, but with this difference: that they never varied in their effects, unlike the physical senses of Matter which only give him uncertainty, and which are the principle instruments of his errors.

Besides, how could he come to understand the men who'd preceded him or who lived far away, if not by the aid of writing? We should agree, however, that these men, like those in the past or at a distance, can have Interpreters or Commentators who like them were taught the true Principles of this Language, and who use it in conversation, thereby bringing time and distance closer together.

This is one of the greatest satisfactions that true Language can give us, because this voice is infinitely more instructive; but it's also the rarest, and among men skill in writing is far more common than skill in oration.

The reason for this is that in our present state we can only rise by degrees; and indeed, in connection to Language sight is below hearing because, in Nature it's by hearing that man obtains the living explanation or intellectual sense of a Language conveyed through speech, whereas writing only gives an indication of it, as it only offers the eyes a lifeless explanation and material objects.

Be that as it may, by means of speech and writing, which belong to true Language, man can instruct himself on everything connected to the most ancient things; for nobody spoke or wrote more than the first men, although nowadays there an infinitely more books than before. It's true that among Ancients and Moderns there are many who've distorted this writing and this Language, but man can identify those who've made these terrible mistakes, and because of that he'll clearly see the origin of all the Languages of the Earth, how they departed from the original Language, and the connection these departures had with the darkness and ignorance of Nations, which threw them down into the abyss of the sufferings they complain about, instead of attributing the reason to themselves.

He'd also learn how the Hand which struck these Nations down only intended to punish them, not to deliver them forever to despair; for once His Justice was satisfied, He returned their first Language to them, and with even more breadth than before, so that they could both atone for their errors, and also have the means to preserve themselves from a similar error in the future.

I only spent so long on this as I was allowed to expand further on the endless advantages contained in the various means this Language uses, through the ears or through the eyes. Nevertheless, if we realize that, in return, it demands the complete sacrifice of man's will; if it can only be understood by those who've forgotten themselves to allow the Law of the active and intelligent Cause, which should govern man as it does the whole Universe, to act fully upon them; we should realize it can't be known to many. However, this Language doesn't exist for an instant without acting, either through conversation or writing. But if man closes his ears, and looks for writing in Books, how could the true Language be understandable to him?

The Uniformity of Languages

An attribute such as that I've just outlined can't suffer from being compared to any other. It's for this reason that I believe myself well-founded in declaring it to be single and unique, untouched by any variation which men can try to introduce.

But it's not enough to have proved the need for such a Language in intellectual Beings for them to express their abilities. It's not even enough to have proven its existence by saying that it was from this Language that all true Legislators and other famous men drew their Principles, Laws and resources for all their great actions. No, its reality also needs to be shown in man himself, so he can no longer be in any doubt. He must be shown that the many Languages in use among his fellow men only vary in their physical expression, in speech and writing. However, so far as the Principle is concerned, there are none who have strayed from it; they all follow the same path, and it's absolutely impossible for them to travel down any other; in other words, all the Nations on Earth have only one Language, though there are barely two who can understand one another.

Grammar

It can't be denied, indeed, that a Language, however imperfect, is governed by Grammar. Now, since Grammar is nothing more than the result of the order inherent in our intellectual abilities, it relies so closely on their inner Language, that one may regard them as inseparable.

It's therefore Grammar which is the invariable rule of Language across all Nations. It's this Law on which they must rely, even if they make the worst use of their intellectual abilities or their inner, secret Language; for since this Grammar only directs the expression of our ideas, it doesn't care if they conform or not to the Principle which gives them life. Its function is simply to render that expression regular; and this can never fail to happen, for, when Grammar acts, it's always correct, or it says nothing.

For proof, I'll only use what enters into the composition of a sentence, or what is commonly known as *parts of speech*. Among these parts of speech, some of them are fixed, fundamental and indispensable to complete the expression of a thought, and they are three in number. The rest are only accessories; and their number hasn't been completely determined.

The three parts which are fundamental to a sentence, and without which it completely impossible to express a thought, are the active noun or pronoun, the verb which expresses the manner of existing, as well as the actions of Beings, and finally the passive noun or pronoun which is the subject or object of the action. If any man examines this proposition as closely as he judges appropriate, he'll see that a sentence can never be constructed without containing an action, that this action can't be imagined if it isn't done by an agent which performs it, and then followed by an outcome which is, must be, or could be the result. If any of these three parts are removed we wouldn't obtain a complete idea of the thought, and then we'd sense that something was missing from the order our mind needs.

Indeed, a noun or a substantive on its own communicates absolutely nothing if it isn't accompanied by an agent which operates on it and by a verb which indicates how this agent is operating on this noun and makes use of it. Remove one or the other of these three signs, and the sentence will offer no more than a truncated idea. leaving our mind to wait for the rest, whereas with these three signs alone we can complete a thought, because we can represent the agent, the action and the subject or the object. It's therefore clear that this Law of Grammar is invariable, and from whichever Language an example is chosen, it will conform to the Principle that I've just laid out, since it comes from Nature itself and from the fundamental Laws laid down in man's intellectual abilities.

Now let's reflect on everything I've said about weight, number and measure. Let's see that these Laws include man in their empire given all that is within him and all that comes from him. Let's also remember what I said about the famous *Ternary* and its universality. Let's consider whether there's anything it doesn't apply to, and then let's learn to have a nobler view going forward of the Being who, despite his degradation, can cast his gaze that far, who can bring such knowledge to him, and take in such an extensive view.

Now, you could argue that there are times where the three parts I say are essential in a sentence are not always all present; that there are often only two, sometimes only one, and even occasionally none at all, as in a negation or affirmation. But this objection doesn't stand when we observe that in all these cases, the three fundamental parts still retain their power and that its Law still endures, because those parts of speech which are not expressed are implied, and they'll still keep their place, and even that it's only in their tacit reference to them that the others have their effect.

In reality, when I respond to a question with just a monosyllable, this monosyllable will always present the image of the ternary Principle, since it always refers to an action relative to what was said to me, and it's in the question itself that the parts of speech tacitly understood in my response can be found. I won't give any examples, since the Reader can provide his own easily enough.

And so, I see in every sentence the strongest evidence of the three signs of the agent, the action and the product; and since this order is common to all thinking Beings, I can confidently say that when even when they'd like to, they can never deviate from them.

I'm not talking about the order in which these three signs should be arranged to conform to the order of the things they represent; this order has evidently been distorted over time at man's hands, and almost every National Language varies on this point. But since the true Language is one, the arrangement of these signs wouldn't have been subjected to all these differences had man known how to preserve it.

However, it shouldn't be believed that even in the true Language these three signs had always been set out in the same order as they are in our intellectual abilities; for these signs are only their physical expression, and I'm certain that the physical could never follow the same path as the intellectual; that is, that the product could never be subject to the same Laws as its Generating Principle.

But the superiority it had over all other Languages is because its physical expression would never have varied, and this expression would've followed the order and the Laws which are its own and specific to its essence, without any changes. And as we've already seen, this Language would've had the advantage of being safe from ambiguity, and would've always had the same meaning, because it's linked to the nature of things, and the nature of things is invariable.

The Verb

Among the three fundamental signs which control every expression of our thoughts, there's one which merits our attention the most, and which we'll now examine. It's the one which links the two others, and is the image of action among our intellectual abilities, and the image of Mercury among the physical Principles; in other words, it's the part of speech called the *Verb* by Grammarians.

It mustn't be forgotten that, since it's the image of action, all physical work is founded upon it; and since the property of action is to do things, its sign or image represents what is being done.

So, if we reflect on this sign's properties in the composition of a sentence; if we see that the stronger and more expressive it is, the more the results which come from it are physical and marked; if we perform this experiment which is easy to do, even in everything subject to the power or conventions of man, the result is regulated, determined and animated principally by the Verb. Finally, let the Observers see if it isn't through this sign called a *Verb* that everything we know to be the most intellectual and active within us is seen; if it isn't the only one of the three signs which can strengthen or weaken an expression, whereas the noun of the subject and object, once given, always remains the same. This is how we may judge if we've been right in attributing action to it, since it truly is its depositary, and its help is clearly required for anything to be done, or to be expressed even tacitly.

This is the place to note that the reason why the indolent Observers and speculative Kabbalists find nothing: it's because they always speak, and never VERBIZE.[83]

I won't expand further on the properties of the *Verb*. Given what I've said, any pair of intelligent eyes can make more important discoveries and prove to themselves that at every moment of his life, man represents the physical image of the means by which everything was born, acts, and is governed.

This, then, is another Law to which all Beings which have the privilege of speech must submit; and that's why I said that all the Nations on Earth have only one Language, though the manner in which they express themselves is universally different.

Accessory Parts of Speech

I haven't spoken at all about the other parts which enter into the composition of sentences. I simply spoke of them as accessories, only serving to assist expression, to give more weight to the weakness of words, and to detail some of the relationships between actions; or, if you will, as emphasizers and repetitions of the three parts we recognized as being essential to complete the image of any thought.

---

[83] Saint-Martin uses the word '*Verbent*' from a fictitious verb '*Verber*', 'to verb'. This comment sheds some light on the practices of the Elus Cohen. Being brought up in the Catholic tradition, which, unlike the Protestants, attribute a quasi-magical quality to the Mass, Saint-Martin would have been at home with the wearing of elaborate robes, the use of candles and incense, the intoning of important words of power (remember that all the sections of the Mass considered to be important, or establishing an 'as above so below' relationship with Deity, such as the Gospel, the words of Consecration and the Invocations, the words are always intoned or vibrated rather than spoken). It therefore comes as a surprise to find him speak disparagingly about the Kabbalists (thought we should note he adds the word 'speculative', perhaps to suggest the 'armchair' types who only read books rather than those who engaged in active theurgical practices). While Pasqually's Treatise has a distinctly Kabbalistic flavor to it, the doctrines laid out are quite different, and in many cases diametrically opposed to the teachings of the Kabbalah. The numerical system is completely different; the Four Worlds are never explored; Evil is seen as dual rather than reflective (as in the *Klippoth*); and key points of study, such as the *Merkabah* or the *Shemhamphorasch* are ignored completely. It wasn't until his move away from theurgical practices and his embrace of the writings of Böhme, that Saint-Martin took on a more Kabbalistic viewpoint.

Indeed, everyone should know that the Articles, as well as the endings of nouns in Languages which don't have Articles, serve to express the number and gender of nouns, and to determine the essential relationships between the agent, the action and the subject; that Adjectives express the qualities of nouns, that Adverbs are the adjectives of the verb or of action; and finally, that the other parts of speech form the connections within the sentence and make its sense more or less expressive, or the complete sentence more harmonious. But as the use of these various signs isn't uniformly common to all Languages; and as they're connected far more closely to a Nation's customs and habits, as everything linked to the physical must have variations, they can be admitted to the class of fixed and unmovable parts of speech. And so, we won't use them in the proofs we are bringing to the unity of man's Language.

Universal Relationships of Grammar

Nevertheless, I urge Grammarians to consider their Science with a little more attention than they have no doubt given it up till now. They do admit that Languages come from a source superior to man, and that all its Laws are dictated by Nature; but this vague feeling has produced almost no effect in them, and they're a long way from suspecting all they might find in Languages.

If you'd like to know the reason, it's because they do with Grammar what the Observers do with all the Sciences; that is, they quickly glance at the Principle, but not having the courage to stare at it for long, they lower their eyes to the physical and mechanical details, which absorb all their attention and leave the most important one, intelligence, hidden.

If only the Grammarians could be persuaded that the Laws of their Science come from a Principle just like all the others, they'd discover an inexhaustible source of light and truths, of which they barely have the least idea.

The small number of truths offered to them must appear sufficient to put them on the path. If they'd actually seen the representative signs of the abilities of intellectual Beings in them, they could've seen the same thing in relation to Beings which aren't intelligent. They could then receive a clear idea of the Principles which have been established about Matter, by simply considering the difference there is between the noun and the adjective. The noun is the Being or the innate Principle; the adjective expresses the abilities of any kind which might be in this Principle. But what must be carefully observed, is that the adjective can't itself join with the noun, just as the noun alone is powerless to produce the adjective; both need a superior action to bring them together and link them. It's only by means of this action that they can be united and show their properties.

Let's note, too, that it's the work of thought itself and intelligence to use adjectives appropriately; that is, it's thought which perceives them or creates them and communicates them in some way to the subjects it wants to apply them to; and let's recognize in this the immense property of that universal action which we've indicated above, since it's certain that we'll find it everywhere.

Furthermore, this same action, having communicated the abilities to the innate Principles, or put another way, the adjectives to the nouns, can extend, diminish and even completely remove them at will, and so make the Being return to its initial state of inaction, a clear enough picture of how it really works on Nature.

But in this, Grammarians could also see without fear of error, that the adjective, which only describes the quality of the Being, can't exist without a Principle, that is, a subject or noun; whereas the noun can quite happily be included in a sentence without any qualities or adjectives. From this they could see a connection with what we discussed about the existence of immaterial physical Beings independent of their physical abilities. Then they might also understand what we said about the eternity of the Principles of Matter, even though Matter itself can't be eternal, for since it's only the result of a union, it's nothing more than an adjective.

From this, they can then see how it's possible for man to be deprived of his first attributes, since it was by a Superior Hand that he had been clothed with them in the first place; but also recognizing with even more certainty his own inadequacy, they'll acknowledge that to be reestablished in those same rights, it's essential to have the help of that same Hand which deprived him of them, and Who only asks him, as I said before, for the sacrifice of his will for them to be restored to him.

In the six Cases, they could still find the six modifications of Matter, as well as the details of the acts of its formation and of all the cycles it undergoes. Genders will be for them an image of the opposing Principles which are irreconcilable; in other words, they could make many observations of this kind, which being neither the result of the imagination nor of man-made theories, would convince them of the universality of the Principle, and that everything is led by the same hand.[84]

The True Language

But having established, as I've done, this unique and universal Language offered to man, even in the state of privation to which he is reduced, I should expect my Readers to be curious about this Language's name and type.

As to the name, I can't satisfy them, having promised myself not to name anything; but as for its type, I can assure them that it's that Language in which, as I've already said, each word contains the true meaning of things, and indicates them so well that it makes them clearly understood. I'll add that it's what is the object of desire of all Nations on Earth, which secretly directs men in all their Institutions, which each of them carefully cultivates in private without knowing it, and which they all strive to express in every work they create; for it's so deeply engrained in them that they can't produce anything which doesn't bear its character.

I can therefore do nothing better to give knowledge of it to my fellow man, than to assure them that it results from their very essence, and that it's because of this Language alone that they are men. So therefore, let them see if I was speaking incorrectly when I told them that it's universal; and if in spite of the incorrect use they've made of it, they could ever forget it completely, since to do so would require them to take on a different nature; and that is all I can say in reply to the present question. Let's continue.

---

[84] While everyone is familiar with nouns, verbs, adjectives, pronouns and adverbs, these last two comments may need an explanation. Firstly, the comment about gender refers to the fact that all nouns in French are one of two genders, masculine or feminine. There is no particular logic to the assignment: for example, a tree is masculine; a flower is feminine. However, English has no such distinction; and in other languages there can be three genders, masculine, feminine and neuter. As for cases, different languages have different numbers. In English, the cases have all but disappeared. In the sentence 'He gave him his coat', 'He' is nominative or the subject, 'him' is accusative or the object, and 'his' implies a kind of genitive, or possession. For example, common cases found in languages may include: Nominative (Who), Vocative (Addressee), Accusative (Object), Genitive (Possessive), Dative (To whom), Ablative (Movement away), Locative (Where) and Instrumental (With what), which very loosely reflects the old adage about what to include in an article to cover all important points: who, what, when, where, how and why.

The Works of Man

I've said that this Language manifests itself in two ways, like all other Languages, that is, through verbal expression and through writing; and as I just said a moment ago that all man's works bear its imprint, we should review some of them in order to see all the better, false though they are, the relationships they have with their source.

Let's first consider those of man's works which being the image of the verbal expression of the Language we're considering, should give us the most correct and elevated idea of it. Next, we'll consider those related to the characters or writing of this Language.

The first type of these works generally includes everything regarded by men as the outflowing of genius, imagination, reason and intelligence, and generally anything which is the subject of all possible types of Literature and the Fine Arts.

In this type of man's output, which all appear to be a class apart, we nevertheless see the same purpose prevailing, and we see them all animated by the same motive, which is that of painting, of proving their subject and convincing us of its reality, or at least giving it the appearance of such.

Intellectual Products

If the partisans of one or other of these types of products are sometimes guilty of jealousy, and work to establish their reputation by pouring scorn upon the other branches which they haven't cultivated, it's clearly a wrong that they do to knowledge, and we can't doubt that among the results of man's intellectual abilities, those which are preferred are the ones which, rather than taking away from the others, support themselves with their aid, and thus offer a taste which is more solid, and beauty which is less open to interpretation.

This notion is certainly the one held by all men who are judicious and endowed with good taste; they know that it's only through an intimate and universal union that their works can find more power and more consideration, and for a long time is has been accepted that all areas of the Arts are connected and communicate their aid to one another.

And indeed, it's a feeling which is so natural to man that he carries it everywhere with him, even if he goes in a direction this Principles disavows. If an Orator wanted to condemn the Arts, he'd have to show himself to be an accomplished artist; if an Artist wished to disparage eloquence, nobody would listen to him if he did not use its Language.

However, even though this useful observation is correct, since it has only been made vaguely, has produced almost no results; and as with everything else, men are used to making absolute distinctions, treating each one of these various parts as so many objects which are not connected with each other.

It isn't that we shouldn't find different kinds work among these products of man's intellectual abilities, and that everything should only be of the same subject. On the contrary, since these abilities are themselves different from one another, and since we can see strong differences between them, it's natural to think that their results must reflect this difference, and that they can't resemble one another; yet at the same time, since these abilities are fundamentally connected and it's completely impossible for one to act without the help of the others, we can see that the different products need to show their common connection, and that they all indicate the same origin.

But I've already said too much about a subject which is only incidental to my plan. I'll return to the examination I've begun concerning the relationships found between the one universal Language and man's various intellectual products.

Of whatever kind these products are, we can reduce them to two classes to which all the others will belong, because in everything that exists, since there can only be the intellectual and the physical, all man knows how to produce will never have anything other than one of these two as its subject. And indeed, everything of this kind that men imagine and produce every day is limited to instructing or moving, reasoning or touching. It's absolutely impossible for them to say or create something outside of themselves which does not have as an aim one or other of these two points; and whatever divisions are made between man's intellectual creations, we'll always see that they either serve to enlighten and lead to an understanding of certain truths, or to subjugate intellectual man by the physical and make him experience situations in which he's no longer master of himself, he's under the spell of the voice speaking to him, and blindly follows the good or evil enchantment which carries him along.

We will attribute to the first, or intellectual class all works of reason, or in general all that should only proceed by axioms, and all which is limited to establishing facts.

We will attribute to the second, or physical class all which has the purpose of making impressions of some sort or another on the heart of man, and to move him in some manner.

Now, in either of these classes, what does its Composer wish to accomplish? Isn't it to showcase their subject from such luminous and seductive angles that the man who meditates on them can't contest their truth, nor resist the power and attraction of the means used to charm him? What resources do they use to do this? Don't they take the greatest care to get closer to the very nature of the subject which concerns them? Don't they work to get back to its source, to penetrate its very essence? In other words, don't all their efforts aim to make the expression agree so well with their concept, and to render it so natural and real that they can be sure of affecting their fellow men in such a way as if the subject itself were in front of them? Don't we ourselves feel this passionate effect upon us to a greater or lesser extent, depending on how close the Composer has come to achieving his aim? Isn't this effect general, and aren't there many stunning works of this nature all over the Earth?

That for us, then, is the image of the abilities of the true Language we're talking about, and it's in these works of men and in their efforts that we find traces of everything that has been said about the accuracy and the power of its expression, as well as its universality.

We shouldn't dwell upon this inequality of impressions which arises from the differences in idioms and in man-made Languages found among different Nations, since this difference in Language is only an accidental defect and not one of nature. Besides, as man can succeed in erasing this defect by familiarizing himself with those idioms which are foreign to it, it can do nothing against the Principle, and I don't fear saying that all the Languages on Earth are so much evidence which confirm this.

Poetry

Although I've reduced the linguistic output of man's intellectual abilities to two classes, speaking and writing, nevertheless I haven't lost sight of the multitude of branches and subdivisions they both have, as much because of the number of different subjects which are within the province of our reasoning, as by the infinite number of nuances which our sensory organs can receive.

Without enumerating them or examining each one individually, we can consider the most important Principle from each class, such as Mathematics from among the subjects of reasoning, and Poetry from among those relating to man's sensory ability. But since we discussed Mathematics earlier, I'll refer the Reader to that section, so he can confirm anew the reality and universality of the Principles I'm setting down.

So, next I'll focus on Poetry, seeing that it's the most sublime output of man's abilities, which comes closest to his Principle, and which by the transports it makes him feel, best proves to him the dignity of his origin. But just as this sacred Language still ennobles itself by raising itself up to its true goal, so too it loses its dignity in lowering itself again to fictitious and contemptible topics, which it can't touch without soiling itself as if by prostitution.

The very people who've dedicated themselves to it have always declared it to be the Language of Heroes and of beneficent Beings which they've depicted as watching over man's safety and preservation. They've felt its nobility so greatly that they haven't even feared to attribute it to Him whom they regard as the Creator of All; and it's the Language they've preferred to choose when they declared His oracles, or when they wished to offer Him homage.

Yet do I need to warn you that this Language is different from that trivial Language which the men of the various Nations use to contain their thoughts? Don't we know that it's a result of their blindness that they thought by doing this they were enhancing its elegance, when all they were doing was overwhelming their work, and that this superfluous attention to which they subjected us, which was intended to impress our physical sensory abilities, couldn't help affecting our true sensibilities just as much.[85]

But the Language of Poetry is the expression and voice of those privileged men who, nourished by the continual presence of Truth, portray it with the same fire which serves as its substance, a living fire and thus the

---

[85] Although Saint-Martin's father initially guided him towards a career in jurisprudence, he was unimpressed by the profession, and shortly after completing his studies and beginning work as a King's Advocate in Tours, he sought to change careers, becoming a commissioned soldier. His dislike for the profession is clearly seen in this passage, where he compares the sublimity of poetry, which through its use of metered language outside of daily interaction can transport us, with the artificially circuitous and long-winded legalese of the government bureaucrat or legal contracts which still plague us some 240 years later.

enemy of cold uniformity, because it controls itself in all its actions, creating itself unceasingly, and as a result is always new.

It's in such Poetry that we can see the most perfect image of this universal Language we are trying to uncover, since when it truly achieves its goal, there's nothing which shouldn't bow down before it; since it has as its Principle a devouring fire which accompanies all its steps, which must enervate, dissolve and inflame everything, and even the first Law of Poets is to not sing when they don't feel its heat.

It isn't for this fire to produce identical effects everywhere; for as all things are in its province it yields to their different natures. But it must never appear without fulfilling its goal, which is to bring everything along behind it.

Let's now see if such Poetry could ever have arisen from a frivolous or corrupt source; if the thought which gives birth to it doesn't have to be of the highest degree of elevation, and if it'd be true to say that the first man must have been the first Poet?

Let's see, too, whether human Poetry could itself be that true and unique Language which we know belongs to our species. No, without a doubt, it's only a feeble imitation; but since among all the fruits of man's labor it's the one which is closest to its Principle, I've chosen it to give an idea of what is most appropriate for him.

Also, it can be said that these man-made measures which men use in the poetry they've created, imperfect as they appear, should at least offer us proof of the precision and accuracy of the true Language whose weight, number and measure are invariable.

We could also remember that, since this Poetry applies to all objects, the true Language whose imperfect image it is must with good reason be universal and can embrace everything which exists. Finally, it'd be through a more detailed examination of the properties associated with this sublime Language, that we could come closer to its model and read directly from its source.

It's there that we would see why Poetry has had such a hold over men in all ages, why it has worked so many marvels, and where that general admiration comes form, which all the Nations on Earth have for those who have distinguished themselves in it, which would extend our ideas about the Principle which gave it birth even further.

We'd also see that the use men often make of it defiles and disfigures it to the point of making it unrecognizable, which would prove to us that, for them, it's not always the result of this true Language which concerns us; that it's a profanation to use it in praise of men, an idolatry to dedicate it to passion, and that it should never have any other purpose than to show men the asylum from which it descended with them, in order to inspire in them the virtuous desire to follow its tracks and return there.

Written Characters

But it's enough for me to have set out the path, so that those who've any desire can penetrate much further along it. Let's move on to the second manner that the true Language should manifest itself, that is, in written characters.

I'm not afraid of saying that these characters are as varied and multiplied as everything which is contained in Nature, that there isn't a single Being which can't find its place there and serve as a sign in it, and that everyone and everything will find their image and their true representation there, which brings these characters up to such an immense number, it's impossible for a man to keep them all in his memory, not only because of their enormous number, but also because of their differences and their strangeness.

When we might suppose, moreover, that a man could retain all those he had encountered, he couldn't boast that he had nothing further to learn about them; for every day Nature produces new things, all of which by showing us the infinite number of things, also reminds us of the limit and deprivation of our species which could never succeed in embracing everything, since here below he can't even manage to know all the letters of his Alphabet.

The variety of these things contained in Nature encompasses not only their form, as we can easily see, but also their color and the place they occupy in the order of things; which means that the Writing of the true Language varies as much as the multitude of nuances which we can see in material bodies, since each of these nuances carries just as many different meanings.

Finally, the characters it uses are as numerous as the points on the horizon; and as each of these points occupies a place which is its alone, each of the letters of the true Language also has a meaning and an explanation which is specific to it.

But I must stop, O Holy Truth, for it'd be usurping your rights to publish your secrets even in an hidden manner, for it's for you alone to reveal them to whom you please, and how you please. As for me, I must limit myself to respecting them in silence, and to gathering all my desires so that my fellow men might open their eyes to your light, and that, disenchanted by the illusions which seduce them, they might be wise and fortunate enough to prostrate themselves at your feet.

Therefore, still taking prudence as your guide, I will say that it's this infinite multitude of characters of the true Language and their enormous variety which has introduced such great diversity into human Languages, that few among them use the same signs, and even those which agree on this point still vary in their quantity by accepting or rejecting some signs, each according to its idiom and its particular spirit.

But, just as the characters of the true Language are as many as the Beings contained in Nature, so it's also certain that none of these characters can originate anywhere other than this Nature, and that it's here that they draw everything which serves to distinguish them, since outside of Nature there's nothing physical. It's also because of this that, despite the variety of characters that human Languages use, they can never go beyond these same limits, and that it's always by means of lines and figures that they have to create all their man-made signs; which proves in the clearest manner that men can't invent anything.

Painting

We'll convince ourselves of all this with a few observations on the Art of Painting, which we may regard as having taken its origin from the characters of the Language in question, just as human Poetry took its origin from its verbal expression.

If it's certain that this Language is unique and as old as time, we can't doubt that the characters it uses were the first models. The men who are devoted to studying it have often needed to help memory by using notes or copies. Now, it's in making these copies that they need the greatest accuracy, since in this multitude of characters which are sometimes only distinguished by the slightest differences, we can be sure that the slightest alteration could misrepresent and confuse them.

We can sense that if men had been wise, they wouldn't have made any other use of Painting, and even in the interest of this Art, they'd have been content to limit themselves to imitating and copying these first characters; for if they are with reason so fastidious in their choice of models, where could they find truer and more regular ones than those which express the very nature of things? If they were so refined in their choice of quality and use of colors, where could they better address this than in forms which each bore its own color? Finally, if they wanted lasting images, how could they succeed better than in copying them from subjects which are always new, and which they could compare with their Painting at any time?

But the same carelessness which had distanced man from his Principle also distanced him from the means given him to return to it. He lost his confidence in the true and luminous guides which, supporting his pure intent, would surely have led him back to his goal. He no longer sought his models from among useful and beneficial subjects, and from which he would continually obtained help, but instead used fleeting and misleading forms, which by offering him only uncertain traits and changing colors, open him up each day to varying his own approaches and despising his works.

This is what happens each day when he intends, as he does, to draw quadrupeds, reptiles and other animals, as well as all the other Beings which surround him; because this occupation, as innocent and agreeable it might be in itself, accustoms man to fixing his gaze on what is foreign to him, and makes him lose not only sight, but also the very idea of what is appropriate; that is, the things man is occupied with drawing today are only the appearance of those he should be studying every day; and the copy he makes of them should, according to established Principles, be inferior to his models, so that it's nothing more than the likeness of a likeness.

Nevertheless, it's by this crude Painting that we can perfectly convince ourselves of the incontrovertible Truth discussed above, which is that men invent nothing. Isn't it a fact that they almost always compose their paintings using physical Beings? Is it possible for them to find their subjects elsewhere, since, as Painting is simply the Art of the eyes, it can only be concerned with the physical realm, and as a result only be found in the physical?

Can it be said that the Painter can not only dispense with looking at physical subjects, but by raising himself above them, he can take subjects simply from his imagination? This objection would be easy to destroy; for let's give his imagination the freest rein, and permit it to wander wherever it will, and I ask whether it'll ever create anything which is outside of Nature, and if we'll be in a position to say that his imagination had actually created anything. No doubt it has the ability to represent bizarre Beings and monstrous composites, of which Nature truly offers no examples. But won't these fantastical Beings themselves be the product of parts brought together? And of all these parts, would there ever be any which weren't to be found among the physical things of Nature?

It's therefore certain that in Painting as well as in all the other Arts, man's inventions and works are never anything more than transpositions, and that far from producing anything himself, all his works are limited to moving things around.

Now, man can learn to calculate the value of his works in Painting just as in the other Arts, and in giving himself over to this delightful occupation, he'll cease to believe in the reality of his works, since this reality isn't even found in the models he selects.

It's unnecessary, I think, to say that this crude Painting still contains strong signs that it descends from a more perfect Art, and in this sense, it's further proof of this superior writing, connected with the one and universal Language whose properties we've already shown.

Indeed, it requires a resemblance to physical Nature in everything it represents. Wanting nothing which would shock either the eyes or the judgement, it includes all the Beings of the Universe, and has even raised its daring hands up to paint superior Beings.

But it's then that Painting is truly reprehensible, because firstly being unable to make these superior Beings visible except by physical and sensory traits it has then debased these Beings in man's eyes, who can only know them through the sensory ability of his intelligence and never in a physical sense, since these Beings don't live in the physical Realm.

Secondly, when Painting took it upon itself to represent them, where did it find the model for the bodies they didn't possess yet it nevertheless wished to give them? There can be no doubt that it was from among the material subjects in Nature, or what is the same thing, in the Painter's unbridled imagination, but which in its very disorder could only ever use the physical Beings which surround man today.

What relationship, then, could there be between the sublime model and the image which has been substituted for it, and what notions must these kinds of image have given birth to? Isn't it evident that this is one of the deadliest consequences of man's ignorance, which has exposed him the most to idolatry, and which endlessly works to bury him in darkness?

And truly, what can dead Matter and lines drawn from the Painter's imagination produce, other than forgetting the simplicity of Beings whose knowledge is so necessary to man, and without which his entire species is given over to the most awful superstition? And isn't it how man's steps, uncaring as they appear, gradually lead him astray, and throw him over precipices whose edges he no longer sees?

Coats of Arms

Man was therefore not content with confusing crude Painting and the work of his hands with true characters copied from Nature itself. He also misunderstood the Principle from where these true characters draw their origin. Seeing, indeed, that he was master of using at will all the different traits of this physical Nature to compose his pictures, he was feeble enough to rely with complacency on his work, and at the same time forget the superiority of the models which he should have chosen and the source which could produce them; or rather, having lost sight of them, he no longer even suspected their existence.

The same must be said about Coats of Arms, which also takes its origin from the characters of the true Language. Common man, puffed up with pride over the nobility of his Arms, as if their signs were real and they truly carried with them the rights which prejudice attributes to them; and letting himself be blinded by the childish distinctions which he attaches to these signs, he forgot that they were but the sad images of the *genuine arms* physically awarded to each man to serve as his defense, and to be at the same time the seal of his *virtues*, his power and greatness.

Errors Regarding The True Language

Finally, he did the same thing with the verbal expression of this sublime Language from which we saw poetry came. Arbitrary words and man-made Languages took the place of the true Language in his mind; that is, these man-made Languages had no uniformity nor any connection, either in expressions, or signs, or generally in their universal relationship with the Language of the intellectual abilities of which they are simply a distorted imitation. Hence the notion of the Principle of this unique and universal Language which alone could enlighten him, having been erased in him, he could no longer distinguish this true Language from those he'd invented.

Now, if man is limited enough to place his works alongside those of the true and invariable Principles, if his audacious hands believe they are equal to those of Nature, if he has even nearly confused the works of Nature with either the general or the particular Principle which manifests them, we should not be surprised that all his notions are so confused and so clouded, and that not only has he lost the knowledge and understanding of the true Language, but even that he is not convinced that one exists.

The Means of Recovering the True Language

At the same time, if this true Language is the only one which could return him to his rights, restore him to possession of his attributes, make him know the Principles of Justice and lead him to an understanding of everything that exists, it's easy to see how much he is losing in moving away from it, and if he should have any other resources other than to devote every moment of his life in taking care to recover an understanding of it.

But, however immense, however terrifying this path may be, there is no man who should give himself over to despair and discouragement, since I've already said that this very Language is man's true domain; that he's only been deprived of it for a time; that far from being forever stripped of it, on the contrary he's constantly offered a Hand to lead him to it; and truly the price attached to this grace is so modest and so natural that it's further proof of the goodness of the Principle which requires it, since it's limited to asking man not to compare the two distinct Beings which compose him; to recognize the differences of the Principles of Nature and the differences they have with the superior temporal Cause of this very Nature; that is, to believe that man is not Matter, and that Nature does not walk alone.

Music

We still have to examine one of the products of this true Language whose notion I'm tasked with recalling to men, which is the one which is connected to its verbal expression, which regulates its strength and measures its pronunciation. This, then, is the Art we call *Music*, but which among men is still only an image of true harmony.

This verbal expression can use words without the sounds being heard. Now, it's the intimate connection between them which forms the fundamental Laws of true Music; it's this which we imitate, as far as we can, in our artificial Music, in the care we take to Paint with sounds the sense of our man-made words; but, before demonstrating the main defects of this artificial Music, we're going to run through some of the true Principles it offers us; and by means of this we can discover the powerful connections to all that's been established, and convince ourselves that it still belongs to the same source, and that it's therefore one of the resources available to man. It's also through this examination that we'll see that, admirable enough though our talents might be in the imitation of Music, we still remain infinitely below our model; which will show man whether this powerful instrument was only given to him for childish amusement, or if, at its origin, it wasn't destined for a more noble use.[86]

The Common Chord

Firstly, what we know in Music by the name of the common chord, is for us the image of that First Unity which enclosed everything within Himself and from Whom everything comes, in that this chord is singular and unique and is entirely complete in itself, without needing help from any sound other than its own; in a word, its intrinsic value is unalterable like Unity; for one mustn't count the transposition of some of its sounds as an alteration, when the results are chords of different names, so long as this transposition doesn't introduce a new sound into the chord, and as a result can't change its true essence.

Secondly, the common chord is the most harmonious of all, the one which alone suits man's ear, and which leaves nothing to be desired. The three first sounds which compose it are separated by two intervals of a third

---

[86] In Saint-Martin's tour of music, which he uses as the last of the Seven Liberal Arts & Sciences, it might be worth remembering that Music was considered the last of these, and he ends with a discourse on this topic. All we know of Saint-Martin's musical abilities is the fact that he played the violin, and not well according to his own judgement, his childhood frailty denying him the ability to obtain a good vibrato out of his instrument. On the other hand, it would be very unusual for an aristocrat of the time not to learn a keyboard instrument, and there is every probability that Saint-Martin also played the harpsichord well enough to entertain his guests at his frequent *Salons*.

which are distinct, but which are linked to one another. That is the repetition of everything which takes place in physical things, where no physical Being can receive or maintain its existence without the help and support of another physical Being like itself, which reanimates its power and sustains it.

Finally, these two thirds are surmounted by an interval of a fourth, whose sound which ends the chord, and is called an *Octave*. Although it's only a repetition of the fundamental note, it's nevertheless this octave which indicates the completion of the common chord; for it essentially derives from it, in that it's included in the original sounds which the resonating body makes to be heard above its own.[87]

So, this Quaternary interval is the Principle agent of the chord. It's placed above the two ternary intervals, to preside over it and to direct its action, like that active and intelligent Cause which we've seen dominate and preside over the dual Law of all physical Beings. Like the Cause, it can't endure any mixing, and when it acts alone, like this universal Cause of time, it's certain that all its results are regular.

I know, however, that this octave, being really only a repetition of its fundamental, can be omitted if required and not counted among the sounds which compose the common chord. But firstly, it's this note which essentially completes the scale; and moreover, it's necessary to include this octave if we want to know what the *alpha* and *omega* are, and have clear proof of the unity of our chord, all because of a calculation which I can't reveal other than to say that the octave is the first agent, or the first organ by which *ten* has been able to come to our knowledge.

Nor, in the physical picture I am presenting, should we expect complete uniformity with the Principle of which it's only the image, because then the copy would be equal to the model. But also, although this physical picture is inferior, and moreover is subject to variation, it exists no less complete, and represents no less the Principle, since the instinct of the senses supplies the rest.

It's for this reason that, having presented the two thirds as being connected to one another, we can't say it's critical that they both be heard; for we know that each of them can be played separately without the ear suffering, but the Law's no less true for that, because this interval played in this manner still preserves its secret relationship with the other sounds of the chord to which it belongs; and so, it always presents the same picture, but we now only see a part of it.

---

[87] That is, its harmonic.

We can say the same about omitting the octave, or even all the other sounds of the chord, and only keeping one of them, because a sound heard alone is not a burden on the ear, and besides, it could itself be considered as the generating sound of a new common chord.

We've seen that the fourth dominated the two lower thirds, and that these two lower thirds were the image of the dual Law which governs the elemental Beings. Isn't it here, too, that Nature shows us the difference between a body and its Principle, by making us see one in subjection and dependency, whereas the other is its leader and support?

Indeed, by their difference these two thirds show us the state of perishable things in physical Nature, which only exist through the unions of various actions; and the final sound formed by a single Quaternary interval, is a new image of the First Principle; for it reminds us of His simplicity, greatness and immutability, as much by rank as by *number*.

It isn't that this harmonic fourth is more permanent that all other created things; once it becomes physical it must pass away; but that doesn't prevent the fact that, even in its fleeting action, it paints the essence and stability of its source to the mind.

We therefore find in the combination of intervals in the common chord everything that's passive and everything that's active, that is, all that exists and all that man can imagine.

But it's not enough for us to have seen the representation of all things both general and specific in the common chord. By further observation we can also see the source of these same things and the origin of this distinction, which was made before time between the two Principles, and which manifests itself every day in time.

To this end, let's not lose sight of the beauty and perfection of this common chord which draws all its benefits from itself alone. We can easily realize that if it had always remained in its nature, order and harmony would've existed forever, and evil would be unknown, because it wouldn't have been born; in other words, only the action of the Good Principle's abilities would've been manifested, since it's the only real and true one.[88]

---

[88] While it wouldn't be possible to give a music lesson at this point, a few reminders might be in order to help those who have only a passing understanding of this Art. If the common DoReMi names are used, we will remember that a scale is made up of 8 notes, beginning and ending on the same note, only higher. This is called an Octave. The first note (Do) is also called the Tonic or the Fundamental, and this is why Saint-Martin equates it with Unity, or the First Cause, from which all else derives. We should remember that Pasqually's and Saint-Martin's systems are based on number, and music is the ultimate expression of numbers in harmony. The common chord is the one made up

The Seventh Chord

How is it that the second Principle became evil? How can it be that evil was born and appeared? Isn't it when the upper and dominant sound of the common chord, the octave, was removed and another sound was introduced in its place? Now, what's the sound which replaced the octave? It's the note which immediately precedes it, and don't we know that the new chord which resulted from this change is called a *seventh chord*? We also know that this seventh chord tires the ear, keeps it in suspense, and asks to be saved, in Artistic terms.

It's through the opposition of this dissonant chord and all those that derive from it, to the common chord that all musical works originate, which are nothing more than a continual game, not to mention a battle between the common chord and the seventh chord, or all the dissonant chords in general.

Surely this Law, indicated to us in Nature, is an image of the universal production of things? Why wouldn't we find the Principle here, just as we found its assemblage and constitution in the order of the intervals in the common chord earlier? Why, indeed, clearly grasp the Cause, origin and results of the universal temporal confusion? We know that in physical Nature there are two Principles which are ceaselessly opposed, and that it can only be maintained through the help of two contrary actions, from which the combat and the violence we see comes about. Isn't this reflected in the mixture of regularity and disorder which harmony faithfully represents to us through the combination of consonances and dissonances which comprise all musical works?

Nevertheless, I flatter myself that my Readers are intelligent enough to see only the images of higher things which I've shown them here. They'll no doubt see the allegory when I tell them that if the common chord had remained in its true nature, evil would still not have been born, for according to the established Principle, it's impossible for the specific Law of musical order to be equal to the superior order which it represents.

---

of Do-Mi-So-Do'. It is made up of two Thirds and a Fourth, given that both notes are counted, so although the distance between Do and Mi is two, we count Do-Re-Mi. So, Do-Mi is a Third, Mi-So is a Third, and So-Do' is a Fourth (So-La-Ti-Do'). Now, if we replace the 8th note (the Octave) with the note below it, the 7th (Ti), we now have a Seventh Chord, which sounds incomplete to our ears, and can only be resolved by replacing the 7th once more with the 8th or Octave. If this appears hard to follow, it may be useful to write out the following in a line: Do Re Mi Fa So La Ti Do' where Do' is the Octave. Then write the numbers 1 – 8 underneath from left to right.

Also, as musical order is founded on the physical, and the physical is only the product of several actions, if it only offered a continual stream of common chords to the ear, it wouldn't be shocked, it's true; but apart from the boring monotony resulting from this, we wouldn't find a single expression or a single idea in such music. Indeed, it wouldn't be Music at all to us, since Music is generally all that is physical, and incompatible with the unity of action, as well as the unity of agents.

So, by accepting all the Laws necessary for the creation of musical works, we can nevertheless apply these same Laws to truths of another order. It's for this reason that I'm going to continue my observations on the seventh chord.

The Second

By putting this seventh in place of the octave, we saw that this put a Principle alongside another Principle which, according to all the illumination of sanest reason, can only result in disorder. We saw this even more clearly when noting that this seventh which produces the dissonance is also the sound which immediately precedes the octave.

But the seventh which has such a relation to its fundamental can also be regarded as a second, in relation to the octave which is its repetition; then we recognize that the seventh is not the only dissonance, and that the second also has this property; and so, all diatonic proximity is condemned by the nature of our ear, and wherever it hears two neighboring notes sound together, it'll be shocked.

Then, since in the scale only the second and the seventh can be found to have this relationship with the tonic or with its octave, which makes us see clearly that any result and any output, in terms of Music, is based on two dissonances, from which arise all musical reactions.[89]

---

[89] Here, Saint-Martin is pointing out that notes which are next to each other on the scale, or a Second, jar our ears when played together. The interval must be at least a Third for it to sit well with our hearing. This is called Consonance, and applies to the Third, Fourth, Fifth, Sixth and Octave (or Do-Mi, Do-Fa, Do-So, Do-La, and Do-Do'). This leaves two notes in the scale which are considered Dissonant: the Second and the Seventh (Do-Re and Do-Ti). However, Saint-Martin points out that the reason these both jar the ears is because they're in fact both the same interval, being consecutive notes, and therefore both are really Seconds. Now, this fits with his belief that '2' is the number of confusion. Saint-Martin also tells us that, if we build the Seventh out of three Thirds, being Do-Mi, Mi-So, So-Ti, by using musical convention to count two notes twice, we arrive at three Thirds, or the number Nine, which we will recall is the number of Earth, the physical realm, and the circumference.

Dissonance and Consonance

Then, carrying this observation across to physical things, we'll see from the same evidence that they've never been able to and never can be created except from two dissonances, and try as we may, we'll never find a source of disorder other than the numbers associated with these two types of dissonance.

Moreover, if we observe that what is commonly called a seventh is in fact a ninth, given that it's the combination of three very distinct thirds, we'll see if I've deceived my Readers by telling them previously that the number *nine* was the true number of extent and of Matter.

If, on the contrary, we want to look at the numbers of the consonances or sounds which harmonize with the fundamental, we'll see that they're four in number, being the third, the fourth, the perfect fifth and the sixth; for here we shouldn't speak of the octave as an octave, since it only a convention of the specific divisions of the scale, where an octave is not different to the fundamental whose image it is, unless we wish to see it as the fourth of the second tetrachord; which changes nothing about the number of the four consonances which we're establishing.

As much as I'd like to, I could never expand on the infinite properties of these four consonances, and this truly distresses me, because it'd be easy for me to show you their direct relationship to *Unity* with striking clarity, to show how universal harmony is connected to this Quaternary consonance, and why it's impossible for any Being to exist in good condition without it.

But at every step prudence and duty prevent me, because in these matters a single point leads to all the rest, and I'd never have undertaken to discuss any of them, if the errors with which human Sciences poison my species hadn't led me to come to its defense.

Nevertheless, I've undertaken not to end this book without giving some more detailed explanations about the universal properties of the Quaternary. I'm not forgetting my promise, and I intend to fulfill it so far as I am

---

Now, to go a little off topic, there is a most curious phrase in the *Exsultet*, or the 'Easter Proclamation' sung at the Paschal Vigil: "O truly necessary sin of Adam, destroyed completely by the death of Christ." In other words, it was preferable for Adam to sin so that mankind could experience Christ's coming to Earth, over Adam not sinning at all and there being no coming of the Christ. The suggestion that perhaps we need to encounter Evil, or Dissonance to be able to identify Good, or Consonance, is a theme which comes late in this book. So, here we find Saint-Martin pointing out that, without the constant use of dissonance as a vehicle to provide satisfaction to the ears by resolving it into consonance, music would be very boring indeed; and by implication, not to experience Evil could lead us not to seek Good.

permitted to do so. But for now, let's return once more to the seventh, and note that if this makes a diversion from the common chord, it's also because of this that crisis and revolution take place, out of which should come order to restore tranquility the ear, since following the seventh it's absolutely necessary to return to the common chord. I don't regard what is called a succession of sevenths as being contrary to this Principle, since it's nothing more than a succession of discords, which can only ever end with a common chord or one of its derivatives.

It's therefore this very dissonance which reflects what takes place in physical Nature, whose career is but a succession of disturbances and restorations. Now, if this same observation previously showed us the true origin of physical things, if it now shows us that all the Beings of Nature are subject to that violent Law which presides over their origin, their existence and their end, why can't we apply the same Law to the entire Universe, and recognize that if it was violence which brought it into existence and which sustains it, must it also be violence which works its destruction?

This is what we hear at the moment a piece of Music ends, for there's normally a confused interval, a trill between one of the notes of the common chord and the second or seventh of the dissonant chord played by the bass which usually maintains the tonic to finally lead everything back to the common chord or Unity.

We should also note that, since after this musical cadence, everything must return to the common chord which restores everything to peace and order, we may be sure that after the crisis of the Elements, the Principles which were in combat must similarly recover their tranquility, from which, applying the same concept to man, we should learn how much a true understanding of Music could keep him from a fear of death, since this death is only the trill which ends his state of confusion, and leads him back to his *four consonances*.

I've said enough for my Readers to understand, and it's up to them to push the limits I've set for myself. I can hope as a result that they won't consider dissonances as being defects in Music – since it's from these that it draws its greatest beauty – but simply as an indication of the conflict which reigns in all things.

They'll understand that even in harmony, of which the Music of the senses is but the image, we should find the same opposition of dissonances to consonances; but far from causing the slightest flaw in it, they're its food and life, and the mind will only sense the action of many different abilities which mutually support rather than fight against each other, and which, through their union, give birth to a multitude of results which are always new and always striking.

This is therefore only a very abbreviated extract of all the observations which I could make of this kind about Music, and the relationships to be found between it and some important Truths; but what I've said about it's sufficient to see the reason for things, and to teach men not to isolate the various aspects of their knowledge, since we've shown them that they're all simply different branches of the same tree, and that the same imprint appears throughout.

Pitch

Should we now speak about the darkness in which the Art of Music still is? We could start by asking Musicians what their rule is to get the pitch; that is, what's their *middle A* or their *tuning fork*; and if they don't have one, and being obliged to guess one, do they think they have something fixed of this kind? So, if they don't in fact have a fixed pitch, this means the numerical relationships they can get from their relative pitch, and the sounds correlating to it are no longer true sounds, and the Principles which Musicians give us as true from the numbers they've accepted could also be connected with different numbers, depending on whether the *relative pitch* was higher or lower; which makes most of their opinions about the numerical values they attribute to different sounds completely uncertain.

However, I'm only speaking here of those who've tried to evaluate different sounds by the number of vibrations of the strings or other sounding parts; for then a fixed pitch is needed for the experiment to work. Consequently, it'd be necessary to have sounding parts which were essentially the same, so that one could rule on their results; but as these two means aren't given to man, seeing that Matter is only relative, it's clear that everything established on such a basis would be open to many errors.[90]

---

[90] There are two kinds of pitch, perfect or fixed, and relative. Most instruments in an orchestra need to be tuned to a common pitch, so that they can play in harmony. The oboe, being a reed instrument, and therefore has no need to tune, plays a middle A, and all the other instruments are tuned to this note. String instruments all have an A string, and brass and non-reed wind instruments have sliders to adjust pitch. If there's no oboe, a tuning fork, which when stuck emits an A, is used. Some people also appear to have an innate ability to identify A, and they are said to have 'perfect' or 'absolute

Principles of Harmony

Therefore, it wasn't in Matter at all that we should have sought the Principles of harmony, for, according to all we've seen, since Matter is never fixed, it can't offer a Principle of anything. But it was in the very Nature of things where everything being stable and always the same, we only need eyes to read the truth in it. Finally, man would've seen that he had no other rule to follow than that which he finds in the dual relationship of the octave, or in that famous dual reason that is written on all Beings, and from which the triple reason has come; which would have shown him once again the dual action of Nature and this third temporal Cause universally based upon the two others.

Artificial Music

There I will end my observations on the defectiveness of the Laws which man's imagination has been able to introduce into Music; for everything I could add will still lead to this first error, and it's clear I can't add anything of further use to it. I'll only warn Composers to reflect well on the nature of our senses, and to observe that that hearing, like all the others, is susceptible to habit; and that as a result they could've been wrong about it in good faith when they made rules out of random things, and made assumptions which time alone would've made them think they were true and regular.

Nevertheless, it remains to me to examine what use man has made of this Music, with which he almost universally occupies himself, and to see whether he's ever suspected its true purpose.

---

pitch'. Relative pitch is a skill which most musicians possess. Once a pitch has been played and identified, a person with relative pitch can subsequently identify any note or pitch. Now, the tuning fork was invented by John Shore in 1711. However, the Well-Tempered system of tuning, named after J.S. Bach's pieces of the same name, where all twelve intervals in the octave are equally spaced, only came into standard use in the late 19th Century. Indeed, it was felt to be banal and boring to 18th Century ears. Then, Meantone tuning was the most prevalent, which focused on accuracy in the sound of Thirds, at the expense of other intervals. This also meant that some keys sounded normal, while others sounded awful since the intervals weren't equidistant. While Saint-Martin acknowledges that some work was being done on vibration and comparing different instruments, he rightly points out that, since they are man-made and therefore subject to variation (mass production was a long way off), it would be difficult to draw any accurate conclusions from such comparisons.

Aside from the innumerable wonders it's capable of, it knows a strict Law, which is the strict measure from which it can absolutely never deviate. Doesn't that alone tell him that it has a true Principle, and that the hand which directs it is above the power of the senses, since the senses have nothing that is fixed?

But if it comes from Principles of this kind, then it's certain that it should never have another guide, and that it was made to be forever united with its source. Now, since as we've seen, its source is that first and universal Language which indicates and represents things in their natural state, we can't doubt that Music was the true measure of things, as writing and speech express their meaning.

It's therefore only by applying itself to this fertile and invariable Principle that Music could preserve the rights of its origin, and fulfill its true function; it's then that it would have been able to paint striking likenesses, and all the abilities of those who listened to it would've been completely satisfied. In other words, this is how Music would've worked the marvels it's capable of, and which have been attributed to it across the ages.

As a result, in separating it from its source, in only seeking themes for it in artificial sentiments or vague ideas, it's been deprived of its first support, and its means of presenting itself in all its brilliance has been removed.

Also, what impressions, what effects does it produce in man's hands? What ideas, what sense does it offer us? Apart from the Composer, are there many ears which could understand what they hear expressed in generally accepted Music? And as for the Composer himself, having given himself over to his imagination, does he ever lose the sense of what he wrote, and what he wanted to convey?

Nothing is therefore more imperfect or defective than the use men have made of this Art, specifically because they were so unconcerned about its Principle, they didn't seek to support one with the other, and they believed they could make copies without having the model before them.

It's not that I blame my fellow men at all for seeking within the infinite resources of artificial Music that pleasure and relaxation which they can offer, nor would I wish to deprive them of the help which, despite its imperfections, this Art can bring to them every day. It can, I know sometimes help to revive in them some of those faded notions which, being better refined, should be their only sustenance and which alone can support them. But to this end I'll always urge them to raise their minds above what their senses hear, because man's element is not in the senses. I'll urge them to believe that however perfect their musical performances are, there are some of *another and more regular order*; that it's not even by reason of a closer or lesser conformity with them that artificial Music engages us and causes some measure of emotion.

Musical Measure or Beat

When I emphasized the preciseness of the measure which controls Music, I didn't lose sight of the universality of this Law. I intended on the contrary to return to it, to show that when it embraces everything, it also has distinct characters everywhere. And there's nothing here which doesn't conform with everything that we've established. We've seen measure take its place among man's intellectual abilities, and counted among the number of Laws which direct him. We've been able to determine from this, that since these intellectual abilities resemble the abilities of the superior Principle from which man receives everything, this Principle must also have its own measure and its own specific Laws.

From this, if superior things have their own measure, we should no longer find it surprising that the inferior and physical things they've created are also subject to them; and as a result, that we'd find in this measure a strict guide for Music.

But, however little we reflect on the nature of this physical measure, we'll soon see the difference between it and the measure which rules the things of a superior order.

In Music, we see that the measure – or beat – is always the same; that once movement has been established it perpetuates and repeats itself in the same form and the same number of beats. Then everything appears to be so regulated and so precise that it's impossible not to feel its Law, and be certain of the need for it. This regular beat is also so well-suited to physical things, that we see men using it with all of their work where the action is continuous. We see this Law is like a support for them on which they can happily rest. We can even see them using it in their most menial tasks, and it's then we can truly see the advantage and usefulness of this powerful aid, since with it, the action seems to lighten the heavy labor which, without it, would seem unbearable to them.

Physical Measure

But this, too, is what can also help us to learn about the nature of physical things; for, to show us such an equality of action, and may I say such servitude, is to show us clearly that the Principle within them isn't the master of that action, but rather that it's controlled and compelled, which takes us back to what we've seen in the various parts of this book regarding the inferiority of Matter. So, it actually shows us a marked dependency and all the signs of a passive existence; that is, as it doesn't have its own action, it has to wait to receive it from a superior Law which can dispense it and which commands it.

Secondly, we can note that this Law which rules the march of Music, manifests itself in two ways, or through two types of time signatures known under the names of 2/4 (or two-four) time and 3/4 (or three-four) time. We won't include common time (4/4 time), nor all the other subdivisions which could be made, and which are only multiples of the two first time signatures. Even less can we allow a measure of one beat, since physical things are neither the result nor the effect of a single action, but only arise and subsist by the means of several actions combined.

Now, it's the number and the quality of these action which we find revealed in the two different types of time signatures associated with Music, as well as in the number of beats that these two time signatures contain. And surely, nothing would be more instructive than to observe this combination of two and three beats in relation to all which exists physically; for here again we'd clearly see the dual reason and the triple reason governing the universal course of things.

But these points have been gone into in too much detail. I would only ask people to evaluate those who surround them, and never to communicate any knowledge to them which should only be the rewards for their desires and efforts. With this in mind, I'll quickly conclude what I have to say about the two physical measures of music.

In order to know which of these two measures is used in a piece of Music, we have to wait until the first bar is completed; or what is the same thing, that the second bar has begun. It's only then that the hearing is attuned, and can sense which number to apply. For, so long as a measure has not reached its end like this we can never know what its number is, as it's still possible to add more beats to what went before.

Doesn't this also show us in Nature that oft-repeated truth, that the properties of physical things aren't fixed, but only relative, and that they're only supported by each other. For unless this were true, any one of their actions on appearing would show its true character, and wouldn't wait to be compared with another to make itself known.

Intellectual Measurement

Such is therefore the interiority of artificial Music and all physical things, in that they only contain passive actions, and their measurements, although determined in themselves, can only be known to us in relation to other measurements to which they're compared.

Among things of a superior order completely outside of the physical, this measurement shows itself under more noble traits. There, each Being has its own action, and also has a measurement in its Laws which is in proportion to this action. However, at the same time, since each action is always new and always different to the one which preceded it and to the one which follows, we can see that the measurement associated with them can never be the same. So, it's not in this class that we should seek that uniformity of measurement which we see in music and in physical things.

In perishable Nature everything is dependent, and can only execute things blindly, through the necessary union of several agents which are subject to the same Law. Since these always come together in the same manner and for the same purpose, they can only produce the same result, so long as they don't experience any disturbances or obstacles in the accomplishment of their action.

The Works of Man

In imperishable Nature, on the contrary, everything is alive, everything is simple, and therefore each action carries all its Laws with it. That is, that the superior action itself rules its measurement, rather than the measurement ruling the inferior action, or Matter and all passive Nature.

Nothing more is needed to sense the infinite difference which there must be between artificial Matter and the living expression of this true Language which we are telling men is the most powerful of the means given them to reestablish them in their rights.

Let them therefore learn to distinguish this unique and invariable Language from all the artificial products which they constantly put in its place. The former, carrying its Laws with it, only ever has the correct ones which conform with the Principle which uses them. The rest are created by man while he's in darkness, and he doesn't know if what he creates conforms or not to this superior Principle from which he is separated, and which he no longer knows.

Then when he sees the works of his hands vary, and the abuses he makes of Languages multiply to infinity, as much in the use of Speech as in Writing and Music; when he sees all the human Languages come into existence and die in succession; when he sees that here below we only know the *number* of things, and that almost all of us die before ever knowing their *names*, because of this he won't believe that the Principle, by means of which he gives life to his products, could be subject to the same changes and the same darkness.

On the contrary, he'll accept that since he can only create anything today through imitation, his works will never have the same solidity as the true originals. Then, observing that it's not possible for everyone to visualize the original model in the same place, he'll realize why the copies are all different; yet he will sense none the less that this model, being at the center, always remains the same, like the Principle whose Laws and Will it expresses, and that if men were courageous enough to draw nearer to it, they'd see all those differences, which only existed because they were so far away from it, disappear.

Then he'd no longer attribute the properties of the invaluable seed which is within him to habit and example; but on the contrary, he'd agree that it's these very habits and examples which degrade and obscure the properties of this true, simple and indestructible seed; in other words, if man had anticipated all these obstacles, or if he'd had sufficient strength to overcome them, he'd have a Language in common with all his fellow men, like the essence which constitutes them and establishes a universal similarity between them.

Rights of the True Language

It is, indeed, the unity of the Principle and the essence of men which best makes them sense the possibility of the unity of their Language, since if by the rights of their nature, they can have all the same ideas of the Laws of Beings, the true rules of Justice, and their Religion and their worship; if they can indeed hope to recover the use of all their intellectual abilities, in sum, if they're all moving toward the same goal and all have the same work to do, yet they couldn't accomplish this without the help of Languages, this attribute must be able to act through a uniform Law, similar to the universality and intimate unity of all their knowledge.

Also, without recalling all that we've said about the superiority of this true Language, we'll believe that we can understand clearly enough how it must be unique and powerful, by repeating that it's the only voice which can lead man to Unity, and to the Source of all Powers; that is, to the *root* of this square whose sides it's man's task to go all around, and whose properties and *virtues*, as I've promised, I'm about to explain here.

Properties of the Universal Number

We previously saw full enough details about the relationships of this square, or this Quaternary number, with the Causes outside of man and with the Laws which rule the course of all the Beings of Nature; but we've learned enough from all that has preceded not to have any further doubt that this universal symbol must have even more interesting connections for man, in that they are more direct for him, and concern him personally.

There's therefore nobody who can't recognize a very great affinity with the fourth of the ten pages of that Book which, before man's condemnation, was always open and intelligible to him, but which today he can no longer read nor understand, except through the succession of time. We'll even see with equal ease a striking similarity to that powerful spear which man possessed at the time of his original birth, and the laborious search for which is the sole object of his temporal journey, and the first Law of his condemnation.

Moreover, a connection may also be found with this fertile center which man occupied during his glory, and which he will never again know fully without returning there.

And truly, what can better remind us of the eminent rank where man was placed at his origin than this square? This square is sole and unique, as is the root of which it's the product and image; and the place where man lived is such that one could never compare it with anywhere else. This square measures the whole circumference; and man in the bosom of his empire embraced all the regions of the Universe. This square is formed with four lines; and man's post was marked by four lines of communication which extended from the center to the four cardinal points of the horizon. This square comes from the center and is clearly indicated to us by the four musical consonances which occupy the exact center of the scale, and are the key agents of all the beauties of harmony; and the throne of man was at the very center of the Country of his dominion, and from there he governed the seven instruments of his glory, which I previously designated under the name of seven trees, and which a great number will be tempted to take as the seven planets, but which however are neither trees, nor planets.[91]

One can therefore no longer doubt that the square in question is the true sign of that place of delights, known in our Realms under the name of *Earthly Paradise*; that is, of this place of which all Nations have a notion, which they each represent in fables and various allegories according to their wisdom, their enlightenment, or their blindness; and which the simple Geographers have innocently looked for on the Earth.

Therefore, we should no longer be surprised by the immensity of the privileges which we have attributed to the square in the various parts of this book where we've spoken about it. We should no longer be surprised, indeed, that if it's from One Single Principle that all Truths and all Lights descend, and that the Quaternary symbol is His most perfect image, this symbol could enlighten man on the knowledge of all four Natures; that is, on the Laws of the immaterial order, the temporal order, the physical order and the mixed order, which are the four columns of the building. In other words, we must agree that the one who can possess the key to this universal

---

[91] In Christian terms, the reference to '7' in this context could refer to the Seven Gifts of the Holy Spirit. However, it is more likely that Saint-Martin was following Pasqually's comments in his *Treatise*. The Master held the number in high regard, and even devoted most of a Chapter to it in his book. He says Noah's second family consisted of seven sons, which he described as the "Seven Spiritual 'Pillars' who would support the universe and preserve it from God's punishment." They also "formed a 'type' of the seven Superior Spiritual Beings" of the highest or denary class, the first Spirits emanated by God, and which He used as Agents of His Will. Later, Adam was put in charge of these powerful Beings. Pasqually goes on to mention, among others: 7 Days of Creation, 7 Spiritual Gifts, 7 Archangels, 7 Angels, 7 Seraphim, 7 Cherubim, 7 Spiritual Places, 7 Thrones, 7 Dominions, 7 Powers, 7 Judges of Israel, 7 weeks of Daniel, 7 days of the week, 7 Fathers of the Early Church, the 7-branched candlestick of the Temple, the 7 days in the moon's quarter, and others. Now, despite Pasqually's and Saint-Martin's constant avoidance of referring to Kabbalistic teachings, there cannot be a single Reader with the least knowledge of this area who hasn't immediately recognized in the lists above the correspondences given to the 7 Lower Sephiroth on the Tree of Life. And Saint-Martin himself makes allusion to 'Seven Trees'.

number would no longer find anything hidden from him in everything that exists, since this number is the very number of the Being Who produces everything, operates everything and embraces everything.

But however innumerable the advantages which are attached to it may be, and however powerful this true and unique Language which leads it may be, such is the unhappy state of present day man, as we know, that not only is he unable to reach the end or even take a single step along this path, without another hand than his opening the entrance to it, and supporting him during the entire length extent of his journey.

We know, too, that this powerful hand is that same physical Cause, both intelligent and active, whose eye sees all, and whose power supports everything in time. Now, if its rights are exclusive, how can man in his weakness and the most complete privation in Nature, continue alone without such a support?

He must therefore recognize here once again both the existence of this Cause, and the crucial need he has of its help to reestablish himself in his rights. He'll be similarly obliged to confess that if it can fully satisfy his desires concerning the difficulties which disquiet him, the first, most useful of his duties will be to renounce his fragile will, as well as the false gleams with which he seeks to color its misuse, and to rely completely upon this powerful Cause, which today is the sole guide he has who can take him.

And truly, this is the Cause which is appointed to repair not only the harm that man has allowed to take place, but also those he has done to himself. It's this Cause which continually has its eyes upon him, as it has upon all the other Beings of the Universe, but to which this man is infinitely more precious since he is of the same essence, and is similarly indestructible. Of all the Beings which are connected to the square, they are the only ones endowed with the privilege of thought, while this perishable Nature is to their eyes like nothing and like a dream.

How much will his confidence grow in this Cause, in which all powers reside, when he learns that it perfectly possesses this true and unique Language which he has forgotten, and which today he is obliged to recall laboriously to his memory; when he knows that he can't know its first syllable without this Cause, and above all when he sees that it inhabits and sovereignly governs that fertile square, outside of which man will never find either rest or Truth.

Then he'll no longer doubt that in approaching it, he is approaching the one true light he can hope for, and with it he'll find not only all the knowledge we've spoken of, but much more importantly, knowledge of himself, since that Cause, though connected to *the source of all numbers*, is nevertheless especially proclaimed everywhere by the number of the square, which is at the same time *the number of Man*.

If only I could put down the veil with which I must cover myself, and say the Name of this Beneficent Cause, Power and Excellence Himself, on Whom I'd dearly love to be able to fix the eyes of the whole Universe! But, although this Ineffable Being, the Key to Nature, the Love and Joy of the simple, the Flame of the Wise, and even the Secret Support of the blind, never ceases to support man in all his steps, as He supports and governs all the acts of the Universe, nevertheless, the *Name* which would best make Him known, were I to profess it, would result in the greatest number to deign to add faith to their *virtues* and distrust all of my doctrine; and thus, to state it more clearly would be to remove the aim I had to have Him honored.

Therefore, I prefer to rely on the insight of my Readers. Very assured that, despite the envelopes with which I've covered the Truth, *intelligent* man can understand it, true men could appreciate it, and even corrupt men could at least not prevent themselves from sensing it, because all men are C-H-R.[92]

Conclusion

SUCH is the summary of the reflections which I've proposed to present to men. If my commitments had not prevented me, I'd no doubt have been able to cover a much wider field. Nevertheless, in the little that I've dared to tell them, I flatter myself that I've only offered them what they'll all feel within themselves when they want to seek it with courage, and protect themselves at the same time from blind credulity and making hurried judgements, two vices which both lead to ignorance and error.

Hence, if I didn't have my own conviction as proof, I always believed I'd recalled them to their Principle and to Truth.

Indeed, it'd be to never deceive man, to show him so forcibly the privation and misery he'll suffer so long as he ties himself to fleeting and physical things, and to show him that surrounded as he is by this multitude of Beings, only he and his guide possess the privilege of thought.

---

[92] See comment on page 35.

If he wishes to be convinced, let him refer to everything he sees around him in this physical class; let him ask the Elements why, enemies as they are, they find themselves united for the creation and existence of bodies; let him ask the plant why it vegetates, and the animal why it wanders on this surface; let him even ask the stars why they shine and why, form the moment of their existence, they haven't stopped following their courses for a single moment.

All these Beings, deaf to the voice which interrogates them, will each continue to do their work in silence, but they will give no satisfaction to man's desires, because their silent deeds only speak to his physical eyes, and teach nothing to his mind.

Moreover, let man ask of that which is infinitely closer to him, that is, this physical envelope which he laboriously wears upon himself. Let him indeed as why it's attached to a Being with which, according to the Laws which constitute it, it's so incompatible. This blind form won't explain this new doubt any better; and will still leave man in uncertainty.

Now, is there a state more burdensome and at the same time more humiliating, than to be relegated to a Region where all the Beings which inhabit it are so many strangers to us? Where the Language we use to talk to them can't be understood by them; where man chained in spite of himself to a body which has nothing more than any other product of Nature, drags around a Being with which he can't even converse?

Thus, despite the greatness and beauty of all these works of Nature, among which we are placed, since they can neither understand us nor speak to us, it's as if we're in the middle of them as if in a desert.

If the Observers had been convinced of these truths, they'd never have sought in this physical Nature for those explanations and solutions it could never give them; nor would they have sought in present-day man the true model of what he should be, since he is so horribly disfigured; nor explain the Creator of things through His material creations whose existence and the Laws being dependent, can't show us anything of Him who is everything in Himself.

Then to tell them that the very road they've taken is the first obstacle to their progress, and distances them completely from the path of discoveries, is to tell them a truth which they would easily agree with, if they cared to consider it.

At the same time, since they can't deny they have an intelligent ability, isn't telling them that they are created to know everything and to embrace everything, to speak to them in the Language of their own reason? An ability of this order wouldn't be as noble as we believe it to be, if among fleeting things, there were some which were above it; and man's continual efforts work, as if naturally, to deliver them from the unwelcome shackles of ignorance, and to bring them closer to knowledge, as if they've striving for a domain which seems to be their own.

If they have so little to applaud concerning their successes, they shouldn't attribute this to the weakness of their nature or the limits of their abilities, but solely to the false path they are taking to try to reach their goal, and because they don't pay enough attention to the fact that each class has its own measurement and Law. So it's up to the senses to determine physical things, because so far as they can't be felt by the body they mean nothing. But it's up to the mind to judge intellectual things which the senses can't know; and to want to apply the Laws and measurement of one of these classes to the others is evidently to go against the order dictated by the very nature of things, and as a result to stray from the only means there is to discern the Truth.

I've therefore believed I was simply offering my fellow men Truths which were easy to perceive, by telling them that what they seek is only in the center, and that for that reason, so long as they do nothing other than go around the circumference, they'll find nothing, and that this center which must be unique to each Being was indicated by the universal square which shows itself in all that exists, and is found written everywhere in indelible characters.

If I've shown them only some of the means to study this fertile center, which is the only Principle of light, it's because, outside of my obligations, it was to slow them down by not revealing more, for most certainly they'd not have believed me. So, I promised myself that I'd call on them to undertake their own studies, and never, as a man, have I claimed to have any other rights.

But few though the means I've given them and the steps I've had them take along this path might be, they can't fail to gain some confidence from them, by seeing just how much they've discovered with their own eyes, and the use we've made of them across so great a number of different subjects.

For I do not presume that this field, by reason that it's so infinitely vast, could seem impracticable to them, and it'd be contrary to all the Laws of

Truth to claim it was the multitude and diversity of objects which was forbidden to man's knowledge. No, if man was born in the center, there's nothing he can't see, nothing he can't embrace; on the contrary, the only fault which he can commit is to isolate and dismember the parts of Science, because that is to attack his Principle directly, in that he is then dividing Unity.

And in this sense, let my Readers decide between their path and mine; since, despite the prodigious variety of points which I've dealt with, I've united all of them and created only one Science, whereas the Observers have made a thousand of them, and every question they ask becomes the subject of a new doctrine and study.

Nor do I need to point out to them that after all the observations I've shown them about the various human sciences, they should assume I've at least some understanding of them. They can, from the marked reserve which prevails in this book and the veils which are spread over it, further assume that I'd probably have had rather more to say than they've seen, and more than is known in general.

However, far from scorning them, considering the darkness in which they still find themselves, my only wish is to see them leave it and place their steps on paths which are more luminous than those where they presently crawl.

Similarly, although I've had the good fortune to have been led further along the path of Truth than them, far from puffing myself up with pride and thinking I know something, I openly admit my ignorance to them, and to avoid their suspicions about the sincerity of this admittance, I'll add that it'd be impossible for me to delude myself in this matter, because I have proof that I know nothing.

That's why I've said so often that I don't claim to lead them to the goal. It's enough for me to have, in a way, forced them to agree that the blind march of human Science takes them even further still from the goal they seek, since it leads them to doubt if there even is one.

From this I oblige them to admit to themselves that in stripping the Sciences of the one Principle which governs them, and from which they're inseparable, far from becoming enlightened, they're only falling back into the most terrible ignorance, and that it's only by becoming distanced from this Principle that the Observers laboriously search everywhere, and that they almost never agree.

It's therefore enough, I repeat, to have revealed to them today the knot of difficulties which stop them. In future, Truth will spread its rays more abundantly, and *in its time* it will take back the empire which the vain Sciences contend for against it today.

For my part, not being worthy of consideration, I've had to limit my efforts to making them sense that it exists, and that man, in spite of his wretchedness, could convince himself of this every day of his life if only he could better control his will. I therefore believe that I'd enjoy the most delightful reward if everyone, after reading this book, would say to themselves in the secret place of their heart, that there is one Truth, *but I can speak to something better than men to know this.*

www.ingramcontent.com/pod-product-compliance
Lightning Source LLC
Chambersburg PA
CBHW050615300426
44112CB00012B/1507